Nixon and the
Environment

Nixon and the Environment

J. BROOKS FLIPPEN

University of New Mexico Press

Albuquerque

© 2000 by University of New Mexico Press

All rights reserved.

First edition

Library of Congress Cataloging-in-Publication Data

Flippen, J. Brooks, 1959–

    Nixon and the environment / J. Brooks Flippen.—1st ed.

      p. cm.

Includes bibliographical references (p.) and index.

    ISBN 0-8263-1993-9 (alk. paper)

    1. Environmental policy—United States. 2. United States—
Politics and government—1969–1974. 3. Nixon, Richard M.
(Richard Milhous), 1913–   I. Title.

    GE180 .F55 2000

    363.7'056'097309047—dc21

00-008607

For Celeste

Contents

Acknowledgments

Nine years ago I began research for this book naive to the task ahead. I now know that no one completes such a project alone, that every author is indebted to a number of individuals and institutions for support and assistance. Professors Keith Olson and George Callcott of the University of Maryland, the former my dissertation director, guided my efforts from the start. The staff at the Nixon Presidential Materials Project of the National Archives helped on a daily basis as I waded through the thousands of pages of documents in their possession. At various points in my research, I had the good fortune to deal with the Library of Congress, the Manuscript Division of the Allen Library at the University of Washington, the Muskie Archives at Bates College in Lewiston, Maine, and the Richard M. Nixon Presidential Library in Yorba Linda, California. In each instance the staff was courteous and professional. Institutional support came from the Oklahoma Foundation for the Humanities and Southeastern Oklahoma State University's Office of Institutional Research and Planning. I wish to thank the former Nixon administration officials, environmentalists, and Muskie aides who were kind enough to grant a struggling young writer an interview, and the very competent staff at the University of New Mexico Press who, in the end, helped bring this project to fruition. Certainly no writer can claim a better editor than my own, Durwood Ball. Finally, I owe a great deal of debt to my parents and my family. My wife, Celeste, patiently read every draft, offering insight that tremendously improved the final product. In the end, I hardly completed this project alone, yet the responsibility for any shortcomings rests solely with me.

Nixon and the Environment

Introduction
"A Wholesale Change in Values"

It was one of the largest demonstrations in American history—an odd gathering of businessmen, housewives, college students, children, workers, and radical antiestablishment militants. Indeed, the amazing turnout represented every strata of American society. In New York, over 100,000 people participated in festivities in Union Square. In Washington, thousands gathered on the mall. In cities from Philadelphia to Los Angeles, a citizenry often divided over issues such as the Vietnam War, racial desegregation, and the economy united in an event part celebration and part earnest protest.

In recent years Earth Day earns only scant notice from an apathetic and preoccupied American public. The first Earth Day on April 22, 1970, however, was different—a significant event in American history and one worthy of the tremendous attention it received. Drawing an estimated twenty million participants and involving over ten thousand schools and two thousand colleges and universities, the first Earth Day and its surprising success represented in many respects the emergence of a powerful new environmentalism.[1] Since the days of President Theodore Roosevelt many Americans had recognized the need to use resources judiciously. They had appreciated that America's natural bounty had limits, and long since had adopted the basic wise-use doctrine of conservation. The many participants of the first Earth Day, however, had broader concerns. They realized that the unrestrained urbanization and industrialization characteristic of the nation's post–World War II economic boom mandated more than the simple need to use natural resources wisely. It demanded broader protection for overall environmental quality, protection for the intrinsic condition of the nation's air, water, and land. Expanding upon the tradition of Progressive-era preservationists, these new environmentalists viewed the earth as an ecosystem with humanity only a part, a part that nevertheless threatened the whole.[2]

The magnitude of the first Earth Day—the apparent breadth of public concern—surprised many observers, for the problems on which the demonstration focused had multiplied rather suddenly, paralleling the nation's rapid postwar economic growth. In the decade and a half after the conclusion of hostilities, the United States emerged as the "affluent society," in the words of Harvard economist John Kenneth Galbraith. By 1960, the nation's population had increased by thirty-five million, with the population growth approaching that of India. The census that year reported a population of 180 million, almost a 20 percent increase over the previous decade. The gross national product was 500 million dollars, more than double the 200 million dollar GNP in 1945. The median family income approached fifty-seven hundred dollars, an increase of almost 50 percent adjusted for inflation.[3]

This growth had a tremendous impact on the way Americans regarded their environment. Rising standards of living allowed more recreational time as well as greater discretionary income. Americans had more time for qualitative experiences along with material necessities, and thus they possessed the means for a greater appreciation of environmental amenities. A host of new appliances appeared on the market—automatic washing machines and dryers, dishwashers, waste disposal units, power lawn mowers, and many others—all significantly reducing the time necessary for normal domestic chores. At the same time the average work week declined from forty-four to almost forty hours. The result was a boom in the recreation business. The making and servicing of pleasure boats, camping equipment, sporting goods, and hunting and fishing gear became multimillion-dollar businesses. Americans purchased almost four million pleasure boats in the 1950s alone. In short, they now had the opportunity to enjoy the outdoors as never before.[4]

The growth in automobile ownership made a retreat to more natural surroundings much easier. From 1945 to 1960 the number of cars increased by 133 percent. Middle-class America now meant two cars, each successive model longer and wider, with more gadgets and bigger fins. The government did its share to facilitate easy access to nature, passing the massive Highway Act of 1956, which provided for thirty-three billion dollars to construct over forty-one thousand miles of new interstate roads.[5] Vacations in the country were no longer the exclusive domain of the super-wealthy. Although few Americans yet saw the recreation business itself as a threat, most Americans now realized that the environment offered more than simply the extraction of natural resources.

America's phenomenal growth following the Second World War did more than stir a new-found appreciation of nature. It also noticeably began to affect overall environmental quality, to erode the very intrinsic value of nature that Americans were just learning to appreciate. The expansion of the population and economy contributed to massive suburbanization. In time, this growth brought more than simply a comfortable lifestyle; it also brought unforeseen environmental consequences.

Suburbs were not new to America. Satellite communities had grown around American urban centers since the days of horsecars and trolleys. The new migration after the Second World War, however, dwarfed these earlier movements. Mass produced and prefabricated, and best represented by the Levittown community on Long Island, suburbs offered affordable homes away from the problems of inner cities. After fifteen years of depression and war, America had a severe housing shortage. Together with the spread of the automobile, the new suburbs offered a solution. During the 1950s, suburbs grew six times faster than established cities, with a total of eighteen million new suburbanites. By 1960, one-quarter of Americans lived in such suburban homes. Americans now spoke of a "megalopolis" to describe the miles of sprawling single-family homes that surrounded established urban centers.[6]

The new suburbanite, however, faced a cruel paradox in his or her existence. Economic growth had made suburban life possible, but it also threatened the amenities that he or she had sought in the first place. Landowners, real estate developers, financial institutions, and utility companies all fostered more intensive use of land. Local governments joined in with the hope of securing more tax revenue from higher land values. Two-lane roads became four-lane roads and shopping centers replaced open fields. By 1960, over two thousand shopping centers had sprung up in previously undeveloped land. Billboards, part of the growth of the advertising industry during the same period, soon blighted what natural beauty remained. Suburbia had become in many ways just like the urban areas from which it grew.[7]

The nation's growth contributed to the deterioration of environmental quality in other ways. In many areas construction of waste-treatment centers did not keep pace with the greater population density. This meant that many communities simply dumped raw sewage into nearby rivers and lakes, magnifying the problem of water pollution. The dumping of such sewage led to eutrophication, the overfertilization of water plants. The resulting algal growth blocked the sun from deeper plants, whose subsequent death and decay eliminated the remaining oxygen in the water. This ensured the death of any aquatic wildlife, including fish. In time, the water was devoid of all life, its ecosystem destroyed.

More people and more suburbs often meant more waste, more trash. Municipal waste—residential, commercial, and institutional refuse—constituted millions of tons a year, the elimination of which composed a municipal expense that only education and roads surpassed. During the 1950s, Americans, with their appetite for automobiles, junked almost as many cars per year as they manufactured. Most communities disposed of their waste in city dumps, incinerators, or landfills. Open dumps contributed to disease, contaminating the surrounding water tables, while municipal incinerators often lacked even the most rudimentary pollution-control equipment. Although they were the best alternative, sanitary landfills were the most expensive, and rarely did municipalities allocate adequate funds.[8]

The greatest threat to the quality of the nation's air, however, was not municipal waste, but the growth of the automobile so crucial to the development of suburban life. The internal combustion engine produced unhealthy levels of hydrocarbons, carbon monoxide, and nitrogen oxide vehicular-exhaust emissions. In certain urban areas on hot days the result was a gray, choking haze, air pollution that decreased visibility and irritated eyes. Residents in the rapidly growing community of Los Angeles soon coined a term for this nasty vapor—*smog*, an amalgam of smoke and fog—a term Americans throughout the country soon recognized and adopted.

The automobile was not the only culprit. The electric-power industry, together with other heavy industry, also contributed. America needed her heavy industry to construct suburbia, and it, in turn, needed its electricity; both saw a significant increase in the 1950s. Most of these industries burned fossil fuels, and in doing so contributed to the problem. The burning of oil, gas, and coal released particulate matter and sulfur oxide into the air. This produced an acrid yellow gas, especially from those plants burning high-sulfur coal.[9] Many large industrial cities had reeked with this foul stench since the dawn of the Industrial Revolution, but in the postwar years the problem only compounded, much to the chagrin of the nearby populace.

This manifold threat to the nation's environmental quality—the complex problems facing America's air, water, and land in the postwar world—ensured a popular protest for adequate reform. It was not until the 1960s, however, that the problems worsened to the point that any significant national movement emerged, a movement that ultimately culminated in the first Earth Day in 1970. In 1962, a former researcher for U.S. Fish and Wildlife Service, Rachel Carson, published *Silent Spring*, a text that bemoaned the environmental impact of indiscriminate insecticide use, but had ramifications far beyond the agricultural community. Carson shocked many Americans with her warning that the impetuous pace of human development threatened the natural world. Quickly a best-seller, *Silent Spring* arguably opened the eyes of the American public to the problems that accompanied the prosperity of the postwar world.[10] The Carson book found a receptive audience in the 1960s, an era rapidly evolving as one of the most rebellious, tumultuous decades in American history. Growing numbers of Americans, most notably many among the nation's youth, countered traditional assumptions by rallying against the evils they perceived in American life. The repression of African-Americans and women, the apparent pointless-ness of the war in Vietnam, the greed of large corporations, and the drudgery of the average middle-class existence—all increasingly galvanized the young into a potent cultural force that welcomed the basic tenets of the new environmentalism. For many, America needed fundamental change, with protection for environmental quality only one among many examples.[11]

As the 1960s progressed, the problem of environmental deterioration was increasingly before the public, from new collegiate-level courses in "environmental science" to a wave of best-selling books in the wake of *Silent Spring*. The National Advertising Council released a poignant commercial that depicted an American Indian looking out over a littered landscape, a tear rolling down his cheek. Environmental degradation, whether a messy oil spill on pristine beaches or mountains of rusted automobiles taller than nearby buildings, made great copy for television; it was sure to win viewers, a fact not lost upon network executives. Not surprisingly, polls soon registered growing public concern. In 1965, over a quarter of respondents surveyed indicated that they thought air pollution was a serious problem in their own community. For water quality, the figure was over one-third. By 1967, half of the respondents indicated a serious problem in both areas, and by the following year the figure had risen to two-thirds. Respondents did not list environmental deterioration as the most important problem facing the nation, but their growing concern was obvious.[12]

The result was tremendous growth in environmental organizations, both in terms of the number of organizations and the membership within each. Prior to 1960 an average of only three new conservation groups per year appeared on the American scene. Throughout the remainder of the 1960s, the average was eighteen. The number of environmental journals and periodicals skyrocketed. Older conservation organizations, such as the National Audubon Society, the National Wildlife Federation, the Sierra Club, and the Izaak Walton League, were slow to adapt to the new environmental awareness, and, when still advocating the wise-use doctrine or pressing for resource development, often found themselves at odds with the new environmentalism. Frequently focusing on specific, narrow interests such as national parks, their efforts failed to appreciate the diversity of the threat to environmental quality and thus capture a broader audience. Relations were at times strained. When young, long-haired environmentalist Joe Browder, typical of the new generation of activists, arrived in Washington, the established groups hardly welcomed him. Browder, who later founded the Environmental Policy Institute, was, they claimed, part of a communist plot to infiltrate the groups. He shared, it turned out, the same last name as communist leader Earl Browder, making him an easy target for conservative conservationists.[13] In 1969, tensions between longtime Sierra Club president David Brower and his board of directors exploded into public view with allegations of financial mismanagement. The dispute was, in fact, as much ideological, prompting Brower to form the Friends of the Earth, a new, more confrontational organization.[14]

In spite of tensions, however, over time most of the traditional organizations began to adapt their message and found that their membership rose. The Wilderness Society, for example, doubled its membership over the decade, while the Sierra Club and the National Audubon Society more than doubled theirs. "We cannot suitably quarrel with youth who seek a new direction," concluded the Wilderness Society.[15] The National Wildlife Federation, which had worked with industry to protect wilderness areas for hunting and fishing, slowly began to adopt a more youth-oriented approach, eventually championing causes such as recycling. The new environmentalism did spawn radical elements that rejected compromise and the incremental advances of political policy and legislation in favor of a more extreme approach, occasionally even violence. By the end of the 1960s, however, this element remained small and out of the mainstream, and failed to exert much influence.[16] Despite all their differences, environmentalists remained "quite united," according to Brower. His successor at the Sierra Club, Philip Berry, concurred: "There was a lot of common action and agreement."[17] In short, the environmental movement, largely united and obviously growing, appeared to be by the end of the decade a political force hard to ignore.

The potential of this grass-roots environmentalism was evident from the start, its successes slowly building as the movement grew. In the 1950s, preservationists succeeded in blocking construction of two dams that promised to destroy the natural ecosystem of the surrounding lands. A proposal to flood the Dinosaur National Monument with a dam at Echo Park near the Utah-Colorado border galvanized a resistance that surprised the dam's proponents. Similarly, a proposal to build a dam at Hell's Canyon on the Snake River in Idaho sparked an unexpected degree of outrage. Fifty years before, Sierra Club founder John Muir had led a committed band of preservationists in an unsuccessful attempt to block the damming of the beautiful Hetch Hetchy Valley in Yosemite National Park. The success of his philosophical descendants, if nothing else, indicated that a new day for environmental advocates was approaching.[18]

By the 1960s, environmentalists found a friend in President Lyndon Johnson. With a new faith in government activism, the Great Society witnessed the first significant legislation to address the problem of pollution. New laws to create air and water quality standards were revolutionary for their day, if not stringent enough to meet the growing problem. Laws to protect unspoiled wilderness from development, to create a permanent fund for the purchase of parkland, to limit solid waste, and to create a wildlife-refuge system were critical steps in the evolution of federal environmental policy.[19] Most notably, Johnson's Interior Department secretary, Stewart Udall, emerged as a forceful champion of the natural world, in many respects challenging the dominant utilitarian biases of his predecessors. Environmentalists had, according to the Sierra Club, "no stauncher friend."[20] Perhaps even more apparent to the public was Johnson's wife, Lady Bird. Although many first ladies had adopted a pet cause, Lady Bird's was unique—the preservation of the country's natural beauty. Chairing a presidential commission and hosting a White House conference on the subject, Lady Bird helped pass legislation to limit roadside blight. Her real significance, however, lay in the example she set. The American people should, she insisted, care about their environment.[21]

Congress, of course, played a major role. In most respects, bipartisan support existed for each legislative initiative. Still, taking the lead was Maine Democratic senator Edmund Muskie. Environmental quality was not yet a major political force, but the former governor of Maine already had a long record of activism that proved his interest was genuine. Born and raised in the town of Rumford, Maine, a town so polluted that the stench from its timber industry permeated the daily lives of its citizens, Governor Muskie had made the pollution of his state's rivers a cause célèbre. Elected to the Senate in 1958 and appointed four years later as chair of the Subcommittee on Air and Water Pollution of the Senate Public Works Committee, he was in a position to place his imprint on virtually every pollution bill before Congress. Together with his colleagues in the executive branch, he helped lay the foundation for an environmental policy that the nation needed.[22]

It was, however, still only a foundation. The problems continued to grow throughout the decade, fueling the development of the environmental movement and leading ultimately to the first Earth Day, an unmistakable signal that environmentalism had arrived. Despite a decade of growing concern and accomplishment, for many Americans the thousands gathered in Washington, New York, and other cities on that April day in 1970 served as a wake-up call, an alarm signaling both the pressing nature of the problem and the urgency for additional action. The sheer size of the turnout ensured significant media coverage, but the demonstrators themselves devised tactics to seize headlines. At the University of Minnesota, members of the "Students for Environmental Defense" conducted a mock funeral service for the internal combustion engine, lowering an engine into a coffin buried in downtown Minneapolis. A New Jersey housewife spent weeks sewing red banners with black skulls and crossbones, banners that she then placed on dredging equipment which she believed sullied nearby beaches. Self-styled Yippies at Indiana University were more aggressive, plugging municipal sewage pipes with concrete, while their more orderly colleagues tossed birth-control pills at the crowds. Protesters intended such actions to garner attention—and their efforts proved successful. All three major television networks devoted considerable coverage to the event, while the public broadcasting stations devoted all of their daytime programs to the protection of environmental quality.[23]

The first Earth Day was a fitting culmination to a popular movement, a demonstration that ecology had achieved political capital as never before—and, not surprising given the incredible turnout, politicians listened. Both houses of Congress adjourned for the day, allowing their members to participate in the various activities, invariably extolling their own interest in the matter. Politicians of every stripe, from liberal South Dakota senator George McGovern to conservative Arizona senator Barry Goldwater, found themselves in agreement—if only for a day. Federal officials were not the only ones rallying to the environmental bandwagon; state and local officials added their collective voice to the chorus of environmentalism. Massachusetts' legislature unanimously amended the state constitution to declare a pollution-free environment a constitutional right. The Albuquerque, New Mexico, City Commission slashed public transportation fares to one cent for the day as an incentive to use mass transit and as a symbol of its support.[24] Many of the promises and speeches proved banalities, but the importance of environmentalism as a political issue was hard to deny.

Inside the White House, the approach of the first Earth Day posed a dilemma for President Richard Nixon. The first-term Republican, like many politicians in Washington, recognized the opportunity the occasion posed to sway a wide segment of voters. Environmentalism, it appeared, was particularly strong in critical electoral college states, including Florida, California, New York, and much of New England. Indeed, with polls indicating that the environment was a key issue among the nation's youth, Earth Day offered a chance to score points with an important demographic group, a voting block not traditionally allied with Nixon. The idea of an Earth Day had grown from the original plan for a large "teach-in," a public gathering popular at many large universities at the time. In such events, more common as protests against the Vietnam War, students boycotted classes to attend meetings, where activists led panel discussions, symposia, and lectures. Coordinating the logistics for a "national teach-in on the environment" — Earth Day, as they named it — was a Harvard University graduate student, Denis Hayes, an ambitious and intelligent twenty-five year old who recruited a number of volunteers from Stanford, his undergraduate alma mater. Earth Day, in short, appeared as youth oriented as the nation's burgeoning environmentalism itself, and thus for a conservative administration constituted a rare opportunity. As the ultimate commander-in-chief of America's forces in Vietnam, Nixon was more often than not the object of such a collegiate "teach-in," not a willing participant. He could not, in short, easily ignore it.

Ever the astute politician, Nixon had recognized the potential power of the new environmentalism sweeping the country even before Hayes and the others began molding their "teach-in" into the truly momentous event it became. In addition, his political opposition stood poised to take advantage of the situation if the administration somehow appeared indifferent. Predictably, Muskie prepared an offensive, planning to venture to Harvard and the University of Pennsylvania for speeches demanding additional environmental protection. As Harvard was a well-known bastion of antiwar radicalism, no national politician had visited the campus since the dovish Democratic senator Eugene McCarthy in 1968. Muskie was well known nationally, and Nixon ardently believed him to be his most likely opponent in the coming 1972 presidential elections.[25] Muskie's aides — themselves with Harvard connections — ensured the senator that the majority on campus "have little faith in revolution," and would cheer a politician brave enough to support directly the environmentalists' mantra of a "wholesale change in values." "Most of these kids have roots in the system," one assistant wrote; they would reciprocate at the polls.[26] Muskie had not joined Wisconsin Democratic senator Gaylord Nelson as one of Earth Day's top proponents, top aide Leon Billings recalled, but he recognized it "as an opportunity to provide political strength to his lonely crusade."[27] Other presidential-caliber Democrats planned to make the most of the occasion as well. Minnesota senator Hubert Humphrey scheduled a major speech at an Indiana high school, while Washington senator Henry Jackson planned the same at the University of Washington. Senator McGovern scheduled his address for Purdue University, while Massachusetts senator Edward Kennedy chose Yale University. The Democrats knew the power of this political bloc, Nixon assumed, and to ignore it completely might prove foolish.

On the other hand, however, Hayes and the other organizers, while denying their event as a partisan affair, had not exactly welcomed the administration's overtures in their preparations. They had publicly trashed the administration's environmental efforts to date as a "billow of smog," and had turned down an invitation to meet with John D. Ehrlichman, Assistant to the President for

Domestic Affairs and one of Nixon's closest advisors. Such an impertinent snub to an incumbent presidential administration did not seem to bother them. "We didn't think we had anything to chat about," a spokesman for the organizers sarcastically explained.[28] Such comments reinforced the belief in the White House that environmentalists were "social activists on the left side of the political spectrum" harboring a natural antagonism difficult to bridge. Still remaining were serious questions about whether Nixon could reach America's youth in any event, especially if the reaction of the Earth Day organizers was any indication. So many other factors—the war, the administration's position on civil rights—played into the equation. Any efforts might simply prove futile, a waste of time.[29]

Worse was the possibility of alienating traditional conservative allies. Many industries anticipated facing the full wrath of environmentalists' anger on this, their designated day. Dow Chemical, which had suffered protests against its manufacture of napalm and chemical pesticides, figured the best defense was a good offensive, sending its public relations team into overdrive to present the most environmentally friendly face possible. Other companies more readily participated, reflecting a market-savvy realization of their own consumers' concerns, if not a genuine concern for environmental quality. On the other hand, however, much of American industry feared that such a wide popular demand for environmental protection might result in additional burdensome regulations, regulations that had the potential to slash employment and hamper the economy. They did not want to appear to counter publicly such a popular movement as the new environmentalism, but neither did they plan to support a president who actively and ardently pushed the environmental agenda. Nixon realized that various industry representatives and a number of conservatives had already voiced in private, if not in public, their displeasure over the administration's environmental accomplishments to date. To appear at the forefront on Earth Day might risk pushing them into direct opposition.

As Earth Day neared, the debate raged within the White House. The first to recommend a strong administration response in favor of Earth Day was aide Christopher DeMuth, who recommended to Ehrlichman and Deputy Assistant to the President for Domestic Affairs John Whitaker, his immediate supervisor, that Nixon deliver a "substantial presidential address." Ehrlichman had just appointed Whitaker as the White House's top environmental advisor, and Whitaker, in turn, had realized the intelligence of DeMuth. A recent graduate of Harvard and the same age as Hayes and the other Earth Day organizers, DeMuth argued that a forceful presidential response before the day itself would ensure the "supremacy of the moderate students," not the radical fringe. DeMuth promised to keep in close contact with various congressional leaders and with his contemporaries in the Earth Day national headquarters in Washington.[30]

Whitaker quickly agreed with DeMuth. A former advance man and scheduler with the Nixon campaign, the forty-three-year-old Whitaker was born in beautiful Vancouver, British Columbia, and held a doctorate in geology from Johns Hopkins University and a long-standing interest in environmental protection. As a boy, he had been shocked by the unsightly grit and grime of the large eastern seaboard cities. His subsequent career in geology had led him to many of the world's most beautiful locales, and by the time of Earth Day Whitaker had found in his assistant DeMuth an instant ally.[31] Ehrlichman, however, was another question. A year older than Whitaker, he also had a background in the environment; he had served for fifteen years as an attorney with a specialization in land-use law. He too recognized the importance of cleaning up the environment and the political potency of the new environmentalism, but as a closer aide to Nixon and with responsibilities beyond simply natural resources, Ehrlichman had reservations about such a strong endorsement as the one Whitaker and DeMuth proposed.

Ehrlichman worried that preparations for Earth Day were not sufficiently bipartisan. Not only had Hayes personally scorned the White House, but the original idea for a day devoted to the environment had come not from Hayes's youthful staff, but from Democratic senator Nelson. Nelson had not agreed with his protégé's ill treatment of Nixon's assistants and had helped recruit California Republican congressman Paul McCloskey as a formal cochair. With a Democrat and Republican officially at the helm, Nelson hoped his colleagues from both sides of the aisle would recognize the importance of the day and look past partisan antics.[32] This did not convince Ehrlichman, who warned Nixon that the entire affair had the potential to turn "anti-Administration."[33] Although Nelson had emphatically stressed the need for bipartisanship, he had come uncomfortably close, in Ehrlichman's eyes, to encouraging the same radical elements the administration feared. In a speaking tour the previous year, for example, Nelson had remarked that youthful activism promised to take leadership away from "indifferent, venal men who are concerned with progress and profit for the sake of progress and profit alone, and who consider the environment the problem of birdwatchers and butterfly chasers."[34] Rather than directly endorsing Earth Day, Ehrlichman concluded, Nixon should organize federal workers' participation, but personally remain aloof.

Nixon made no immediate decision, allowing the debate within the administration to spread. Secretary of Interior Walter Hickel, together with his chief advisor, Undersecretary Russell Train, argued that Nixon should declare Earth

Day a national holiday and issue an executive order directing government employees to aid their local efforts. "This action would be beneficial not only to our fight for the environment," Hickel wrote, "but also to our continued efforts to involve young people in national concerns."[35] Hickel noted that the Interior Department had already formed a student advisory body termed the Student Council on Pollution and the Environment (SCOPE). In addition to SCOPE, the Interior Department had arranged a series of nine regional seminars on the environment in cities from Boston to San Francisco—and in not one had the participants turned antiadministration. With still no decision from Nixon, Whitaker wrote Train to ensure that, at the very least, the department adequately publicized the seminars, including mailing environmental organizations press releases of its efforts. If nothing else, this would help inoculate the White House from possible criticism.[36]

Nixon recognized that preparations were necessary in any event, and thus he could not delay his decision. Weighing the options, Nixon decided on a middle course, a low-risk plan along the lines of what Ehrlichman recommended. The White House would ensure the active participation of its key staff, who would speak throughout the country lauding the president's concern for environmental quality. Nixon, however, would remain quiet, neither issuing an executive order nor even making an official statement beforehand. If it appeared that events were proceeding smoothly—that is, with little violence or criticism of the White House—then Nixon might issue a quick statement to the press, hopefully in time for the evening news. A certain amount of criticism was inevitable, Nixon assumed. He had promised a major environmental address in the future and had his staff actively preparing a program of legislative initiatives. It was an agenda, Nixon hoped, that would establish his environmental credentials regardless of his response to Earth Day, a complete program sufficient in its own right to win the environmental vote. If he tried to steal some of the spotlight on Earth Day, an event for which he had contributed nothing, some would criticize him for grandstanding.[37]

Whitaker and DeMuth had their marching orders. They sent a memorandum to the departments of Interior, Agriculture, Labor, Transportation, and Health, Education and Welfare requesting each to develop a plan of action for the coming day. DeMuth, in turn, would coordinate publicity. The administration, Whitaker wrote DeMuth, should "hit Carson, Cavett and the think-type programs." It should include "young fellas" in its agenda, not simply higher administration figures. DeMuth notified Patrick Buchanan, a young aide and speech writer, that if any administration figure were asked about Earth Day, he should respond positively, noting that Nixon planned future environmental initiatives. To ensure that no administration figure encountered a hostile reception for which he was unprepared, Whitaker instructed DeMuth to "categorize our potential speakers as 'establishment' or 'teach-in' types."[38]

Preparations proceeded according to plan, although not without worries. The Vietnam War continued to rage, with protests on the rise. In the months before Earth Day, Nixon had increased the withdrawal of American troops as part of his "Vietnamization" of the war, but a string of ugly incidents, including the infamous My Lai massacre by American troops, undercut any positive effects domestically. In San Diego, student radicals burned a bank; at Kansas State, others burned down the ROTC building; at Yale, still others set afire books in the Law School library; at the University of California-Berkeley, they fought police for six hours in an antiwar protest.[39] In the eyes of many administration officials, courting the nation's youth appeared to be an increasingly perilous proposition. The student leaders of SCOPE, Hickel recalled, had grown "so hostile some of my aides wondered if they were going to 'occupy' [my office]."[40] Nixon had planned to attend his daughter Julie's graduation from Smith College, but the Secret Service had advised him that ugly protests might mar the event. Radicals in Boston had threatened to bus 200,000 protesters to the college if any member of the presidential family attended. "Fuck Julie," chanted thousands of young Bostonians led by recently acquitted Chicago Seven defendant Jerry Rubin. The thought of scores of young people on yet another protest—whether in support of environmental protection, or whatever—terrified many industry representatives, who began to prepare for the worst-case scenario. Owners of the Forest Industries building in Washington began to board up their first-floor windows, but settled for setting up fir trees in front of the glass. Most officials in the White House had by this point accepted the argument of Whitaker and others that some form of participation was wise, but Vice President Spiro Agnew remained a vocal opponent of any action whatsoever. He was insistent to the end that given the likelihood of violence, any involvement would prove a mistake.[41]

These were serious worries for the White House's environmental staff. For Nixon, however, they warranted little of his time. As meticulous and organized as ever, and with his decision made, Nixon turned his attention elsewhere. Indeed, Nixon faced a critical decision, one that for him surely dwarfed his administration's response to Earth Day. The National Security Council had informed him of the damage done by communist supply lines through Cambodia, and Nixon wrestled over the possibility of invading that ostensibly neutral country. With much of America apparently radicalized by the continued fighting, a decision to intervene might pour fuel on the fire. Earth Day would certainly command attention, but Nixon had his mind on other matters.[42]

Nixon had not announced his decision by the time Earth Day arrived, and for this one day nothing competed for the public's attention. Hundreds of administration staffers fanned out as planned, their scripts in hand. His own speech scheduled for Harvard, Train recalled that the staff was "very engaged around the country."[43] William Reilly, who later headed the Environmental Protection Agency under President George Bush, gave a speech on solid waste, prompting a man in the back to ask, "Mr. Reilly, where were you when it was garbage?" It was, Reilly recalled, "my baptism under fire."[44] Any such fire, thankfully, was not real; the White House's fear of violence proved to be unfounded. Only a handful of incidents nationally resulted in arrests—an amazing fact given the magnitude of the turnout. When protesters blocked access to part of Boston's Logan airport, police arrested thirteen. A young Florida man faced jail for violating a local sanitary code. His crime was protesting the thermal pollution of Biscayne Bay by showing up at a utility company's offices with a cart of decaying fish and a dead octopus.[45] Overall, Hayes and the other organizers were ecstatic, describing the event as the largest, cleanest, and most peaceful demonstration in American history.

With neither the major riot so many feared nor a significant Vietnam story, the media had more time to assess and critique the event, and the focus quickly turned to the administration. Ignoring the administration's efforts, the headline declared neglect by the White House—the very criticism Nixon had hoped to avoid. His actions—or, more correctly, lack of action—ensured condemnation. In the end, despite the best efforts of Whitaker and DeMuth, only two cabinet members gave speeches on the environment, Secretary of Transportation John Volpe and Hickel. Hickel's topic did little to appease critics: support for the Alaskan oil pipeline, a major privately funded engineering project that required federal permits. This, environmentalists argued, would destroy the pristine beauty of America's last wilderness. Aware of the possibility of a fuel shortage, Nixon approved of the speech. Hickel, the ex-governor of Alaska, wanted to use the opportunity to argue that construction posed no hazard. With campus unrest prevalent and his speech scheduled for the University of Alaska, Hickel was, according to Whitaker, "understandably nervous." Nixon made no statement or proclamation, although White House proclamations appeared that week for National Boating Week and National Archery Week. The speeches of the many participating subcabinet officials, of Whitaker, Train, Reilly, and of other prominent individuals friendly to the White House reaped little coverage.[46]

"There was little doubt," Whitaker later wrote, "that the Nixon administration took its licks on Earth Day." CBS's much-admired newsman Walter Cronkite characterized the crowds as "predominantly anti-Nixon." Newsman Daniel Schorr added that while the event offered a rare chance for reconciliation between the nation's youth and its presidential administration, "they went their polarized ways." White House correspondent Dan Rather was more pointed, describing Nixon's reaction as "benign neglect." In many instances, the speakers themselves added jabs at the White House. Addressing a crowd in New York City's Bryant Park, noted author Kurt Vonnegut, Jr., remarked, "If we don't get our President's attention, this planet may soon die . . . I'm sorry he's a lawyer; I wish to God that he was a biologist." Protesters in Washington threw oil on the front steps of the Department of Interior, a mess maintenance crews rapidly bathed away before television cameras arrived. Most politicians, in the vein that Nelson intended, avoided direct criticism of Nixon, but for many of the younger protesters, tying environmental protection in with criticism of Nixon's war policies was hard to resist. As organizer Hayes concluded, "We cannot save the environment as long as the war goes on."[47]

The week of Earth Day, White House staffers participated in a symbolic cleanup of the polluted Potomac River, with the media properly alerted. The administration, the staged event seemed to declare, did care, after all. The White House had scheduled the event prior to Earth Day, and had in fact touted it for some time to all who would listen. After the criticism of the day, however, the cleanup appeared to be a lame attempt to shield the administration from further rebuke, far from any genuine expression of concern.[48]

It made no difference. On the night of April 30 — only eight days after Earth Day — Nixon went on national television to announce his decision to send troops into Cambodia. It was not an "invasion," Nixon assured his audience. The troops would leave once they had disrupted the enemy's supply lines into neighboring Vietnam. "We will withdraw," he promised. The following morning, speaking to supporters, Nixon made an offhand remark describing student protesters as "bums," a slur the press readily quoted. A reaction to these developments was inevitable, but no one expected the uproar that followed. Viewing the Cambodian excursion as an escalation of the conflict, not a way to a quicker victory, campuses throughout the nation exploded. Students at 450 colleges and universities immediately went on strike. In California, the situation was so bad that Governor Ronald Reagan ordered the entire statewide university system closed. On May 4 the blaze turned to conflagration as National Guard troops at Kent State University in Ohio opened fire on student protesters, killing four.[49]

The entire episode shook Nixon and shocked the country. The United States appeared on the verge of revolution, and, as tempers flared, leaders called for calm. Nixon, unable to sleep early one morning, ventured out unannounced to protesters at the Lincoln Memorial, trying in vain to reach an accord. He cared for the same things they did, he explained, turning to his environmental agenda as evidence of a common denominator. California had the most beautiful beaches in the world, Nixon stated, pointedly adding that he had ordered the San Clemente beach opened as part of "our whole 'quality of life' environmental program."[50]

Nixon's attempt to divert the handful of war protesters with his care for the environment had as little effect as Earth Day in diverting attention from the Cambodian attack. Despite the pressing nature of the problem and the apparent wide-spread American interest, the reality was that public concern for the environment faded when other urgent problems commanded attention. In the words of Sierra Club's Berry: "That stupid war eclipsed the movement."[51] America's new-found interest in preserving environmental quality was a significant development in the nation's social and political evolution, a real break from the assumptions and opinions of the past. With the problem of environmental deterioration a genuine threat to the nation's future, the first Earth Day was, indeed, a momentous event. Ironically, it just did not appear so two weeks later, a fact that no doubt registered with Nixon. For the media and much of the public, it suddenly did not matter that critics accused the Nixon administration of neglecting Earth Day, which was forgotten in the wake of the Vietnam War.

In the end, the story of the first Earth Day tells a great deal about the Nixon administration and the emergence of the modern environmental movement. In a sense it demonstrates both the strengths and weaknesses of the new environmentalism, as well as the manner in which Nixon approached it. Nixon, the consummate political animal, gave no indication of sharing the concerns and hopes of the thousands who gathered on that April day in 1970 but rather gauged his response according to political expediency. Politics inevitably surrounded the day, just as the new environmentalism changed the political dynamics of the era. For many on the White House staff, the matter of environmental protection was more than just politics, but it was, nevertheless, the desire for partisan advantage that consumed the commander-in-chief. The story of the first Earth Day provides ample evidence of Nixon's desire to win the environmental vote, the strength of the Democrats as they resisted his efforts, and the rapidity with which critics condemned the White House. It illustrates, paradoxically, the important nature of the cause as well as the fleeting nature of public vigilance. If nothing else, it demonstrates the critical place of the Nixon administration in American environmental history.

I

"Ecology Has Finally
Achieved Currency" 1969

Political expediency was nothing new to Richard Nixon. If anything, his rapid political ascent reflected a keen ability to recognize public opinion and capitalize on it. Baptized into the world of politics at the outset of the Cold War, first elected to the House in 1946 and the Senate four years later, Nixon emerged a fierce anticommunist. Smart enough to avoid the demagoguery of Joseph McCarthy, he recognized at the same time the political power of the vein tapped by the Wisconsin senator. Parlaying both his fame on the House Un-American Activities Committee and his well-known partisanship into the vice presidency under Dwight Eisenhower, Nixon cultivated his reputation as a shrewd politician and an expert on foreign affairs. It was an age of backyard bomb shelters, blood-curdling rhetoric, and an arms race that for the first time threatened total Armageddon. Nixon, as the chief inquisitor of suspected spy Alger Hiss and a vice president with more international experience than any other, promised the staunch defense America demanded while accusing his opponents of the opposite. He appeared, not coincidentally, a man for his time.

The time, of course, reflected little of the environmental concerns that later captivated America on the first Earth Day. A man of his generation, Nixon did not recognize the growing threat that ironically paralleled his own political growth; he had no reason in the early postwar years to champion the natural world in Washington. Unlike many of the environmentalists he later faced, Nixon had no personal experience with the problems of urbanization or industrialization. The place of his youth, an agricultural community outside Los Angeles, was "idyllic," Nixon later recalled. The beautiful San Bernardino Mountains rising to the north and the spectacular Pacific Coast lying only a few miles to the west, the area might have instilled in the boy a love of nature if not an awareness of the threat it faced. An ambitious youngster, however,

Nixon was more often than not inside studying, his academic interest political science, not physical science. Unlike many rural boys, he enjoyed neither hunting nor fishing. From a family of modest means, he had to work both before and after school in any event. There was little free time for any recreational activities. Not once did he venture to the mountains and, rarely, to the ocean.[1]

Faced with questions of conservation early in his career, Nixon's actions reflected none of the certitude characteristic of his foreign policy. Just as many Republicans, Nixon favored state ownership of "tidelands oil," the valuable oil deposits in the submerged coastal lands claimed by the federal government. This placed him at odds with the Sierra Club, which assumed that Washington was less likely to exploit rapidly the reserves. Nixon's stance won him the friendship and financial support of major oil-company executives throughout his years.[2] When the roots of the modern environmental movement began to emerge with the Hell's Canyon and Echo Park controversies in the 1950s, Nixon sided with those favoring construction. A private citizen throughout most of the 1960s, having lost his bid for the presidency to John Kennedy at the outset of the decade, Nixon remained active in Republican circles and in the international realm. He did not, however, play any role in the nation's first significant pollution legislation, a product of the turbulent decade and an indication that environmental quality was about to explode as a pressing national issue.[3]

Nixon was not philosophically against conservation nor did he later think the initial legislation to protect environmental quality was frivolous. It was simply politics. Nixon's California constituents, sensing huge profits, demanded state control of tidelands oil. To take the opposite position was to court political suicide. While he consistently voted against many conservation projects to please fiscal conservatives, he shrewdly supported those benefiting his own constituents, most notably the Whittier Narrows Dam, the San Antonio Canyon Dam, and the Live Oak Flood Control Channel. "These three projects are vitally important to my district," Nixon stated, requesting federal funds and conveniently forgetting the pleas of others.[4] After Republican resistance to federal funding for reclamation cost the party western congressional seats in the 1956 elections, *Business Week Magazine* reported that Nixon "was arguing right up the cabinet for a turnaround on public power."[5] Out of office in the 1960s, Nixon recognized the growing conflict in Indochina, not the nascent environmental movement, as his platform for political rebirth. In short, unlike foreign policy, Nixon had no interest in natural resources, and his policies consequently lacked any firm footing. He appeared, as one angry constituent complained to Eisenhower, "too willing to sacrifice your principles for a few votes."[6]

The election year of 1968 offered candidate Nixon little incentive for change.

As polls indicated, a growing number of citizens recognized that deterioration in environmental quality posed the potential for ultimate destruction. The momentous events of the year, however, appeared to offer that possibility immediately, framing the campaign for both Nixon and his Democratic opponent, Vice President Hubert Humphrey. Beginning with the enemy's "Tet Offensive" in Vietnam, extending through the assassination of renowned civil-rights leader Dr. Martin Luther King and the riots that followed, and ending with the brawling disaster of the Democratic National Convention in Chicago, the months of turmoil before the election left many voters hungry for a new direction, for a solution before the nation ripped itself apart. Nixon, attuned as ever to public opinion, cast himself in this role, a role that relegated the environment to secondary status.[7]

Neither candidate, of course, opposed environmental protection; both the Democratic and Republican platforms professed a concern. With his record in the Johnson administration and a running mate none other than Edmund Muskie, Humphrey obviously held the upper hand, with more incentive to raise the matter. The Democratic platform was more specific in its calls for federal action, and Humphrey's Senate career included support for a number of wildlife bills, a fact not lost on the growing number of environmentalists. "The record of the Democratic administrations is impressive, with the record of the last four years particularly outstanding," campaigned Muskie, fully realizing that the war in Vietnam overshadowed any such claims.[8] Under attack from many in his own party for his support of the war, a defensive Humphrey had little opportunity to recast the debate. On only two occasions did he raise the environment — the dedication of a Texas park in August and an Oregon dam in September. Even then, the war seemed to permeate his comments. "Pollution is a form of aggression," Humphrey declared. "Just as we condemn military aggression, we must condemn the aggression of persons — nations and businesses alike — that destroy the life-giving resources of air, water and land."[9]

Nixon's campaign literature virtually ignored the environment, as did the candidate himself. Raising the issue in only one of his eighteen "Nixon Speaks Out" radio addresses, he stressed instead two themes: a return to law and order and a "peace with honor" in Vietnam. Although he provided no details on how to accomplish this, the campaign was sure to resonate with voters. Avoiding the Republican platform's call for more environmental activism, Nixon promised to slash Johnson's Great Society programs. He disdained "nattering nabobs of negativism," appearing, as he so often had in the past, a man for his time.[10]

His course was, once again, smart politics. The environment indeed played little role in the election, as the issue of peace — both domestic and international—commanded the attention of voters. With a record seventy-three million citizens voting, Nixon won a close election, just as he had lost one to Kennedy eight years before. Nixon captured 43.4 percent of the popular vote to Humphrey's 42.7 percent and third-party candidate George Wallace's 13.5 percent. Nixon's national tally surpassed Humphrey's by only 510,000 votes, an amazingly slim margin given the turnout but a victory nonetheless. Nixon had finally achieved the pinnacle of American politics but now faced the problem of governance, a task far more complicated than campaigning. With the breadth and consequence of the nation's difficulties so great that they even obscured the real menace of environmental decay, Nixon had his task cut out for him.

On the morning after his election, Nixon took his first step as a representative of the people and not a practitioner of partisanship, adopting as his "great objective" the task of "bringing the American people together." "This will be an open administration, open to new ideas, open to men and women of both parties, open to critics as well as those who support us," Nixon confidently declared. Given the rhetoric of the campaign, the message was as ironic as it was portentous. But with the fractured nature of American society, it was an appropriate sign for a nation in need of hope.[11]

The president-elect's many skeptical critics did not see it this way. The thought of a Nixon administration struck fear in the hearts of many activists who had embraced the Great Society's reforms. In their minds, Nixon, the apparent right-wing zealot, the man who had made a career of battling communism, and the man who recently had spoken vaguely, and for many, ominously, about a return to "order," would certainly signal the emergence of a right-wing backlash domestically. Muskie, for one, approached the new administration with "great apprehension," fearing that "the programs would be gutted."[12] Because Nixon's "philosophy on natural resource management received such scant attention during the election campaign," the Sierra Club complained, "there is little on record by which to form a judgement."[13] Whether fear of the unknown or simply sadness at the apparent demise of the Great Society, to many skeptics any hope for future reforms would surely have to wait until after the dreaded tenure of the Nixon years, his comments notwithstanding.

Although Nixon had no hope of answering such pessimistic predictions from his reform-oriented detractors, his remarks were more than mere meaningless platitudes by a demagogue still delirious from his victory the night before. Nixon was never the reactionary that opponents painted him; he still remained a shrewd politician, savvy to the winds of public opinion. He did not intend to let the Great Society remain unchecked, but neither did he intend to launch a conservative reign of terror.[14] Such policies would unnecessarily provoke anger and resentment at a time when divisiveness threatened the very fabric of the nation. If anything, the Eisenhower years—a period of prosperity— had taught Nixon the power of moderation. Eisenhower's brand of conservatism was, by its own admission, "dynamic," not akin to the firebrand antigovern- ment rhetoric beginning to blossom in some quarters in reaction to the John- son era. To assault all federal programs was to throw the proverbial baby out with the bathwater, to ignore the Great Society's accomplishments for fear of its transgressions. In Nixon's view, this would not prove wise for the nation or for his own administration's political future. In the words of daughter Julie: "Al- though my family entered the White House with great hopes that my father could help with the healing process, we never underestimated the divisions caused by war and decades of racial injustice, nor forgot that the President who had lived in the White House before us had been broken by the bitterness and the unrest."[15]

On the day after the election, Vietnam stood as the first order of business. With his considerable expertise in foreign policy, Nixon had firm ideas on how to proceed, with Korea as the model for an armistice and an indefinite division of the country.[16] As president, however, Nixon would have to deal with all the issues, a task for which he was unprepared. He might avoid issues such as the environ- ment in an election, but as chief executive he clearly could not. After a brief vacation to Key Biscayne, Florida, Nixon began the job of putting together his administration, its officials, and its policies. This process first demonstrated that the environment could no longer be ignored. Despite its relative insignifi- cance in the election, it was indeed a pressing national issue. For environ- mentalists, the transition period and the first few months of the new Nixon administration served as the catalyst for a greater public activism. For Nixon, recognizing this, it was the catalyst for a new political strategy, one that in the end proved his postelection promises of moderation more than meaningless piffle.

Upon returning from Florida, Nixon appointed a series of transition task forces to provide overviews of various issues and to make the first policy sug- gestions. Each was to submit its report before the inauguration. One such group was the Task Force on Natural Resources and Environment, a group of twenty academicians, environmentalists, and corporate executives chaired by well-known environmentalist Russell Train.[17] A graduate of Princeton Univer- sity and Columbia University School of Law, Train held both strong Repub- lican and environmental credentials. A Republican judge, his interest in the environment grew from an African safari he took in the 1950s. This led him to organize the African Wildlife Leadership Foundation and, in 1965, to accept the top post at the Conservation Foundation. On December 5, a month after the election, Train's group issued its conclusions, with the first sentence setting the tone: "The Task Force recommends that improved environmental management be given high priority by the new Administration." The report was clear that the problem was no longer simply a matter of conservation of natural resources, but the larger task of maintaining and improving environmental quality. "The stake is no longer simply the protection of wildlife and forests," the report read. It involves "our standard of living, the health and quality of the life of our people." The world was at a turning point, as unchecked pollution "will eventually destroy the fitness of this planet as a place for human life."[18]

The report was as blunt and forceful a statement of environmentalism as Nixon had ever read. It noted, correctly, that public concern was on the rise, and that solutions were possible politically. The new administration should focus on the problem of urban growth, the driving force behind the myriad threats to the natural world. Nixon should appoint a "Special Assistant for Environmental Affairs," one individual charged with coordinating a diverse agenda. He should also expand former First Lady Lady Bird Johnson's Citizen's Advisory Committee on Recreation and Natural Beauty into a Citizen's Committee on the Environment. To act quickly offered political rewards, the report emphasized. An appendix with polls indicated public concern and published charts on the increasing number of state referendums.[19] The overall conclusion was obvious: the administration should take the lead against environmental degradation, for the good of the country as well as for the administration politically.

The thought of selecting one individual as an environmental coordinator had occurred to Ehrlichman, who agreed with the report's conclusions and who, himself, had only been on the job for a matter of days. By the time of the report, Nixon had found time for only two key substantive appointments, Ehrlichman's as top domestic advisor and that of H. Robert Haldeman as chief-of-staff. Unlike Ehrlichman, Haldeman had no experience or interest in environmental matters, although with credentials in advertising he undoubtedly knew what struck a chord with the public. Ironing out jurisdictional responsibilities was bound to create at least some tension, however, and Ehrlichman's appointment miffed Vice President Agnew, who had assumed himself the final arbiter of all matters domestic.[20] Nixon, nevertheless, focused on other key assignments, and, in regard to environmental quality, this in large measure meant the Secretary of Interior.

On December 11, a week after Train's task force issued its report, Nixon announced his cabinet selections. For Secretary of Interior, Nixon chose Alaska governor Walter Hickel. Hickel was in some ways a natural choice. A self-made man, the forty-nine year old had served as western regional coordinator of Nixon's campaign. He was from a western state, the traditional locale from which nominees hailed, and, as Alaska governor, was familiar with federal land and natural resources.[21] He was, however, far from a consensus candidate, and the resulting uproar over his nomination was Nixon's first indication that "bringing the American people together" was an easier slogan than policy. If the task-force report had not convinced Nixon of the importance of the environment as an issue, the tumultuous struggle waged against Hickel's nomination proved beyond a doubt that it should command the embryonic administration's attention.[22]

Resistance to Hickel centered on his prodevelopment gubernatorial record. Under Hickel, the state of Alaska unsuccessfully challenged a Department of Interior policy that halted all land withdrawals from the public domain until the federal government resolved native land claims and disputed oil rights. He opposed a strict nondegradation policy in regard to the federal water pollution law, and publicly encouraged oil development on Alaska's pristine North Slope. Reports indicated that Hickel had investments in oil stock, which raised questions of conflict of interest, and that he was a close ally of James Watt, chair of the Natural Resources Committee of the U.S. Chamber of Commerce and an ardent critic of strict enforcement of oil and water pollution legislation. In short, critics argued, he would sacrifice long-term interest for short-term gain, and the national interest for the interest of Alaska.[23]

Hickel did not help his cause. In a press conference a week after the nomination, Hickel decried "conservation for conservation's sake," a comment that provoked a storm of protest. Although his confirmation hearings had not yet begun, prominent newspapers condemned the nomination. The appointment, the New York Times declared, "has confirmed the worst fears of those who regard the restoration and conservation of a ravished continent . . . as priority business for this generation of Americans."[24] Key senators found their offices flooded with letters of protest. If confirmed, one citizen wrote Gaylord Nelson, Hickel would "bomb pollution control and resource conservation back to the Stone Age."[25]

When the confirmation hearings began, Hickel did his best to allay such fears. "All decisions I make will be governed by the broad national need and interest," Hickel declared on his first day of testimony. Promising to maintain the Alaskan "land freeze" and to divest himself of any investments that gave the appearance of impropriety, Hickel declared his full support for tough oil and water pollution legislation. Oil executives had not dominated his state government, he noted, but in reality had constituted only a small percentage of gubernatorial appointments. Facing hostile questioning, most notably from Senator George McGovern, Hickel remained dignified and restrained, assuring the committee that he was as genuinely concerned about the environment as they.[26]

Hickel's defense had as little effect in mollifying critics as had Nixon's post-election comments a month before; indeed, both efforts appeared to be astonishing denials of their respective pasts. Like Nixon's remarks, however, Hickel's comments were more than simple political expediency. Some truth existed in what Hickel said, although lost to environmental critics at the time. Alaska, both in its size and relative lack of development, was unique, and while Hickel's own record raised doubts about his partiality, environmental protection and economic growth were not mutually exclusive given proper planning. Alaska's situation did not directly translate into the lower forty-eight states, and Hickel's actions in regard to the former did not necessarily preclude a forceful environmental policy for the latter. As one aide to Muskie reluctantly acknowledged, nothing in Hickel's background was "capricious or excessive to date."[27]

This meant nothing to his critics, who perceived his appointment as evidence of Nixon's true intentions. The Izaak Walton League and the Sierra Club, along with other conservation organizations, remained adamantly opposed, ultimately delaying the final vote until three days after the inauguration. Hickel was the only cabinet member so delayed, an embarrassment to both Hickel and Nixon. In the end, however, critics could not derail approval, as the Senate Interior and Insular Affairs Committee voted to recommend confirmation 14–3, and the full Senate complied 73–14. The majority of the senators concluded that Hickel at least deserved the opportunity to prove himself an honest public servant. "My impression," Muskie declared before the vote, "is that there will be nothing strong enough to deny him the confirmation." Given his promises, "we will just have to give him a chance."[28] His nomination approved, Hickel invited every member of the Senate committee to lunch, placing in each chair a copy of his confirmation hearings entitled *How to Get a Job in Washington in Three Days.* "You have never seen twelve guys laugh so much in your life," recalled one Hickel aide.[29]

On January 20, 1969, Nixon took the oath of office as the nation's thirty-seventh chief executive. Continuing in the vein promised the day after the election and with as much goodwill as evident in Hickel's luncheon, Nixon again issued a call for an end to divisiveness, for healing and moderation. Whether impressed by Train's task-force report or the strength and intensity of Hickel's environmental opposition, Nixon pointedly included environmental protection in his comments, a noticeable break from the past. "In rebuilding our cities and improving our rural areas; in protecting our environment and enhancing the quality of life; in all these and more, we will and must press urgently forward," Nixon declared.[30]

Pressing forward, as fate would have it, was not an option at the outset. On January 28, 1969, only eight days after the inaugural and the day after Nixon's first official news conference, crude oil from a Union Oil Company well off the coast of Santa Barbara, California, began to leak from the sea floor, forming a large oil slick. Heavy winds spread it over twenty miles. Soon washing ashore, the slick killed a variety of marine life and soiled beaches renowned for their beauty. The disaster was, in fact, no greater than several oil tanker spills the world had suffered but, with the scenic beauty of the Californian coast as a backdrop, it still made for great television. Birds covered with sticky oil struggled for life; dead seals floated ashore; enraged Santa Barbara housewives cried for the cameras. The oil spill's cost to the environment was immense, but in a sense the tragedy served a purpose, for as the oil spread, so did national outrage. Although many may not have recognized it at the time, the Santa Barbara oil spill was the seminal event that environmentalists had sought. It shocked Americans, placing environmental protection on the front burner in a way it never had been before, turning a concerned public into an activist one. "Santa Barbara's oil disaster has pointed up for the world the fact that our technology can get us in serious trouble—trouble we can hardly repair," noted National Audubon president Dr. Elvis Stahr. "Santa Barbara's voice has been heard more loudly than any voice of protest in years." The spill had, in short, "a special impact." The spill, according to the Sierra Club, represented "an historic opportunity to dramatize the nation's need for a better and more livable environment." Park Service director George Hartzog was more philosophic: "Ecology has finally achieved currency."[31]

All eyes turned to the new administration, which immediately came under attack. Slow to recognize both the severity and significance of the spill, the White House once again found itself on the defensive, only weeks after Hickel's confirmation. For two days the administration did nothing, and it took six days for Hickel to fly to California and inspect the damage—the spill worsening by the hour. After a flight over the beaches and a meeting with angry citizens, Hickel denied their requests for an immediate ban on drilling in the channel, but instead asked the oil companies to suspend voluntarily their operations.

When only six companies complied, outrage grew, and the lobbying began. Santa Barbara's Republican congressman Charles Teaque met with Nixon and pressed for a permanent cessation to all drilling. Nixon, aware of the importance of California politically, waited for the press photographers to arrive, and then promised action. The next day Hickel announced the complete suspension of all drilling in the channel. It was, Hickel later acknowledged, "a slow start."[32]

Nixon was as angry as the Santa Barbara citizens. The Johnson administration had negotiated the oil leases in the first place, but his administration was taking the heat. Appointing a panel under his new science advisor, Dr. Lee DuBridge, to recommend ways to restore the beach and prevent similar spills in the future, Nixon hoped to counter charges that his administration had not acted forcibly enough. "We are going to do a better job than we have done in the past," Nixon stated in a veiled reference to his predecessor.[33]

Despite Nixon's hopes that Hickel's announcement had put the matter to rest, the White House's actions only engendered more carping. Hickel had promised a suspension—not a permanent ban. Citizens assumed that the administration would wait until the furor died down, and then allow resumption of drilling. This appeared the case when two weeks later Hickel ordered all five wells on Platform A, the main source of the leak, reopened and pumped "at maximum rate." It did not matter that DuBridge's panel had recommended the action and that it was sound strategy to relieve subterranean pressure and guard against a worse disaster. The administration simply appeared indifferent, an angle much of the media reported.[34] "I was with the Administration and you in your nomination problems," one Californian wrote Hickel, "but you can be sure that my opinion of you and others that I have supported will change if the off-shore drilling is not stopped."[35]

Recognizing an opportunity, Democrats moved quickly to capitalize off the groundswell for additional action. As chairman of his pollution subcommittee, Senator Muskie called public hearings to investigate the disaster. "To those of us who have been trying for several years to legislate in this area," Muskie stated, "[the spill] is another justification for broadened Federal responsibility to cope with pollution disasters." Muskie announced that, like Hickel before him, he planned to inspect the damage personally, to ensure "first-hand knowledge of the present episode."[36] Democratic California senator Alan Cranston and others proclaimed that they supported legislation to ban permanently all drilling in the Santa Barbara channel while instituting a "moratorium on drilling in all other federal tidelands in California until there are assurances that drilling will not endanger the environment."[37] The Sierra Club concurred, adopting a resolution that declared, "The nation's tidelands and outer continental shelf are being exploited with the same unbridled singleness of purpose that left much of America's landscape ravaged in the last century."[38]

While such lobbying bordered on hyperbole, clearly the administration had to do more. The actions of Muskie particularly bothered the White House. "Nixon always had Muskie on his mind," Train remembered.[39] In late March, two months after the blowout and as crews continued the momentous task of cleaning up, Nixon visited the damaged beaches, wading through the muddy and oily waters with television cameras in tow. The same day Hickel announced that Nixon had approved an "ecological preserve," a two-mile-wide buffer zone where oil companies could not drill in the channel. Hickel assumed that such efforts to appease public sentiment were inadequate given the attention the spill earned, and advocated public review of all future drilling leases. Taking what actions he could on his own, Hickel approved tougher Interior Department regulations, including more casing on wells, additional required testing, and mandatory warning devices. Nixon, however, refused his secretary's suggestion for public review of leases, once again hoping that his administration had already answered critics.[40]

As Hickel predicted, however, the issue continued to fester. In early April, after assurances by geological experts that his actions were sound environmentally, Hickel allowed the resumption of drilling on five of the Santa Barbara leases. It made no difference that all five were well removed from the original blowout, that they had passed environmental scrutiny, that Interior had just instituted stricter regulations, or that the suspension remained in place for the sixty-seven other leases, the overwhelming majority. The action still made national news and appeared as though the administration proceeded exactly as critics had predicted: waiting for the furor to pass and then continuing with business as usual.[41]

In reality, however, the persistence and intensity with which environmentalists approached the issue surprised and conflicted many in the administration, with the internal White House debate anything but usual. On one hand, the issue had clearly hurt the administration politically, despite the efforts it had taken. To shut down the leases permanently, however, not only ended access to the valuable resources there, but also might make the government liable to the companies, which had paid millions for the right to drill. If the government rescinded the leases permanently, pressure might build to do the same elsewhere, an obviously untenable solution given the nation's dependence upon foreign oil. No easy solution existed, and thus the issue simply remained on the table. While the temporary suspension remained, the White House was at least happy to see the matter, with no new developments, finally fade from the news.[42]

For the White House the successive controversies of Hickel's nomination and the Santa Barbara oil spill had cost the administration political capital but had taught a valuable lesson. Just as the transitional task force had noted, the environment was no longer simply an issue best ignored. The administration should embrace the new environmentalism, take the offensive, or risk being run over on an issue that increasingly appeared politically potent. This was a real problem, Nixon complained to Ehrlichman as the oil-spill crisis unfolded. The Democrats had many "good ideas . . . for domestic programs," including the environment, and the administration's "slow start might allow the opposition to seize the initiative."[43] Ehrlichman quickly called a series of meetings with cabinet secretaries and other high-ranking executive officials to discuss domestic initiatives. At the recommendation of New York senator Daniel Patrick Moynihan, who had emerged as an informal advisor, Ehrlichman invited the conservationist Train to ensure an adequate discussion of environmental policy. With the Santa Barbara oil spill as the backdrop, Train made the case for an activist agenda. Now elevated to Undersecretary of Interior as an overture to environmentalists still angry over Hickel, Train stood with Whitaker as a secure and reliable advocate within the administration. No consensus existed regarding specifics, but all concurred with Train that the administration needed a comprehensive environmental program.[44]

The first step was to organize the White House staff. Soon after his appointment, Ehrlichman had enlisted Egil Krogh, a thirty-year-old attorney, as one of his assistants. In May, Ehrlichman designated the environment as Krogh's main responsibility. Krogh's job was to coordinate a task force charged with producing a comprehensive package of proposals, a complete legislative agenda that Nixon hoped to unveil early the following year. Presenting a complete program in an "environmental message to Congress"—something no president had ever done before—would address the breadth of the problem, not to mention the likelihood that it would capture the headlines.

The trouble, of course, was that preparation for the amalgam of issues required considerable time, and in the interim the Democrats were on the move. By May, Senator Henry Jackson had introduced legislation to create a Council on Environmental Quality (CEQ), a three-person advisory body to coordinate environmental policy in the executive branch.[45] Over eighty executive branch agencies or departments had, in varying degrees, responsibilities for the environment. The problem was multifaceted, and, as the original transitional task force had noted, duplication and overlap of programs was common. Krogh's new task force included representatives from many of the relevant departments, and while the members were young and energetic, they were relatively lower-level experts on specific areas, unable to facilitate the overall coordination necessary. Jackson's council, designed as a more formal, permanent entity, more precisely fit the bill, a fact not lost upon environmentalists and many in Congress. A warm reception on Capitol Hill, therefore, greeted Jackson's bill, as the media and many political pundits praised the proposal. "Allow me to congratulate you on your legislation to establish a Council on Environmental Quality," former Secretary of Interior Stewart Udall, a well-known champion of environmental quality, wrote Jackson. "I ask of you," a Jackson constituent added, "please, please, please, please do something [to assist passage]."[46]

As Jackson addressed environmental organization, Muskie moved more directly in response to the Santa Barbara crisis, proposing legislation mandating complete company liability in the event of an oil spill. In January the House had passed a bill establishing partial liability, which Ehrlichman and other top administration officials favored, but after the infamous spill, Muskie had countered with a proposal that insisted upon complete company liability short of "acts of God" or the consequences of war. By May, Muskie's version, termed the Water Quality Improvement Act, had gained strength in the Senate, adding to his reputation as "Mr. Clean" and "Ecology Ed." President Nixon, Muskie told the press in May, was entitled to a "honeymoon," but time was running out for needed action. Pollution was one result "of our urban crisis," Muskie declared, and while Nixon had promised action, "we ought to be getting it before long."[47] Muskie had proved his environmental credentials before the emergent political benefits, and he appeared in no rush to relinquish his crown as the nation's most forceful environmental advocate.

The claims of a muddled bureaucracy did not shock Nixon, who had campaigned on promises of more efficiency. For Nixon, the bureaucratic quagmire that characterized the existing environmental establishment was indicative of the entire executive branch, and begged for a more comprehensive reform. Taking the first step in April, Nixon appointed the President's Advisory Council on Executive Organization, a study group chaired by former Litton Industries CEO Roy Ash and charged with making specific recommendations for overall executive branch organization, environmental policy included.[48] Like Krogh's task force, however, the Ash Council, as it was popularly known, required months of preparation before any significant proposals were ready, and, as the reception given Jackson's and Muskie's respective bills indicated, the White House had little time to dally. On May 29, therefore, Nixon issued an executive order creating his own White House coordinating body, the Environmental Quality Council (EQC). As the transitional task force had recommended months before, the order also expanded Johnson's Citizen's Advisory Committee on Recreation and Natural Beauty into the Citizen's Advisory Committee on Environmental Quality (CACEQ). Consisting of selected cabinet secretaries and chaired by science advisor DuBridge, the EQC would control policy as the Ash Council and Krogh's task force completed their respective preparations.[49]

For many in the White House, environmental policy increasingly appeared to be a potpourri of disparate and complicated problems united only in the sense that not one offered an easy solution. On one hand, with the relative strength of the political opposition, Ehrlichman and other top administration figures realized the need for immediate action, something to counter the public relations debacles and the apparent inactivity of the first few months. On the other hand, every specific initiative carried with it a possible economic cost, a potential downside best not forgotten in the rush to win the political initiative. This invariable fact hindered a solution to the Santa Barbara crisis and complicated an array of specific issues that arose simultaneously. The result was that all too frequently in the first months of the administration, the White House was forced to delay action, to appoint study groups or task forces to define options—beyond the umbrella efforts of Krogh's group. Many environmental organizations, focusing narrowly and entirely on the threat to nature, failed to appreciate the administration's attempts to compromise between legitimate but competing interests. They demanded action, immediate and unabridged, and thus for the White House the political initiative appeared as remote as ever.

By early summer, administration-appointed committees studied an array of problems, from environmental annoyances to lethal threats, each demanding the White House's attention and each with the potential to alienate an important constituency. The Garwin Committee, named for its chair, the renowned physicist Richard L. Garwin, wrestled with the proposed supersonic transport. The sleek plane was a technological marvel, able to jet passengers across the Atlantic in just over two hours, carrying almost three hundred passengers and traveling up to a breathtaking eighteen hundred miles per hour. It stood to revolutionize the airline industry, if it were not for the fact that its attendant sonic boom and excessive engine noise were intolerable to most Americans. The SST's principal manufacturer, the Boeing Corporation, noted its economic importance as ardently as the National Audubon Society and the Sierra Club noted its environmental hazards. At the grass-roots level, people from around the country formed the Citizen's League against the Sonic Boom (CLASB), a group led by a Harvard University physicist. A formidable opponent, CLASB soon proved as adept at raising funds as lobbying Congress. The White House had to decide whether to let the contract for development, and, without a ready solution, first required further study.[50]

The Mrak Commission, named for its chairman, chemist Emil M. Mrak, simultaneously investigated the problem of pesticide use. No one could doubt the benefits that chemical pesticides offered the American farmer. Proclaimed as miracles of modern science, they protected a wide range of crops from insect damage. Because of its ability to kill malaria-bearing mosquitoes and protect the Southern cotton crop, the chlorinated hydrocarbon DDT won for its inventor the coveted Nobel Prize. The agricultural community insisted that pesticides were absolutely essential, a claim that environmentalists countered with equal vigor. Noting that many of the chemicals were persistent—that is, they remained in the organism once ingested—environmentalists argued that they posed a threat to those higher in the food chain, including man. Armed with a slew of studies and backed by the emotional pull of Carson's best-selling *Silent Spring*, critics prepared to take on the powerful agricultural lobby, a force in Washington for decades. The struggle had already begun in New York and Michigan, with the latter state concerned over traces of the chemical found in trout. In Wisconsin, the controversy had flared into acrimonious litigation, which continued as Nixon took office and set an ominous tone for debate at the national level.[51] The question threatened a true political brawl, and all looked to the new administration—which, unfamiliar with the issue, again required further investigation.[52]

These were not the only issues complex enough to warrant delay when the political initiative urged action. By early summer, additional committees studied the future of the Florida Everglades and the equally troublesome matter of timber supply. The Everglades had been a cause célèbre for the National Audubon Society for years, and with good cause. At the tip of mainland Florida, the Everglades National Park's 1.4 million acres composed a unique and multifarious ecosystem, home to over twenty-two endangered species of fish and wildlife and an array of exotic tropical flora. Essentially an aquatic park unlike any other in America, the Everglades and its inhabitants depended upon a supply of water from the sloughs and sawgrass savannahs of the Big Cypress Swamp to its north and west. The problem lay with the phenomenal growth of Miami, which threatened the Big Cypress and thus indirectly the Everglades. At the center of this growth was the proposed Miami jetport, planned for only six miles north of the Everglades and in the heart of the Big Cypress. A mammoth project, the jetport would occupy over thirty-nine square miles, an area larger than the city of Miami itself. With runways six miles long, it would handle the largest and fastest jets, over two hundred thousand commercial flights a year. The entire complex would prove large enough to hold the major metropolitan airports of New York, Los Angeles, and Washington combined. It promised an economic boon and an environmental disaster—in short, another issue that the administration had no intention of approaching unprepared or in a haphazard manner. The Leopold Commission, a joint Department of Interior-State of Florida investigation named for its chair, the Florida ecologist Luna B. Leopold, thus faced the task of unraveling the tangle of competing interests, finding a solution acceptable to both developers and environmentalists.[53]

The issue of lumber supply, meanwhile, had already landed the administration in court, and the White House recognized that the prudent course was one with caution. On one hand, the nation faced a severe lumber shortage, as the expanding economy's clamor for wood-based products led to calls for additional harvests on U.S. Forest Service land.[54] On the other hand, the administration faced the mandate of the Wilderness Act. Passed five years before, it was one of the early political hallmarks of the nation's new environmentalism. In creating the National Wilderness Preservation System, the act required a ten-year study of all large and undisturbed "primitive" or "roadless" forests for possible protection, a task that was sadly behind schedule.[55] As much of this land was prime Forest Service land, the stage was set for a political fracas to rival that over pesticides. Environmentalists had already fired the first volley, filing suit when the Forest Service, utilizing a narrow interpretation of the law, allowed harvesting on forests potentially eligible for the Wilderness System.[56] In Congress, timber proponents answered with legislative proposals to finance an increase in logging. This legislation was, according to Train, "bad practice environmentally." It would, Nixon acknowledged, "touch a lot of raw nerves." It certainly did with the Sierra Club, which indulged in a little hyperbole: "This bill could well rule out the creation of future national park, recreation, and wilderness areas in the forested portions of the public domain." Still, for the White House, the economic reality remained. The wholesale price for softwood lumber had risen over 30 percent since early the preceding year, and the lumber situation appeared, indeed, ominous.[57] It was, in short, a classic case of economy versus environment, a strong economic need pitted against a new constituency that the administration hoped to win. No easy solution existed, as the White House scrambled for an acceptable program. This would once again take time, however, with the only immediate solution the appointment of the Softwood Lumber and Plywood Task Force, yet another study, another delay, necessary before policy implementation.

The most frustrating issue—and the most damaging to the administration's hopes of capturing the environmental initiative—was the proposed Alaskan oil pipeline. In the wake of the Santa Barbara disaster, much of the public was hardly sympathetic to the idea of increased use of this fossil fuel, often demonized not only for its infamous spills but as the lifeblood of the air-polluting internal combustion engine. Added into the equation was the proposed route of the pipeline: from Prudhoe Bay on Alaska's North Slope southward eight hundred miles to Valdez, the northernmost ice-free port in the nation. Here truly lay the last pristine wilderness in the United States, the exemplar of all the Wilderness Act intended to protect. It was a land of roaming caribou and soaring eagles, and from any angle a subterranean hot-oil pipeline was not an easy fit. "It is important," the Wilderness Society rallied its members, "that citizens in Alaska and throughout the nation express their concern."[58]

The White House recognized both the symbolic and ecological importance of maintaining the integrity of this wilderness. It was also, however, aware of another reality, that of the nation's energy needs and the economic potential of the area. A decade before, worried over the nation's increasing reliance upon foreign oil, the government had established an import quota. While this had induced American refiners to utilize domestic reserves at a faster rate to meet growing demand, by the end of the Johnson administration it had also resulted in an ominous decline in the nation's reserve supply. Foreign producers, meanwhile, had formed the Organization of Petroleum Exporting Countries (OPEC), a cartel that threatened to raise prices. The possibility of a significant new domestic source, therefore, understandably drew the attention of the administration—as well as those sensing a profit. Leading oil companies quickly formed a consortium to exploit the new fields, the Trans Alaska Pipeline System (TAPS), just as the possibility of huge earnings exacerbated the issue of Native American land claims. For a decade Alaska's natives had complained that the state's creation had robbed them of land, and now they claimed a significant share of the potential oil profits. The situation was controversial enough that former Secretary of Interior Stewart Udall had issued a "land freeze" denying any withdrawals from the federal domain pending a resolution of the matter. To many in the administration, Udall's order was political more than practical. Issued after Johnson's decision not to seek reelection, it was a way to ensure his own environmental agenda no matter which party won the election, and a chance for the Democratic Congress to exert more influence. Regardless, in any respect, the entire issue was indeed an administrative quagmire: environmentalists opposed construction and favored the "freeze"; the state and its natives took the opposite positions, albeit at odds in sharing the spoils.[59]

The inevitable result was another committee, this one's task even more complicated than the rest. Nixon had no doubt that the Department of Interior should lift the "freeze" and allow construction. He just insisted that the job be done without harming the environment. "It is urgent that we consider now the ways in which we can explore and develop . . . the oil reserves of northern Alaska," Nixon wrote Hickel in May, adding, "without destruction and with minimum disturbance." Nixon and environmentalists disagreed over the possibility of this last caveat, but they both turned to the new North Slope Task Force for a solution.[60]

The delays, while necessary, were truly frustrating. By June, reports reached Ehrlichman that key Democrats, including Senators McGovern and Muskie, planned criticism of the White House for its apparent lack of activity. Under assault on many fronts and with a president increasingly sensitive to adverse publicity, this was the last thing the administration needed.[61] If Nixon enjoyed a "honeymoon," by summer it had long since ended. Aware of his predecessor's political demise, Nixon had hoped to become a popular chief executive, excising the country from Vietnam without conceding defeat and rolling back the Great Society without neglecting the problems it intended to solve. On every front, however, impatient critics demanded immediate action. In many respects, Nixon had quickly become a man as hounded as President Johnson before him, and, to the lone occupant of the Oval Office, the focus of so much wrath, the entire world appeared in opposition. Hecklers appeared to stalk him everywhere; his every action seemed to provoke a firestorm. For Nixon, liberals, driven by emotion and never open to rational explanations, would not wait for fiscally sound solutions. Conservatives, demanding an immediate end to welfare programs, would not wait for answers that the majority of Americans would embrace, ones that attacked the bureaucracy while still protecting the truly needy. Youthful war protesters were the worst, more intent upon disruption than policy, unable to wait for an acceptable agreement before a complete and immediate troop withdrawal. Nixon increasingly believed that much of the public simply did not appreciate the administration's efforts and the time necessary for adequate programs. Monitoring press coverage daily, Nixon's anger threatened to boil over, with a more vengeful, less accommodating persona emerging, one more along the lines of what critics had expected at the outset. Now maintaining a list of "enemies," Nixon began down the slippery slope that would ultimately lead to his political demise, ordering illegal wiretaps and the Internal Revenue Service upon his most vocal critics.[62] The White House's varied committees promised the possibility of grand accomplishments on behalf of the environment, but the likelihood of appearing as an environmental ogre only added fuel to Nixon's already bright fire.

The best defense was a good offense, Ehrlichman assumed, turning to Krogh's task force for a possible legislative initiative that would silence critics such as McGovern and Muskie before they caused additional damage. The fact remained, however, that Krogh's task force was still no better prepared to offer a specific proposal than were the committees that the White House had just appointed.[63] In fact, Krogh had found the mandate of producing a comprehensive environmental agenda onerous, and longed for a new challenge. Ehrlichman, aware of his young assistant's desire, agreed to transfer Krogh to the issue of narcotics. With former Harvard professor Timothy Leary urging the country's youth to "tune in, turn on, and drop out," the issue of drug use offered an emotional appeal even greater than that of environmental protection, and Krogh readily accepted. To continue the complex task of molding a comprehensive environmental agenda, Ehrlichman turned to John Whitaker, then serving as secretary to the cabinet.[64] With his geology background and record of support for Nixon, Whitaker was the obvious choice, and, in the end, a wise one. Over the next several years, he proved a consistent advocate of environmental protection, an ally to environmentalists in an administration often regarded as more foe than friend.

In the summer of 1969, however, Whitaker inherited the same complex problems that had confounded his predecessor. A complete package of proposals for Nixon's planned environmental offensive was still months away, and with every passing week the administration found itself further on the defensive. The Sierra Club, for one, did not believe administration inaction was the result of a lack of preparation; it was, rather, "a failure to make commitments."[65] Nixon remained largely transfixed by the quandary of Vietnam, with his youthful critics now planning a "moratorium," a massive antiwar protest that would flood Washington and encircle the White House. This provided great play for the media, diverting public attention from the environment—but not stopping the substantive debates just then forming in Congress. Nixon had little time for the specifics of these debates, but Ehrlichman, Whitaker, and the other assistants entrusted with responsibility for environmental protection realized that turning the issue to their political advantage remained a goal, not reality.

By summer, the reality in Congress was that Jackson's bill to create a Council on Environmental Quality had grown from a simple reorganization proposal into a forceful statement of a national environmental policy. When the Senate Interior and Insular Affairs Committee, which Jackson chaired, reported out the bill in early July, it included not only provisions for a CEQ, but also provisions declaring it a national policy to protect environmental quality. More significantly, the new bill included an "action-forcing mechanism," a requirement that, before any large federal project, the government issue a "finding" concerning its probable environmental impact. The House version did not include this latter provision, but the Senate passed it easily, as environmentalists lauded Jackson and his fellow Democrats for strengthening the legislation.[66] For his considerable efforts in this and other endeavors, the Sierra Club awarded Jackson its John Muir Award, named for the famous late nineteenth-century naturalist. The award was indeed an honor, given the significant accomplishments of Muskie and an array of Jackson's Democratic colleagues. In accepting the award, Jackson added a slap at the White House, warning members to guard against an erosion of gains during the Nixon administration.[67]

The turn of events annoyed the White House, for Nixon's own advisory body, EQC, had neither settled the problem of bureaucratic organization nor won the support that Jackson's CEQ now engendered. Without appreciating the importance of the "action-forcing mechanism," the administration's objections focused on this proposed rival body, which the White House argued duplicated its own. Jackson was swift in defense of his proposal, arguing that Nixon's EQC had no full-time support staff. Composed of cabinet members, each hoping to curry favor with the president, EQC would, Jackson predicted, bog down in interdepartmental disputes or simply acquiesce to Nixon's every wish. Cabinet members would not have "the time and energy to provide the continuity of effort required," their ultimate advice "compromised."[68]

As administration officials testified against the CEQ provision, Ehrlichman realized that continued resistance threatened to undermine once and for all the White House's lofty rhetoric, giving credence to the opposition's criticism that Nixon never backed up his words with actions. As DuBridge wrote Nixon, "Opposition to the bill would appear to put you in the position of being against activities aimed at improving the environment," which was not wise politically.[69] It was, for Nixon, an awkward situation. He wanted off the defensive, but by summer recognized that some truth existed in what Jackson and the others claimed. EQC indeed appeared ineffective. Fearing that it had become "bogged down with a shotgun approach to all environmental problems," Nixon told DuBridge that he was "anxious that the Council come up with three or four hard programs." The council, Nixon ordered, was to "pinpoint areas where something can be quickly accomplished."[70] In addition, Train, a man he had grown to respect, was to take part in all deliberations. Nixon knew that Ehrlichman and DuBridge were correct; if Jackson's bill passed the full Congress, he would have to sign it. He was just anxious that from EQC and other independent committees studying the problems of environmental degradation, someone provide a solid initiative, a proposal that would end the criticism he had already come to expect.

It was Moynihan, the senator turned presidential confidant, who recognized the opportunity for action. Although he appeared the embodiment of all

Nixon despised, a liberal Democrat, an elite New Yorker closely associated with the eastern intellectual community, his intelligence and independent mind intrigued Nixon, who had by this point hired him as a top assistant for urban affairs. Moynihan now proved his value, arguing that population control underlay all environmental problems, and that no one to date had addressed the matter. It was an astute observation. Author Paul Ehrlich's 1968 text, *The Population Bomb*, had sold over three million volumes, and its bleak forecast that "hundreds of millions of people are going to starve" had clearly hit a nerve with the public.[71] Although such pessimistic predictions were certainly open to question, one could not ignore the possibility of a Malthusian nightmare—or the public's fear of it.

Like so many other environmental issues, the matter was complex. It was foolhardy, Nixon recognized, to wade unadvisedly into the waters of abortion and birth control, awash in the controversial seas of religion and morality. On the other hand, Congress once again threatened to act first, in this case members of his own party. The House Republican Task Force on Earth Resources and Population had held hearings on population growth, and its chairman, Texas Republican George Bush, had already called for a greater emphasis on family planning. The Democrats, outside of concurring with calls for increased funding, had accomplished little. Indeed, no president had ever mentioned the issue—and therein lay the opportunity. If he were to address Congress on the matter, appoint a Population Commission as Moynihan recommended, the initiative would be his. His message would do little more than what members of both parties had already advocated, and the appointment of another committee, another investigation, was hardly provocative—but the symbolism was hard to deny. He would stand as the first president to note the problem, a significant event in itself.[72]

On July 18, Nixon delivered the first presidential message on population growth ever given to Congress. He highlighted a bevy of grim statistics, and instructed his EQC to explore the relationship between population growth and environmental quality. No American family, Nixon declared, should lack family-planning assistance due to financial need. Calling for Congress to create a twenty-four-member Commission on Population Growth and the American Future, with its report due in two years, Nixon promised increased funds for family planning.[73]

The message did not please everyone. To avoid the obvious pitfalls, Nixon made no plea for zero population growth, claimed by some as the ultimate solution to the "crisis." His call for voluntary reduction in family size was, according to scientists at the John Muir Institute's Conference on Population Growth, "insanity." The only real solution, they argued, was mandatory birth control in underdeveloped nations of the world, and, four years before *Roe v. Wade*, easy and legal abortions in the United States. Nixon had done nothing more than call for another environmental committee that would produce pages of recommendations but little substance.[74] In protesting, the scientists were correct that Nixon's message was not radical, but, at the same time, they neither appreciated Nixon's position nor the importance of what he did do. This importance lay, as Nixon anticipated, in its symbolism. Sufficient or not, a presidential message still highlighted the seriousness of the problem; it stimulated debate, if nothing else garnering attention for critics as well as supporters. Nixon may not have received all the praise he sought, but he nevertheless aided the cause of the very critics he endured.

In the long, hot summer of 1969, symbolism was all Nixon could count on; he suffered critics on every front. When the Apollo mission successfully landed on the moon, Nixon spoke with the astronauts by telephone — and on national television. "This certainly has to be the most historic telephone call ever made from the White House," Nixon began. When they returned to Earth, Nixon flew to the South Pacific to greet personally the returning heroes — once again on national television. Nixon had taken absolutely no role in the space program, but he recognized a public relations opportunity. He also recognized a public relations debacle. When Senator Ted Kennedy drove off a bridge on Chappaquiddick Island in Massachusetts late the night before the lunar landing, killing a young female companion and raising questions about the senator's drinking, womanizing, and, obviously, his culpability in the tragedy, Nixon ordered Ehrlichman to "get it properly exploited."[75] Nixon was not about to miss an opportunity to get off the defensive or put his opponents on it.

As summer turned to fall, Secretary Hickel spotted an avenue for action beyond symbolism. In many ways, Hickel as an environmental advocate was still as hard to envision as Moynihan as a White House assistant. Lambasted by environmentalists at his confirmation hearings months before, one could hardly blame Hickel for harboring a grudge, for crossing environmentalists at every turn. This was not the case, however, as Hickel drew from his experiences not a burning desire for retaliation but a keen awareness of the potency of the new environmentalism. He, like no one else, had weathered a firsthand encounter with this new political reality. Like his boss in the Oval Office, he was not about to let an opportunity pass by.

The national parks, Hickel suggested, offered an excellent means by which to demonstrate the administration's commitment to environmentalism. Conveniently ignoring that his recommendation expanded his own authority, Hickel proposed a new program to improve and expand the National Park System.

The proposal was certainly reasonable, for many of the more popular parks were virtually under siege, burdened by congestion and, in this sense, victims of their own success. A program "to bring parks to the people" would prove popular, Hickel argued, and, because the cost of acquiring new parkland escalated every day, it would save money in the long run. Hickel had already issued new policy directives, including better mass transportation services, more corporate participation in nature preservation, and more coordination with schools and universities, directives that had won rave reviews from the Wilderness Society and the Sierra Club.[76] The next step was up to Nixon. The idea had merit, Nixon agreed, but its cost was worrisome. In any event, the Department of Interior should publicize immediately that it had issued its directives only with the president's personal knowledge and consent.[77]

The Miami-jetport proposal particularly angered Hickel. The Everglades was one of the crown jewels of the Park System, and Hickel had no intention of letting it deteriorate during his watch. When the Leopold Commission issued its report in September, a report that stressed the destruction of the fragile ecosystem, Hickel pressed his case with the White House. Dade County, the location of the proposed airport, overwhelmingly supported construction, Hickel wrote Ehrlichman. It was, however, a largely Democratic stronghold, and would probably not support the administration in any event. Sufficient lands were available north of Miami, in Republican areas and only six miles from downtown. Florida governor Claude Kirk, fearing a negative impact on tourism, supported a move, while environmentalists had united into the "Everglades Coalition," an umbrella organization of twenty-one environmental groups in opposition. Jackson's Senate Interior Committee had held hearings on the issue and was on record as strongly opposed, with other Democrats pushing the matter before a media prepared to publicize it. "I intend to fight for the preservation of the Park," promised Muskie, "not only for the benefit of wildlife, but also for the benefit of present and future generations."[78] The entire scenario did not take long to convince Ehrlichman that Hickel was correct; it was important environmentally and an excellent opportunity to get off the defensive. On September 10, therefore, Hickel, Transportation Secretary Volpe, and Governor Kirk jointly announced that the administration and the state of Florida supported moving the airport, music to the ears of environmentalists.

The problem was the Dade County Port Authority (DCPA), which insisted on the original site. Florida law permitted the DCPA to operate the facility on its own, subject only to Federal Aviation Administration (FAA) regulations. As the DCPA funded the jetport through local bond issues and its own revenues, there appeared little that federal or state authorities could do, Hickel's advocacy aside. The DCPA, anticipating astonishing growth, was in no mood for

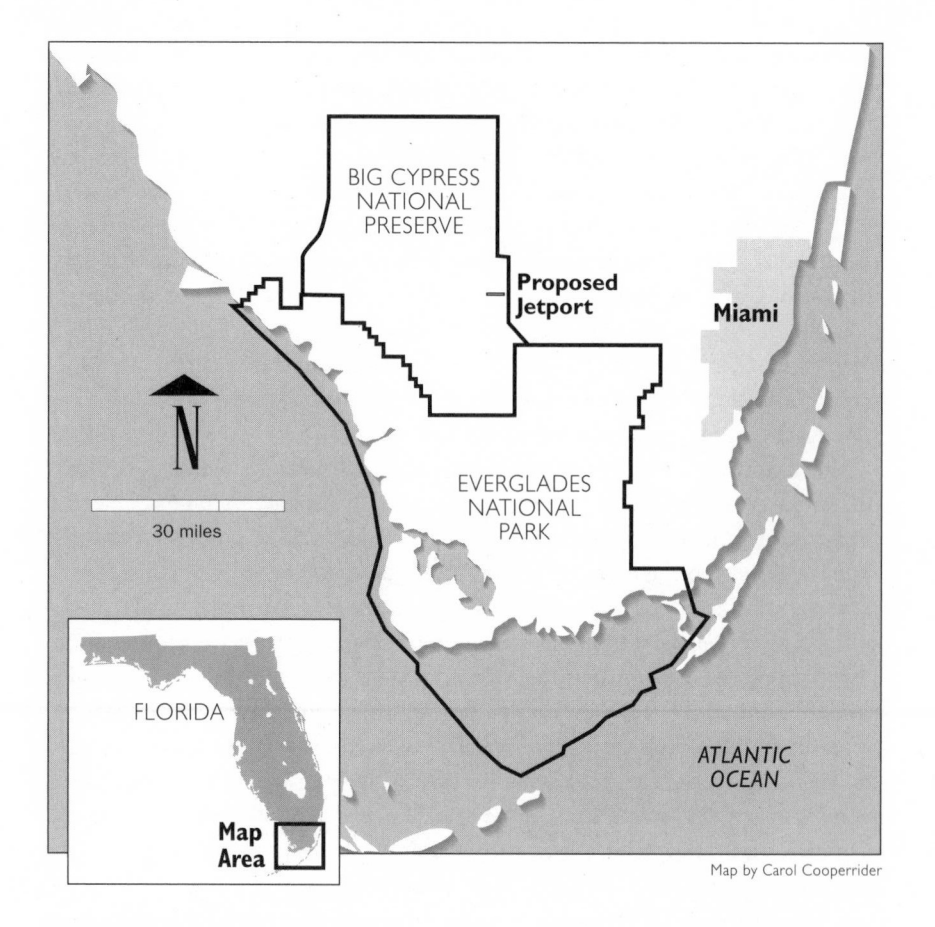

Map of Big Cypress Preserve and Everglades National Park. (Courtesy Everglades National Park, National Park Service.)

concessions. "A new city is going to rise up in the middle of Florida . . . whether you like it or not," claimed Alan Stewart, DCPA director.[79] For local Dade residents, the impact on the Everglades was a small price to pay for the bonanza they anticipated. When critics argued that the noise would drive alligators away, Stewart reportedly commented that he would buy the alligators earmuffs. For Stewart, environmentalists were "butterfly chasers" and "yellow bellied sapsuckers." Why not, he sarcastically asked, build an astrodome next to the runways where environmentalists could chase their butterflies unmolested?[80]

The DCPA was ready for a fight, but Hickel was up to the challenge. There was a way to overcome such stubborn resistance, Hickel convinced Ehrlichman. While the FAA had no environmental regulations, it might still use what leverage it had. It could slow down the approval process, restrict flights, add other burdensome regulations, in short do everything it could to make continuing at the present location a costly and ineffective solution. In addition, the DCPA had planned on using Army Corps of Engineers equipment in its construction, equipment that the Corps might deny.[81]

It was a devious, hard-ball tactic, but in the words of one aide, it put the administration "on the side of the angels" — and it appeared to work. Serious negotiations quickly commenced, with the DCPA more open to compromise. Construction on the airport's training facility had already begun, and questions revolved around compensation for money spent as well as the possibility of allowing the training facility to remain in operation. Whitaker, new to the job but now intricately involved, worried over the long-term implications for other airport-site controversies. A solution was not yet at hand, but at least now, thanks in large part to Hickel, one appeared possible.[82]

In the interim, Hickel pressed on with other suggestions for environmental advocacy. Existing water pollution law mandated that the Interior Department recommend to Congress a program to protect the nation's estuaries.[83] With this report due, Hickel argued, another opportunity existed for immediate action. Almost three-fourths of the nation's population lived in coastal states, the Great Lakes included. In the previous thirty years this population had grown by almost 80 percent, 30 percent higher than the national rate. With the nation's postwar affluence, beach cottages and high-rise hotels grew where before only sand dunes stood. In short, the problem was more than just the rivers; it involved the land along the water. Beaches, wetlands, the tidelands in general — these were the endangered lands of America, the battlegrounds for environmentalists of tomorrow. The administration, Hickel recommended, could act first, preempt the issue with a proposal for coastal zone management.[84]

Whitaker thought the proposal unnecessary, for his task force anticipated a more comprehensive proposal for overall land use, the coastal zone included. Ehrlichman, however, recognized that South Carolina Democrat Ernest Hollings was considering a similar bill, and to hesitate was to lose an opportunity to boost the administration. In any event, coastal zone legislation probably stood a better chance of passage than any broader proposal. Marine biologists and oceanographers had formed an effective lobby in Congress and were adept at capturing public sympathies. Members from land-locked states dominated the Senate and House Interior committees and would prove less likely to object to restrictions that did not directly affect their own constituencies.[85]

The bill the White House proposed was more carrot than stick. Rather than forcing a national plan upon states that understandably worried about federal limits on their growth, it provided federal assistance in the development and operation of state coastal zone plans. As Hickel recommended, the bill mandated that the Department of Interior oversee a program of direct grants, 50 percent of the cost incurred in the development of the plan, and upon the department's approval, 50 percent of the annual operational cost. The bill specified criteria for approval, including protection of ecologically fragile areas, the plan's supersedure over any countervailing local zoning, and compliance with all relevant federal regulations. Each state, however, was free to participate in the program or not.[86] Hickel had smartly crafted the bill; it addressed an issue that needed attention, and did so without overtly threatening state authority.

Approaching an issue diplomatically was never Hickel's forte, however, and now, committed to environmental protection, his blunt advocacy annoyed many in the White House. "The Administration must face up to its natural resources and environmental responsibilities," Hickel wrote Nixon. "We must plan and act in terms of altered priorities."[87] Nixon agreed, but wondered if the need to launch an environmental offensive had blinded his secretary to fiscal constraints and the pressing realities of other obligations. The press certainly noticed Hickel surprising advocacy, as the *Christian Science Monitor* concluded that "events so far indicate Hickel is a very good Secretary." He was, in short, "trying hard to make a good record." Such reports only partially pleased his superiors. "This worries me," Nixon wrote Ehrlichman in reply. "He may be caving in too much to his critics."[88] On the one hand Hickel helped the administration's battered environmental reputation, but on the other his advocacy appeared at times to know no restraints. "Secretary Hickel has serious differences of opinion with the Bureau of the Budget," Ehrlichman wrote Chief of Staff Haldeman. It was a matter, Haldeman replied, that Nixon wanted to address personally.[89]

It was for the White House the same old dilemma, the same matter that had compelled delay when the administration remained so obviously on the defensive. All recognized the environment as an issue that continued to grow, but differences of opinion existed on the degree to which the administration should allow its advocacy to affect the budget, the economy, and an array of other issues. By fall, Congress faced a slate of proposals, an agenda that made the administration's ongoing studies all the more urgent. The environment had become, in the words of one reporter, "the fastest moving bandwagon in Congress this year." Hickel was hardly alone. Senators and congressmen of both parties were "scrambling aboard, eager to protect something we once took for granted and now suddenly consider sacred and fragile as motherhood."[90] Nixon was not about to challenge something as sacred as motherhood, but he realized the economy as no less sacred, if for no other reason than some truth existed in the old axiom that people voted according to their wallets.

The summer had ended, but for the administration the heat continued; even with the agony of Vietnam aside, it was simply not a good fall for Nixon. Congress resisted Nixon's nominees for the Supreme Court; it shredded his proposal for welfare reform—and, in environmental policy, it, not the administration, dictated events. The efforts of Hickel and Moynihan had helped establish at least some record of environmental advocacy, but as the administration's varied committees finally issued their reports, the Democrats pressed their advantage. As the year wound down, the White House was able to make several long-awaited decisions, but, wrestling with the dilemma of environmental advocacy, it found that these decisions only compounded its environmental woes.

In September Nixon announced his decision on the SST. The Garwin Committee questioned the plane not only because of its sonic boom and jet noise, but also because of its cost.[91] These were concerns, Nixon acknowledged, but they should not prevent a contract with Boeing Corporation for the development of a prototype. Nixon had originally hoped that the matter could be settled "thoroughly and dispassionately, but quickly."[92] As the months had passed, however, he had grown to recognize that this was not possible, and had searched for a way to approve the project without incurring the wrath of environmentalists, in the words of Chief of Staff Haldeman, "a SST game plan."[93] For Nixon, focused as ever on international affairs, the specter of an American airline industry at the mercy of foreign competitors was too important to ignore. The Anglo-French Concorde and the Soviet TU-144 both proceeded well, and despite the recommendation of his administration's committee, the tradeoff environmentally was necessary. He would not, however, request substantial

funds for the plane in the coming fiscal year. "Carry-over funds" from the previous year would hopefully suffice, allowing the administration to avoid further antagonizing a constituency it still hoped to win.[94]

This was not about to mollify the SST's supporters. Muskie and leading congressional Democrats lambasted the decision. In an article written for *Trial
Magazine*, Muskie pounded Nixon as hypocritical, on one hand giving "lip
service" to environmental protection, while on the other working against it.
"Technology must be the servant of man, not his master. It must enhance the
quality of life, not destroy it," Muskie wrote. Anxious to undercut the administration's new position, the Environmental Defense Fund filed a Freedom of
Information Act request for all documents utilized in the administration's deliberations. In a move that foretold Nixon's later defense in the Watergate controversy, the White House objected, claiming executive privilege.[95]

This blow to the administration's hopes of winning the environmental initiative was not irreparable, the White House hoped. When the Mrak Commission concluded that persistent chemical pesticides posed a sufficient threat to
the environment to warrant a complete ban, the White House ordered the cancellation of all residential uses of DDT, the most egregious of all such pesticides. It also promised to eliminate all but the "essential" use of DDT by the end
of 1970. Four days after the announcement, Whitaker urged White House
Counsel Charles Colson, hired recently for improved public relations, to publicize the action "with the conservation lobby." "I assume we should be saying,
'look boys, we've done something' to these people."[96]

Once again, however, the administration was in for disappointment. The Environmental Defense Fund, this time joined by the Sierra Club, the National
Audubon Society, and the Izaak Walton League, filed suit, arguing that the administration's decision did little to thwart a major threat to the public health.
Not only did the order fail to include the use of DDT on cotton, the largest single use of the chemical, it allowed for protracted cancellation hearings under
existing law, hearings in which the use in question could continue pending a
resolution. While technically temporary, a suspension order was the answer,
they claimed. If nothing else, it would at least halt all uses immediately.[97]

It took little time for this to dawn on the American chemical industry, as six
DDT manufacturers immediately appealed the ban, setting into motion cancellation hearings that legal experts predicted would last over two years. This infuriated environmentalists and their champions on Capitol Hill. As one aide to
Senator Nelson remarked, "With the quality of the environment certain to be
the most important issue of the 1970s, it seems to me [the administration] is
using poor judgement in continuing to drag its heels."[98] The matter clearly had

not unfolded as the White House hoped, another thorn in its side rather than salve to its wounds.

The passing months had done little to cool tensions over the Alaska pipeline, which remained the most complex environmental issue facing the administration, as well as its biggest impediment to the political initiative. The administration's North Slope Task Force issued its final report in September, stipulating a number of requirements that the oil consortium, TAPS, must meet for the Interior Department to lift the "land freeze" and allow permits for construction.[99] On this issue Hickel and Nixon agreed; in both men's views the problem remained a matter of how best to protect the environment—but with the pipeline itself a given. When it came to his home state, Hickel's new-found environmentalism had its limits.

To ensure environmental protection, Hickel sent Train on two investigative missions to Alaska, and in public hearings on each he found himself bombarded with critics on all fronts. Clearly, the administration could not please everyone. The task force's stipulations included the revegetation of disturbed terrain, the protection of stream beds and fish-spawning areas, the free movement of wildlife across the pipeline corridor, and a ban on the use of harmful chemicals. Problems still remained, however. How could TAPS, for example, avoid damage to permafrost with a subterranean hot pipeline? What about seismic activity and the possibility of earthquakes? What about the possibility of a leak on the marine leg of the journey to the West Coast? Equally as significant, what of the claims of the Alaskan natives? Without an agreement on this latter point, the answers to the rest were moot.[100]

Hickel did his best to facilitate solutions to the myriad of complex problems. A pipeline raised in portions on platforms above the ground might answer a lot of the problems, Hickel argued. At Whitaker's suggestion, Hickel agreed to another long-term study of the environment, this time of the entire Arctic region, a "master plan" to protect the environment "under the assumption that pipeline construction . . . will be taking place in the next few years."[101] TAPS, meanwhile, agreed to abide by all stipulations, and proposed that the Interior Department lift the "freeze" for the necessary right-of-way, but only grant permits for construction section by section. This would allow construction to begin on those areas where permafrost was less of a problem, while granting additional time to answer the more serious environmental objections. Sensing that once construction had begun—even if it was just for the necessary construction roads—the momentum would prove difficult to halt, the leaders of the Izaak Walton League, the Wilderness Society, the Sierra Club, and the National Audubon Society wrote the Senate Interior Committee. The "freeze," they argued, was the last defense against the wholesale disposal of Alaskan public lands on the nineteenth-century "first come-first served" basis.[102]

It was no coincidence that critics turned to Jackson's Senate committee; the matter was not entirely up to the Department of Interior. In an effort to assure environmentalists and calm detractors, Hickel had promised not to lift the "freeze" and grant construction permits without the approval of the House and Senate Interior committees—and Jackson, the newly minted John Muir Award winner, took this responsibility seriously. Hickel, Jackson complained to Ehrlichman, was "very difficult to deal with."[103] Still, the committee would acquiesce to TAPS's request, allowing Hickel to lift the "freeze" and grant permits in sections for road construction. When TAPS met all environmental problems and when all concerned agreed on land claims, construction on the pipeline itself might commence. This was a reasonable decision, the House Interior Committee concurred.[104]

The matter of native land claims remained mired in acrimonious negotiations, and an adequate solution to the environmental problems was not imminent, yet the decision outraged the pipeline's critics. In Jackson's mind, however, his committee had done nothing to abdicate its environmental responsibilities. With his eye on Congress, Jackson was aware that environmentalists would soon hold a trump card, a means to ensure Alaska's environment regardless of his committee's decision.[105] As the end of the year approached, all indications pointed to the passage of his bill to create a Council on Environmental Quality. It was not just the proposed CEQ, however, that gave Jackson so much confidence. The bill, now known as the National Environmental Policy Act (NEPA), promised to pass both houses strengthened beyond what even Jackson had anticipated, beyond the version passed in the Senate in the summer. Proclaiming it the nation's policy to protect environmental quality, the bill now popular in Congress no longer required the government to issue a "finding" of environmental impact before the approval of any large federal project. It now mandated a "detailed statement," an exhaustive study that had to include possible alternatives to the proposed project. The bill obligated the government to circulate the statement among the public before approval by the proposed CEQ. If passed, it would stand as one of the nation's most important environmental laws, a cornerstone of the nation's policy for years to come. In short, it appeared that pipeline critics would soon have the means to demand adequate environmental protection and ensure compliance—the actions of Jackson's committee aside.

The "bandwagon" of environmentalism sweeping Congress, Jackson assumed, assured that the conference committee then meeting to iron out the differences between the House and Senate versions would return a bill favorable to environmentalists. In fact, he assumed, he had already overcome the single biggest threat to the bill, a threat not from opponents of stringent provisions, but, ironically, from his colleague in the struggle to protect the environment, Muskie. Muskie's Water Quality Improvement Act, then still under debate, called for a different version of an executive environmental council, not a three-person CEQ, but a five-member Office of Environmental Quality. It was no small dispute, for if Muskie's bill and council prevailed, future environmental issues would fall not under Jackson's Interior Committee, but Muskie's Public Works Committee. In this respect, the struggle was one for environmental prestige, a struggle between the John Muir Award winner and "Mr. Clean."[106] "Scoop [Jackson] wanted a piece of the action," recalled Muskie aide Billings, with Muskie "not too happy about Jackson cutting into his issue." The solution was a compromise that allowed both bills to proceed. To achieve this end, both senators agreed that Jackson's bill would specify his CEQ as the major body for policy considerations, while Muskie's bill would specify his OEQ as the major body for enforcement and support staff. At Muskie's insistence, the agreement provided for a stronger environmental impact–statement requirement in Jackson's bill and otherwise supported the strongest provisions possible.[107]

With leading Democrats on the same page and with the public receptive, Whitaker was blunt with Ehrlichman. The opposition had "run over" the administration. Witnessing a competition so keen that even Muskie and Jackson were struggling among themselves for advantage, Train agreed. Immediate action was still necessary to "take the initiative away from the Democrats" and "identify the Republican Party with concern for environmental quality."[108] It was by November a familiar refrain, but, at last, one that this time carried some weight; Whitaker's task force had finally completed its preliminary agenda for a comprehensive environmental program and it was ready for Nixon's review. For the first time, the administration stood on the brink of a true offensive. Nixon, who up to this point had only concerned himself with environmental policy in a cursory manner, took the sixty-five-page volume with him on Thanksgiving weekend to Key Biscayne.[109] It commanded his full attention, a positive sign for environmentalists if nothing else.

The White House planned Nixon's environmental address for early February, and throughout the waning days of 1969 Whitaker, Ehrlichman, and their staffs worked on final preparations and revisions. Duly impressed by the task force's report, and, as always, aware of political opportunities, Nixon had one additional chance to divert attention from Jackson, Muskie, and the Democratic juggernaut. Just after Thanksgiving, Congress passed new, stronger wildlife legislation. The bill expanded the nation's endangered-species lists to include mollusks and crustaceans, and more importantly prohibited the importation of species considered in danger of extinction on a worldwide basis. With over 275 species of mammals and 300 species of birds threatened around the globe, wildlife advocates had lobbied for the bill for years. It was a solid piece of legislation with little apparent economic cost, and the White House had no doubts that Nixon should sign it. Apart from Hickel, however, the administration had taken little role in the bill's passage, and Whitaker worried that the media would praise its "large Democratic sponsorship." The wise course was not to stage an elaborate signing ceremony as Hickel recommended, but a private one. This allowed the White House to control coverage by mailing environmental groups pictures of the signing ceremony. With less traditional coverage and fewer Democrats present, more credit flowed to the administration.[110]

On December 5, 1969, Nixon signed the Endangered Species Conservation Act of 1969, his first chance to sign into law significant environmental legislation.[111] It was not, however, his last. Twelve days later the conference committee working on NEPA submitted its report, which included almost all the stringent provisions upon which Jackson and Muskie had agreed. Under pressure from the House conferees, the report added the qualifying phrase "to the fullest extent possible" to its impact statement requirement, and it mandated each agency to "consult" with CEQ, not receive its approval. In all other respects, however, the report was as forceful a statement of environmental policy as supporters had hoped.

The committee report sailed through both houses of Congress, reaching Nixon's desk just after Christmas. Once again, Nixon faced a decision on a bill largely authored and supported by his political opposition. Surprisingly, no one in the White House recognized the significance of the impact-statement requirement, the only true coercive portion of the bill and the one in which environmentalists placed so much faith.[112] No executive agency recommended against approval, despite potential conflicts with the new CEQ. In the years to come, Nixon would come to regret this oversight, but at the end of his first year in office, the bill appeared only a minor nuisance. Another environmental council—and, if Muskie's water pollution bill were later to pass, the possibility of a third—promised duplication and overlap. Nevertheless, the nation needed a coherent environmental policy and Nixon still held the right to appoint the new council's members. He might simply deactivate or ignore one of the bodies if jurisdictional issues hampered efforts. In any event, as Whitaker noted and Ehrlichman agreed, to veto the bill was to court political disaster, for the environmental "bandwagon" ensured a congressional override. A veto would cast Nixon as anti-environment just as the administration was finally prepared to unveil its long-awaited program. An opportunity still existed, Whitaker and Ehrlichman agreed. Just as with the endangered-species bill, Nixon could co-opt the legislation as his own. If he were to stage properly the signing ceremony, choose his words wisely, and follow with credible appointments, NEPA could work in the administration's favor.[113] Coupled with his coming environmental message to Congress, it would finally win the political initiative that the White House had so long sought.

The end of the year brought a number of retrospectives in the press, accounts of how far America had traveled and how far she still had to go. It was a time of reflection, and for many a time of hope in finally leaving a tumultuous decade full of tragedy at every turn. Few pundits stressed the environment as they attempted to summarize America's condition, yet the changes of the decade had altered forever the way Americans perceived the natural world around them. It had ended with what before was inconceivable: the conservative Nixon, a man with no environmental background, interest, or expertise, committed to a program of environmental protection. The administration, Nixon promised in an end-of-the-year news conference, would always do what was right rather than what was popular. The environmental issue, he assumed, was definitely popular, an excellent issue that offered outstanding political benefits and a powerful new constituency. For many in the White House, it was also right. If properly balanced with the economy and other pressing obligations, it promised the nation benefits to match the political payoff.

The end of the year was for Nixon as hopeful a time as it was for many Americans. The criticism was relentless and the pressure unabated, but, in Nixon's view, reason for optimism existed. He had at last, he believed, recognized a reaction to the antiwar radicalism that had plagued him throughout the year. He had appealed to this "silent majority" in a nationally televised speech, and the overall result was positive. Gallup polls indicated his approval ratings were on the rise.[114] Clearly he had turned the corner, with the new year, and, indeed, the new decade full of promise. The environmental issue was only a case in point. He had clearly suffered on the issue, his efforts to win the political initiative stymied by the reality of economic considerations and a Democratic opposition poised for the attack. His administration had, nevertheless, made progress, and with his comprehensive program now ready for Congress and the public, it would soon be he, not Muskie, Jackson, or the other environmental heroes of the day, on the attack.

2

"A Johnny-Come-Lately"
January–April 1970

The new year dawned slowly for most Americans. For many the first day of the new decade was a holiday, a day to relax and watch college-football bowl games on television. As Texas defeated Notre Dame in the Cotton Bowl and Penn State downed Missouri in the Orange Bowl, the only news of the day was the controversy over which of these two undefeated gridiron victors warranted the title of national champion. In Washington, journalists had little to report. With Nixon at his San Clemente, California, home, Vice President Agnew visiting troops in Vietnam, and members of Congress scattered throughout the nation, the *New York Times* pronounced the capital a "vacuum," devoting much of its coverage not to hard news, but to the "mood of the nation."[1]

For Nixon, the slow news day was a unique chance to seize the headlines—a perfect opportunity to sign the National Environmental Policy Act. Few developments competed for the nation's attention, and, with opponents on vacation and the ceremony three thousand miles from the focus of national debate, Nixon could turn coverage to his advantage, away from the true Democratic genesis of the bill. In addition, signing NEPA on the first day of the new decade offered symbolic significance. If he were to highlight properly the signing as only the first action of a new era in which the government would protect America's environmental heritage, the press would focus on the future, in which the administration planned an environmental offensive, and not on the past, in which the White House had encountered little but environmental criticism.[2]

Calling reporters to the "Western White House," Nixon chose his words carefully. "It is particularly fitting that my first official act of this new decade is to approve the National Environmental Policy Act," Nixon's began. "By my participation . . . I have become convinced that the nineteen-seventies absolutely must be the years when America pays its debt to the past by reclaiming the purity of its air, its waters and our living environment." Nixon said nothing of his earlier resistance to NEPA, conveniently forgetting that his administration had testified against the executive branch advisory body it created, the Council on Environmental Quality. The bill, he now declared, "gives us a good statement of direction," while the new CEQ would enjoy a "close advisory relation to the President." The administration, Nixon concluded, "is determined that the decade of the seventies will be known as the time when this country regained a productive harmony between man and nature."[3]

Nixon had played no role in the passage of NEPA, but, recognizing its popularity, now sought to cast it as his own, portraying it as a demonstration of his personal concern for environmental quality. Chatting with reporters after signing the bill, Nixon told how he had recently taken a friend, Charles "Bebe" Rebozo, on a drive through the countryside of Orange County outside Los Angeles. In ten years, they had agreed, development would scar forever the beauty of the land, an occurrence not unique to southern California. With NEPA and a slew of legislation planned in the near future, Nixon promised, his administration would not let such a tragedy unfold.[4] With his official statement only briefly commending Senator Jackson, the chief architect of the bill, and with his informal comments bordering upon self-congratulation, the law appeared as much a victory for the administration as one for the nation.

Although somewhat disingenuous about his motives, Nixon was correct that NEPA stood as a cornerstone for future environmental policy. Failing along with much of the public to appreciate the true significance of the law—its impact statement provision—Nixon praised its forceful statement of environmental policy and its creation of CEQ. Much of Nixon's remarks focused on the promise of this new council, concluding that any further advisory body was a "mistake."[5] The Jackson-Muskie compromise the previous year had allowed NEPA to proceed but had also pledged that if Muskie's Water Quality Improvement Act were to pass, another council, the Office of Environmental Quality, would exist as support staff for NEPA's CEQ. To Nixon, who had already created his own cabinet-level Environmental Quality Council as well as Whitaker's White House task force, OEQ was another layer of unnecessary bureaucracy. Nixon's criticism was the only hint of his earlier resistance to NEPA and a clear slap at his rival Muskie.

Muskie and Jackson defended their agreement, trying their best to note both the necessity of the additional body and the administration's earlier resistance to NEPA. They did not succeed, however, in blunting praise for the administration. Nixon had cleverly cast himself as the key player in the drama, a role that most Americans apparently accepted. Letters of commendation poured into the White House from all quarters. Minnesota governor Harold LeVonder wrote Nixon of his "sincere appreciation for taking this important step." John Nanna, mayor of Dobbs Ferry, New York, lauded Nixon for his "leadership in the environmental field." The *New York Times* reported in a January 4 editorial that Nixon's action in signing NEPA and his pledge to combat pollution "offers new hope that environmental problems will be given top priority." Three weeks later, the paper added another editorial praising the administration's environmental record.[6]

Wasting no time in pressing his advantage, Nixon surprised critics with his appointments to the new CEQ. Signing the bill was a political fait accompli, administration opponents correctly assumed; when the glare of publicity dimmed, Nixon would show his true colors and appoint weak members reticent to stand up to industry, or, worse, individuals openly hostile to federal regulation. It was an understandable but unwarranted worry. Enjoying the laurels pouring in from around the nation, Nixon had no intention of undermining his NEPA rhetoric. His selections would prove to the public that his commitment was legitimate. Foremost among the three members chosen—the choice most welcomed by environmentalists—was the administration's own Undersecretary of Interior, Russell Train, as CEQ chairman. Everyone knew where Train stood on the environment; he was, as Whitaker later recalled, "for the environment first, Nixon second." Not only did he bring impeccable conservation credentials, his brief stint with the Department of Interior underscored his intention to press the environmental agenda from within the executive branch. At Interior, Train had welcomed Hickel's surprising environmental advocacy, but had clashed with his boss personally. If nothing else, the two had completely different styles. The Ivy League-educated Train was refined and soft-spoken. Hickel was a "rough and tumble westerner," the only member of the cabinet not to hold a college degree. "Wally shot from the hip," in the words of an aide. Hickel's outspoken style frequently antagonized many of his colleagues, even those with whom he agreed. Train approached Whitaker privately about the transfer, and Ehrlichman thought the position a perfect fit.[7] Joining Train were Gordon MacDonald and Robert Cahn. MacDonald was a geophysicist and member of the Environmental Studies Board of the National Academy of Science, then serving on the faculty of the University of California at Santa Barbara. Cahn was a Pulitzer Prize–winning conservation reporter for the *Christian Science Monitor*. Together the appointees stood as a formidable trio, not one a lackey to industry. They were to "carry the ball," Nixon instructed them in the Oval Office, to "get the administration out front on the environment."[8]

A strong CEQ was critical for a forceful administration policy, but questions remained about implementation of NEPA nevertheless. Here again Nixon moved quickly to give teeth to his rhetoric, issuing an executive order "for the protection and enhancement of environmental quality." Clearing up all possible confusion with Nixon's old cabinet-level EQC, the order defined CEQ's specific relationship with other agencies and clearly established not only the dominance of the new council over the old but the importance of NEPA in the daily function of all facets of the executive branch. Each agency, the order mandated, was to review its own regulations, eliminating all that "prohibit or limit full compliance with the purposes and provisions of [NEPA]." More than simple consultation with CEQ, the legislative mandate, each agency was to comply with precise guidelines for the preparation of impact statements, guidelines to be issued by CEQ and to include the requirement of public hearings. CEQ was to "coordinate" all federal environmental programs, monitor agency compliance, and enjoy a close working relationship with the White House.[9] Thanks to Nixon's order, CEQ was no paper tiger, staffed instead with strong environmental advocates and placed at the heart of the federal bureaucracy. Clearly Nixon had done more than simply comply with a political fait accompli; his actions were more a sign of what he planned for the future than a reaction to what had taken place in the past.

The future, Nixon promised in his first State of the Union Address on January 22, was bright, despite the trauma of the previous years. Conspicuously avoiding Vietnam, concluding only that "prospects for peace are far greater today than they were a year ago," Nixon invoked the image of a prosperous America with the "best clothed, best fed, best housed people in the world." Standing before a packed joint session of Congress and with television capturing his every word, Nixon spoke of an America with little inflation and crime, an America with improved health, faster transportation, and superior education—and, as a key factor, an America with a cleaner environment. Wealth, Nixon insisted, was not synonymous with happiness, and economic growth was desirable only if it improved the "quality of life." This included not only population, which he had addressed the previous year, but wise use of land and technology. Congress and the administration, therefore, should work together to develop a "national growth policy" to enable government "to influence the course of human settlement and growth so as positively to affect the quality of American life." Toward this end, Nixon insisted, the nation needed more parkland. "As our cities and suburbs relentlessly expand those priceless open spaces . . . are swallowed up, often forever." If the government did not act, "we will have none to preserve."[10]

For the first time in history, a president stressed environmental quality in an official State of the Union address. The message harkened back to his NEPA comments three weeks before, and once again cast the White House at the forefront of environmental activism. The press and the public responded positively, as Nixon anticipated, leaving the administration's opponents flustered. Clearly enjoying the prime-time, uninterrupted exposure, Nixon had reason for optimism—if not for the rosy scenario that his comments promised. His message was smartly crafted, for the new year had brought nothing to diminish the force of environmentalism. Everywhere the problem of environmental decay was before the public. In the first few weeks of the year, scientists at the University of Wisconsin warned that modern society threatened to alter forever the world's atmosphere, with possible tragic results. Popular author Anne Morrow Lindbergh called for a "revolution in values" to save the planet's "dying environment." Renowned British historian Arnold Toynbee wrote of the commonality of all nations—capitalist and communist—in "suffering from a polluted environment." Ministers across a wide spectrum of Christian denominations spoke of the "link between faith and ecology," admonishing their flocks to embrace preservation. "The raping of natural resources for personal gain," concluded one pastor, "is essentially sinful." Under pressure from citizen groups, local governments from New York to California allotted a greater portion of their budgets to waste management, recycling, and zoning.[11] Environmental groups thrived, with the Sierra Club announcing on New Year's Day that its rapidly growing membership necessitated a restructuring of its national organization.[12] So popular did the issue appear across all socioeconomic levels and all geographic regions of the country, pundits declared that "no clear opposition" to environmentalism existed. According to one Washington correspondent, "both parties seem to be competing to embrace the anti-pollution drive."[13]

For many in the White House, the president's long-anticipated environmental offensive could not have come at a better time. His address tapped into a popular vein, one that promised to unite a nation still largely divided over the tumultuous events Nixon's comments conspicuously avoided. Nixon was correct that for the moment Vietnam was relatively quiet, and, compared to the vitriolic dissension of the previous year, the nation appeared oddly calm. Nevertheless, for much of the public, inundated with sensationalist news coverage and carrying memories of recent turmoil, the glorious future Nixon envisioned appeared almost a utopian dream, far removed from the fractious nature of American society. Protests over African-American civil rights often earned front-page coverage, with the militant Black Panther movement intimidating a white middle class critical to Nixon's political future. Each week seemed to bring disturbing reports of new movements—protests for women's rights, protests against drug and sexual prohibitions, protests against the capitalist system in general, and even protests with no clear focus or agenda, nothing more than random violence and youthful rebelliousness.[14] Each protest—each constituency—demanded a response, and the development of a political agenda was no simple task. For many in the White House, environmental advocacy was a political guaranty in a Washington where an astute politician could take little for granted.

Nixon fully appreciated the importance of the environmental issue, but had not forgotten the lessons of the previous year: no easy solutions existed; each environmental issue carried with it possible economic costs; and the Democrats had no intention of abdicating their environmental leadership without a struggle. Fully prepared by a year of study, the administration should move judiciously, Nixon believed. It should not rush pertinaciously to embrace environmentalism at every turn, but rather couch its agenda in the best possible terms. In Nixon's mind, the search for broader context did not preclude a solid legislative agenda, nor did such an agenda mandate ignoring economic reality. Now prepared, the White House could win the political initiative by dictating the debate, highlighting those issues on which it agreed with environmentalists while downplaying those where disagreement reigned. It could publicize its proposals and attack those of the opposition. Success was a matter of timing, wording, and properly crafted legislative detail.[15]

In public, White House aides worked to build publicity for Nixon's environmental message to Congress. When a CBS documentary in late January featured Muskie and criticism of the administration's environmental record, Ehrlichman dispatched Moynihan and Hickel to the Sunday morning news show *Meet the Press* to counter the charges. "The administration will be devoting an increasingly larger proportion of its energies to the problems of the environment," White House aides promised.[16] By late January, the debate over the administration's response to Earth Day had begun in earnest, as reports suggested the event might surpass all previous expectations. Aware that the day offered the possibility of a perfectly timed demonstration of the administration's commitment, but that it also portended the possibility of riotous disaster, Nixon slowly settled in on his carefully orchestrated middle-of-the-road approach. This, he felt assured, wisely prepared the White House for all contingencies, both from charges that it had ignored a seminal event in American environmental history or had embraced a chaotic and violent protest that it should have foreseen. When questioned about the event, aides were to respond, "The administration supports the environmental movement and will take the initiative with the upcoming February environmental address."[17] In Nixon's view, the administration was now proactive, not reactive, aggressively working for the political offensive but wisely calculating all ramifications.

As if planned to fit into the White House's unfolding strategy, only weeks before Nixon's address, the departments of Interior and Transportation announced that they had finally reached an agreement with the Dade County Port Authority over the proposed Miami jetport, one of the previous year's most well-publicized controversies. In exchange for the DCPA's cooperation in moving the complex, the administration agreed to allow the training facility to operate until the state had finalized a new location. The administration promised to reimburse the DCPA for the thirteen million dollars it had already spent on the Everglades site and to cease all pressure from the Federal Aviation Administration and the Corps of Engineers. All parties agreed that any new jetport would meet exact environmental regulations.[18]

The pact pleased Nixon and garnered positive publicity. Telephoning Hickel and Transportation Secretary Volpe the following day, Nixon told the two that the agreement was a good example of the interdepartmental cooperation necessary if the administration were to win the environmental initiative. The White House quickly released a presidential statement praising the pact as an example of the administration's commitment to environmental protection. The press release lauded the work of the environmental organizations active in the struggle and the "individual citizens whose hard work and concern for the environment made this agreement possible." "This is part," the statement read, "of the broad new approach we must take to make certain that our environment is treated with greater wisdom and care."[19] In the press conference that followed the announcement, Hickel promised further administration action to protect the entire Big Cypress Swamp, the water lifeline to the Everglades, whose pollution was arguably a greater threat to the area's ecosystem than the jetport itself.[20]

The White House had as much reason for satisfaction at the timing of the announcement as pride in the accomplishment. Much of the work leading to the pact had taken place the previous year under a constant cloud of environmental criticism, but with the final agreement within weeks of both Nixon's State of the Union Address and his planned February environmental message to Congress, the timing was undeniably perfect, lending credence to administration rhetoric. Congratulations rolled in. Anthony Wayne Smith of the Everglades Coalition, a Florida organization that had spearheaded the opposition, lamented the temporary operation of the training facility but agreed with Whitaker that the pact was "the best way to settle this matter."[21] Smith and others within the environmental opposition knew that without the administration—or, more precisely, the efforts of Hickel and Volpe—the DCPA would have held firm and jets would have landed where cranes and pelicans now flew.

The administration had proven itself vital to the struggle—and the White House was determined to make sure all knew.

The real test of both Nixon's political strategy and the veracity of his commitment to environmental protection was not the jetport controversy, however. Although the administration had appointed the Leopold Commission the previous year to investigate the Everglades matter, it was not debate over the administration's position that had caused the major delay in consummating the pact, but rather the dogged resistance of the DCPA. For the White House, implementation of policy, not definition, had ultimately proved the primary obstacle. Just as in the previous year, however, the real test would arise from other more controversial matters that did not lend themselves as readily to policy consensus. The fact that the White House now had an agenda ready for a political offensive did not alter this essential fact. A year of study had not, indeed could not, prepare the administration for every emergent issue. In the weeks before the environmental message, it was the unexpected—problems outside the planned legislative calendar—that posed the greatest challenge to Nixon's rhetoric and his strategy.

Two proposed reclamation projects were particularly difficult to reconcile with the administration's stated environmentalism. Both were as controversial as the Alaska pipeline and the other policy disputes still simmering from the previous year, and all were potential fodder for Democratic criticism. The Cross Florida Barge Canal and the Tennessee-Tombigbee Waterway promised significant economic benefits, and each came with a constituency more potent than even the DCPA. Brought to the attention of the White House only weeks before Nixon was to unveil his program, each also promised an environmental battle royal. Enjoying the wave of environmentalism sweeping over the public, local opposition to both projects was rich with contributions and publicity and was emboldened to take on the powerful financial interests supporting construction. It mattered little if the administration otherwise had a battery of legislative proposals; the controversies were sure to engulf the White House.

The Cross Florida Barge Canal and the Tennessee-Tombigbee Waterway were new to the Nixon administration, but were hardly new proposals. Proponents had lobbied for both projects for years, with their arguments difficult to deny. Congress had debated the possibility of a canal to cut across central Florida since the early nineteenth century, first as a means for shippers to avoid West Indies pirates and then as a tool for economic development in its own right. In the early twentieth century, the Corps of Engineers noted the feasibility of connecting the Atlantic and Gulf coasts through the Oklawaha River basin, but questioned the cost. Only after President John Kennedy, in an effort to win Florida votes in the 1960 election, promised to make the project a priority, did the Corps of Engineers revise its cost-benefit analysis and openly support construction. Congress first appropriated funds in 1962, and President Lyndon Johnson turned the first spade of earth two years later. The plan called for a canal to run 107 miles up the Oklawaha, cut across central Florida, and eventually emerge near the mouth of another river, the Withlacoochee. One hundred fifty feet wide and twelve feet deep, the canal required dams to flood over twenty-seven thousand acres of wild swamp and drain forty-five miles of the Oklawaha. Six years into construction in 1970, the project enjoyed the unanimous support of Florida's congressional delegation, an array of citizen groups along the canal's proposed path, and, by all estimates, a sizable percentage of the electorate in a key political state.[22]

A half-century before Congress first debated the Florida canal, French settlers in the mid-eighteenth century noted the economic advantages of connecting the north-flowing Tennessee River and the south-flowing Tombigbee River. Joined by a canal, the rivers would constitute an eastern alternative to the Mississippi River, relieving traffic on the continent's major interior artery and spurring economic development from the Gulf of Mexico to Ohio. Having conducted eight feasibility studies between 1913 and 1966, the Corps of Engineers stood firmly behind the project, as did a vocal alliance of supporters united behind the Tennessee-Tombigbee Development Authority. Although Congress had not yet allocated funds by 1970, it had first authorized the project twenty-four years earlier. Proponents, therefore, were impatient and stood as a formidable, well-financed lobby, prepared just as their colleagues in Florida to pressure the new administration in Washington.[23]

Compared to the long history of support for both projects, environmentalist opposition was fairly recent, but, as the White House was keenly aware, no less compelling. Just as Nixon planned to lay claim as the nation's environmental champion, the Florida Defenders of the Environment presented the White House with a 150-page critique of the Florida canal, an intelligent treatise that challenged Nixon to live up to his rhetoric. The detailed report painted a bleak picture of the canal's impact. Because the western section of the canal would fill with groundwater, the report claimed, salt water from the ocean and pollution from boats would contaminate the drinking water of nearby towns. Contamination of the Oklawaha meant Armageddon for the wildlife dependent upon it for habitat—panthers, black bears, otters, bobcats, herons, alligators, and other unique species. The dams would block upstream migration of fish, while the canal would serve as a conduit for serious pest infestation. Eutrophication, the overall result, would destroy what remained of the natural ecosystem. The

Oklawaha, the report reminded the White House, was one of Florida's two remaining wild rivers, one of the nation's only semitropical streams and invaluable in its own right. In any event, much of the expected economic boom was specious, for destruction of the environment would eventually lead to a reduction, not an increase, in the recreation industry.[24]

As the Florida Defenders of the Environment mobilized against the Cross Florida Barge Canal, the Committee for Leaving the Environment Natural — "CLEAN," as they were known — organized against the Tennessee-Tombigbee Waterway. Led by members of Mississippi State University's Biology Department, CLEAN lobbied the White House with a similar story of ecological genocide. The proposal, CLEAN argued, required the excavation of more earth than did the construction of the Panama Canal. Creating a total of 40,000 acres of flat water surface, it would eliminate 170 miles of tributary streams and 140 miles of the Tombigbee's main stem, ultimately increasing siltation and destroying the river system's biodiversity. Subsequent navigation would increase turbidity, waterborne pollutants, and bank erosion, with the end promising the death of fish, wildlife, and the entire natural ecosystem.[25] Like the Florida canal, the project would ultimately stand as a monument to man's careless exploitation of the natural world.

The administration's course was clear, Whitaker and Hickel agreed. To advocate either project was to play the hypocrite, substantiating criticism that the administration was all talk and little action. Ignoring Nixon's strong stance in support of NEPA and the Everglades, congressional Democrats had reacted to the State of the Union address with attacks reminiscent of the previous year, claiming that the administration never backed up its rhetoric with substance. "I don't see how anyone can find fault with [Nixon's] goals and objectives," Senator Jackson commented. "What it boils down to is how are we going to implement it." Fully aware that the White House planned to unveil an extensive environmental agenda in only a matter of days, Muskie noted the past, not the future: "To date no substantive environmental program has received meaningful support from President Nixon or his cabinet." Rhetoric, Muskie argued, was not enough. "We cannot expect to whip the public into a fervor of anticipation and not deliver the environmental improvement our words promise." In a press conference to comment on the administration's record, Senate Democratic leader Mike Mansfield was more open about Nixon's efforts to seize the initiative, but no less critical. Nixon was a "Johnny-come-lately," Mansfield stated. His record still paled in comparison to the Democrats.[26]

Such criticism was, in retrospect, inevitable with Earth Day and an off-year congressional election approaching. Indeed, for the first time, the Democratic criticism reflected a growing defensiveness, in a sense an acknowledgment that the administration's growing accomplishments were cause for concern. At the end of his tumultuous first year in office, Nixon was optimistic that with a new decade came a new opportunity, that finally he would emerge as the popular chief executive envisioned only twelve months before. Although only weeks old, the new year had not completely disappointed him. Protests continued unabated, and whether the problem was Vietnam, crime, the economy, or racial relations, solutions remained elusive. Still, a new Gallup poll placed Nixon's public support at 61 percent, with disapproval at only 22 percent. According to Gallup, Nixon was the public's "most admired man," a surprising accolade undoubtedly welcomed at 1600 Pennsylvania Avenue.[27] With his attention still largely focused on foreign policy, Nixon may not have placed the environment as critical to these figures, but to Whitaker, Hickel, and the other environmental advocates within the administration, the president's actions of late explained his amazing endurance in the face of such vocal opposition. To switch course now—to come out in favor of the Cross Florida Barge Canal or the Tennessee-Tombigbee—was to risk losing both the ground gained and the agenda still planned.

The Tennessee-Tombigbee was the greater of the twin threats, Whitaker believed, "bothering me personally in the gut."[28] For Hickel, it was the Florida canal. Straight on the heels of his jetport victory, Hickel "is looking for a reason to conclude that the environment is being damaged and then plans to take action," Whitaker wrote Train. The Florida canal was unwise, Whitaker agreed, but its strong support among the state's elected officials was cause for worry. If the White House did not consult them, "they will probably go out of their minds." The entire scenario had the familiar ring of the Everglades controversy. "No question about it," Whitaker concluded, "the Cross Florida Barge Canal will be this year's jetport."[29]

As Whitaker, Hickel, and Train lobbied Ehrlichman, events continued to unfold. The Florida Defenders of the Environment joined forces with the Environmental Defense Fund and filed suit under the newly passed NEPA. The Corps of Engineers had not complied completely with the law's impact-statement mandate, the suit claimed, and construction should halt pending adequate study. Only weeks after the signing of NEPA, critics had awoken to the reality of the sword the law provided them. It was the first such use of the law, but it would not prove the last. Launching their attack in the courts of law and public opinion, critics also convinced developers of the magnitude of the groundwater problem, and several major financial backers began to balk. The future of the Florida canal appeared increasingly in doubt, regardless of any potential administration action.[30]

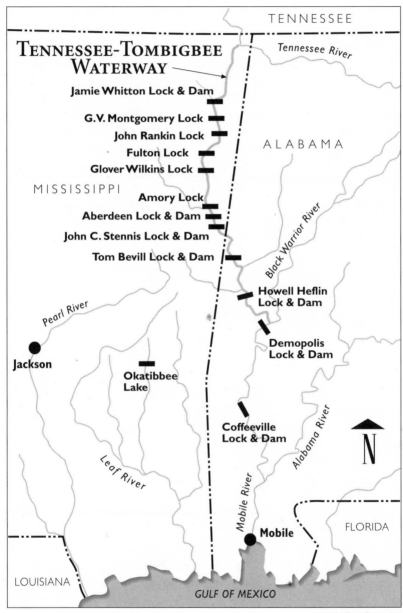

Map of the Tennessee-Tombigbee Waterway. (Courtesy Mobile District, U.S. Army Corps of Engineers.)

The White House could afford to wait in regard to the Florida canal, Ehrlichman concluded, but the Tennessee-Tombigbee was another story. Alabama governor Albert P. Brewer and the Tennessee-Tombigbee Development Authority continued to lobby the administration for sufficient funds to commence construction, and Bureau of the Budget director Robert Mayo concurred. Nixon, meanwhile, had his own motives. Support for the project, Nixon assumed, helped undercut a political rival, former Alabama governor George Wallace. His eye ever on the political ramifications of each issue, Nixon intended not only an environmental offensive, but a concerted effort to win the entire South for the Republican Party, part of the administration's celebrated "Southern Strategy." With the South traditionally a Democratic bastion, Nixon's hopes rested with a series of decisions popular to southerners—decisions such as support for the Tennessee-Tombigbee. Brewer made a convincing argument of the popularity of the project despite environmental objections, and Nixon assumed that environmentalists in the southern heartland were less influential than in other areas of the country. The time, it appeared, was right to move. Heeding the warnings of his environmental advisors, however, the plan was to include only one million dollars in the coming fiscal year, a figure high enough to break ground but hopefully low enough to avoid the ire of environmentalists. Much of the focus would then fall on Congress, buying the White House time. A similar plan in regard to the SST had not diverted condemnation the previous year, but hopefully the coming environmental address would overshadow the budget request and blunt criticism.[31] Whitaker and Hickel may not have agreed, but the plan exemplified Nixon's environmental strategy: it was carefully crafted and cunningly planned.

By early February, the administration's well-planned media blitz not only prepared the public for the address, it also assured that all criticism went answered. In an interview with *U.S. News and World Report*, White House science advisor Dr. Lee DuBridge claimed that criticism of the administration's record indicated no appreciation for the complexity of the science involved in environmental protection. The White House had delayed, DuBridge argued, to assure realistic and proper legislative proposals. The best was yet to come. Urging Train and Hickel to write articles defending the administration's record in such popular magazines as *Field and Stream* and *Readers Digest*, Whitaker instructed White House spokesman Ronald Ziegler to stress Nixon's "pollution solutions," a catchy phrase that the media would quote.[32] On February 4, Nixon issued an executive order mandating that all federal facilities, by the end of 1972, meet air and water pollution standards set by the Department of Health, Education and

Welfare. In a formal press conference, Train praised Nixon's record and promised additional action. "This order," Train stated, "makes it clear that the President does not expect Federal facilities simply to meet some minimum requirements, but to exercise leadership and to show the way in meeting air and water quality standards."[33] To help publicize the administration's concern, Nixon invited the governors from Illinois, Wisconsin, Michigan, and Indiana to join him in attending the first official meeting of CEQ on February 6, with pollution in the Great Lakes the topic for discussion. After the meeting, Nixon informed the press that Train, still popular with environmentalists, greatly impressed him with a lengthy presentation on Lake Michigan's problems.[34]

As the administration's well-honed strategy unfolded in public, in private final details remained. Although the legislative package prepared for presentation covered the gamut of environmental problems, several notable proposals that Ehrlichman had hoped to include in the address, were, in fact, not ready for submission to Congress. This was in one case particularly troublesome, for the Democrats had just introduced their own version and thus threatened to preempt the administration once again. For almost a century America had recognized the need to protect portions of the public domain from commercial development, but with the new urban sprawl characteristic of the modern age, a growing chorus insisted that environmental quality demanded broader protection for all land. Throughout much of the nation, only local zoning restricted private land use. Often uncoordinated with no explicit environmental provisions, these restrictions afforded little protection to ecologically fragile areas, many of which extended through several local jurisdictions. Whitaker's task force had recognized this problem for some time but had found workable solutions elusive. The issue involved individual property rights protected by the Fifth Amendment and the possibility of federal coercion of local or state prerogative, never an attractive option for a purportedly conservative administration.

Democrat Jackson was the first to navigate the trepid waters of land-use legislation, proposing a bill just before Nixon's address that met with considerable acclaim, much to the chagrin of the administration. "Intelligent land use planning and management," Jackson stated, "provides the most important institutional device for preserving and enhancing the environment."[35] In a sense, Jackson's bill provided the specifics for a "national growth plan" that Nixon's State of the Union avoided. The bill called for a national policy to encourage and assist the states in the development of "statewide land use plans." It provided that the Water Resources Council administer a program of three-year grants to cover two-thirds of the cost of plan development, after which not to exceed 50 percent of the cost of implementation. If states did not develop adequate plans within three years, they faced a 20-percent reduction in entitlement programs, with the choice of programs left to the president. Jackson denied conservative criticism that the bill gave the federal government, not the states, primary authority, and quoted Victor Hugo in pressing his case: "Nothing in the world is so powerful as an idea whose time has come."[36]

The address Nixon finally delivered to Congress on February 10 omitted any land-use proposal such as the one Jackson introduced, but his unequivocal message left no doubt that, in his eyes, the environment's time had come. "Like those in the last century who tilled a plot of land to exhaustion and then moved on to another, we in this country have too casually and too long abused our natural environment," Nixon's message began. "The time has come when we can wait no longer to repair the damage already done, and to establish new criteria to guide us in the future." The message dovetailed nicely with both Nixon's NEPA comments and his State of the Union address, stressing once again the administration as the nation's leading environmental champion. In a press conference to announce the transmittal of the message, Nixon was not about to let reporters miss the significance of the occasion, whether specific proposals were omitted or not. "This is the most far reaching and comprehensive message on conservation and restoration of our natural resources ever submitted to Congress by a President of the United States," Nixon proudly declared.[37]

The statement was exactly correct. Nixon's program consisted of thirty-seven proposals divided into five major sections: air pollution, water pollution, solid waste management, parks and recreation, and a final section on government reorganization and citizen activism. The package may not have covered every issue that warranted attention, but no president before—or since—has offered such an extensive, coordinated legislative agenda. In retrospect, not every bill offered was sufficient to address the specific problem at hand, and most, for varying reasons, faced tough roads to passage. Collectively, however, the program promised to strengthen greatly the nation's ability to combat environmental degradation. Nixon's motives may not have always been pure, but this mattered little when it came to forceful provisions on the floor of Congress. Overall, Nixon had reason for pride, his political opponents reason for concern, and the nation reason for relief.

Of all the environmental problems plaguing the nation, air pollution was arguably the most pernicious. Jackson may have thought land-use planning was the key weapon for environmental protection, but Nixon recognized that pollution in all its varied forms galvanized public opinion to a greater degree. Not surprisingly, therefore, new, strong federal air-pollution legislation stood as the linchpin of Nixon's program. Along with water pollution, it commanded the greatest media coverage and debate. Nixon's proposal was not the first federal foray into the problem; in fact, its greatest strength lay in addressing the weaknesses of previous law. Nevertheless, Nixon's proposal was revolutionary in the power that it gave to Washington, a surprise from a self-described advocate for states' rights, but a power that was necessary given the record of the government to date.

By Nixon's election, approximately 100 million automobiles and trucks poured over 180 billion pounds of contaminates into the air, choking Americans with unhealthy levels of hydrocarbons, carbon monoxide, and nitrogen oxide vehicular-exhaust emissions. Combined with sulfur oxide from stationary, coal-burning industrial sources, such vehicular pollution was no longer simply a nuisance; it was a genuine threat to public health.[38] Existing law was inadequate to address the problem. Just as Nixon unveiled his program, New York University scientists released a study concluding that uncontrolled pollution damaged heart and artery tissue, hindered the development of fetuses, and potentially altered chemicals within the body's hereditary material. Such sensational studies, not unique, often embedded themselves in the nation's consciousness by a competitive media in search of ratings. Not coincidentally, as Nixon's agenda arrived on Capitol Hill, network television ran a fictional film entitled "A Clear and Present Danger." The plot did not involve communist subterfuge or a nuclear doomsday, as the title suggested, but rather the threat from polluted air. The film utilized "real smog scenes," the producers readily acknowledged.[39]

The first foray into federal air-pollution legislation had come only seven years before, but in those seven years Congress had revisited the issue several times, in each instance strengthening existing law but soon finding the new program itself inadequate. The Clean Air Act of 1963, supported by President John Kennedy, empowered HEW to hold a series of public hearings, and, ultimately, to issue injunctions. In reality, however, extended hearings proved a procedural nightmare. In addition, the law required states, not HEW, to initiate proceedings. Afraid of losing key industries to less vigilant neighbors, states were understandably reluctant and few hearings resulted. In any event, the law provided no specific mandates for automotive companies, which simply ignored the legislation.[40] With these problems, it took only two years for Congress to move again, this time under the tutelage of Kennedy's successor and fellow Democrat, Lyndon Johnson. The Motor Vehicle Air Pollution Control Act of 1965 authorized HEW to establish emission levels for new motor vehicles. Again, however, problems emerged. The law required automakers to meet the standards on only one representative prototype engine, and thus companies were under no pressure to meet the standards on mass-produced, production-line models or under realistic conditions. Regardless, HEW proved slow to set the standards themselves, and critics bemoaned the lack of any legislation pertaining to the other culprit, the malodorous, sulfur-laden black smoke bellowing from factories across the land.[41]

Once again, Congress took only two years to strengthen federal law, this time with the Air Quality Act of 1967. The approach now was not specific emission standards, but ambient standards for overall air quality. Under the new law, HEW was to establish air quality regions, regions that might embrace part of a state, a whole state, or, in the broadest configurations, extend across state lines. The states within each region would then establish ambient standards for that region, and, if they failed to do so, HEW would in their place. To assist states in setting appropriate limits, the law provided for HEW to research and publish criteria on the effects and extent of each major pollutant. To replace the burdensome conference enforcement procedure that had existed since the first law four years before, the new legislation empowered HEW to instigate court action if the pollution posed "an imminent and substantial endangerment" to life or health, and if the polluter in question had failed to address adequately a 180-day abatement notice. Overall, the new law was a significant improvement, but once again problems were soon evident. HEW found publishing criteria on pollutants more difficult than anticipated, and states, still reluctant to challenge industry, did not exactly rush to fill the void. By Nixon's election, less than 25 percent of the projected ninety-one air quality regions had firm standards, with many too lax for the increasingly vocal environmental movement. HEW had not instigated one enforcement proceeding under the new regulations, and, in fact, only a total of ten since the original 1963 law. Critics still demanded tight controls on all specific sources of pollution, from assembly-line vehicles to industrial sites. Federal law had advanced significantly by Nixon's election but needed revision again.[42]

Nixon recognized this from the outset, and while ignorant of the possible specifics, always anticipated a strengthening of the 1967 law as a cornerstone of his environmental program. As Whitaker's task force had worked out the details the previous year, Nixon had conferred with Moynihan about possible options. While others outside the White House fretted over Nixon's conservative credentials, inside Nixon had already acknowledged that any solution "was going to cost billions."[43] Impressed by independent automaker William Lear's attempts to build an unconventional, non-polluting car, and convinced that the major auto companies were dragging their feet in this regard, Nixon ordered the new CEQ and the Office of Science and Technology to coordinate a separate federal development program. If nothing else, Nixon believed, the effort put additional pressure on the automotive industry. Ehrlichman applauded the idea and suggested that Nixon unveil the program in his environmental address.[44]

The legislation Nixon proposed in his message to Congress addressed all the major failings of existing law, and, in doing so, signaled a significant extension of federal authority and jurisdiction. The 1967 law was a "useful beginning," Nixon's address stated, "but has a number of shortcomings." In solving these problems, national ambient air quality standards were necessary, eliminating weaker restrictions where they existed, but allowing for stronger standards where desired. In reaching these ambient standards, set by the federal government, states would have to establish specific emission standards for all stationary sources of pollution while requiring auto companies to face assembly-line testing of emission-control systems. Auto companies would, in the interim, face tighter 1973 and 1975 model-year emission standards. Washington, the message went on, should have the authority to regulate fuel contents and additives, a clear reference to leaded gasoline, and should have expanded authority for enforcement. The message called for a five-year research program and promised advances in the future. The plan was, in total, a solid initiative, more than what many Democrats demanded and a strong case for the administration as environmental champion.[45]

Although disagreement over the capabilities of various pollution abatement technology raised the possibility that the government might set standards too high for industry, a potentially explosive issue in the future, few in the administration questioned the approach of the air-pollution proposal itself. For the White House, settling on a legislative initiative had proved relatively uncontroversial. The same was not true for the second major cornerstone of Nixon's program, water pollution. Here, although no doubt existed that sufficient technology existed, debate was more elemental. No consensus emerged over the manner of regulation, the cost of a sufficient cleanup, or the appropriate financing methods—the heart of the legislative proposal. The result was a bill that greatly expanded federal power but still reflected a conservative concern for the budget, a bill establishing a strong regulatory program, but arguably falling short of the expenditures necessary to complete the task.

The problem of water pollution was no less pressing than the threat to the nation's air, and equally complex. The lack of adequate municipal waste-treatment centers and the continued dumping of raw sewage into rivers and lakes contributed to eutrophication, but did not constitute the only explanation. In addition to municipal waste, agricultural runoff—nitrogen- and phosphorus-based fertilizers and, worse, more toxic pesticides—compounded the problem. Strip mining and water reclamation projects, such as the Cross Florida Barge Canal and the Tennessee-Tombigbee Waterway, disturbed critical water tables and silted rivers and streams. Likewise contributing were minerals loosened by broken overburden, phosphates from widespread detergent use, and the growing threat from an array of recreational activities. Industrial by-products such as mercury, used in the production of chlorine, made solutions more problematic still.[46]

With such a potent combination of variables, Nixon's water pollution proposal was, like his air pollution bill, not the first federal endeavor into the matter. Indeed, Nixon's proposal sought once again to strengthen Washington's role by filling the voids in existing law. Federal water pollution legislation had, like that for air pollution, emerged incrementally, with each successive step building on its predecessor but in the end proving inadequate. Although attempts to thwart water pollution stemmed from the colonial era, when Massachusetts prohibited the dumping of raw refuge into Boston Harbor, not until after the Second World War did the nation's economic growth mandate federal action. In 1948 and 1953 Congress offered states limited low-interest loans and technical assistance for the construction of municipal waste-treatment facilities, but it was not until 1956 that legislation with permanent authority passed. This legislation authorized federal grants to states, expanded the earlier technical assistance, and provided for federal enforcement in interstate waters. The new law was not, however, equal to the task. Despite the new grants, construction costs remained considerable, and few states developed sufficient programs. Similar to air pollution, enforcement rested with cumbersome conference proceedings initiated by states. With growth unabated, the quality of the nation's waters only worsened.[47]

The nascent environmental movement of the 1960s and a sympathetic president in Democrat Lyndon Johnson assured reform, which came with the Water Quality Act of 1965 authored by the Nixon administration's leading nemesis, Muskie. This legislation created the Federal Water Quality Control Administration (FWQCA) in HEW, bypassing the burdensome adjudication of state-initiated conferences, and required states to develop within two years quality standards for interstate waters and their tributaries. What the legislation did not do proved its downfall, however, namely providing sufficient funds for cash-strapped states. Despite increased appropriations the following year, the costs for construction of adequate facilities remained high, and states still hedged by adopting weak plans or, worse, failing to comply altogether. To encourage enforcement, Johnson transferred the FWQCA to the Department of Interior, but reorganization only disrupted operations. A diverse array of critics, from the League of Women Voters to organized labor, demanded precise effluent standards on all sources of pollution, with the necessary funds from Washington. By Nixon's election, in short, questions over jurisdiction, the manner of regulation, and, most critically, money commanded the new president's attention.[48]

The solution, Nixon's message outlined, was a ten-billion-dollar program for the construction of waste treatment centers, four billion in federal lump-sum payments, a billion a year for the next four years, with the remainder from the states and municipalities themselves. To encourage local communities to issue bonds to cover the costs, Nixon proposed the creation of an Environmental Financing Authority. If a municipality were unable to sell its own tax-free bonds, the EFA, as the entity of last resort, would buy them and then sell them on the taxable market. Turning to industrial and agricultural pollution, the message proposed precise effluent standards set by Washington, a significant break from the ambient standards employed previously. Violators were to face swift punishment, for the proposal armed investigators with subpoena and discovery power and the Department of Interior with the power to levy fines up to ten thousand dollars for every day of noncompliance. Federal jurisdiction would cover "all navigable waters," not simply those that were clearly interstate. Together, the message read, the program illustrated a "simple but profoundly significant principle: that neither a municipality nor an industry should be allowed to discharge wastes into those waterways beyond their capacity to absorb the wastes without becoming polluted."[49]

A simple principle perhaps, but the internal administration debate it generated far outstripped that in regard to air pollution. Muskie was on record as supporting legislation providing direct federal grants and greater appropriations, and Hickel thought the administration figures conservative as well. To the secretary, the annual appropriation debate had grown so rancorous it could no longer guarantee sufficient funding. In its place, Hickel argued, the administration should provide one-time contracting authority of ten to fifteen billion dollars. With thirty-year financing, the government would pay the principal on bonds for the construction of municipal treatment centers that the state and local governments issued. These governments would, in turn, pay the interest.[50] This was not wise, Secretary of Treasury David Kennedy countered, for the plan would have an adverse effect on the municipal bond market. It would, the Bureau of the Budget added, make it difficult to resist similar proposals for mass transit, hospitals, education, and other programs difficult to meet through the normal budget process. Ehrlichman and Whitaker noted that the idea in essence required the relevant congressional committees to abdicate their review authority, an unlikely occurrence under any circumstance. In any event, Hickel, as abrasive as ever, did not help his cause by advocating his proposal and the need for larger appropriations in public—before Ehrlichman and Nixon had made their decision.[51]

Others in the administration faulted the notion of precise effluent standards, advocating instead an effluent fee or permit system. This alternative, supporters insisted, relied on more effective financial incentives, making technological experimentation more likely and litigation less so. To Ehrlichman, however, such a plan constituted a new form of taxation, not only disrupting committee jurisdiction but placing the White House in an uncomfortable political situation. Most environmental groups favored the straight regulatory approach previously employed in pollution legislation, and while this was sure to meet some resistance with industry, direct regulation was less controversial with the public. The entire proposal, Secretary of Commerce Maurice Stans strenuously argued, ran roughshod over the interest of industry—and ultimately over the interest of the administration. Industry was not the enemy, the evil black knight pictured by critics, but a willing partner in the cleanup effort. Its cooperation was necessary for success. Aware of the new regulatory powers about to emerge, Stans remained a firm proponent of Department of Commerce jurisdiction, the possibility pleasing to the department's business constituency but anathema to most environmental groups. At the very least, Stans argued, Nixon should create a National Industrial Pollution Control Council (NIPCC) composed of industry leaders and under Commerce jurisdiction, to "provide an effective liaison with the Federal Government."[52]

It was a complex problem, and the lack of administration consensus underscored the reality that any direction the White House turned would anger someone. In the end, Nixon's proposal in many ways embraced the position of environmentalists, a strong and direct regulatory approach. To calm industry, Nixon accepted the idea of a NIPCC, but assumed strict supervision by CEQ. NIPCC members would, in Whitaker's words, "be brought into really small, private meetings with Train," who would impress upon them the president's desire to control pollution.[53] Politics demanded that the administration "be harsh on industry to abate pollution," Nixon told his advisors, and to do otherwise allowed "Muskie and the Democrats to seize the initiative."[54] Harsh on industry or not, Nixon could not bring himself to accept the appropriation figures that various scientists, Democrats, and environmental groups requested. To allocate additional monies for the construction of waste treatment centers was to burst the budget, necessitate higher taxes, and court economic disaster. His position was principled but, in the end, the Achilles' heel of the entire proposal. With the continued growth of suburban America, the situation demanded more aggressive federal funding, an argument that Muskie was prepared to press to a receptive public. A billion dollars a year barely surpassed previous appropriations, and given the fact that a third of the nation's sewage went untreated and half of the existing water treatment plants were still overloaded, the magnitude of the problem demanded more money. The National League of Cities and the United States Conference of Mayors estimated that by 1975 national needs would surpass three times the total Nixon proposed. By the end of Nixon's term, estimates of the total cost ran as high as sixty billion dollars.[55] The administration proposed, in short, a solid regulatory agenda that was, ironically, impotent to carry out its own stated goals.

Nixon's third major proposal was less ambitious than either his agenda for air or water pollution, but no less significant. Solid waste — whether junked automobiles, discarded beverage cans, or the tons of generic garbage accumulated daily by every major city — did not necessarily pose the direct and immediate health hazard of polluted air and water, but, as an eyesore alone, demanded attention. Each year America threw away an amazing 80 million tons of paper and paper products, 100 million automobile tires, 30 million glass bottles, and millions of junked automobiles and major appliances, all for a grand total that approached four and a half billion tons. Lady Bird Johnson, the former first lady, had made litter a cause célèbre, and had assisted in the passage of the Solid Waste Disposal Act of 1965. This legislation created the Bureau of Solid Waste Management in HEW to aid states with a modest program of research, training, and technical assistance, but the program remained from the outset underfunded and beset with morale and personnel problems.[56] To Muskie and many Democrats, the solution lay in new legislation to expand federal funding for collection and elimination projects. To Nixon, however, this constituted the "old way." Proposing an extension of the 1965 law rather than new legislation, Nixon called for a "redirection of research" into recycling. Worried about the budget, Nixon recommended against "pouring more and more public money into collection and disposal of whatever happens to be privately produced and discarded." New thinking, not new money, was the answer. Turning to CEQ, Nixon announced that he had asked the new agency to recommend a solution to the problem of abandoned automobiles, some way to remove the rusted hulks of vehicles blighting much of the American landscape.[57]

Nixon's proposal was, in one sense, before its time. Anticipating the day of curbside recycling pickups and biodegradable packaging, it was absolutely correct that innovations promised to revolutionize the way America dealt with its trash. The country first needed the technology to make such efforts cost-effective, however, and only further study offered answers. Washington had a role in this regard, and Nixon recognized it. At the same time, however, his proposal did not appreciate the pressing need for additional financial assistance. Not only was research itself costly, but in the interim the problem worsened by the hour. Americans already discarded over five pounds of trash per capita daily, a figure expected to double by the end of the century. With the population approaching 200 million and advancing in its own geometric fashion, the status quo promised nothing but disaster. New technology was no guaranty, and years might pass before recycling proved profitable in the market.[58] Although Nixon conveniently ignored it, Muskie had already issued a call for more intensive recycling research, supplementing his plea for expanded disposal facilities. Together, at least in this regard, the two boded well for the future of recycling, if not for the additional financial allocations that the problem of solid waste disposal also mandated.

The fact that the fourth section of Nixon's environmental agenda dealt with the issue of parks was hardly surprising. The press had reported Hickel's parks advocacy the previous year, and Nixon had raised the matter in his State of the Union. The message to Congress only added the specifics. "I propose," the message began, "that we adopt a new philosophy for the use of Federally-owned lands, treating them as a precious resource . . . which should be made to serve the highest possible good." To accomplish this, the address announced an executive order creating a Property Review Board. The board was to identify all underutilized General Services Administration property and make recommendations for disposition. Much of this property would become parkland, often in congested areas virtually devoid of nature. It was, as Hickel had recommended the previous year, a perfect way to "bring parks to the people." Train would serve on the board, as would sundry economic and administrative advisors. Washington should also have the option, Nixon later added, to convey surplus real property to local governments at discounts up to 100 percent. Localities could thus obtain federal land at no charge, allowing them to use their own money to obtain matching grants from the Land and Water Conservation Fund, the six-year-old federal reserve designed to assist communities in acquiring natural areas. Congress, Nixon went on, should increase this fund from 200 million dollars to 300 million dollars, with the money coming from outercontinental shelf oil and gas-leasing receipts. Finally, all federal agencies should pay rent for space assigned by GSA, an incentive for disposal.[59] "When in doubt," Whitaker recalled Nixon's instructions, "make a park out of it." For Nixon, it was arguably one of the few areas of environmental interest that transcended political expediency. In the words of Whitaker: "He felt very strongly about parks, particularly because he'd been brought up in a reasonably poor environment and he realized that the folks in his area couldn't afford a trip to Yellowstone or the great pristine parks, so somehow we had to bring the parks to the people." Politics or genuine concern, the fact remained that Nixon had already devoted as much, if not more, personal attention to parks than any other environmental issue, with its inclusion in the environmental message expected.[60]

The entire dilemma—from air pollution to crowded parks—required restructuring the federal bureaucracy, Nixon's message concluded. This was an undeniable truth, and a proposal largely expected given the president's efforts to date. The message noted CEQ and the Ash Council, whose recommendations for executive reorganization still pended, and announced the imminent appointment of the NIPCC, presented as an assurance for industrial compliance and not a conduit for legal exception. In any event, the message emphasized, solutions ultimately rested with the public. Everyone should become involved, for the problem "presents us with one of those rare situations in which each individual everywhere has an opportunity to make a special contribution to his country." In the end, public activism was vital for success. "This is our task together."[61]

Solutions indeed required public involvement, but, coming from a president who at that time failed to embrace fully the rapidly approaching Earth Day, the statement was somewhat ironic. Nixon was correct to encourage popular enthusiasm, in politics the lifeblood of accomplishment, but to date the White House had sought more to capitalize off the groundswell of grass-roots environmentalism than encourage it. Still, on the other hand, the parks proposal alone was enough to counter any rhetorical hypocrisy. Urbanites did have few open areas for recreation, and transferring GSA property was a viable alternative for parks, one that, Nixon knew, reaped political dividends. In this sense it was a stroke of genius, making something of value where before none existed, winning support with virtually no economic costs. More significant, however, was the call for increased funding for the Land and Water Conservation Fund. Since its inception, the LWCF had suffered annual appropriations far behind that authorized in the original legislation.[62] The nation's parks remained overcrowded and poorly maintained while potential additions continuously fell to the spread of suburban sprawl, despite the intent of the original statute. Nixon's proposal may not have provided what all the nation's parks needed, but, in helping to fulfill the promises of the past, it increased the promise of the future.

In total, there was much to applaud in Nixon's environmental agenda. Unveiling it as a coordinated package of legislative initiatives in an official message to

Congress assured not only political credit to Nixon, but another front-page story for the environment. Just as another Republican president, Theodore Roosevelt, had used the presidency as a "bully pulpit" more than half a century before, so had Nixon. Nixon's motives may not have been as pure as his predecessor's, but the message rang true all the same. Problems existed with the agenda, and in no way did it serve as a panacea for all that ailed the nation's environment. In any event, the program now lay with Congress, where strenuous debate was sure to follow. Nixon's program may not have concluded the journey, but for environmentalists it was a step in the right direction.

The reaction to Nixon's message reflected its relative strengths and weaknesses. For the most part, the agenda won the praise it deserved. The *Washington Post*, not always a friend to Nixon, termed the agenda "forward-minded." The White House, the *Post* correctly acknowledged, "has taken us a long way." The *New York Times*, more muted in its commendation, could not ignore the reality that Nixon had raised the standard in environmental protection. While noting Nixon's budgetary restraint, most specifically in regard to water pollution, the *Times* spoke of "the President's laudable purpose." The *Times* editorial concluded: "President Nixon deserves praise for giving an unprecedented emphasis to the environmental needs of the country. But if the country is really to make peace with nature, as he wisely counsels, he will have to demand for the purpose, in far greater quantities than he has yet suggested, the chlorophyll of good green cash."[63]

Industry, for the most part, did not share this perspective. While welcoming the NIPCC, auto companies complained that the administration's environmental zeal meant more costly cars, prices up to 10 percent higher. If the administration persisted, the inevitable result was the "eventual elimination of every independent [automobile] company in the United States."[64] Such predictions undoubtedly frightened the public—as intended—but in a sense stood as the best counter to critics who painted the entire program as irresolute and feeble. This image of weakness was exactly the one that the administration's political opponents wished to advance, but given the real strengths of many of Nixon's proposals, criticism was difficult.[65] If nothing else, Nixon's rhetoric mirrored their own. To criticize harshly Nixon's program risked appearing overtly partisan, but to do nothing risked abdicating the issue. Critics, understandably, had to walk a fine line. In public Muskie began by lauding the message and promising bipartisan cooperation, only then adding that additions were necessary. Turning attention to the Democratic Congress and the amendments he thought necessary, Muskie promised, "We want to take advantage of the high level of public interest in this subject this year." In private, his aides assured him that Nixon's message contained "nothing new, imaginative or interesting that is not contained in your legislative package," in short nothing to diminish Muskie's own stature on the issue.[66]

"Has the President preempted the environmental issue?" CBS newsman Roger Mudd asked Muskie a week after Nixon's address. The political initiative did not matter, Muskie replied, although the question itself—inconceivable only a year before—undoubtedly bothered "Ecology Ed."[67] Letters of congratulations arrived at the White House daily, including many from the nation's leading environmental organizations. "The Nixon message," the Sierra Club proclaimed, was a "clear warning" to the Democrats. "They will have to re-double efforts if they expect in November to tell voters, as they have in the past, that they are doing the most for solutions of environmental problems."[68] For Whitaker and his young staff, who had worked long tedious hours for almost a year, such praise certainly appeared to vindicate their efforts. When Trout Unlimited, a conservation group of fishermen, wrote to congratulate Nixon, Colson summed up the view from the White House: "We are really scoring points with these groups." Acknowledging the acclamation pouring in from around the nation, Nixon encouraged his staff to continue the offensive; after all, introducing legislation was one thing while congressional passage was another. "Okay, get going," was the mandate from the Oval Office.[69]

Nixon might have paused to enjoy the situation. For once the White House appeared to have the upper hand, with the environmental message a conduit to many elements of the public stringently opposed to the administration on other issues. The greatest of these issues, the Vietnam War, remained relatively quiet, and compared with the previous year at least, dissension paled. It was almost as if Nixon's "Silent Majority" speech at the end of the previous year had silenced critics and calmed tensions beyond the most optimistic predictions. Problems remained of course, but Nixon's approval ratings indicated solid support, and, with Earth Day looming, the environmental message promised only to augment the numbers. In the shadow of the turbulent 1960s, in an era of war and social upheaval, Nixon had found precious little opportunity for reprieve. The first weeks of the new decade had largely turned in Nixon's favor, in no small part due to his popular environmental offensive. Nixon might have relaxed, but he recognized that the struggle had only begun. Flying to Key Biscayne and the Bahamas with his family to celebrate daughter Patricia's impending twenty-fourth birthday, Nixon called Whitaker personally to invite his family to join them. For a president known as inaccessible to all but his top aides, the invitation was a clear sign of approval. A thoughtful gesture, Whitaker later recalled, that "makes you feel good." Nixon was "as happy as he could be." The break, however, only lasted an extended weekend. It was then back to the office and work, back to the task at hand.[70]

As if the eye of a hurricane were passing, any opportunity for satisfied reflection proved fleeting. In the weeks following Nixon's address, as winter turned to spring, the administration found itself once again under attack, wrestling with events that divided the nation and promised to overwhelm any political momentum the administration enjoyed. The change was not due to any diminution of the environmental threat or any shift in the administration's strategy. As Earth Day approached, no shortage of pundits existed to point out that the threat remained. Popular actor Eddie Albert, for one, announced a new production company to make antipollution films for theaters and schools, an action that promised to keep alive the spirit of the present generation well into the future. Undergraduates at San Jose State University in California held a week-long "survival fair" in anticipation of the designated day. Denis Hayes and the national staff of Earth Day reported that preparations proceeded well, with increasing numbers of politicians wishing to take part.[71] Earth Day loomed not as an event of less significance, but one with more.

Comfortable with his middle-of-the-road approach to Earth Day, and assured that his legislative package sufficiently demonstrated his administration's concern, Nixon forged ahead with his environmental offensive. Taking every opportunity to advance his standing, Nixon gave no indication of any policy shift in the weeks following his address to Congress. Indeed, when lawmakers, following the momentum of public opinion, passed two new environmental bills—both largely shaped by Democrats and containing provisions that Nixon thought excessive—Nixon overlooked his objections and signed them into law. In March, Nixon signed legislation creating the Commission on Population Growth and the American Future, which he had proposed in his population address the previous year. The law was not, however, the same bill that the White House originally supported, containing new provisions encouraging zero population growth. Aware of the potential implications for the politically explosive matter of abortion, Nixon had resisted them the previous year. Now, in the wake of his address to Congress and in anticipation of Earth Day, Nixon claimed that he "welcomed" the additions.[72] In April, Nixon signed Muskie's Water Quality Improvement Act. As passed, the bill mandated absolute company liability for oil spills, not the partial liability that the administration favored. As part of the Muskie-Jackson NEPA compromise the previous year, the bill also provided for an Office of Environmental Quality as support staff for CEQ, the additional layer of bureaucracy Nixon had warned against in his

NEPA comments and had resisted consistently. Now, however, facing a potentially much larger water pollution struggle with Muskie over funding for waste-
treatment facilities, Nixon signed the bill, conserving both his energy and his
goodwill with environmentalists for the certain future battle.[73] The Water
Quality Improvement Act of 1970 was a significant improvement in the struggle against oil pollution, and Nixon was correct to sign it. Although his own
legislative victories remained few, his acquiescence to the actions of others had,
if nothing else, enhanced his image as an environmental advocate and kept his
environmental offensive intact.

The sudden downturn in the administration's fortunes was due not to any
shift in environmental policy, or for that matter to the environment in any respect, but to the old familiar nemesis, Vietnam. On February 12, only two days
after Nixon's environmental address, the North Vietnamese broke the relative
calm with a long-feared offensive. The attack came not in Vietnam, where it
had been expected, but in neighboring Laos. Nixon had for months authorized
a secret war against communist guerrillas in this ostensibly neutral nation. In
the wake of the new assault, he ordered B-52 bombings—the first such use of
the aeronautical dreadnoughts outside of Vietnam. Difficult to contain, the
news sparked outrage in the American public, with critics interpreting developments as an escalation of the war. After first denying that Americans were
engaged in ground warfare in Laos, Nixon begrudgingly acknowledged combat and American deaths there, further antagonizing the peace movement. If
this tempest were not enough, Cambodia, another neighbor of Vietnam, suffered a military coup that, while bloodless, threatened further to destabilize the
area. Both Laos and Cambodia contained the infamous Ho Chi Minh Trail, a
crucial enemy supply route into South Vietnam. With the new North Vietnamese offensive, the military argued that the rapidly deteriorating situation
required additional troops, and in the case of Cambodia ground forces for the
first time.

Anticipating a "gathering spring storm of antiwar protest," Nixon grew increasingly frustrated, not only by the new wave of critics who did not agree
with the urgent need for decisive action but by the slow pace of peace negotiations.[74] In the secret Paris talks, Hanoi's negotiators appeared to procrastinate
deliberately, with the administration's promised announcements of overall
troop withdrawal neither encouraging peace nor pacifying the peace movement. As criticism grew, the Senate Foreign Relations Committee voted to re-
peal the Gulf of Tonkin Resolution, which the Johnson administration had
once called the "functional equivalent" of a declaration of war. Nixon insisted
that, because he inherited the war, he did not need justification to continue it.

The vote was, nevertheless, another reminder of the limitations that his policy faced and the sudden reemergence of popular protest. From the outset Nixon had assumed that he would see the "light at the end of the tunnel" by early 1970 and a peace settlement by the November congressional elections. Now the tunnel only seemed darker, with the congressional elections a potential public rebuke.[75]

Frustration flowed from other sources as well; the weeks following Nixon's environmental address brought more unexpected bad news. First, a Moynihan memorandum to Nixon, leaked to the press, proved a public relations debacle. The memo noted the growing anger and alienation of many African-Americans and recommended a policy of "benign neglect" to cool tensions. Taking the comments out of context, critics seized upon the opportunity to paint the administration as racist, uncaring, and brutal. The Senate then rejected the nomination of G. Harrold Carswell for the Supreme Court, the second rejection of a Nixon nominee for the Court vacancy and a humiliating defeat, the first time since 1894 that two consecutive appointments had met this fate. With critics uncovering a Carswell connection to white supremacist groups, the White House appeared once again as reactionary. If this were not enough, the Apollo XIII moon flight suffered an onboard explosion, and the crew aborted the mission. Although the flight had nothing to do with the White House, the disaster compounded a national sense of pessimism, and Nixon suffered the consequences. As he had benefited from the Apollo triumph of the past, so did he endure the failure of the present.[76]

The sudden turn of events left Nixon angry and bewildered. In late February, just after his environmental address, his approval ratings peaked at 66 percent. Two weeks before Earth Day, a Gallup poll placed the figure at 53 percent, a significant drop in less than two months. In the East his numbers fell below 50 percent. Poll respondents cited the administration's handling of the Vietnam War and a general sense of Nixon as a "passive president," with the latter reason rather ironic given the administration's recent environmental activism.[77] It appeared that despite the White House's environmental efforts and the popular environmentalism sweeping the nation as it prepared for Earth Day, much of the public quickly returned to the view that critics had of Nixon at the outset. He remained to many not the moderate that his recent environmental rhetoric and agenda suggested, but still a right-wing reactionary bent upon dismantling reform and intensifying the war. Despite the political gains Nixon had briefly enjoyed, his environmental record in the end paled in the strong light of war, race, money, and other controversial issues of the day.

In this sense, the story of Earth Day and the momentous events that followed are hardly surprising. Ignoring the many positive aspects of Nixon's environ-mental program, much of the public, angry over Nixon's conduct in other are-nas, was quick to carp when the administration failed to embrace fully the day's festivities. Nixon did not adequately demonstrate his commitment to environ-mental protection on the very day the nation publicly declared its own, a mis-take hard to deny. Earth Day on April 22, 1970, was an important event in American environmental history, deserving the full attention and endorsement of all levels of government, the president of the United States included. This ac-knowledged, however, in many respects Nixon still did not deserve harsh de-nunciation. The significance of Earth Day lay in its manifestation of popular environmentalism, a concern that spawned the requisite governmental re-forms. During his brief tenure in office, Nixon had already signed crucial legis-lation, proposed more, and, in attempting to win the political initiative, raised public consciousness. Worried about persistent opposition and criticism, Nixon unwisely avoided a full embrace of the national celebration. Launching his agenda had, nevertheless, helped launch the movement that Earth Day rep-resented.

"Every day is the last—make it count," Nixon confided to himself.[78] It was an admirable credo by which to live, even if for the administration Earth Day had passed as a day best forgotten. It also implied an essential truth: that each day carried with it new opportunity, a new chance to forget the past and move for-ward. Nixon spent little energy worrying about Earth Day criticism, instead fo-cusing on his decision to send ground forces into Cambodia. He recognized well the lesson of the preceding months, that while environmental quality was important politically, his future ultimately lay with other issues. In the end, the criticism Nixon faced over Earth Day was but a summer shower compared to the hurricane of hostility that followed in the wake of his Cambodian incur-sion. If Earth Day obscured Nixon's solid legislative agenda, so did the riots and deaths at Kent State obscure Earth Day. It was all somewhat ironic. Nixon was, finally, in his strongest position to proclaim himself the nation's leading envi-ronmental champion, yet faced criticism on Earth Day. Earth Day represented the overwhelming popularity and force of the nation's new environmentalism, yet that environmentalism itself appeared insignificant given the explosive de-velopments of the day. For the administration, the new day appeared no better than the old.

3

"All Politics Is a Fad"
May–December 1970

Walter Hickel was angry. Nixon's decision to invade Cambodia not only sparked tragedy at Kent State University, the secretary fumed, it completely alienated much of America's youth and ripped apart a nation whose divisions the administration's environmental advocacy had just begun to bridge. For over a year Hickel had diligently worked to reach the youthful dissenters, yet, as campuses exploded, his efforts all seemed to come to naught. Earth Day was a "day of hope," Hickel later recalled, which Nixon's Vietnam strategy instantly obliterated. "Earth Day raised expectations. The Cambodian invasion crushed them."[1]

Never one to endure quietly, Hickel quickly drafted a letter of protest to the White House, circulating a copy to his staff for comment. The letter noted the Department of Interior's efforts to involve young people in environmental policy and claimed significant success. If Nixon continued to "alienate those who could be our friends," he erased the gains so arduously attained. The administration must, Hickel wrote, "learn from history" and "communicate with youth and listen to their ideas and problems." Obviously annoyed that Haldeman had denied his request to meet with the president the previous day, Hickel concluded his letter by declaring that the close involvement of the cabinet was vital for success.[2]

What happened next is debatable. The Associated Press picked up the letter, obtained by the *Washington Evening Star*, and the story appeared as front-page news across the country on May 7. Just as the four Kent State students were laid to rest, and with the White House under siege, the president's own Interior Department secretary was on record in opposition. The leak was all a big mistake, Hickel explained to Nixon. Learning of the letter, the *Star* had called the Interior Department's Public Information Office to request a copy. Without both a director or instructions, PIO staffers had requested a copy from the steno-graphic pool, which had mistakenly released it. Hickel had no reason to cross his boss, Hickel's assistants maintained. "He was savvy enough to know that re-leasing it would take him out of play." Nixon was "pissed," according to one de-scription, refusing to believe that with Hickel's well-known capacity to speak his mind, the chain of events was anything but purposeful.[3] Ehrlichman agreed, suggesting that Hickel had given the letter directly to Bobbie Hornick, a female *Star* reporter who had impressed him. Hickel, Nixon told Haldeman, had gotten "too big for his britches." White House staff were to ignore him. "Be extremely cold," Haldeman quoted Nixon as saying. "Obviously he knew about it. Give him hell."[4]

Nixon wanted Hickel to resign. The secretary's brashness grated, and Halde-man agreed that his independence was a potential threat and that his manage-ment style was too lax. Hickel acknowledged as much. "I never had a whole lot of friends over there [at the White House]," he remembered. "I am a top-down manager," not one "for details." The applause Hickel received for his surprising environmentalism diverted attention from the White House and underscored the sense that the secretary was not a team player. The letter had won for Hickel the national spotlight, casting him as the new darling of administration critics. He was, Ehrlichman later recalled, like a "pop hero," granting interviews with-out fully retracting his letter.[5] If Hickel would not resign, Nixon instructed Haldeman, "behind the scenes encourage his enemies." Spokesmen should "build him up as incompetent" and "keep the pressure on." After Hickel stated publicly that he had no intention to resign, Nixon instructed Ehrlichman to tell him that he had no choice. It was already May, Hickel responded, too late in an election year for him to reenter Alaskan politics. With the matter at an appar-ent impasse, a tense telephone call soon provided a compromise. Hickel could stay "until after the elections." The time would allow him to prepare for his de-parture and shield Republicans from the political fallout that would certainly follow his termination.[6]

Hickel won a brief reprieve, but Nixon immediately began considering his replacement, and rumors of dissension within the administration spread. At first Nixon thought Robert Mayo the ideal candidate. As director of the Bureau of the Budget, Mayo had proved himself a "good bureaucrat." He was, in a sense, all that Hickel was not. Mayo understood the need for fiscal restraint and was meticulous with specifics. Although he frequently disagreed with his col-leagues, he was unlikely to take the dispute public. The drawback, of course, was his lack of natural resources policy experience, although, in Nixon's opin-ion, "Russell Train could handle the substance."[7] A final decision could wait, but Train obviously stood in good stead with the president. For this—an ally amidst the apparent turmoil—environmentalists were thankful.

Reports of Hickel's imminent political demise were, nevertheless, disturbing to many environmentalists, the assurance of Train notwithstanding. Just as they had rallied against him in the confirmation battle, so did many environmental organizations ironically lobby on his behalf in Cambodia's wake. "Allow us to commend you for having the honorable Walter J. Hickel in your cabinet as Secretary of Interior," Anthony Wayne Smith, president of the National Parks and Conservation Association, wrote Nixon. "In the short period of his tenure, Mr. Hickel has achieved real stature as a conservationist and an environmentalist."[8] Given Hickel's public defense of the Alaska pipeline, not every organization shared Smith's zeal. To David Brower, Hickel's record remained "horrible."[9] Faced with the prospect of someone worse, however, most acknowledged that his accomplishments outweighed his transgressions. Joe Browder, then conservation director of the new organization Friends of the Earth, believed Hickel's metamorphosis was an attempt to compensate for the widely held perception of him as an anti-environmentalist. Hickel had "considerable genuine interest." Others were less charitable, but acknowledged his overall record as a pleasant surprise. In the following months, the White House received over seventeen thousand letters concerning Hickel, with the overwhelming majority strong in his defense.[10]

The turbulent days following the Kent State tragedy, Nixon later recalled, "were among the darkest of my Presidency." His unplanned early morning sojourn to the Lincoln Memorial was only one indication of a man suffering a tremendous burden. Hickel's criticism may have spoken for many Americans, but in no way did it reflect the anger, the righteous indignation, aimed at the occupant of the Oval Office. The ferocity of protest "stunned' Nixon's advisors, the *New York Times* reported.[11] A line of busses parked end to end once again surrounded and protected the White House, just as they had during the Moratorium march the year before. Inside, one Nixon aide remembered, "it was like a war." Smoke filled the air with protest chants and cherry bombs audible from the outside. When one guard in the Executive Office Building dropped a tear gas canister, the staff had to evacuate, their eyes burning and red. In Georgetown the National Guard lined M Street and Wisconsin Avenue; in Potomac Park police arrested hundreds, herding them into RFK Stadium, quickly dubbed by protesters a "concentration camp."[12]

The fighter in Nixon wanted to lash out, to meet the protesters head on, and to put them in their place. After all, Nixon had support as well. Vice President Agnew urged a combative stance, and only two weeks after the tragedy more than 100,000 pro-Nixon demonstrators marched in downtown Manhattan, led by helmeted construction workers carrying signs that read, "America. Love it or leave it." Former President Lyndon Johnson wrote of his support, and, most happily for Nixon, polls indicated more citizens approved of the Cambodian operation than disapproved.[13] Nixon might have met anger with anger—but wisely chose to diffuse tensions. The protesters undoubtedly incensed Nixon, bringing out in Hickel's words, "the dark side" of his personality.[14] They understandably exacerbated the resentment, the sense of paranoia, that had increasingly characterized the president since the previous year. An offhand remark to a supporter in the middle of the crisis reflected Nixon's true feelings: protesters were "bums." Indeed, Haldeman later recalled the period as a turning point for Nixon, who privately determined to use whatever means he could to defeat his enemies. Haldeman may have been correct, but the public Nixon recognized the need for restraint. Outside of the ill-advised "bums" comment in an unguarded moment, Nixon's statements were mostly conciliatory. They may not have bridged the chasm that the invasion widened, but they wisely avoided further provocation.[15] By the end of June, Nixon promised, troops would withdraw. His political instincts intact, Nixon calmly stayed the course in domestic policy. Outside of Hickel, the White House's environmental staff conducted business as usual.

The administration's environmental strategy remained steadfast despite the tumult that surrounded the White House, but the climate for environmental activism had suddenly changed. More than on just the obvious level—Vietnam and its attendant disruptions or the impending fate of Hickel—the White House had, in a sense, played much of its hand in launching its long-awaited agenda. For almost a year Whitaker and his team had labored to construct a comprehensive program, and, as the designated day for unveiling it approached, the White House had worked to build anticipation. Now the day had passed, along with Earth Day. Nixon had earned his headlines, however brief, and the environmental issues were once again before Congress. The Democratic reaction would undoubtedly center on specific provisions—the minutia of detail that might disrupt the delicate balance of competing environmental and economic factors that the administration had worked so hard to achieve, and the narrow specifics that had the potential to cast the president as an opponent of environmentalism despite his record. In addition, the courts increasingly loomed as another venue for the matter, an area of diminished dominion for the White House. The administration's strategy to win the political initiative rested on careful timing, wording, and detail—with circumstance taking all three increasingly out of the White House's control. Although from an environmental perspective it was imperfect, the administration's program promised much for the nation's environmental quality. Its continued value as a political weapon was, however, as problematic as promising.

The task of implementing the program fell largely on those responsible for creating it. The White House's Domestic Council met each morning at 7:30. Ehrlichman, the chair, sat at one end of the table while George Shultz, director of the Office of Management and Budget, sat at the other. Between them sat the array of officials responsible for specific policies, including Whitaker, now with the title of Deputy Assistant to the President. Working with Whitaker was an able staff, including a number of young assistants who later went on to distinguished careers in government.[16] Across Lafayette Park from the White House, CEQ met, with Train as its chair and driving force. With Ehrlichman, Train, and Whitaker at the fore, the environment enjoyed a triumvirate considerably more friend than foe. From the various cabinet members came the spectrum of advice, often with the departments of Interior and Commerce diametrically opposed. Commerce Secretary Stans remained wary of his colleagues' environmental advocacy, far from convinced that his new NIPCC effectively blunted what he saw as the threat to his constituency, American business. For the environmental staff, Stans remained a "knee-jerk big business guy," the perpetual opponent, "always on the other side."[17] Nixon was not above the fray, but continued to have little time for the matter relative to other issues, a fact hardly surprising given the events of the day. Instead, the president preferred to issue his mandates from option papers created and disseminated by Ehrlichman and his staff. The process was efficient management—broad policy decreed from the top with specifics delegated to those with more interest and expertise. Nixon made clear what he expected from the issue: a strong but reasonable environmental policy, one sure to reap political dividends. His staff had come through with a solid program; now it settled in to the difficult tasks of congressional passage and implementation.

Nixon was content with his Domestic Council, but had broader concerns about efficient management of policy. The Domestic Council itself was a new Nixon creation, and, along with the Office of Management and Budget, part of a more extensive executive branch reorganization. By spring 1970, the Ash Council, appointed the previous year, had begun to issue its recommendations, which collectively promised to transform further the landscape for environmental advocacy. Nixon had already endorsed the Domestic Council and OMB, but, if he accepted the rest of the Ash Council's suggestions, environmentalists would have more to applaud than the administration's extant staff.

If Nixon proceeded, implementation of any policy would emerge radically different, indeed significantly strengthened. It would, Nixon hoped, reinforce his legacy and brighten his troubled political fortunes.

Over eighty federal agencies dealt with pollution, an intolerable situation that assured jurisdictional overlap and dispute. The egregious problem was included among the Ash Council's first recommendations. Over a year before, Nixon had met with Roy Ash, the council's chair, and identified natural resources as a priority.[18] If the administration could not adequately implement its environmental policy, programs developed by Ehrlichman, Whitaker, or Train would make little difference. The Ash Council's recommendations were extensive—and controversial. Most important was the creation of an Environmental Protection Agency, an independent body concerned with pollution abatement and with jurisdiction over all monitoring, research, standard-setting, and enforcement. The Ash Council also proposed expanding the Department of Interior into a Department of Natural Resources, which ultimately would include a new ocean agency to coordinate marine policy, the National Oceanic and Atmospheric Administration. The idea of a Department of Natural Resources was hardly revolutionary. Conservationists had lobbied for its creation since Franklin Roosevelt's administration, although in each instance congressional proponents of the status quo, seeking to protect existing committee jurisdictions, blocked reform.[19] Now, with the blossoming of the environmental movement, the prospects for success appeared brighter.

Brighter perhaps, but no less controversial. The proposals sent shock waves through the executive branch as each agency and department gauged their own individual prospects. Their reactions were fairly predictable. Under the Ash Council's plan, EPA drew most heavily from HEW and the Department of Interior, although the Atomic Energy Commission and the Department of Agriculture also lost significant jurisdiction. From Interior came the Federal Water Quality Administration, while HEW lost the Bureau of Water Hygiene, the National Air Pollution Control Administration, the Bureau of Solid Waste Management, and the Bureau of Radiological Health.[20] The proposed DNR had an even greater impact, most notably on the Department of Agriculture, which forfeited the Forest Service, the Rural Electrification Administration, and the Soil Conservation Service. The plan cost the Department of Defense the Corps of Engineers and the Department of Transportation the Coast Guard, while it transferred the independent Atomic Energy Commission to the new department. The Ash Council rejected the possibility of a joint Department of Environment and Natural Resources, arguing that protection of environmental quality and efficient management of natural resources posed conflicting mandates. Although Whitaker and Ash had originally supported this larger department, Nixon had turned against the idea, convinced that it posed too unrealistic a disruption of the existing congressional committee structure. It was, Whitaker acknowledged, "a sticky political wicket."[21]

The proposals were outrageous, Secretary of Agriculture Clifford Hardin argued, harming farmers who were sure to retaliate politically. The departments of Transportation, Defense, and HEW concurred that problems existed, but, resigned at least to the creation of EPA, were less vocal in their dissent. Characteristically, Stans protested the lack of any role for the Department of Commerce. Reiterating the position he had taken earlier in regard to the NIPCC, Stans wrote Nixon, "It is essential that the Commerce Department actively participate in the policies, interfaces and actions relating to environmental control."[22] Specifically, Commerce should have jurisdiction over the National Oceanic and Atmospheric Administration, or NOAA, an argument to which most environmental organizations were, in the words of the National Wildlife Federation, "unalterably opposed."[23] With much of the public debate centered on NOAA, the Department of Interior, anticipating a bounty of administrative authority, countered the other departments with equal vigor, insisting upon the Ash Council's recommendations. A jurisdictional quagmire had degenerated into a struggle for power, and all looked to the White House as the arbiter.[24]

With the status quo clearly unacceptable, Nixon first proposed NOAA within the Department of Commerce. Although environmentalists protested, Stans was persuasive, and, in any instance, Nixon believed that industry's strength in the Senate Commerce Committee and the House Merchant Marine and Fisheries Committee portended an unsuccessful fight for the alternative. Nixon next proposed EPA, with Train in a press conference describing it as proof that the environment remained a high priority. The new agency, Nixon maintained, would not conflict with CEQ, but augment it. CEQ would continue as the central body for the formation of policy, while EPA would serve as the "main line agency for policy implementation."[25] The proposal for a DNR, Nixon decided, would have to wait. Still angry with Hickel, the thought of enlarging his authority was not an attractive alternative. In any event, it was best to propose officially the DNR as part of an overall cabinet reorganization, which the Ash Council continued to study. If the reaction of the cabinet secretaries was any indication, the proposal would also engender strong resistance in Congress, and the White House intended major proposals for revenue sharing in the near future. Nixon fully intended to pursue the DNR, but to do so now risked alienating potential allies on other issues.[26]

Nixon introduced NOAA and EPA in early July as reorganization plans, not separate congressional legislation. As such, neither held cabinet status, but both automatically became operative in sixty days without a formal congressional objection. In the case of EPA this seemed unlikely. Muskie and most Democrats supported a similar independent agency, and Nixon's actions left them little room for criticism. The White House had seized the day again, leaving Muskie only to retort that it was a "useful beginning," a refrain reminiscent of his reaction to Nixon's environmental address.[27] As congratulations arrived, an obviously pleased Whitaker thanked Ash, saying, "I think we can all look back with justifiable pride and tell our grandchildren about EPA."[28] Although another pollution agency undoubtedly would have emerged from Congress in any instance, the administration's proposal warranted Whitaker's pride. In just one quick maneuver, Nixon had unraveled the jurisdictional quagmire that characterized the federal government's pollution-fighting bureaucracy. He had established an agency with enough independence and enforcement power to answer the clarion call of the day, a legacy that remains today.

"EPA looks very good," Whitaker wrote Ehrlichman, "but NOAA is a bit shaky."[29] Indeed, if EPA met smooth sailing in Congress, NOAA faced rough waters. Rather than letting Commerce Department jurisdiction of NOAA pass in the glow of EPA, most environmental groups protested fiercely. According to the Izaak Walton League, Stans protecting the ocean was akin to the fox guarding the hen house. The situation was, in short, "the beginning of a national program for the development and exploitation of the seas."[30] Gaylord Nelson introduced a resolution of disapproval, which gained considerable media coverage. Unable to attack Nixon on EPA, prominent Democrats also noted the lack of a DNR proposal, attempting to turn it to their advantage. Former Secretary of Interior Stewart Udall wrote in a *Newsday* article that the omission was due to vindictiveness, an attempt to punish Hickel. Ignoring the well-known fact that the Ash Council's DNR recommendation was still before the White House, Udall argued that by punishing Hickel, Nixon hurt the very cause he claimed to protect. It was, Udall maintained, a prime example of the way the White House silenced environmentalists within its midst.[31]

In the end, NOAA emerged from Congress as Nixon proposed. Nevertheless, the controversy had, in a sense, stolen the administration's thunder, robbing Nixon of the full political benefit that he sought and that his EPA proposal deserved. Although Nixon received praise for his new environmental agency, the debate over NOAA jurisdiction and the delay of the DNR—comparatively insignificant in the larger scheme—nevertheless blunted credit for what one might argue as Nixon's most significant environmental accomplishment.[32] EPA was not a Democratic initiative reluctantly accepted, as was the case with

NEPA. Rather, Nixon had been proactive and forceful. With his legislative program before a Democratic Congress ready to respond, and with a divided nation in turmoil over his Vietnam policy, Nixon recognized EPA both as a solution to a real problem and a valuable political opportunity. Although he had in large part accomplished the former, he was less successful with regard to the latter.

Congressional passage of EPA was, of course, only the beginning. With operations set to begin within a year, the new agency needed a top administrator, a critical choice. For the White House the job description required someone experienced and popular. Scanning Congress, Whitaker rejected Texas representative George Bush as "tainted with oil."[33] Stans approached Hickel about the job, but Hickel was unclear whether Stans's comments represented a passing thought or an official inquiry from Nixon. Although he was not interested, Hickel later speculated, the offer made perfect sense as a way to remove him from Interior without any political ramifications.[34] Regardless, in time, Nixon settled on Warren Knowles, the progressive Republican governor of Wisconsin. When offered the job, however, Knowles cited poor health and declined, leaving Deputy Attorney General William Ruckelshaus as the leading candidate. Ruckelshaus, Whitaker argued, was an excellent choice; he had developed in the Indiana Attorney General's Office a solid reputation for vigorously enforcing environmental statutes. In any event, to choose some other Republican with less experience would appear "simply to pay a political debt."[35]

Whitaker was correct that Ruckelshaus met the White House's criteria well. The thirty-eight-year-old Princeton University and Harvard Law School graduate had worked closely with the Indiana Board of Health for years, playing a critical role in that state's air and water pollution enforcement. Coupled with his solid environmental credentials was an impressive Republican pedigree, including service as a GOP state representative and U.S. Senate candidate. Tall and bespectacled, he appeared serious and intellectual. Now an assistant U.S. attorney, Ruckelshaus benefited from an active lobbying campaign by an old friend and career U.S. Health Service officer, Jerry Hansler. While Hansler won the backing of major environmental organizations, Attorney General John Mitchell, Ruckleshaus's boss at the Department of Justice, strongly supported his candidacy.[36] Ehrlichman agreed, and the White House had its man.

The debate then turned to the best location for EPA's central office. To Whitaker, placing it in "one of the heartland states" had a strong "public relations impact." OMB disagreed, maintaining that anywhere other than Washington was more costly, and that it "could not keep a leash on them."[37] This argument resonated with the White House, but congressional Democrats debated the jurisdictional implications of the new agency. Several committees claimed oversight, a situation that Muskie recognized as potential "chaos."[38] A solution to all such environmental problems, Muskie and others maintained, was the creation of a Joint Committee on the Environment. This in itself raised problems, however, as a number of contenders vied for the chairmanship. As Nixon could attest, when the fight came to power and control in Congress, the status quo ruled. The committee remained only a possibility, but Democrats proved that not only the administration wrestled with the politics of environmental reorganization.[39]

The end of the summer had arrived by the time the White House settled on Ruckelshaus, an appointment most environmentalists welcomed, but in the interim politics continued to unfold. The turmoil of the spring slowly began to fade, but, in regard to the environment, the heat on the administration grew from more than the infamous Washington summers. The reaction to Nixon's environmental offensive had begun in earnest, and whether the administration's problems arose from the reemergence of controversial issues still simmering from the previous year, or the direct reaction of Democrats to Nixon's legislative agenda, the reality was that any momentum the White House enjoyed quickly evaporated. As Nixon launched a public relations blitz stressing "what is right" with America, administration critics predictably countered with what they saw as wrong with the administration's program.[40]

From its first year in office, the administration knew all too well those issues likely to raise the ire of environmentalists. On many matters its concern for the economy risked alienating the very voters that its environmental offensive intended to win. Conspicuously lacking from Nixon's environmental message were such problems as the Alaska pipeline, the timber harvest, DDT, and the SST, all unresolved and thus continuing sources of friction. As part of its strategy, the White House hoped to downplay these issues; it could not, however, completely avoid them. Just as in the past, they remained a thorn in the administration's side. Defending its position as best it could, the White House only hoped that these issues would not completely undermine the goodwill that its legislative program and EPA engendered.

The disposition of public lands was especially problematic, more so even than the Alaska pipeline, which had caused such anguish the year before. In fact, the focus of the pipeline controversy had moved away from the administration to the courts and Congress, and thus the debate at least temporarily posed less direct negative publicity. With his clearance to lift the land "freeze" from the Senate Interior Committee, Hickel planned to issue the permits for the necessary road construction and endure the wave of criticism that would surely follow. Learning of his plans, Muskie had already launched a salvo. "I was disturbed," a Muskie press release read, "to learn that Secretary Walter Hickel plans to issue a permit for the Trans Alaska Pipeline System." Conveniently omitting the role of the Johnson administration, the statement added, "It reminds me of the kind of mistakes the Interior Department made when it granted oil drilling permits for the Santa Barbara Channel."[41]

Just as Hickel prepared to make his announcement, however, litigation made the decision moot. Five native villages north of Fairbanks filed suit to block the permits, claiming that TAPS had not recognized their land and that they had not agreed to any right-of-way. Acknowledging that the matter demanded a definite resolution of conflicting land claims, Congress debated a bill that provided the Alaskan natives a direct land grant, a cash payment, and a percentage of royalties from mineral leasing on federal lands, while allowing withdrawals for one of the various federal public land systems. With the proverbial devil in the details, the legislation unleashed furious lobbying, not only from the state of Alaska and the Alaskan Federation of Natives, which sought to assure their share of the oil bounty, but also from environmentalists who sought protection for the largest allotment possible. Answering fire with fire, the Wilderness Society filed its own suit arguing that pipeline construction should not commence without an adequate environmental impact statement under NEPA. Nixon had signed NEPA never anticipating its use to obstruct a project he supported, but to environmentalists no such reservations existed. TAPS, for its part, was having its own difficulties in meeting the official environmental stipulations issued by the Interior Department the year before. Hampered as much by mismanagement as by science, TAPS reorganized as a new corporate entity, the Alyeska Pipeline Service Company. This, it hoped, facilitated all phases of its operation, assisting in litigation, lobbying, and research. In short, the pipeline issue remained a complex and volatile combination of factors, but an issue that had one advantage for the administration as the year progressed: it was increasingly as much a matter for lobbyists, lawyers, and legislators as for the White House.[42]

The most obvious of all the public land issues, the national parks, posed less of a problem. Indeed, if one area of Nixon's agenda won strong praise in the months following his address, it was his proposal on behalf of the nation's parks. Nixon's plan to expand funding for the Land and Water Conservation Fund passed Congress overwhelmingly, giving his environmental program one of its first legislative victories. In Congress, bipartisan support included both Muskie and Jackson, with the latter declaring himself "delighted" by Nixon's proposal. "As our population moves toward the 300 million mark," Jackson stated, "the resources of the Land and Water Conservation Fund must increase also to meet the needs of future generations."[43] Politicians did not need to look far to recognize the growing popularity of parks. In New Jersey, citizens passed a 100-million-dollar bond issue to expand the state's park system. In Virginia, the state legislature adopted a ten-year plan to improve its existing parks as well as to add twenty more by the national bicentennial in 1976. The Canadian House of Commons complained that Americans purchased an alarming percentage of that nation's valuable open spaces, while the World Wildlife Fund urged all nations to create more parks.[44] Aware, therefore, that his proposal to convert underutilized federal land into new parks enjoyed wide popular support, Nixon agreed to a suggestion by his chief speech writer, Raymond Price, to label his program "Nixon's Legacy of Parks." A catchy phrase, the name helped publicize the administration's efforts, serving as a "powerful selling point in 1972."[45]

Posing the greatest dilemma were the millions of other acres within the public domain. Since the days of the Articles of Confederation, when the colonial legislatures ceded their western claims to the nascent federal government, Washington had dealt with the proper disposition of these lands, an issue that only became more complex with the spread of the country westward. Throughout the nineteenth century, the question was simply to whom to give the land, which individuals and corporations best promoted economic development. Slowly, however, the nation came to view these lands in a broader perspective and to assume that permanent public management, not private ownership, best served the national interest. The question now was specifically how to manage these lands, to what use the public should put them. This issue, no small question, became another political quagmire for the Nixon administration by mid-1970.[46]

The Bureau of Land Management and the Forest Service controlled vast expanses of western lands, indeed in some states, such as Nevada, the majority of land. More so than the National Park Service, however, both of these agencies lacked a clear mandate guiding management policies. The Multiple Use-Sustained Yield Act of 1960 commanded the Forest Service to give equal consideration to five resources—recreation, range, fish and wildlife, water, and timber—but otherwise provided little specific guidance on balancing these divergent and often conflicting interests.[47] With the advent of environmentalism and passage of the Wilderness Act, with its call for withdrawal of wilderness lands, the task was only compounded. For many environmentalists, wilderness carried almost sacred connotations, with its preservation approaching a religious crusade. As one author would later write, "Our lives are inextricably tied to trees and forestlands, spiritually, aesthetically, and because of the benefits they afford. The union between trees and people took place before the dawn of civilization, and, with few exceptions, our lives are entwined with trees and forestland ecosystems from the cradle to the grave."[48] Many faulted the Forest Service for favoring its traditional role as timber supplier at the expense of its other valuable tasks. A University of Montana School of Forestry report charged that the agency paid only "lip service to multiple use principles," while one of the Forest Service's own periodic study groups drew essentially the same conclusion.[49]

The BLM domain, meanwhile, had served for years as prime grazing and mining land, but environmentalism posed once again a contentious challenge to tradition.[50] For much of the nation's history, stock concerns enjoyed no restrictions on public land grazing. The Taylor Grazing Act of 1934, which led to the formation of the U.S. Grazing Service, the BLM's antecedent, sought regulation to avoid over-use, but essentially only codified the interests of livestock owners. The infamous "Dust Bowl" of the Great Depression taught the importance of soil conservation, but did not prepare the bureaucracy for the new wave of public interest that the BLM now faced, the new environmentalists who valued the land's natural ecosystem, its habitat for wildlife, and its natural beauty. If this were not enough, a growing number of westerners resented federal authority in all respects and actively encouraged a return to federal disposal and private and state control. Not coincidentally beginning in Nevada, ranchers protested the dictates of the BLM and organized a potent lobby that matched the zealousness of wilderness advocates, a precursor of the famous Sagebrush Rebellion a decade later.[51] The stage was set for another drama of environmental politics, one that Nixon's environmental program not surprisingly avoided but one that was sure to cast him as someone's antagonist.

The first act of the drama had already begun the previous year, when the Forest Service, hoping to alleviate the nation's lumber shortage, began harvesting timber on land that, according to the Wilderness Society, warranted protection under the Wilderness Act. The dispute had led to a lawsuit over the Forest Service's narrow interpretation of the law, a legislative battle over a bill to increase the timber harvest, and, for the administration, the appointment of a task force to study the issue. Now, as the summer began, developments once again commanded the administration's attention. The Softwood Lumber and Plywood Task Force reported that, because of the severity of the potential lumber shortage, congressional action to ensure an adequate harvest merited Nixon's support. Congressmen from strong timber-producing states, including, surprisingly enough, the environmentalist Jackson, also sought a greater harvest.[52] Convinced by the task-force report and afraid of higher home prices, Ehrlichman concurred. HUD Secretary George Romney issued a statement that the bill was crucial "to build the homes America needs." Agriculture Secretary Clifford Hardin agreed that the bill now had the administration's "complete approval."[53]

With the administration now on record in support of the bill, its opponents recognized an excellent opportunity to blunt the administration's environmental offensive. "The timber-cutting bill is the first major environmental legislation to move before Congress since President Nixon signed NEPA," an indignant Muskie announced. "If the law for environmental quality is to be meaningful for the country, it cannot be ignored or circumvented as was done in this case." As Muskie inquired whether timber legislation required a NEPA impact statement, the Conservation Coalition, an ad hoc alliance of ten environmental groups, began an intense lobbying campaign, aimed in no small part at the administration.[54] In the end their efforts proved successful, as the House rejected the rule under which it was to consider the bill. By refusing to take up the measure, Congress, at least temporarily, killed it.[55]

The episode cost the White House political capital, but the problem remained. As the administration suffered its congressional loss, the United States District Court ruled against the Forest Service and in favor of the Wilderness Society in its year-long court battle. The Forest Service could not harvest timber on land contiguous to designated "primitive" areas until it had complied with all studies as required under the wilderness law. Although not specifically mentioned in the Wilderness Act, these areas of "de facto wilderness" deserved study for possible protection in the Wilderness System. On the offensive, the Sierra Club added another lawsuit, this time arguing that the clear-cutting practices of U.S. Plywood-Champion Papers in Alaska's Tongass National Forest violated the Wilderness Act and NEPA. Concerned that this litigation threatened to exacerbate an already perilous lumber situation, the administration argued that clear-cutting was not only legal, but necessary for regeneration and the orderly management of tree species intolerant of shade.[56]

Challenged in both Congress and the courts, the administration struggled to make its case to the public while simultaneously diffusing tensions, a tack that in a sense embraced opposing goals and thus assured failure. On one hand, Train and his CEQ colleague Robert Cahn met with environmentalists to discuss the possibility of an executive order protecting at least some "de facto wilderness," an action that CEQ endorsed but one that placed it in direct conflict with the Forest Service. Promising to propose additions to the Wilderness

System in the near future, the White House reiterated its support of the Wilderness Act. On the other hand, the White House backed a proposal of the National Forest Products Association (NFPA) to "make a start at increasing timber production through administrative action."[57] Rather than pushing legislation to increase the annual timber harvest, which would engender more congressional criticism and litigation, Nixon should simply order higher funding for the Forest Service's "cultural practices," such as earlier planting, more sprucing, and additional pruning. This allowed Nixon in good conscience to order unilaterally an increased cut from national forests. Charles Colson, counsel to the president, liked the idea. "Personally, I am convinced we are better off this way than walking back into the hurricane that will ensue in Congress."[58] As Nixon ordered the Department of Agriculture to arrange an increased harvest, members of the Council of Economic Advisors held a formal White House press conference to publicize the task force's conclusions. While this afforded the administration a chance for justification, Whitaker thought such a public display unwise. The issue "cuts both ways as a national story," and thus the proper course was "low profile with no briefing." To put it simply, "the lumber people will like it, the environmentalists won't."[59]

As if to prove Whitaker correct, the timber industry applauded Nixon's order while most environmentalists condemned it. James Turnbill of the NFPA wrote Nixon that the decision "gratified" him, for the task force's conclusions "generally substantiate the contentions of wood producers and users over the past several years." Michael McCloskey of the Sierra Club saw it differently. An increased harvest "quickened liquidation of old growth," and, taken with the administration's position on clear-cutting, cast Nixon as an opponent of wilderness, his public support of the Wilderness Act notwithstanding. In Congress, Republican John Saylor labeled Nixon's order "disastrous," trying to accomplish "by executive fiat what could not be done legislatively."[60]

In the year since the White House first broached the issue by appointing a task force to define policy, it was no closer to an adequate solution than it was at the outset. On one hand, the Housing and Urban Development Act of 1968 had called for the construction of twenty-six million new housing units, an undeniable factor in the dramatic rise in lumber and home prices. On the other hand, however, some truth undoubtedly existed in the claim that the problem was also one of inflation, caused in part by speculation in timber based on the new housing legislation. If nothing else, the timber industry had a long history of famine rhetoric.[61] In recognizing new home sales as a key indicator of a healthy economy and as concerned with inflation as the public, Nixon's decision to pursue the increased harvest was understandable, although from an environmental perspective it was counterproductive. It was obviously a difficult decision for the White House, one that Nixon might omit from his environmental address, but one that commanded attention nevertheless.

Commanding the most attention in the summer of 1970 was the final report of the Public Land Law Review Commission (PLLRC), a report that assured the timber debate and all public-lands disputes significant publicity, much to the chagrin of the Nixon administration. No one anticipated a report friendly to environmentalists, least of all the White House. Congress had created the PLLRC in 1964 as a compromise with the Wilderness Act's opponents, most notably Colorado Democratic congressman Wayne Aspinall. When this opposition acquiesced to the new wilderness law, Congress created a commission to review all public-lands regulations, a body chaired by Colorado's most famous environmental critic. With Aspinall in charge, the PLLRC not surprisingly included strong representation from western mining and ranching states. Supporting the commission was an advisory council composed almost 90 percent by industry representatives and with only one member an environmentalist. Aspinall clearly intended the study to recommend more industrial access to public lands and assured the mining industry that its final conclusions would not encroach upon its interests.[62] Now, in the summer of 1970, Aspinall wrote Nixon that the commission's recommendations were ready and that he wanted, in the words of one aide, "as much fanfare as possible."[63]

The White House stalled. On one hand, it obviously wanted to avoid antagonizing environmentalists just as Congress took up the administration's environmental program. On the other hand, as Whitaker warned, Aspinall "controls with an iron hand virtually all natural resource related legislation and funding in the West." The president had no choice but to accept the report publicly or risk endangering his broader program. "It's too late to make points," Whitaker concluded, "but let's try to break even."[64] Ehrlichman agreed, and in late June Nixon received the report before the press in a Rose Garden ceremony. Nixon chose his words carefully, however, speaking in generalities and avoiding a direct endorsement. "It is essential to plan now for the use of [public lands], not to do it simply on a case by case basis, but to have an overall policy."[65] To this extent, as Nixon knew, both Aspinall and his critics agreed.

In the end, the PLLRC did not directly attack environmentalism in its three-hundred-page report, *One Third of the Nation's Land*, but did endorse a program that elevated economic use of the public lands above all else. While paying lip service to environmental goals and advocating a Department of Natural Resources, the PLLRC declared that "multiple use has little practical meaning as a planning concept or principle." Citing the "dominant use" as that which provides "the greatest public benefit," it stressed the economic and monetary importance of the public lands. While the commission did not embrace calls for complete state authority, a movement that would later culminate in the Sagebrush Rebellion of the late 1970s, states should nevertheless enjoy an "effective role" in managing federal land, with no federal regulations counter to state and local zoning. "Mineral exploration and development," the commission went on, "should have a preference over some or all other uses on much of our public lands." Relying on the private sector, the government should issue "a continuing invitation" for development, minimizing its royalties. Pouring gas on an already bright fire, the commission recommended that timber "should be managed primarily on the basis of economic factors," in short to assure the maximum yield of board feet. In a similar vein, the government should limit public access to grazing lands "so as to avoid unreasonable interference with authorized livestock use." Failing to stress the importance of natural watersheds and the wildlife that depended upon them, the commission bluntly proclaimed that it was "unnecessary to retain public land for watershed purposes."[66] Overall, the PLLRC issued a direct challenge to the very constituency that Nixon's agenda courted, providing a call to arms for environmentalists. In doing so, it also published a welcomed political manifesto to the western ranchers, miners, and industrial interests critical to Republican hopes for the coming election. In short, it galvanized debate, with the White House positioned uncomfortably in the middle.

Reaction to the PLLRC report was swift. "A bland and unctuous document," one reviewer claimed, "weighted heavily on the side of mining, timber and other commercial users." According to *Sports Illustrated*, Aspinall as chair of the study was "a little like letting a rabbit decide the disposition of a lettuce field." To state the obvious, the report "encourages commercialization." Sensitive to such criticism, Aspinall defended his commission, arguing that it only recognized the need to balance commercial use with recreational and environmental aims, and that the public should not lose sight of the economic importance of the land in its frenzy for environmentalism. Taking pains to rebut each individual conclusion, the Sierra Club was blunt with its reply. The PLLRC's report was "anti-environmental."[67]

For the most part, other than officially receiving the report, the White House did not have to accept or endorse publicly anything that the PLLRC recommended—and, gauging the political reaction, it wisely did not. Only in one respect did the administration have to act: the controversial debate over the grazing fee, the price the government charged ranchers to graze their livestock on public lands. Here emotions ran particularly high, and here, with the

PLLRC report, any hopes the administration had of avoiding the issue died rapidly. Just before leaving office in 1968, Stewart Udall commissioned a study to determine an appropriate fee for grazing on BLM and Forest Service lands. Its conclusions shocked the livestock industry. The fair market value, the study concluded, was $1.23 per Animal Unit Month (AUM), approximately the amount of forage consumed by one cow or five sheep in one month. With the BLM AUM set at $0.33 and the Forest Service at $0.72, Udall ordered three scheduled fee increases phased in over a ten-year period to make up the difference. After Udall ordered the first scheduled increase amidst a chorus of protest from stockmen, the issue—the problem—fell to the new administration. Caught once again in a situation in which he recognized the arguments of both sides, Hickel had stalled against the second increase, waiting, he claimed, for the report of the PLLRC. Now the report was in, however, and his decision had to come.[68]

Nothing more angered ranchers, and with good reason. If implemented fully, Udall's plan promised almost to double the cost of business on Forest Service land while increasing fourfold that on BLM land. In an already competitive business, the industry claimed, the inevitable result was bankruptcy for many small producers. On the other hand, overgrazing posed a legitimate threat to the long-term viability of the nation's public lands, often turning productive grasslands into barren desert, destroying wildlife habitats and the area's entire ecosystem. An increased fee, environmentalists argued, guarded against the menace of overgrazing while providing additional funds for maintenance. It was a persuasive argument, one that even the PLLRC recognized had merit. While not endorsing Udall's scheduled increases, the PLLRC report accepted the fair market value as the key determinant in setting the grazing fee, a conclusion that while unstated thus endorsed at least some increase. While the report then hedged this endorsement by proposing certain "allowances" for stockmen, it nevertheless left the Department of Interior little room but to order the second scheduled increase.[69]

Interior's decision to order the fee increase won the administration few plaudits from environmentalists, who were still angry over the delay in the first place. In fact, the administration's reaction to the entire PLLRC report exposed an essential weakness in its environmental agenda. While much of Nixon's program advanced the cause of environmental protection, its silence in the summer of 1970 on the issue of public lands left unanswered real environmental threats. For one, the nation's mining laws begged for reform, but the administration's program remained silent on the issue. The Mining Law of 1872, approaching its centennial, was antiquated legislation designed to encourage settlement of the West and an affront to environmental protection.

To encourage exploitation, the law provided a claimant with proof of a valu-able mineral discovery title to the land for a nominal sum. With the govern-ment unable either to receive royalties or assess and control the environmental impact, Udall proposed a leasing system similar to that already applied to oil and gas. It was a sensible proposal, but, unfortunately, one that Hickel and the new administration failed to press.[70]

"My land is dying," Dan Gibson, an eighty-year-old resident of Appalachia, declared just before Nixon's election. "The strip miners are killing these old hills, and when they finish there won't be anything left." Gibson had a point. The day after Earth Day, strip mining in West Virginia caused disastrous land-slides and floods. In Kentucky, landowners lobbied their legislature to outlaw the practice, complaining that it depreciated the value of their property.[71] It was a warning with ample evidence, but, nevertheless, a warning that Nixon's environmental program also failed to heed. With new, larger earth-moving equipment, strip miners left much of the nation's public lands a desolate waste-land. Permits to strip federal land doubled in 1970. Mining industries turned lush landscapes into permanent pits, polluted the air with sulfuric acid from oxidized coal, and contaminated streams with chemical-laden overburden. Mirroring clear-cutting, the practice provided a less expensive way to access valuable natural resources, thus promising a quick solution to the needs of the nation's expanding economy and immediate jobs for local communities. Just as its industrial cousin, however, strip mining too left an ecological scar that de-manded attention.[72] Aware of both the economic and environmental reality, the administration's program in the summer of 1970 failed to give the prob-lem the priority it deserved. Even as the administration unveiled EPA and launched its legislative agenda, it could not completely hide those public land issues that posed a threat to both its political momentum and the nation's en-vironment at large.

The political jousting continued; the White House, with its strategy in hand, at-tempted to advance its stated program while Democrats sought to exploit its weaknesses. "Senator," a local New York reporter asked Muskie, "Do you see the environmental problem becoming so political that the results are likely to be watered down in the coming two years?" No, Muskie replied, "the competition for credit" would result in tougher, not weaker, legislation. "We don't have a non-political way, nor do I." The nation would win, Muskie concluded, conve-niently forgetting that he had no intention of losing either.[73]

The stakes, all agreed, remained high. Although some pundits had predicted the issue would soon fade when the cost of the environmental cleanup became apparent, nothing suggested that this was the case as the summer progressed. Taking a page from Orson Welles's celebrated 1938 "War of the Worlds" radio scare, Metromedia Television released a two-hour dramatized documentary depicting the world in 1985. The picture was not pleasant, "a harrowing vision of thousands of smog deaths, power failures, depleted rivers, barren lands and smothered oceans," according to the *New York Times*. Although the show won strong ratings, New York City did not need its police, who were alerted to forestall possible panic. For the more intellectually inclined, booksellers reported a boom in environmental-oriented texts. Running the gamut from serious academic tomes to alarmist, doomsday predictions more akin to television fare, the boom meant, in the words of one reviewer, "a lot of trees cut to print books on trees." Scientists and academics continued to lead the way; the problem, according to one Harvard biochemist, was "overwhelmingly threatening." Popular periodicals such as *Time, Fortune, Life, Newsweek,* and *Look* all ran front-page articles on the dilemma. As the administration wrestled with the grazing fee, the Ford Foundation announced grants of over two million dollars to help fund environmental efforts while the Greek Orthodox Archdiocese of America called on its flock to "harness their intellects and energies" against pollution. In short, the public need only turn on its television, open a book, read a magazine, attend a class, or frequent a church to find itself confronted with environmental degradation.[74]

Naturally, the environmental groups and the policymakers they hoped to sway felt the ramifications. The months after Earth Day witnessed a rapid rise in the membership of national organizations, the collective total later estimated at over 300,000 or an approximately 38 percent increase.[75] Denis Hayes, the youthful coordinator of Earth Day, announced the formation of Environmental Action. Surrendering a tax-exempt status, the new entity was "free to say and do whatever is necessary." Within months it was focusing on the problem of solid waste and publishing its "dirty dozen," companies with the worst pollution records. Drawing the attention of politicians was the League of Conservation Voters, organized to track the voting records of those in Congress and the executive branch. As environmentalist Joe Browder later recalled, the League's founder, Marion Edey, "understood candidates' vulnerabilities." Politically savvy, the League made its presence felt at the outset, helping to defeat in the primary—"a shocker"—Baltimore's congressman George Fallon, a renowned proponent of reclamation works. The November elections were still several months away, but it was no wonder that the competition for political advantage continued.[76]

Predictably, the struggle unfolded on more than simply White House terms;

public lands were not the only threat to the administration's momentum as the summer passed. Nixon's decision to pursue prototype development of the SST and his stance on the controversial pesticide DDT remained irritants for many environmentalists—and opportunities for the administration's foes. Democratic Senator William Proxmire's Joint Economic Committee held hearings throughout June and July on the transport, which did not proceed well for the White House. When pressed, Train acknowledged before the committee that a fleet of SSTs would leave enormous quantities of combustible products in the stratosphere, an acknowledgment that earned him a sharp rebuke from the president. The administration was not advocating an entire fleet, Nixon complained, but only two prototypes, which would cause no such problem. Train apologized, but the damage was done.[77] The administration did prevail in court, where environmentalists failed in their attempt to secure copies of all White House SST-related documents. Although Senator Jackson, whose state included major aeronautical manufacturers, supported Nixon's SST policy, Muskie rallied grass-roots opposition, which now included the new Coalition against the SST, the brainchild of a young Baltimore schoolteacher. "It is disturbing to me," Muskie wrote one constituent, "that we should spend three times as much for an environmental hazard as we spend for air pollution control." In August, the House barely passed the plane, and its prospects in the Senate appeared worse.[78]

For the administration, DDT erupted once again as an issue when the U.S. Court of Appeals ruled in the case the Environmental Defense Fund brought the previous year. Agreeing with the EDF, the court concluded that because the Agriculture Department's cancellation proceedings took so long to adjudicate, the secretary's cancellation order in no way constituted an actual ban. The department should halt usage immediately or provide adequate reason why it would not. The administration had originally intended its cancellation order to soothe environmentalists, but the protracted hearings had only inflamed resistance. Moving once again to recoup the initiative, therefore, the Agriculture Department announced in August that it planned to begin cancellation proceedings for an additional fifty uses, including that for fruits, vegetables and forest trees, expanding its earlier order against residential use. It also reiterated its intention to cancel all but "essential" uses in the near future. It would not, however, order any immediate suspension and would make its case to the court.[79] As the Agriculture Department took this tack, the Interior Department added that it planned to ban sixteen threatening pesticides—DDT included—on land under its control. If the administration intended all of this to calm tensions, however, it was once again in for disappointment. As environmentalists complained, Whitaker mirrored the attitude of his boss. "Why," he wondered, "don't we seem to get any real positive press play?" Science advisor DuBridge summed up frustrations: "Pesticides are straining our image on the whole environmental issue."[80]

Clearly, the White House's political strategy was more difficult to implement than to formulate. Sensing their political might, many environmentalists saw little reason for compromise. As Ruckelshaus later recalled, "It was impossible to go as far as the movement wanted."[81] On one hand, the administration was correct that it supported the development of only two SST prototypes, which alone posed virtually no environmental hazard. In an era of Cold War competition, the possibility of technological inferiority was indeed frightful. The administration had also moved more forcibly against DDT than any of its predecessors, with the promise of more to come, an action that to this extent deserved approbation. On the other hand, however, an effective and successful SST prototype surely increased pressure for a complete fleet, a true environmental hazard. DDT cancellation proceedings did in fact progress at a glacial pace, and the Department of Agriculture had yet to issue any order affecting cotton production, which constituted almost 75 percent of all DDT use. Interior's order regarding public lands was in reality only public relations, a simple codification of rules in effect for years. In a sense, was the glass half empty or half full? Confident in public opinion, environmentalists appeared unwilling to accept anything other than a cup overflowing—bad news for an administration bounced between party politics and environmental realities.

The White House did its best to recast the debate once again, to turn public attention to its strengths. At every instance, however, frustration loomed. Nixon's call for a "national growth policy" in his January State of the Union address was, if anything, visionary. The threat of urban and suburban sprawl involved a number of specific issues including land use, population, transportation, and housing, all of which demanded coordination. The Commerce Department had followed this proposal with a national growth conference at Washington's Watergate complex, and the Domestic Council had formed a subcommittee to work on the problem. By summer, however, the once promising program appeared a shambles, hampered by petty jurisdictional disputes. The departments of Transportation, Agriculture, Commerce, and HUD bickered over control while the issue itself raised questions of federal power. The administration had, of course, initiated individual efforts in many of these areas, but even these appeared increasingly frustrated. A proposal for national land-use planning was still not complete, even as Jackson pushed his version in the Senate. Worried that Jackson might make its own efforts moot as well as hinder its coastal zone proposal still before Congress, the White House sought to work with him, a man whom Nixon admired despite their political competition.[82] Jackson had won Nixon's admiration by supporting administration policies in Vietnam, but Jackson held land-use planning dear to his heart and remained protective of his proposal, refusing to budge. Despite attempts to weaken it, Jackson told the National Wildlife Federation, "My bill is the next logical step in our effort to achieve a quality environment."[83]

The matter of population, meanwhile, remained as troublesome as ever, certainly no hope as part of a national growth policy. Nixon had grudgingly signed a population-control bill in March, but new legislation threatened once again to augment federal funding. Concerned with conservative objections and now questioning whether the problem was distribution and not growth, Nixon initially resisted the new proposal, a position that contributed to "an icy exchange" in a meeting with new Sierra Club president Philip Berry.[84] Nixon had agreed to meet with leading environmentalists, who then among themselves had agreed to avoid grandstanding. The thirty-two-year-old Berry, however, was in no mood to remain quiet. Nixon was blunt, beginning the meeting with a lecture: "All politics is a fad. Your fad is going right now. Get what you can, and here's what I can get you." As Nixon proceeded to explain that he thought the population problem was overblown, Berry seethed. When his turn came to speak, he exploded in a blunt fashion to match Nixon's: "I don't believe what you believe in." For five minutes an "argument" then ensued, before Nixon angrily adjourned the meeting.[85] The encounter appeared to be an unmitigated disaster, but in the end was not. Berry, although arguably disrespectful, made a lasting impression on those in power. "Who is this Sierra Club?" asked an incredulous Henry Kissinger.[86] Recognizing that Berry's anger, although impudent, represented the opinions of many, Nixon's political instincts overcame any personal disdain. Facing resistance even greater than the year before, Nixon once again capitulated and agreed to support the bill. This, he hoped, would silence such vocal carping. Led by Maryland Democratic senator Joseph Tydings, the chief architect of the bill, Democrats nevertheless lambasted the conversion as nothing more than political expediency, which, indeed, it was.[87] For the administration, the result was simply more disappointment.

Turning debate back to the administration's advantage meant, of course, ignoring frustrations and pressing ahead, taking whatever opportunities presented themselves. Although it had already unveiled the thrust of its agenda, the White House continued to search throughout the summer for new, acceptable initiatives, as if to prove correct Muskie's contention that political competition begot stronger federal policy. Advice came from all quarters, but, just as in the previous year, new recommendations often raised new, troublesome questions of economic and political compromise. As experience had already taught the White House, this in itself was frustrating.

The Great Lakes, for one, begged for attention, although to date the administration had taken little notice. The problem was manifold, including corporate and municipal dumping of dredge spoils and the matter of phosphate pollution. Adding to eutrophication, the result was, in the words of one report, "a mat of algae two feet thick and a few hundred miles in extent" during the summer.[88] In their efforts to expand port facilities, cities found it easy simply to distribute unwanted river sludge farther out in the water, a practice that, while cheap, ensured eventual problems. Phosphates, as an integral ingredient in detergents, easily washed into the water and compounded the problem. The cumulative effect was foul to both sight and smell, and local protest naturally developed. In Gary, Indiana, citizens formed Community Action to Reverse Pollution; in Buffalo, New York, the Citizen's Committee on Pollution; in Cleveland, Ohio, the Citizens for Clean Air and Water. Taking pictures and water samples along with petitions, protesters pressured state legislators, who struggled with the problem. The situation clearly demanded stronger federal intervention, another opportunity, Ehrlichman wrote Nixon, "to keep you out front on the environmental issue."[89]

CEQ provided a ready solution for dredge spoils, although phosphates posed more of an immediate problem. To recapture momentum, Nixon ordered CEQ's report "greatly accelerated," and, when it arrived at the end of the summer, Whitaker instructed Colson to "publicize it with the environmental lobby . . . essential because of public interest in the matter."[90] The report pertained to more than just the Great Lakes, restricting dumping in the ocean as well. CEQ recommended specifically banning the dumping of municipal solid waste, while empowering the new EPA to restrict other dumping with permits, under penalty of harsh sanctions. Nixon did not agree with the specific ban on municipal waste, leaving that decision to EPA, but immediately accepted the report's conclusions. He agreed with Whitaker, however, that it was best for publicity purposes to wait to introduce the bill formally until the new Congress early the following year. "The Democrats," Whitaker explained, "don't have enough time to steal something out of the report and put in a bill during this session of Congress."[91]

The phosphate problem was more complex, if for no other reason than it required better coordination with Canada, an equal offender in this respect. Both countries had agreed to a joint study, but, impatient for the report, the White

House wanted immediate action.[92] The problem, Ehrlichman reported to Nixon, was that the detergent industry "is playing a hard-nose game with us." The three leading detergent producers — Proctor and Gamble, Colgate-Palmolive, and Lever Brothers — refused voluntary reductions, which CEQ argued warranted direct legislation. This, in turn, raised the ire of the Commerce Department, which thought such a remedy unnecessarily punitive. Environmentalists demanded a new phosphate substitute, nitrilotriacetic acid, or NTA, but as the detergent industry argued, some studies suggested it was ineffective if not harmful. Canada had already begun use of the substitute, which increased complaints that the administration was dragging its feet. To make matters worse, Bryce Harlow, the administration's top liaison with Congress, quit his post to take a position as a detergent-industry lobbyist, a public relations disaster. The White House sought to advance its agenda, but this issue appeared only to add to its woes.[93]

With Train at the helm, CEQ recommended other possible initiatives, helpful in regaining momentum. One, to solve the problem of junk automobiles, was a federal loan program to help businesses purchase modern metal-scrap shredders. The money, drawn from an increase in the auto excise tax, would also fund a program to improve scrap recycling. Another, to encourage beverage-container recycling, was a ten-cent deposit on all bottles and cans. The White House thought both proposals had merit, but hesitated because of an increased cost to the consumer.[94] When CEQ issued its first annual report in July as required under NEPA, however, the White House quickly recognized an opportunity that it desperately needed for positive publicity. Train thought CEQ's first report best if noncontroversial, certainly neither pushing initiatives that Nixon would reject on fiscal grounds nor advocating a program that usurped what the White House had already proposed. The report, therefore, simply reiterated Nixon's agenda before Congress, and for this reason Whitaker thought it "argues for fanfare." When the NIPCC, by contrast, followed with its first report, a report that spoke of "inconsistent [environmental] standards" and encouraged voluntary regulations, Whitaker's conclusions were markedly different. Much less affording it the publicity granted CEQ, he declared, "I do not even think it is worth the President's time to read it."[95]

The moderate, noncontroversial nature of CEQ's first report in fact belied the growing frustration of Train and his colleagues. In January Nixon had ordered each department and agency to comply with CEQ guidelines on the preparation of NEPA impact statements. In April CEQ had issued these guidelines, requesting a response from each agency by June. Now, in late summer, it was apparent that many of the agencies resented CEQ oversight and deliberately delayed compliance. "Although agency performance has been improving," Train concluded, "it is still not satisfactory." The matter continued to fester, ultimately resulting in CEQ hearings with delinquent departments, but it was already obvious that Train fully intended to fulfill the trust that environmentalists placed in him. Problems undoubtedly lay ahead.[96]

A man with his own frustrations, Hickel did not cower before his superiors, joining CEQ in recommending new initiatives to regain the momentum even as his days in the administration grew short. To appease public-lands advocates annoyed by the PLLRC and the grazing fee, Hickel appointed a committee led by biologist Stanley Cain to investigate the matter of predatory animals. Ranchers, worried about their stock, often used poisons against predators such as wolves. These poisons, in turn, unintentionally killed other species, including those endangered. In some instances the endangered included the predator itself, annoying to ranchers but important to the region's ecosystem. The problem demanded a solution, which, Hickel recognized, would provide another feather in the administration's cap.[97] More significantly, in June, Hickel announced that he had requested the Corps of Engineers to halt construction for fifteen months on the Cross Florida Barge Canal, time for an Interior Department task force to study the environmental ramifications. The Environmental Defense Fund's January lawsuit had already mired construction in litigation, but the canal's many antagonists welcomed the announcement as evidence that the administration acknowledged their position. For the Florida Defenders of the Environment a final decision could wait, but the new development was a positive step, if not a mortal blow, to the hated canal.[98]

Hickel had pressed Nixon for over a year to rescind permanently the remaining Santa Barbara oil leases, still technically under temporary suspension. The White House had remained reticent, however, much to the dismay of the local citizenry. Now, in the summer of 1970, bipartisan support grew for a rescission bill in Congress, which, just as the Florida canal, continued to receive strong publicity. Recognizing that Congress might force his hand and that he was about to lose another opportunity to regain the political momentum, Nixon announced in June what he had failed to do the previous year. Making the most of his decision, he held a formal ceremony with the press present. His proposal to rescind the leases, Nixon declared, "illustrates our strong commitment to use off-shore lands in a balanced and responsible way." The ceremony did not include Hickel, ironically enough, a man who had pressed for the action even before Congress. It was, Whitaker acknowledged, a "very stiff slap" from a still-angry president.[99]

Nixon might have been angry at Hickel or he might have simply been frustrated at the situation itself. Every step the White House took, something arose to destroy any potential political benefits. In August, Congress passed a bill creating a Youth Conservation Corps. Nixon disapproved of the measure; not only was the bill Democratic, it sounded uncomfortably similar to Franklin Roosevelt's New Deal.[100] The measure was popular, however, addressing two problems at once, young people and the environment. As he had shown before, he was not above signing a distasteful bill if he thought it expedient, and so once again new environmental legislation became law. The White House gained little, however. Hickel's youth organization, the Student Council on Pollution and the Environment, released a letter to Congress and the media criticizing the SST as evidence of "misplaced priorities and archaic rationales." Sent on Interior Department stationery, the letter left the impression of interdepartmental conflict, the byline of the press. "We have enough Trojan horses within the walls," complained one White House assistant.[101] As this unfolded, activists, concerned that the NIPCC blocked administration environmental initiatives, attempted to attend one of the council's meetings. Claiming that they could not have an open discussion with the group present, Commerce Department officials denied entrance and a request for a transcript. Reported by the *New York Times*, the incident, Train wrote Ehrlichman, "caused considerable adverse publicity."[102] For every step forward, it appeared that the administration took two steps back.

The apprehension, of course, was over the November off-year congressional elections. Nixon, frustrated by Congress at every turn, recognized the elections as an opportunity to win a Republican majority. The House was hopeless for the GOP, but the Republican leadership thought the Senate encouraging. Vietnam, of course, would play a major role, but, compared to the horrible spring, the foreign-policy arena appeared oddly calm. The withdrawal of troops continued and casualties were down; protests were equally indignant but less violent and, thankfully for Nixon, less frequent. Unlike two years before, more individual contests might turn on domestic affairs. Here the administration was no less frustrated, however. The Senate dealt Nixon's Family Assistance Plan, his ambitious welfare-reform proposal, what amounted to a death blow, and the economy was far from rosy. With both unemployment and inflation at an uncomfortable 6 percent, pundits coined a new word, "stagflation," which obviously did not bode well for the incumbent administration.[103] The environment was not the only issue on which the administration had lost momentum. In short, Nixon needed domestic accomplishments.

For Nixon, the best defense was a good offense. He had to continue advancing his agenda on those issues apparently important, denying the advantage to his opponents, while attacking in general terms the purported evils of society. Vulnerable to charges that he had accomplished little of his own, Nixon thought the broad political attack was best, a return in a sense to his political roots. For Nixon the campaign was about pot, permissiveness, protest, pornography, and patriotism.[104] As protesters shouted, "One, two, three, four, we don't want your fucking war," Nixon bemoaned a "rising tide of terrorism and crime." Here was the old Nixon, releasing the anger and resentment growing throughout his presidency. His divide-and-conquer strategy launched a negative wave of broad attacks largely devoid of rationale and detail. Behind the scenes, however, the political struggle continued on terms more specific. In Congress the coming elections gave new urgency to efforts to gain the domestic accomplishments that Nixon so desperately needed—and to matters of the environment.

As summer turned to fall, a *New York Times* survey reported the environment a key issue in twenty-five states. Environmental Action and the League of Conservation Voters targeted twenty-eight candidates in nineteen states for election or defeat. One, a Democratic candidate for the Senate in New York, ascended above Central Park in a hot-air balloon to demonstrate his concern for pollution. The older environmental organizations, their tax-exempt status challenged by the IRS, were not as direct in their appeals, yet made their preferences known in general terms nevertheless.[105] In Congress, not surprisingly, debate turned to the heart of the matter, the issues that promised to captivate the public to the greatest extent: air pollution, water pollution, and solid wastes. These issues were no longer among those the administration hoped to avoid, and Nixon's agenda was sure to play a critical role in all debate. The political initiative and, perhaps, the outcome of the election lay in the balance.

The problems of the nation's air were hard to miss. As if to give impetus to congressional debate, the worst East Coast smog on record blanketed a broad stretch from Washington to Boston. New York City mayor John Lindsay ordered new traffic restrictions in Manhattan; similar plans were spawned in Baltimore and Boston. In Congress Muskie attacked. "The recent air pollution crisis along the eastern seaboard is a reminder that contamination of our environment is a real danger, and not an issue dreamed up to divert our attention from other pressing concerns." Nixon, while "long on words," had not offered an adequate solution, preferring instead to "drag his feet on the issue."[106] Such criticism was unduly harsh, although understandable; Muskie himself was under attack. Ralph Nader's consumer advocacy organization issued a report highly critical of the senator, painting him as the reason for the weak standards in the existing 1967 legislation. "This fact alone," the report read, "warrants [Muskie] being stripped of the title of Mr. Pollution Control." Such comments from an ostensible ally cut to the quick, for Muskie cared as much about clean air as his reputation. Wasting no time with his response, Muskie proposed new, tougher legislation that in effect raised the ante on Nixon. "Now," Muskie triumphantly declared, "here is a chance for [Nixon] to put his support where his words are."[107]

Nixon's bill, which had already passed the House basically intact, called for national ambient air quality standards, obtained by having the states set specific emission standards for stationary sources and by raising the emission standards for 1973–1975 model automobiles. Muskie's new bill agreed with this, but mandated a 90 percent reduction in hydrocarbons and carbon monoxide by 1975, and a 90 percent reduction in nitrogen oxide by 1976. These figures were, in short, astounding, unrealistic given present technology. The administration did not anticipate reaching such reductions until 1980, with this goal contingent upon the requisite advances. The auto industry in the fall of 1970 simply did not have the means to meet Muskie's requirements, and thus to this extent his drive to ensure clean air and defend his reputation faced probable failure. The bill was still a worthy endeavor, however. In a sense, it assured rapid technological advancements from an auto industry not known for its own initiative. Facing such rigid standards, companies would invest the maximum possible in research. In addition, strong coercion guaranteed a market for pollution-control equipment, thus stimulating third-party innovation. Even if the industry failed to meet the deadlines, the legislation ensured the absolute best possible scenario. While in one sense it guaranteed failure, therefore, in another respect it guaranteed success.[108]

The administration was once again on the defensive. Although its bill was a significant improvement on the original 1967 law, environmentalists quickly endorsed Muskie's version, leaving the White House in the uncomfortable political position of pointing out the true technological limitations. Nixon did not want to support unrealistic legislation, but neither did he want to surrender one of the cornerstones of his program. When the leaders of five major auto companies sought to protest to Nixon in person, the White House stalled, ordering a review of the new proposal. Whitaker, aware that in the last several months the administration had lost momentum, advised that, regardless of the study, Nixon had no choice but to endorse Muskie's proposal. With the election looming, the bill gained tremendous support, and to oppose it would be futile and play into the Democrats' hands.[109]

It was for Nixon a classic Muskie maneuver. As one White House advisor later recalled, "Nixon thought Muskie was pandering on this issue." The senator

was simply trying to top the administration, and did not consider fully the scientific and economic implications of what he proposed. While many of Nixon's
environmental staff perceived Muskie as a man of "great moral commitment"
and understood that he did indeed care about air quality, Nixon "did not have a
lot of intellectual respect for him."[110] For his part, Muskie fully believed that his
bill's standards were technologically possible if the auto companies only applied themselves. Throughout the Johnson administration, he had grown annoyed by what he perceived as a lack of industry initiative, and now, backed by
several scientists who agreed, he intended to give the industry the push it
deserved.[111]

Few in the Senate wanted to challenge a popular environmental bill only
weeks before the election, and thus, in late September, the Senate passed Muskie's
bill unanimously. The stage was now set for a showdown in a conference committee between the House version, largely Nixon's bill, and the Senate version,
largely Muskie's. Predictably, CEQ agreed with Whitaker that fighting stronger
provisions before the election was unwise, while the Commerce Department
recommended fierce resistance. The solution, Ehrlichman agreed, was quietly
to stall the bill until after the elections and then, behind the scenes and out of
the public eye, lobby for the weaker standards. As the White House took this
tack, Nixon issued an executive order requiring low-leaded gasoline in federal
vehicles. He had already proposed a two-cent tax on leaded fuel, and together
the measures helped insulate the administration from possible criticism.[112]

Whitaker had earlier suggested that the best way for the administration to
regain political momentum was to "hit Congress" for inaction. With the election approaching, this was no longer an option. As the conference committee
took up air pollution, Congress passed solid-waste legislation that resembled
Muskie's proposal more than the administration's. The bill authorized a four-
teen-fold increase in funding over a two-year period, from 1971 to 1973, a total
of approximately 400 million dollars for EPA's solid-waste programs. A significant portion of the money was for resource recovery, and thus the bill began to
shift the emphasis from disposal to recycling, a point on which Muskie and
Nixon agreed.[113]

The problem for Nixon was the funding. Way beyond what the White House
proposed in its program, the figures were, in Nixon's view, budget-busters. The
bill still contained so much money for the construction of traditional waste-
disposal plants, he believed, it effectively transferred ultimate responsibility for
this task from the states to the federal government. He wanted to veto the bill,
but once again politics dictated caution. Although EPA planned "Mission
5,000," a program to close five thousand of the country's fourteen thousand
open dumps, the White House had in the end denied CEQ's proposals for junk

autos and beverage cans, questioning their effectiveness and economic impact. To veto solid-waste legislation now would cast him as the anti-environmentalist his critics painted. Once again, he had no choice. In late October, therefore, Nixon signed the Resource Recovery Act of 1970. The law may have made Nixon uncomfortable, but it was a potent response to a real threat; if nothing else, it more than fulfilled the promises of Nixon's February environmental message. Nixon was correct to sign the legislation. Announcing his signature, the White House cited Nixon's "concern for dealing with problems of the environment" as the "overriding factor." The statement was not completely truthful, but in the end it made no difference.[114]

The approaching election helped break the gridlock surrounding much legislation, but it could not advance the water pollution debate so contentious in Congress. If Whitaker wished to "hit Congress" for inaction, in this respect he had cause. With the White House's proposal and Muskie's so divergent on funding for waste-treatment facilities, no consensus was near. The administration needed positive publicity in any event, Whitaker suggested, recommending a documentary film on the problem by Bonanza star Loren Green. Because the film presented his proposal in a positive light, Nixon should notify the press that he saw and recommended it. Besides, "It's much better than those Italian movies he sees at Camp David." CEQ, meanwhile, had a more substantive suggestion. Nixon might use the permit authority granted in the seventy-year-old Refuse Act of 1899 to combat pollution. Never intended in this way, the law established a Corps of Engineers permit program to prevent the discharge of materials from blocking the passage of ships. Nothing, however, prevented its use against pollution, CEQ general counsel Alvin Alm wrote. The old law would, Whitaker acknowledged, allow the White House the upper hand, to claim that the president was doing all that he could as congressional debate—federal inaction—dragged on.[115]

This idea was innovative thinking, something positive as Nixon pounded home the negative thrust of his campaign. Sensing that the momentum was still not in his favor, Nixon campaigned frenetically, unprecedented for a president in an off-year election. His participation would, Nixon hoped, bring his party victory and his administration a friendly Congress. Only then would his agenda—the environment included—win the political initiative and the respect it deserved.

Election day, November 3, proved Nixon's efforts all for naught, his environmental program and political barnstorming notwithstanding. For the House of Representatives, Democrats received 28.9 million votes compared to the Republicans' 24.4 million. In 1968 Democrats had outpaced the Republicans by 1.1 million, and now the total was 4.5 million, hardly a positive sign for 1972. The Democrats' House majority increased by nine seats. In the Senate Republicans gained but two seats despite Nixon's efforts. With the Democrats also capturing eleven additional governorships, the scenario was simply not bright for the White House. More frustration undoubtedly loomed.[116]

Both politicians and pundits began their election postmortem. The importance of the environment was as obvious as the irrelevance of the administration's program. The support or opposition of environmental organizations, the *New York Times* reported, was significant in a score of House races and at least one Senate and one gubernatorial contest. In thirteen states voters approved a total of sixteen environmental propositions, including over one billion dollars in antipollution bond issues, while rejecting only four. Despite public comments otherwise, White House feelings were bitter—and divided. Nixon refused to concede that his strategy had been a mistake, preferring to blame a cadre of lackluster Republican candidates. Others, however, disagreed. The president's negative, go-for-the-jugular attacks had only lowered him into the political muck. According to speechwriter Raymond Price, the "bile" had hurt and the White House needed something "elevating" to talk about, "something that would speak to the hopes, to the goodness, to the elemental decency, of the American people." In short, the president should return to his "bring-us-together themes."[117]

The White House's environmental staff undoubtedly agreed, although they understood more than most the frustration Nixon felt. With regard to the environment, the administration had never left this theme in its view, and had much to show for the nation's environment but little political payoff to match. To gain the respect it deserved, to reverse political momentum, the administration would simply have to persevere and redouble its efforts to win the political initiative. Less than a week after the election, long-time Nixon advisor Herb Klein promised a new emphasis on popular domestic programs and less on law and order. Republican National Committee chairman Rogers C. B. Morton promised the same day that the White House planned more emphasis on environmental protection. In a television interview, Morton suggested shifting defense contract spending to contracts with industry for pollution control, arguably a popular idea with many voters the administration had apparently missed.[118]

Rogers's comments were more than simply idle musing from a Republican on the outside. The election was now over, and Nixon, always one to harbor a grudge, had not forgotten Hickel. The time for his termination had finally arrived, and Morton was in line to succeed him. Two weeks after the election, Hickel ordered eight species of whales added to the endangered species list. With whale products important in the production of soap, beauty cream, machine oil, pet food, and a variety of other products, environmentalists applauded. It was, however, Hickel's last executive order. The next day, summoning Hickel to the Oval Office, Nixon fired him as a military band played on the South Lawn and the music scored the meeting. No one mentioned their earlier agreement to choreograph Hickel's exit; the time had simply come "to make a change." The secretary assumed that the termination would take effect early the following year, but Nixon surprised him by dismissing him effective immediately. The president was civil but angry, instructing his staff that if Hickel tried to contact them, they were to provide "no response, no comment or anything." They should, in short, "act as if Hickel never existed."[119]

Nixon was not the only one angry. Explaining his termination to fellow Alaskans, Hickel complained, "Hell, I just got screwed." Beginning a speaking tour, Hickel sought to highlight the environment and the problems of society. Concerned that possible criticism might add to the administration's environmental problems, White House aides suggested inviting the former secretary as part of an environmental panel in the coming White House Conference on Youth, in the words of one, "a soothing influence on more radical environmentalists." When Nixon rejected this, aides followed with the possibility of "some unofficial mission," something to get Hickel "back in the fold."[120]

The White House did not need to worry; Morton proved a welcomed replacement. Like Ruckelshaus, Morton held strong Republican credentials. A congressman from Maryland's Eastern Shore since 1962 and brother of Kentucky Republican senator Thurston Morton, the fifty-six-year-old Morton had worked as Nixon's floor manager at the 1968 Republican convention, a task that won him the position of Republican National Committee chairman the following year. In Congress Morton served on the House Committee on Interior and Insular Affairs as well as on the Merchant Marines and Fisheries Committee. In this capacity, he helped advance legislation protecting the fragile environment of the Chesapeake Bay. He brought to the position the requisite environmental experience and, unlike his predecessor, a less abrasive personality. Modest and soft-spoken, colleagues later recalled, he was "very charming," a person "nobody could dislike."[121] The greatest attraction for the environmental community, however, was that he "broke the mold" of previous Interior Department secretaries. He was not from the West and thus, in the words of Joe Browder, was "free of the usual Rocky Mountain Republican prejudices." He would not, they hoped, prove beholden to the mining, ranching, and industrial interests so powerfully represented in the PLLRC report. At best he would understand concern for the coasts and the environment in its totality and thus emerge as a man more akin to Stewart Udall than to Wayne Aspinall. With strong support, Morton faced little opposition at his confirmation hearings and soon stood ready to tackle the arduous task ahead.[122]

From a political perspective, the administration's task remained a difficult one indeed, no surprise given the election returns. The remaining weeks of the year brought no respite from the political tailspin in which the White House found itself, although its unrelenting push helped make the waning days of the lame-duck Congress productive for the nation's environment. Productive for environmental quality and yet frustrating for the White House, the end of the year was, in other words, more of the same.

Only a week after the election, Muskie shocked the White House by introducing ocean-dumping legislation—the exact bill that CEQ had just developed and that Nixon planned to introduce early the following year with the new Congress. "I don't know where it leaked," complained Whitaker, who had advised that such a development was impossible. It was not a complete disaster; as the New York Times noted, the bill was "almost a carbon copy of the one the White House intended to send." Still, from any perspective, Muskie had robbed the administration. It was, Whitaker grumbled, "a blatant political attempt to usurp the President," annoying in the very least. Years later, Muskie aide Billings remained coy about just how the senator acquired the bill. "Let's just say we had pretty good access to what was going on down there."[123] Equally annoying was the Senate vote on the SST, a committee vote, as many expected, against funding for the plane. Debate swirled as much around the economic viability of the project as its environmental ramifications, yet to the Sierra Club, the Coalition against the SST, and the rapidly growing number of its opponents, the end result was the same. An angry Nixon vowed to renew debate with the new Congress and the full Senate, but for now the SST appeared doomed.[124]

The SST had driven a wedge between the White House and environmentalists for over a year, yet the desperate struggle for votes only added insult to injury. When the Department of Transportation circulated its environmental impact statement on the plane just prior to the vote, Whitaker warned that many other departments expressed reservations that might earn "scare headlines." A "strong-arm strategy" allowing no such objections would prevent this. A questionable tactic at best, it backfired as the media learned of the effort. Another public relations debacle put the administration on the defensive from charges that it had suppressed the facts. Always polishing the administration's image among environmentalists, Whitaker had unintentionally tarnished it.[125]

The administration once again fought back, but just as before problems emerged. Issuing an executive order, Nixon announced the Refuse Act permit program that CEQ recommended. Although the Corps of Engineers would issue the permits as the law required, EPA would have the power of veto. Making the most of the situation, Nixon attacked congressional intransigence and promised continued support for water pollution legislation still debated. Critics wondered if the new program was in lieu of such support, but neither could they deny Nixon's contribution to environmental protection by increasing the number of EPA enforcement personnel and by requiring companies to report discharges.[126] Likewise, the Forest Service unveiled the Roadless Area Review and Evaluation (RARE), a response to the timber debate and the Forest Service's own conflicting institutional mandates. Seeking to identify at least some of the hotly contested "de facto wilderness" for protection, the Forest Service promised to complete the study by the end of 1972. Because Nixon had rejected an executive order protecting such land and had embraced an increased timber harvest, Ehrlichman applauded the policy. In the very least, he hoped, RARE would avoid further litigation.[127]

By the end of the year, however, Ehrlichman well knew that NEPA worked against the president. Even as the administration unveiled new programs, the law appeared to hinder the White House's efforts to regain political momentum. When the Atomic Energy Commission (AEC) announced in December plans to approve a new nuclear power plant on the Chesapeake Bay in Maryland, the National Wildlife Federation and a local activist group, the Calvert Cliffs Coordinating Committee, sued to block the project. The AEC's new rules for licensing nuclear facilities, which the administration supported, allowed the proposed Maryland plant to cool its reactors with bay water. This process, plaintiffs argued, harmed fish and wildlife and thus required a NEPA impact statement. The White House had just appointed a well-known defender of the Chesapeake Bay as its Interior Department secretary and it had just unveiled a unique attack on water pollution, the Refuse Act program. Here the administration was again, however, cast as more villain than hero.[128]

Just before Christmas and adjournment, Congress passed Senator Tyding's population bill, which afforded the White House another opportunity to lift Nixon's image. The bill's appropriations for family planning were excessive to Nixon, yet, given the political climate, he had no intention of vetoing the legislation. The Family Planning and Population Research Act of 1970 provided a three-year, 382-million-dollar expansion of family planning services and created the Federal Office of Population Affairs, a new agency to work with Nixon's own population commission. As he signed the bill the day after Christmas, Nixon said little of his earlier resistance and his quarrel with the Sierra Club's Berry. Instead, he declared his full support for the measure and underscored his commitment to environmental protection.[129]

More significantly, Congress passed air-pollution legislation that again did not exactly appeal to the administration. The conference committee's final report was, in short, a victory for Muskie, despite the administration's quiet lobbying after the election. In addition to including the provisions on which Nixon and Muskie agreed, the law provided for EPA to set national ambient standards as well as specific emission standards for sulfur oxide from power plants and other stationary sources of pollution. It prohibited states from adopting tougher standards than those set by EPA, but allowed no deterioration in air quality in those states already above national standards. States were to have assembly-line testing of auto emission systems, while EPA was to publish regulations and guidelines for the states as they developed their individual compliance plans. However, the bill also agreed with Muskie's auto emission standards and deadlines for hydrocarbons, carbon monoxide, and nitrogen oxide, the critical and controversial provisions that had so long delayed passage. In a concession to Nixon, the bill provided for the National Academy of Sciences to study the feasibility of meeting the required deadlines and allowed EPA to grant an extension if the company in question had made a good-faith effort to comply but had failed because of a lack of technology.[130]

Nixon faced a scenario that he had seen so often in the previous two years—a bill flawed from his perspective, yet popular with the public. White House advisor Ken Cole was blunt; Nixon had to sign the law to "recoup the initiative." Saying as much for weeks, Whitaker urged an elaborate signing ceremony that would put the focus on the White House and afford another opportunity to "knock Congress for lack of action" on water pollution.[131] A difficult pill for Nixon to swallow, the bill fell behind a radiator in the Oval Office at one point as Nixon debated his response. In the end, after a personal appeal from Kentucky Republican John Sherman Cooper, Nixon finally agreed to sign the Clean Air Act Amendments of 1970 on December 31. In a press conference after the ceremony, Ruckelshaus declared that the White House welcomed the emission deadlines, had not worked against them, and promised vigorous enforcement of the new law.[132]

Conspicuously absent from the ceremony was Senator Muskie. Despite protests from Ehrlichman, Nixon did not invite the chief architect of the bill. Reporters, who referred to the legislation as the "Muskie bill," noted his absence to Ruckelshaus, who tried to deny the obvious. An outraged Muskie sought to block Nixon's credit. "The Senate did not get all it wanted," Muskie told the press. Administration pressure, he said, had forced "the conferees to accept major changes . . . in order to preserve the deadlines." The law "was a product of Congressional initiative," and despite bipartisan contributions, it was "opposed in part by the Administration."[133] Righteous indignation aside, however, Muskie was already in Maine with no intention of returning to Washington. In the words of his aide, Don Nicoll, "It was one of those cases where you took advantage of their behavior pattern." The snub was real, but the outrage was not.[134]

Politics was inevitable, White House aides reasoned. "This Muskie brouhaha," Charles Colson wrote, "could not have been avoided." If Nixon had invited Muskie, the senator "would have hogged the cameras." If he had opted for a private signing ceremony, Nixon "would have received no publicity." Muskie's complaints "looked very petty." Regardless, aides worked to ensure credit for the administration. Ruckelshaus appeared on the *Today Show* and Train on *Meet the Press*. Recognizing the importance of the bill, the White House distributed a press release to fifty prominent environment organizations. The document praised Nixon and omitted Muskie.[135]

The bill, indeed important, was another milestone in the nation's struggle to ensure environmental quality and a fitting conclusion to the year. Nixon endorsed critical legislation that, for the first time, armed the country with sufficient power to address the horrible degradation of its air. However, he did not fully embrace the bill, but rather reluctantly endorsed it for political expediency. Three hundred sixty-four days earlier, on the first day of January, Nixon had signed NEPA, another monumental law in the nation's environmental history but also a bill signed reluctantly. At the end of Nixon's second year in office, one essential political fact remained: Congress and the Democrats still held the political momentum. During 1970 they, more than the administration, saw their bills through to fruition and received the lions' share of the credit.

Nixon was beaten at his own game. He had put forth a solid legislative agenda, but his opponents attacked its limitations, augmented its strengths, and maintained the political initiative. He had arguably done more for environmental quality than any president in history, a fact that few recognized. As if to prove correct Muskie's contention that political competition guaranteed stronger policy, Americans had more reason to face their future with confidence than at Nixon's inauguration only two years before. They had reason for satisfaction—as much as Nixon had for frustration.

Senator Henry Jackson Meeting with Members of the Youth Conservation Corps,
Olympic National Park, 1969. (Photograph by Ira Spring, Edmonds, Washington,
courtesy Manuscripts and University Division, Allen Library, University of
Washington Library, Seattle.)

Senator Edmund Muskie Speaking at Water Pollution Conference, Boston, 1970.
(Photograph courtesy Edmund M. Muskie Archives, Bates College, Lewiston, Maine.)

(*Opposite*) Senator Jackson Trout Fishing, Wenatchee River, Washington, 1969.
(Photograph courtesy Henry M. Jackson Papers, Manuscripts and University Division, Allen Library, University of Washington Library, Seattle.)

President Richard M. Nixon Signing NEPA, San Clemente, California, January 1, 1970. (Photograph courtesy Richard M. Nixon Presidential Materials Project, National Archives II.)

Senator Muskie Conferring with Russell Train, 1970. (Photograph courtesy Edmund M. Muskie Archives, Bates College, Lewiston, Maine.)

Press Conference Following the Signing of NEPA, San Clemente, California, January 1, 1970. (Photograph courtesy Richard M. Nixon Presidential Materials Project, National Archives II.)

President Nixon Signing Clean Air Act, December 31, 1970. Standing behind President Nixon are William Ruckelshaus and Russell Train. (Photograph courtesy Richard M. Nixon Presidential Materials Project, National Archives II.)

White House Staffers Clean Up the Potomac River, April, 1970. (Photograph courtesy Richard M. Nixon Presidential Materials Project, National Archives II.)

President Nixon with John Ehrlichman, 1970. (Photograph courtesy Richard M. Nixon Presidential Materials Project, National Archives II.)

President Nixon Attending Ground-Breaking Ceremonies of the Tennessee-Tombigbee Waterway, 1971. Standing behind President Nixon are Alabama governor George Wallace and Julie and David Eisenhower. (Photograph by Jimmy Oland courtesy Mobile District, U.S. Army Corps of Engineers.)

Construction of Tennessee-Tombigbee Waterway. (Photograph by Adrien Lamarre courtesy Mobile District, U.S. Army Corps of Engineers.)

Walter Hickel, 1969. (Photograph courtesy Institute of the North, Anchorage, Alaska.)

Hickel (far right) Holding Chevron Oil Cartoon with Assistant Secretary Leslie Glasgow. The cartoon depicted Hickel as reeling in the oil industry. (Photograph courtesy Institute of the North, Anchorage, Alaska.)

Cartoon on Hickel. Political cartoonists, such as the Chicago Sun-Times' Mauldin, reflected the sentiment that Hickel had proved as secretary to be a friend of the environment in battles with oil and other industrial interests. (Photograph courtesy Institute of the North, Anchorage, Alaska.)

4

"You Can't Out-Muskie Muskie" 1971

Hope springs eternal. With Republicans largely repudiated at the polls and the administration facing a new Congress that promised more hostility, Whitaker still thought the time right for another environmental offensive. Just as many Americans were optimistic with the new year, Whitaker was confident that the political initiative remained within the administration's grasp. The frustrations of the first two years still flowed from tactics and not goals, he believed, from strategy and not substance. The key remained proper presentation, with the new Congress a fresh opportunity finally to get it right.

A coordinated "game plan to win the environmental issue," Whitaker lobbied, would correct past failings. The "big sticks"—Train, Ruckelshaus, and Morton—should "hit the intellectual news shows," such as those on Sunday morning and on public television. "They should walk the streets and parks for publicity." The "second team," including less visible members of CEQ, EPA, and the Interior Department, "should do all those miserable lunches and conventions that never make more than the local news." Muskie could "go waste his time there." More significantly, the White House should woo Congress as much as criticize it. White House aides might invite congressional staff for a lunch meeting. Nixon could then "drop by on a surprise basis . . . kidding them that they, not their bosses, have got to do the work on environmental legislation." This would certainly leave an impression. In addition, he might invite members of Congress to the White House or even to Camp David for that personal touch that only he could offer.[1]

Whitaker had a point; the administration's relations with Congress were antagonistic at best. The reality remained, however, that the new year and new Congress promised new legislation. No matter the spin, the political initiative did turn on substance, not presentation, on the specific provisions and details that had proved for two years the Achilles' heel of the White House's political

ambitions. In the early weeks of the new year Congress faced a full slate of proposals, unfinished business from the previous legislative session as well as new
bills. The political competition was as keen as ever, promising another productive year if not the political initiative that Whitaker sought.

For Muskie, the key was the unresolved water pollution debate. As aide Leon
Billings advised, "The only must legislation at this point is the water pollution
bill." In spite of the fact that the White House's proposal authorized less funding for waste-treatment facilities, "Congress can be criticized by the Nixon Administration if it fails to act."[2] For Jackson, the crux was his pending land-use
legislation. For others, the new Congress offered new opportunities — bills to
regulate strip mining, revise the antiquated Mining Law of 1872, and, in varying
degrees, expand federal funding across a wide spectrum of environmental
threats.

In public at least, Nixon appeared both chastised and conciliatory toward his
critics. In a bold one-hour television interview with network correspondents
on January 4, he stressed the positive, not the negative, and mentioned his
hopes for new domestic accomplishments. "If we can get this country thinking
of clean air, clean water, open spaces . . . then we will have the lift of a driving
dream." Within days White House aides reported that while Nixon still preferred foreign affairs, he felt the recent election a clear indication that the country wanted him to tackle better domestic problems. The congressional election
was one matter, but the coming presidential race was another.[3]

Although the White House had already unveiled its agenda the previous year,
it too had something new to add. On January 19, Nixon announced his decision
to halt construction of the Cross Florida Barge Canal. In one sense Nixon did
not have to act. Hickel's fifteen-month moratorium was still in effect and, four
days before his announcement, the U.S. District Court for the District of Columbia agreed with the Environmental Defense Fund that construction should
not commence until the Corps of Engineers completed an adequate NEPA impact statement. In another sense, however, a presidential injunction on construction cost little and might pay huge political dividends. The White House
recognized that Florida did not sit squarely within the Deep South political
bloc and that environmentalists were more powerful there than in neighboring states. Given developments, one might consider an injunction nothing
more than bowing to the inevitable. In any event, the Associated Press quoted
Hickel as taking credit for leading the struggle against the project, and thus acting now derailed the still-annoying former secretary as well as would-be congressional critics.[4]

Pleased with his performance the year before, Nixon once again offered an official environmental message to Congress on February 8. The message afforded the chance to reiterate the administration's program to the new Congress as well as add a few new wrinkles to support Nixon's public comments. "The comprehensive and wide-ranging program I propose today builds upon the thirty-seven point program I submitted to Congress a year ago," Nixon declared. Stating the obvious in calling 1970 a "year of progress," Nixon left little doubt that more was necessary, with Congress the culprit for any deficiencies.[5] Most noticeable among Nixon's new proposals was his call for increased funding for waste-treatment centers, an obvious response to the appropriations in Muskie's water pollution bill. Whereas the administration's earlier bill called for a ten-billion-dollar program, four billion dollars in federal funds with the rest from the states, Nixon now proposed a twelve-billion-dollar program, with the federal share at two billion dollars for three years. While this remained roughly half of Muskie's twenty-five-billion-dollar program, the White House hoped that the increased funds demonstrated good faith and deflected criticism.[6]

Nixon's message also unveiled the administration's land-use proposal, the product of a year of study. Unsuccessful in working with Jackson on his bill, the administration proposed a grant program run through the Department of Interior. For five years states would receive a total of twenty million dollars annually to develop land-use plans for all areas of "critical environmental importance." Settling upon the proposal was no small accomplishment; HUD argued strenuously for jurisdiction and CEQ was equally insistent upon strong sanctions for noncompliance. In the end, Ehrlichman decided against both, with the latter due to concerns over congressional objections. In any event, its acrimonious internal debate concluded, the administration now had its proposal to rival Jackson's.[7]

A third major addition to the White House's environmental agenda was pesticides legislation, the debate over agricultural chemicals extending beyond simply DDT. A broad range of pesticides threatened the environment with federal law inadequate to meet the challenge. The Federal Insecticide, Fungicide and Rodenticide Act of 1947, the only applicable legislation, mandated labels to ensure proper use, but provided no enforcement. It allowed cancellation of unsafe substances but, as the struggle over DDT proved, only after prolonged proceedings. Equally significant, the law gave jurisdiction to the Pesticide Regulation Division of the Department of Agriculture. As such, all appropriations fell to the Subcommittee on Agriculture of the House Appropriations Committee. Controlling this subcommittee with an iron hand was Mississippi Democrat Jamie Whitten, an outspoken defender of pesticide use and the author of *That We May Live*, a rebuttal to Rachel Carson's *Silent Spring*.[8]

The administration's bill swiftly addressed the problem. EPA was to classify all pesticides according to the hazards they presented, thus hopefully denying Whitten jurisdiction. Local and state restrictions were adequate for those less dangerous, but only an "approved pesticide applicator" could administer more hazardous chemicals. Armed with the power to inspect manufacturers, EPA was to reject any pesticide that posed an imminent threat to human health, which the administration hoped prevented additional cancellation hearings such as those it had endured over DDT. As for DDT, the federal appellate court ruled just as the administration introduced its bill that the Department of Agriculture had not provided sufficient reason to warrant its refusal to ban all uses immediately. The court, therefore, ordered EPA to hold hearings and determine definitively if the threat warranted an instant prohibition. As the DDT debate continued into the new Congress, the White House obviously hoped that its bill recouped at least some of the goodwill already lost over the issue.[9]

The only other notable addition to the administration's existing program was its ocean-dumping bill, although Muskie's theft of the White House's proposal the previous year made the introduction somewhat anticlimactic. Nixon added a proposal to tax sulfur oxide emissions from stationary sources of air pollution, which Ruckleshaus and EPA recommended, but otherwise the message to Congress remained largely redundant, covering in generalities the need to pass environmental legislation and reminding the public that much of the administration's program still pended before a Congress slow to act. The failure to go farther was the byline of much of the media, conveniently forgetting that while new proposals were few, they helped in part fill the gaps in Nixon's existing program.[10] Nixon's pesticide proposal alone provided a dramatic and vital improvement of existing law, while his new moves against water and air pollution once again proved him more a political pragmatist than the environmental demagogue his opponents painted him. The administration's program was still inadequate, but the additions significantly strengthened it. As Whitaker sought a better strategy to present the White House's program, the new environmental message to Congress spoke at least in part to the substantive details that made his optimism and hope for the political initiative appear so unrealistic.

Nixon understandably had his doubts, however, his new proposals and continued rhetoric notwithstanding. If pragmatism led him to expand his environmental program with the new Congress, it also made it hard for him to ignore that the new year, just as the one before, brought little else to warrant Whitaker's optimism. A Gallup poll only weeks after Nixon's address placed his approval ratings below 50 percent for the first time. The new proposals arguably had little, if any, political effect. Worse, polls placed Muskie ahead in a hypothetical race. In New Hampshire, the first state to hold a primary, the lead was a solid eight points. Touted for some time as "the Democrat's biggest hope for 1972," Muskie now basked in the afterglow of the Clean Air Act Amendments of 1970. Just as thoughts turned toward the presidential election, the North American School of Conservation named Muskie, not Nixon, as its "Conservationist of the Year," an accolade with which much of the public apparently agreed.[11] As his environmental staff counseled perseverance, Nixon for the first time began to question whether the effort was worth it. "I don't believe the public interest is deep," Nixon mused, "though it may be wide in some areas." People cared, but would cast their votes on other matters. Ordering more polling data on public opinion, Nixon's patience was wearing thin. Perhaps change, not persistence, was the answer. The status quo clearly was not.[12]

From a political perspective at least, Nixon had a point. In spite of his program's incompleteness, he arguably had done more in two years than any president in history, certainly enough to place him in league with Theodore Roosevelt and Lyndon Johnson, the only other chief executives with similar claims. From endangered species to population control, the White House had acted. The first president to present to Congress a comprehensive program for environmental protection, he had in just one year signed NEPA, the Water Quality Improvement Act of 1970, the Resource Recovery Act of 1970, and the Clean Air Act Amendments of 1970. He had created EPA and staffed his administration with strong environmental advocates. It was true that many of these accomplishments had more Democratic than Republican geneses and that the administration had in many instances worked to weaken the final result. Regardless, each required Nixon's approval—ultimately granted, whatever the motivation. The fact remains that another president might have acted differently. Without Nixon, 1970 might not have emerged as the "year of progress" that all now acknowledged. Without a doubt, Muskie, Jackson, and the Democrats deserved considerable credit, but, to the extent of his contributions, Nixon did as well.

And yet Nixon was on the defensive and under attack. His popularity at an all-time low, he was, according to Muskie, launching only a "sham attack on pollution," an enemy more than an ally of environmental quality.[13] Even as Nixon presented his new proposals, all indications pointed to more frustration. Far from pleased with the administration's injunction blocking construction of the Cross Florida Barge Canal, the Environmental Defense Fund sued. The injunction was not officially permanent, it worried, and thus at some point construction might commence. The White House had no such intentions, but to critics Nixon was simply not trustworthy.[14] The White House intended its Refuse Act water pollution program to win political points, but as the new year continued the program engendered more condemnation than praise. The program applied only to interstate waters, critics complained, worthless unless it applied to intrastate tributaries. Forgetting the matter of questionable federal jurisdiction, to much of the public the program's shortcomings were evidence of administration malice.[15]

In Congress the picture was no brighter. Noting that CEQ recommended the previous year banning the dumping of municipal solid waste, critics complained about the lack of any such provision in the administration's ocean-dumping bill. The White House, they argued, had weakened its bill despite the gravity of the problem that its own environmental advisors recognized. The administration's new land-use bill, meanwhile, did not deserve their support. Unlike the Jackson bill, it did not apply to all lands statewide, only lands of critical environmental importance. The question of what constituted a critical area was open to debate, and no guarantee existed that states would coordinate all necessary planning. Because the White House had once again ignored the advice of CEQ and struck any sanction provisions from the bill, the government had no way to ensure compliance.[16] Finally, and perhaps most troublesome for the administration, was the warm reception given Muskie when he announced that he supported augmenting federal allocations in his own water pollution bill. In an apparent tit-for-tat response to the White House's new bill, Muskie now argued that his own twenty-five-billion-dollar proposal provided insufficient funds for waste-treatment facilities. Nixon already thought Muskie's existing proposal fiscally unsound, and to him the applause from environmentalists was the sound of a narrow special-interest group increasingly removed from any sense of economic reality.[17]

Environmentalists, it increasingly appeared to Nixon, would always push for more. The administration could never satisfy them. Given new developments as well as the experience of the past two years, it was a difficult argument to counter, any legitimacy to critics' claims notwithstanding. Sensing Nixon's exasperation, Ruckelshaus reluctantly acknowledged the environment as "a negative political issue," but sought to press both the importance of the issue itself as well as the political ramifications of retreat. "You can't win with the environment," Ruckelshaus reluctantly acknowledged, "but they can beat you up with it."[18] Nixon had to continue his efforts, not to win new votes but to weaken the criticism he had no chance of avoiding.

The thought of another offensive as Whitaker urged seemed useless, Nixon assumed. Devoting time and energy to a problem that his own environmental advisors acknowledged promised nothing but admonition made no sense. "The environment is not a good political issue," Nixon bluntly told Haldeman. "I have an uneasy feeling that perhaps we are doing too much." In short, "We're catering to the left in all of this."[19] Change, rather, was the order of the day—and not just in environmental policy. The administration should back away from all its unproductive domestic initiatives, Nixon ordered, and move more aggressively on issues heretofore neglected. Although the most surprising development was the decision to embrace deficit spending to ignite the economy—a Keynesian policy that potentially promised more funds for an array of issues, the environment included—Nixon moved strategically to the right, to win votes with a more conservative domestic agenda. He had already introduced his plan for revenue sharing, returning federal funds to the states for disposal, but now the policy would enjoy a new degree of urgency and a higher level of publicity. No longer on issues such as welfare reform, civil rights, and the environment, the new emphasis was on lower taxes, deregulation, economic efficiency, and, most importantly, an embrace of industry. Returning to his party's core constituency, and, Nixon hoped, the majority of Americans, he would campaign against Washington, not for it.[20]

To Nixon it was revolutionary; to the Democrats it was a counterrevolution. The conservatives in the administration loved it. According to speechwriter Patrick Buchanan, a young firebrand whose star rose rapidly in the White House, Nixon had to date adopted a "liberal domestic program," a slur to those of Buchanan's ilk. Nixon had taken conservatives for granted—"the niggers of the Nixon Administration"—and the new course ensured that they did not revolt and back California governor Ronald Reagan in the Republican primaries.[21]

An angry Nixon charted the new course. The vindictiveness, resentment, distrust of the media and his opponents that bordered on paranoia, and, most importantly, reliance upon cutthroat, dirty politics all remained a constant among the shifting sands of policy. Planning one political attack, Nixon took note of Whitaker in describing his needs to Haldeman: "I wish you could get a personality type like Whitaker who will work his butt off and do it honorably. I really need a son of a bitch . . . who will work his butt off and do it dishonorably." Whitaker had begun to lose influence with his superiors, but still commanded Nixon's respect. Buchanan, on the other hand, increasingly held Nixon's ear. As Nixon sought to couch Muskie as "irresponsible," Buchanan suggested "exaggerating his position."[22] When Buchanan described Ralph Nader as "a demagogue who has eclipsed all visible competition," Nixon instructed Haldeman to "develop a plan for exposing [Nader]." An "unprincipled huckster" according to Nixon, Nader had repaired his relationship with Muskie in light of the senator's new water pollution proposal. He was, in short, "dangerous to the business system so essential to survival of the nation." Haldeman was to "mobilize a business group to finance an effective research and counterattack campaign."[23]

His anger largely masked in public, Nixon's distaste for environmentalists could spontaneously erupt in the White House. In a meeting with CBS executives in March, Nixon declared that he "had no sympathy with environmentalists who were demanding equal time on the air for every reply to every issue." In a clear reference to NEPA's impact statements, he declared that "[environmentalists] have gone too far in many instances." Although we live in a civilized society, Nixon said, "some people want to go back in time when men lived primitively . . . really a very unhappy existence for people."[24]

The immediate cause of Nixon's outburst was obvious. Just as its committee had done the previous year, the full Senate voted to deny funds for the SST, the proverbial nail in the coffin for the project and, in Nixon's view, "the number one technological tragedy of our time." The Department of Interior, meanwhile, circulated its draft environmental impact statement on the Alaska pipeline, which predictably raised the ire of opponents. The statement acknowledged that some ecological damage was necessary, but maintained that it was inconsequential compared to the national security implications of the demand for oil. The draft spent only a few pages on alternative routes, but concluded that construction should commence immediately when Alyeska met the Department of Interior's stipulations.[25] As for the equally controversial Tennessee-Tombigbee Waterway, the Corps of Engineers proposed a three-part impact statement, the first phase an initial overview, the second a more detailed analysis of engineering and design, and the final a review of any problems encountered. Submitting its first phase in March, the Corps declared the environmental consequences surmountable and said that it planned to commence construction. CEQ accepted the initial report, but noted the likelihood of a lawsuit and urged Nixon not to attend groundbreaking ceremonies. After Nixon accepted anyway, Whitaker complained to Ehrlichman that "the President was digging his ditch and fouling up the environment." At the absolute minimum, he should wait until the impact statement was complete. "The meaning of this," Whitaker concluded, "frankly escapes me."[26]

Apparently ignoring the opinions of his own environmental advisors, Nixon could not understand how anyone could object to these projects. Canceling the Cross Florida Barge Canal accomplished nothing, Nixon assumed, and clearly opponents were radicals unwilling to accept any advance in civilization. They were simply naive or, worse, fools harking back to some idyllic time that never existed. In the words of one advisor, Nixon now saw them as part of "the wacko fringe," unable or unwilling to engage in logical discourse and, in short, largely "dippy."[27] Having forgotten or ignored any merit to their claims, Nixon increasingly perceived them as part of the problem and not the solution. The solution, Nixon surmised, was reason, not emotion, logical balance in policy and not uncompromising extremism.

Most environmental groups were hardly extreme. Although an Internal Revenue Service investigation concluded that the majority of environmental organizations should maintain their tax-exempt status, most groups still worried that too direct partisan political advocacy threatened their financial lifeline. Having established the independent Sierra Club Foundation, the Sierra Club more directly lobbied Washington, extreme, if at all, in its opposition to the administration more than in its positions on specific issues. If anything, many radical elements had grown disenchanted with the thrust of the mainstream groups.[28] In the words of one former activist in the Berkeley free speech movement, now an avowed Marxist, "The ecology thing is our last chance, and we're doing the same thing with that as everything else. It's all a lot of talk and a lot of jive." Added another, a former organizer of the first Earth Day, now depressed and cynical in spite of the advances, "I can't relate to [lobbyists and politicians]. They are an elite, talking to themselves." If not "tuning in and turning on," to paraphrase popular LSD guru Timothy Leary, they were at least to this extent "dropping out." Incredibly, given the evident Democratic bias of most environmentalists, others on the fringes of the antiwar movement denounced mainstream environmental organizations as "tools of the Nixon war machine." They were, according to this rather convoluted logic, giving the administration another issue to divert public attention from the heinous crimes of the war.[29]

Nevertheless, there was a grain of truth to Nixon's assumption, at least in the sense that the environmental movement, just as every popular movement of the era, had a small but growing radical element. Its roots were evident even as Earth Day unfolded. The talk here was often of imminent doom, of unavoidable death and destruction. The free-enterprise system itself was at fault and nothing short of its demise could save the planet. These doomsday antagonists were few in number, but the publicity they received gave ammunition to Stans and others in the administration who saw it to their advantage to paint all environmentalists with this single stroke.[30] Industry often applauded the effort. Mobil Corporation ran television commercials that implied environmentalism was radical, angering the Sierra Club. When the Sierra Club spoke of halting growth that threatened the environment, the term it employed, "no growth," won few friends when taken out of context. Philip Berry, with his tenure as head of the organization ending, recalled an angry electric-power industry and tense meetings with the American Management Association trying to explain the rather vague phrase. The Sierra Club was not against economic growth and prosperity, a defensive Berry pleaded.[31] The major environmental organizations were not radical, but they occasionally made themselves easy targets.

Environmentalism, Ruckelshaus later concluded, evolved like many popular movements. Although it began as a grass-roots, mainstream crusade, it soon gained success and thus struggled to maintain momentum. This, in turn, led to more controversial positions and ultimately more polarization. While this analysis is debatable, the fact remains that in 1971 any such evolution was only in its infancy.[32] The year witnessed the birth of Greenpeace and other alternative, direct-action groups, but the publicity they received far outweighed their actual following or impact. The founders of Greenpeace, for example, set out in an antiquated halibut seiner to block underground nuclear tests in the Aleutian Islands. A similar attempt against French testing in the South Pacific found their vessel rammed by a warship. Such sensational exploits made great copy, but for the overwhelming majority of environmentalists the more effective venue remained rather mundane and conservative: lobbying and legislation. In later years, the same sense of urgency and despair that caused many to "drop out" led others to eco-sabotage, romanticized in a 1975 Edward Abbey novel as "monkeywrenching."[33] Whether their tactics included driving iron wedges into trees about to be cut or vandalizing construction sites, here existed the true radicals, the extremists that perhaps support Ruckelshaus's theory.[34] Environmentalism posed no such threat as Nixon shifted policy. Environmentalists were not extremists, and their sin was political opposition more than actual inordinacy. It was for Nixon, nevertheless, a mortal sin, just cause for a detour on the road to reelection.

Nixon had help in charting his new course. Launching a counterattack in the wake of the new environmental restrictions, industry sought to convince policymakers that environmentalists were unreasonable radicals. A reaction by the business community was, of course, only natural. Whether it was farmers threatened by pesticide legislation, the automotive industry by clean-air legislation, the timber industry by public-lands policy, or the myriad of other economic concerns uneasy about the future, a constituency existed to check further environmental advances. At first, business leaders believed environmentalism was only a temporary cultural phenomenon sweeping college-age youth. In the wake of 1970, however, they recognized a need for a rigid, coordinated resistance focused on both the White House and public opinion. Industry opposition, just as environmentalism itself, evolved over time, ultimately culminating in the anti-environmental crusade of the Reagan administration. By the early 1970s, however, it was already a force hard to ignore. "Unless those who know the seriousness of environmental degradation are prepared to meet this new challenge," the Wilderness Society argued, "the Know-Nothings could do great mischief to the forward steps of recent years."[35]

Industry's tactics varied. Business groups distributed literature to teachers and pundits, financed advertising campaigns on television and radio, and published their own magazines, for example Dow Chemical's *Down to Earth* and the Tobacco Institute's *The Tobacco Observer*. They discouraged media reports unfriendly to their cause, which on occasion led to heated debate. The Pacific Gas and Electric Company, for one, attempted to discredit the professional reputation of television producer Donald Widener for his documentary critical of the nuclear industry. The matter finally ended in court with Widener's vindication in 1979. Government lobbying drove home the same point: it was jobs or the environment, a choice that environmentalists claimed was unnecessary. Politicians had to choose. Were they really willing to sacrifice the livelihood of hardworking, decent Americans just to save a few whooping cranes? Only an extremist, a radical, would make such a choice.[36]

Coming off a disappointing election that he attributed in part to a stagnant economy, Nixon was certainly receptive to such logic. He saw warning signs everywhere. The *New York Times*, for example, reported that pollution-control costs placed some corporations in a competitive disadvantage, with their international rivals facing less stringent restrictions. When the polls he commissioned indicated continued public support for environmental protection, Nixon proclaimed the results were inaccurate. They did not, he complained, ask the acid question: would voters still feel the same way if it meant that they lost their jobs? Now doubting that he could achieve both his economic and environmental objectives, Nixon agreed with industry; it was to this extent an unfortunate but necessary choice of priorities.[37]

The Department of Commerce remained industry's conduit to the White House. Administration spokesmen, the department advised, "should stress the seriousness of the consequences to industry, labor, and the economy as a whole," advice that Nixon obviously did not need. Secretary Stans, now sensing an ally in his boss, was more blunt: business had become a "whipping boy for the environment." Environmentalists had "accusatory, hostile public attitudes about business." The administration should respond in an equally hostile and public manner. As Commerce Department spokesmen gave speeches debunking "the myths about the American environment" — including one that "the U.S. environment has continuously deteriorated since the Pilgrims landed at Plymouth Rock"—business leaders grew more hostile in their own public comments. According to one vice president of Weyerhauser, the large timber company, "This uninformed environmentalist phenomenon . . . has the potential to destroy much of the social and economic progress which this nation has made in the past few decades."[38]

Whitaker, just as Ruckelshaus, did his best to stem the tide of retreat. Writing that he knew Nixon "had a concern that overzealous pollution laws would tear down the private enterprise system," Whitaker lobbied that the White House should not abandon its efforts. To Nixon, it was not a matter of completely abandoning environmental protection. In his mind, he just shifted policy emphasis, interjecting a little sanity into a debate dominated by emotional extremists and one that in any event promised little political gold to mine. Nevertheless, Nixon's growing antipathy toward the environmental movement continued and was sorely evident to Whitaker and the others on Nixon's environmental staff. When Gaylord Nelson introduced a congressional resolution calling on Nixon to issue a presidential proclamation declaring the third week of April as "Earth Week," Nixon initially refused, which dumbfounded Whitaker. "It costs us nothing," Whitaker complained. "I think we are painting ourselves into a corner for nothing." Whitaker continued to lobby and reminded Nixon of the success of the first Earth Day and the political criticism he faced. In the end, Nixon reluctantly issued the proclamation.[39] When the NIPCC issued a report concluding that environmental regulations harmed industry and a more "orderly approach" was necessary, Nixon invited its members to the White House to receive the report formally, praising its conclusions. "I express appreciation to the Council for its work," Nixon declared. "We are not here . . . to make [industry] scapegoats for this problem." Only a year before Nixon had distanced himself from a similar NIPCC broadside against environmentalists; now he embraced it.[40]

Friction was bound to develop. As the Izaak Walton League wrote that the NIPCC report "reflects an antiquated myopia which is directly responsible for the magnitude of our problems today," Whitaker, Ruckelshaus, Train, and the others in the White House who agreed found themselves ostracized in a way they never had been before, rebuked more often than applauded. Their efforts to mitigate shifting policy increasingly antagonized their superiors. "I have been receiving a number of disturbing reports about Bill Ruckelshaus's attitude toward industry," Charles Colson wrote Ehrlichman.[41] Worried that Train might make comments against the SST as he had the previous year, Ehrlichman telephoned him to ensure that he did not. Train agreed, but when the court-mandated EPA hearings on DDT began, he was no less vocal in his support of an immediate ban. UPI quoted him as saying that DDT and other pesticides killed over two hundred people annually, a comment that angered the White House. Noting that such remarks appeared critical of the EPA hearings and administration policy in general, Whitaker asked his friend, "Rough day?" Pressing his agenda, Train, like Whitaker, lobbied forcibly against the Tennessee-Tombigbee Waterway, which earned another reprimand. The project, Ehrlichman reminded him, "has tremendous political benefits in the deep South."[42] Joining Train, the administration's Citizen's Advisory Council on Environmental Quality lobbied for additional environmental activism. An obviously annoyed White House bluntly rejected the idea, replying that it considered policy "with respect to overall priorities and expected pay-offs."[43] Nixon had always admired his environmental advisors; now, it increasingly appeared to him, they just did not know when to stop.

CEQ and EPA had, of course, enough independence to advance the cause of environmental protection whatever the shifting priorities of their superiors. To this end, CEQ, already angered by agency compliance with NEPA, tightened its impact-statement guidelines according to the law. The new guidelines mandated that departments wait at least ninety days after the first draft and thirty days after the final draft to commence construction. They were, to Jackson, "a step in the right direction."[44] More significantly, EPA moved forcibly to implement the Clean Air Act, just as Ruckelshaus promised. When EPA released its ambient state standards as required, environmentalists applauded. "These are tough standards," Ruckelshaus proudly declared, a statement undeniably true.[45] When EPA then followed with stringent regulations for how states were to reach the specific 1975 and 1976 auto emission standards, it was clear that it had no plans to buckle under pressure. Even newly appointed Secretary Morton showed a surprising degree of independence, announcing an indefinite moratorium on coal leasing on federal lands. With a reactive leasing policy that allowed application on an individual basis, the Department of Interior had leased more land than the production of coal warranted, thus encouraging speculation. Morton's action at least temporarily addressed this issue, proving again that environmentalists still had friends within an administration that was increasingly a foe. "The environmental crowd in the administration," Train later recalled with obvious pride, "did fairly well in holding our ground."[46]

Reflecting on the growing rift between his agency and the White House, Ruckelshaus recalled that the Clean Air Act was itself a contributing factor. The law was "very complex," granting EPA the primary responsibility for implementation and the establishment of specific standards when before the White House had always played a larger role. Nixon had a difficult time accepting this premise, particularly when he viewed the standards as excessive. In any event, the White House was also critical because of inadequate warning. "This was a fair criticism . . . I might have warned them first." In retrospect, "I was new; everything was new."[47]

Nixon was less gracious. When Ruckelshaus, in one speech, bemoaned "greedy corporations" harming the environment, Nixon ordered a reprimand. "EPA shouldn't demagogue like this." Even as Ruckelshaus announced his tough standards, Nixon met with the leaders of the Ford Motor Company, Henry Ford II and Lee Iacocca. "Whether it's the environment or pollution or Naderism or consumerism," Nixon told the executives, "we are extremely pro-business." Mirroring the comments of Stans, he added, "Environmentalists are a group of people that aren't really one damn bit interested in safety or clean air." Their interest lay "in destroying the system." He would, Nixon promised, protect them from these extreme "enemies of the system." Legislative mandate or not, Nixon made it clear that the White House, not EPA, CEQ, or the Interior Department, set administration policy.[48]

By late spring, with the rift in the administration growing, Nixon had yet to chastise publicly environmentalists to the degree that the Department of Commerce thought appropriate. He obviously agreed with Stans, encouraging his harsh rhetoric while discouraging the opposite from Ruckelshaus and Train. He had not, however, made any major speeches that reflected his true feelings. The White House had issued no proclamations that indicated the magnitude of its shift in priorities. CEQ's William Reilly received instructions to compose a speech attacking the environmental movement, which Reilly then attempted to soften, but in the end Nixon never gave the speech. Nixon's comments, whether to auto executives or to the NIPCC, were to those of like mind, in the White House and largely private. In public, a casual observer might not have discerned any change in administration policy, especially in light of Nixon's second message to Congress and the independent actions of his environmental staff.[49]

Nixon, Ruckelshaus later recalled, "never once asked me if there were a problem with the environment the whole time I was there." It was all politics. "Whether or not it had any legitimacy was irrelevant." As such, Nixon's political instincts told him that while it was expedient to abandon the environmental initiative, it made no sense to antagonize unnecessarily the environmental vote. He wanted his allies to know that he had returned to the fold, and in time administration policy would be obvious to all. Nevertheless, to attack simply to attack, to demonize environmentalists without good cause, was to intensify the inevitable reaction he would have to face.[50] To this limited extent, Whitaker and

Ruckelshaus were correct. While he would not continue the struggle he had endured for two years, the White House still needed a fig leaf behind which to hide, something to deflect as much environmental criticism as possible. Rather than the hostile public attacks that Stans urged, a more appropriate strategy was, in the words of one White House aide, to "maintain to the extent possible the posture of continuing concern for the environment, but stay away from specific issues."[51]

As the White House well knew, avoiding specifics was no easy task, whatever the policy objective. Muskie, Jackson, and others obviously did not share the White House's new attitude, and in any event the new Congress stood ready to place its stamp on a fresh wave of legislation. The congressional wars, in short, continued. Just as Nixon instructed his staff that the environment "was not a sacred cow," his administration made enough concessions to provide the necessary political cover.[52] When the U.S.-Canada Joint Working Group, the group commissioned by both countries the previous year to study Great Lakes pollution, issued its report, the administration endorsed it despite the problems that it posed. The report called for an agreement to reduce phosphates by 80 percent by 1975, an admirable goal but one especially difficult for the administration. By still rejecting the substitute NTA and the tough restrictions that CEQ recommended, it had in a sense endorsed the ends and not the means. Problems were sure to emerge. In another initiative, Nixon issued in June an executive order banning federal contracts, loans, and grants to businesses convicted of pollution-law violations. The order was once again a move in the right direction, although with relatively narrow ramifications, it was as politically symbolic as truly significant.[53]

More significant was Nixon's long-awaited departmental reorganization, unveiled in a special message to Congress. Nixon called for legislators to cut the existing twelve departments to eight, with the State, Defense, Treasury, and Justice departments kept intact, and with the others combined into four new departments: Human Resources, Community Development, Economic Development, and, as the Ash Council had recommended the year before, Natural Resources. Most environmental groups applauded the proposal, as the Department of Natural Resources was in essence a strengthened Department of Interior, most notably including the Forest Service from the Department of Agriculture. Nixon gave this little thought, however, as the proposal was for him a cornerstone of his new conservative agenda. The "bureaucratic elite in Washington," Nixon stated, always assume that "they know what is best for people everywhere." The proposal would check the growth of the federal bureaucracy—the very bureaucracy critical for adequate environmental protection. It was, thus, a welcomed proposal on one hand and somehow suspicious and threatening on the other.[54]

As the farm lobby rallied to protest the proposal, a challenge to existing congressional committee jurisdiction, the dilemma for Nixon was getting it past Congress. This was not the problem with another bill that was introduced simultaneously, a proposal to protect ocean mammals introduced by Oklahoma Democratic senator Fred Harris and Arkansas Democratic representative David Pryor. Here the problem was the likelihood of passage. It was, simply put, bad legislation, an overreaction to environmentalism that the White House was correct to oppose. The bill proposed to ban the killing and importation of all marine mammals, including seals, walruses, sea lions, porpoises, otters, polar bears, and whales. Many of these animals were far from endangered, some were critical to the economy of Alaskan natives, and all were better served by scientific management. A sudden ban would in time lead to overpopulation with its own negative ecological ramifications.[55]

The White House had its own reasons for opposition. The United States was the largest market for ocean mammal products, and, if passed, the bill required the termination of an international agreement with Canada and Japan that prohibited the killing of seals at sea and regulated the hunt on Alaska's Pribilof Islands. Backers had a persuasive case, however, namely large color photographs of the slaughter of baby seals on these islands. For thousands of years natives had surrounded the seals and clubbed them to death. Color photographs of the cute, defenseless baby seals facing their grisly fate on the blood-stained snow struck a chord with an environmental-conscious America, and both Congress and the White House found themselves flooded with letters of protest. "The ladies in the suburbs are really going at it," reported one White House aide. The issue consumed " a ridiculous amount of time." If the issue were clubbing seals, John Dean joked, referring to the famous Black Panther leader, "Bobby Seale might be a more appropriate topic."[56]

It remained no joking matter, however, drawing more attention than Nixon's revolutionary reorganization proposal and ironically captivating a public inundated by the horrors of Vietnam. The administration finally settled on a bill to establish a commission to study the matter and a permit system for proper management, but with emotions running high, debate continued and all bills languished. As with most media-driven sensations, the issue slowly began to fade. This was not until after it had cost the administration political capital, however, despite the White House's own reasonable proposal and the support of the Izaak Walton League, the National Audubon Society, and most major environmental groups.[57]

If difficult to discern in the spring, the real shift in the administration's policy came not with resistance to the Harris-Pryor ocean mammal proposal, but in more subtle ways. With the White House's pesticide bill stagnant in Congress, the victim of a potent farm lobby determined to maintain jurisdiction with the agriculture committees, Ehrlichman decided to resubmit the proposal as an amendment to existing law, not as separate legislation. While apparently insignificant, the move ensured Representative Whitten and his farm allies control. In an effort to appease Oklahoma Republican Page Belcher, a power in the House Agriculture Committee, Ehrlichman also agreed that EPA not require farmers to release on demand information they maintained on pesticide safety. It would, however, have to pay an indemnity to farmers who suffered financially because of a cancellation, and it would have the responsibility for safe disposal. Whitaker recognized that this quietly emasculated the entire program, making the decision to cancel one of cost as much as safety. It was a "nightmare," but in his view no revision meant no bill.[58] In June, Nixon delivered the first energy message ever sent to Congress. While couching his comments in the context of a "clean energy policy" and mentioning the need to develop alternative fuels, the thrust of his program was greater exploitation of oil, not conservation. The nation sorely needed an energy policy, but to Nixon this meant increased leasing of off-shore oil and public oil shale lands. It meant a more active nuclear program and a Department of Natural Resources focused first and foremost on energy, not the environment.[59]

The population bill Nixon signed at the end of the previous year still bothered the White House, which now did all it could to reverse policy. Under pressure, HEW issued guidelines for the newly passed law, which for the first time included means testing for federal assistance. Any family with an income over four thousand dollars was ineligible. Declaring abortion "an unacceptable form of population control," Nixon ordered a ban in military hospitals and urged the defunding of family-planning services that provided it. While in many respects the abortion debate carried as much political clout as the environment, with policy independent, environmentalists objected. According to Stewart Udall, the order was "lamentable" and the Commission on Population Growth and the American Future, which continued its study, "should consider the contribution of [abortion] . . . to reduced population growth."[60] In another vein, Ehrlichman ordered a new internal administration procedure, the Quality of Life Review. On the surface the order simply promised the "proper balance between economic and environmental concerns." In practice, however, EPA was to submit all proposed regulations to the scrutiny of other agencies, a review coordinated by the Office of Management and Budget and led by its new director,

George Schultz. However sensible it appeared, the White House intended the Quality of Life Review as further restraint on the environmentalists in its midst. It was, according to Train, "a troublesome process."[61]

In early July Nixon accepted an invitation to a dinner in honor of Yosemite National Park. Whitaker acknowledged the event as an "easy" way for the administration to maintain the front of environmentalism even as this task became more difficult. Only weeks later, as CEQ warned, the Environmental Defense Fund sued over the Tennessee-Tombigbee Waterway's partial impact statement. Recognizing Ruckelshaus as a potential ally, the plaintiffs wrote EPA to gain its support. "This agency," EPA solemnly replied, "has no authority to prevent its construction." At the same time, the U.S. Court of Appeals for the District of Columbia ruled against the administration in the Calvert Cliffs nuclear power plant controversy on the Chesapeake Bay. The court agreed with the National Wildlife Federation that the Atomic Energy Commission had to complete fully an impact statement before it could license the Maryland facility.[62]

The scenario proved that environmentalists were extreme, the White House believed. Nixon had just noted the importance of nuclear power in his energy message, but environmentalists seemed to care more about fish than the threat to national security. Journalist Tom Shepard had it right, Nixon explained. In an article in popular *Look Magazine*, Shepard wrote that the nation's air and water were cleaner than in the past, that DDT was not harmful, and that population growth in no way threatened a crisis. Environmentalists who argued such were extremists opposed to economic growth. This was what he had been trying to say, Nixon told Haldeman. "We've been sucked in too much on issues such as the environment." Haldeman relayed Nixon's comments to Ehrlichman: "He wants it understood that Shepard writes like the President believes, whereas a great deal of our speech material has reflected programs which in turn reflect the liberal malarkey." Aware of unnecessarily antagonizing the environmental vote, the administration should take care not to appear as part of "a backlash to the environmental movement." It should, rather, cast its comments as "a recognition that complex problems do not deserve simplistic solutions."[63]

The Department of Commerce, Nixon instructed, should undertake a study of the economic impact of environmental regulations, most specifically Muskie's proposed water pollution bill. In fact, Muskie's subcommittee had launched essentially the same investigation, although it was obvious from the start that its conclusions would differ from what Nixon had in mind. To Muskie the question for his hearings was simple: "If people, workers, communities, and industrial plants are to be affected because we have resolved to protect the environment, how and by what means shall their interests, their personal health and welfare, also be protected?" To Muskie it was mostly a matter of compensation; to Nixon it was a matter of less regulation. "Make sure [the study] isn't biased toward the environment," Ehrlichman ordered.[64] As if to make his point, EPA was to assist in identifying "what type of legislative or administrative action may be required to soften any dislocations within the economy." In short, the plan was "to cool off the excesses."[65]

Just as the White House had earlier developed a coordinated agenda of environmental advocacy, it now sought a specific program to check the same. This program was not complete as the summer progressed, but the administration's drift away from its previous stance nevertheless grew more apparent every day. Stans, of course, continued his harsh attacks, in one speech declaring that "the volume of work across the country delayed for environmental reasons exceeds $5 billion," a grossly exaggerated figure. Nixon remained hesitant to match such public rhetoric, but still wanted his message conveyed. When CEQ in August issued its annual report as required by NEPA, Nixon warned against "ecological perfection at the cost of bankruptcy." The nation needed a sense of "realism" and a commitment to maintain "a healthy economy while we seek a healthy environment."[66] EPA, the White House ordered, should change its newly announced regulations for state air-pollution-control strategies. In designing their specific programs to meet the required auto emission standards and deadlines, states should consider "the social and economic impact" of their efforts. EPA should also, the White House ordered in private, appoint more prominent Republicans, specifically several recommended by Kansas senator Robert Dole. "We are very much indebted to him," Ehrlichman noted.[67]

The CEQ report was excellent, according to the *New York Times*, but Nixon's reaction was "timid." He had given it only his "modified blessings." Within the administration, where knowledge existed that Nixon no longer held any concern, modified or otherwise, reaction to the new developments further strained relations between the White House and its environmental staff. Stans's comments were outrageous, Train protested. "Costs are unfairly charged to the environment issue when, in fact, they are due to poor planning and general economic factors." Partisan EPA appointments, Whitaker warned, would cause a "negative public reaction that the choices were made on political grounds rather than on the technical qualifications of the appointee." Ruckelshaus, Whitaker added, "is getting to the point where he simply can't believe the President feels that way." Nixon should meet with him to help calm him down. If the public were only beginning to sense the new reality in the administration, Train, Whitaker, and Ruckelshaus knew the future boded nothing better.[68]

For Nixon, on the other side of the issue, the future looked significantly brighter. If by the fall the public had more reason to note the White House's shifting environmental policy, Nixon was increasingly confident that it did not matter. He had just unveiled a bombshell that promised to alter his political fortunes and historical legacy forever. In a nationally televised speech from the NBC studios in California, Nixon announced that Henry Kissinger had secretly visited the People's Republic of China, the massive communist nation with whom the United States had no diplomatic ties. He would follow with his own visit, the first ever for a president, with both countries hoping at some point to normalize relations. It was a stroke of diplomatic brilliance, recognizing that with mainland China and the Soviet Union increasingly estranged, the overture not only lessened tensions with the most populous nation in the world, it encouraged détente with the Soviets. In fact, Nixon had earlier announced an initial agreement with the Soviet Union to limit antiballistic missile systems as part of the ongoing Strategic Arms Limitation Talks. For a president still mired in the quicksand of Vietnam, the announcements were a dramatic and welcomed break. Neither a political partisan nor a warmonger, Nixon finally stood as he had always envisioned himself: the statesman bringing the possibility of peace.[69]

The public loved it. The response was "amazed but awestruck," in the words of one Nixon biographer. "The politics of surprise leads through the Gates of Astonishment into the Kingdom of Hope," waxed columnist Max Lerner.[70] If a surprise, Nixon's diplomacy was advantageous for both the country and his own political legacy. It was not, however, his only surprise nor his only political success. By the fall, Nixon's strategic move to the right had apparently begun to pay dividends. Whether battling taxes, ranting against forced busing, or denouncing the threat to American business, the new conservative agenda had apparently hit a chord with the public, at least the rural and suburban "silent majority" that the White House courted. The economy remained a barrier, however, and Nixon thought the time was right for another shocking announcement. With inflation unchecked, Nixon once again returned to the national airways. In addition to new tax cuts, Nixon declared, the situation required a ninety-day freeze on all wages and prices, after which Washington would work with business and labor for continued price stability. It was an offer that flew in the face of his stated conservatism, an apparent schizophrenic policy initiative with, at best, limited chances for success. It was also another shrewd political calculation. Although he in a sense denounced government regulation and interference at the same time he imposed exactly that, to much of the public his conservative credentials remained intact. He was operating on their behalf, whether attacking the choking bureaucracy or the stifling inflation, with all irony forgotten. Coupled with his now apparent diplomatic acumen, to many Nixon was no longer the frustrated, struggling incompetent careening toward certain political vanquishment.[71]

The proof was in the polls. Trailing Muskie only months before, his negative ratings above his positive, a new Gallup poll in early October placed his popularity at its highest level of the year, those who approved outpacing those who did not by 19 percentage points. In another poll, Nixon led Muskie 43 to 35 percent. While both his overtures to the communists and his wage and price controls bothered many to his right philosophically, Nixon once again stood atop a reenergized Republican Party, quick to hold "Salute to the President" dinners and raise money on his behalf.[72] With only a year before the presidential election, Nixon suddenly appeared at the top of his game, his policies politically effective if somewhat disjointed.

To Ruckelshaus, the president's new-found success was the proverbial straw that broke the camel's back, the end of any faint hope that Nixon might still return to his original position. While Nixon might tinker with the economy in a way that fiscal conservatives thought improvident, such as deficit spending or price controls, nothing had happened throughout the year to counter the basic thrust of his new agenda—the conservative swing that doomed his environmental program. Campaigning against Washington worked. Earlier in his administration, Ruckelshaus recalled, Nixon "did not feel that strong and so wasn't comfortable taking on a popular issue such as the environment." As he gained strength politically, however, "he felt he could strike out more." Far from challenging his new assumptions about the environment, his success reinforced them. Elections did turn on the economy and foreign policy, and the environment as a political issue was indeed less consequential.[73]

A more confident Nixon meant harsher public rhetoric. In one late September speech to the Economic Club of Detroit, Nixon lashed out at environmentalists as never before. "How many jobs is it going to cost?" Nixon rhetorically asked. "We are not going to allow the environmental issue to be used sometimes falsely and sometimes in a demagogic way basically to destroy the system."[74] It was still not rhetoric to match that of Stans, and Nixon still thought it prudent to avoid unnecessary antagonism. Nevertheless, his true feelings were evident. Environmentalists annoyed Nixon. If they were willing to launch angry salvos at the administration, then he, in his new-found confidence, was more likely to respond in kind.

With battle lines drawn, NEPA impact statements remained the environmentalists' weapon of choice, one of Nixon's chief complaints. Still angry over what they perceived as improper implementation of the Refuse Act's water pollution permit program, environmentalists sued, arguing that a planned permit for the Grand River in northeastern Ohio first required a NEPA statement. Not only did the program fail to extend to intrastate tributaries, the Corps of Engineers made it a sham by issuing too many permits. If EPA could not have complete jurisdiction, at least the threat of an impact statement might make the entire program too expensive to continue. With this litigation just beginning, the Environmental Defense Fund prevailed in its Tennessee-Tombigbee Waterway suit. The court agreed with the plaintiffs that the first stage of the Corps' three-part impact statement was insufficient to meet NEPA's requirements. Whitaker had warned the White House of just this possibility to no avail. Nixon now stood publicly rebuked, having taken part in groundbreaking ceremonies. The administration did enjoy success in one suit, as the court held that allowing clear-cutting in Alaska's Tongass National Forest did not violate the Wilderness Act or NEPA.[75] It was one victory over the Sierra Club that Nixon undoubtedly savored, although, after sixteen months in litigation, it did little to change his opinion of NEPA or environmentalists.

NEPA, Jackson predicted, would remain "one bright spot" if the pendulum continued to swing against environmentalism. Just as the White House viewed the law as an obstacle, Jackson spoke of the need to strengthen it. "As many of you know," Jackson declared in one speech, "the act was designed with the intent of forcing federal agencies to consider the impact of their programs." Aware of EPA's frustration with agency compliance, stronger amendments were necessary to aid the "lawyer-conservationists." Had Nixon known two years before the role that these lawyers would play, he might never have signed NEPA. To the White House, the new decisions of the fall only reinforced impact statements as a "bombshell out of the blue." In fact, Jackson's comments were somewhat disingenuous, for at NEPA's signing he had no more inclination of the law's breadth than did Nixon. Not only was the impact-statement provision largely added at the insistence of Muskie, the courts' decisions had given it a power its framers had not envisioned.[76]

Muskie agreed with his colleague on NEPA and joined him in bemoaning the administration's increasingly antagonistic position. When the *New York Times* incorrectly reported that Ruckelshaus had offered his resignation in frustration, Muskie recognized a political opportunity. The White House, a Muskie press release charged, blocked EPA's statutory obligations. It was obviously a questionable charge, made in reference to the White House's Quality of Life Review. It was also obviously political opportunism, as much as Jackson's public defense of NEPA.[77] Only a year before the presidential election, both Muskie and Jackson sought to position themselves as the solution to Nixon's growing environmental antagonism.

Although they agreed on such issues as NEPA, the political competition between the two Democratic senators was bound to produce an antagonism all its own. Just as Nixon abandoned the environmental vote, Muskie and Jackson sought to carve out their own niche on the issue. The author of the controversial new clean-air law and the driving force behind the most expensive and stringent water pollution bill ever before Congress, Muskie was clearly the front-runner on the issue, undoubtedly the most popular choice of the environmental lobby. As the original author of NEPA and the sponsor of tough land-use legislation still pending, Jackson too had strong credentials. Still, in the words of Muskie aide Billings, the two "held very different views on certain issues." Derisively described as the "Senator from Boeing" for his promotion of the SST and the airline industry, Jackson supported a greater timber harvest than Muskie thought appropriate. On other issues as well the two parted, the latter arguably more stringent in his advocacy. The solution, Jackson decided, was to couch himself as the reasonable environmentalist. Sensing the same environmental radicalism as Nixon, Jackson declared, "I am a conservationist but not a nut." He supported strong laws, but was "fed up with those who think we can solve the problems of environment by shutting everything down." If he could cast Muskie on one extreme and the administration on the opposite, he would stand as the sensible middle. After Jackson became the first to announce his candidacy, news reports spoke of a possible Muskie-Jackson ticket. In reality, however, their confrontation over NEPA two years before still strained their relationship. Although "cordial" according to Billings, no such partnership was a possibility. If their differences over Vietnam and the economy were not enough, their continued competition for the environmental vote—a competition that Nixon had abdicated—precluded it.[78]

As the end of the year approached, Whitaker wrote Nixon that Muskie "has launched a major offensive against you based on the difference between your rhetoric and actions on the environment." Nixon should demonstrate a "personal commitment" or the issue would hurt him in the following year's election. Given that Whitaker knew Nixon's views, it was in a sense an amazing recommendation. The reversals of the year had obviously blunted neither his optimism nor perseverance. It was, of course, sure to fall on deaf ears, just as before. "You can't out-muskie Muskie" was the only reply. The administration should not appear too stringent against environmental protection, Nixon reiterated once again, but it should keep in mind that the environment was a genuine threat to the economy, and, as in the past, promised nothing but headaches politically.[79]

"International affairs is our issue," Nixon told Charles Colson in another statement unnecessary to make. As everyone in the White House recognized, it was a major factor behind the administration's sudden popularity, as obvious as Nixon's reply to Whitaker's continued environmental advocacy. Nixon had never personally devoted considerable time to the environment relative to other issues, and now, convinced of its inconsequence, he devoted even less. Muskie and Jackson might press the matter as the election approached, but he would capture the public with more diplomatic maneuvering. The following year, Nixon announced, he would travel to Moscow for a personal summit with Soviet leader Leonid Brezhnev. It was, all agreed, another welcomed indication of détente. He would also order another forty-five thousand soldiers home from Vietnam by the end of the year. While the war continued and the White House remained committed to a successful negotiated peace, which appeared unlikely any time soon, any troop withdrawals were sure to find a receptive audience, good for Nixon's political future and the nation in general.[80]

If not foremost in Nixon's thoughts and dominating the news, important developments relative to the nation's environment continued to unfold. Jackson's Senate Interior Committee held hearings on revising the Mining Law of 1872, with the administration supporting reform but not the leasing system that most environmentalists advocated. In line with what the Public Land Law Review Commission had recommended the previous year, the administration endorsed a permit system. While this allowed the Department of Interior to inspect the land and establish regulations before mining commenced, it retained the historic domination of mining over other land uses. Also relative to public lands, Secretary Morton ordered the third and final grazing fee increase. It was, however, an increase of only 3 percent, much smaller than originally proposed.[81]

Morton, reflecting pressure from the White House, announced the first "hardship" exemption to the endangered-species law. The law allowed the Interior Department to lift the ban on the hunting of endangered whales when economic hardship resulted. The beneficiary of Morton's leniency raised some eyebrows — Kal Kan, the dog food manufacturer. By the end of the year exemptions appeared almost a matter of course, a total of thirty-seven resulting in the importation of over thirty thousand tons of endangered sperm-whale oil. In an increasingly rare victory for its environmental staff, the White House announced its support for federal purchase of the Big Cypress Swamp. As Hickel before him, Morton thought purchase would be more effective than regulation in protecting this critical watershed for the Everglades. The White House, however, had taken no position, at least not until Jackson and Florida Democratic senator Lawton Chiles announced congressional hearings to push the matter. Legislation to create a federal freshwater reserve would prove popular, Whitaker lobbied. Noting the electoral importance of Florida, he asked, "What better, higher priority than reelection?"[82]

Outside of administration support for the Big Cypress, Whitaker and his allies in the administration had little else to applaud, their ostracization from Nixon and his top aides complete. Nixon signed legislation to protect wild horses on federal lands, but otherwise his every step ran counter to their position. When news reports indicated that New York City mayor John Lindsay planned more money for police and not the environment, Nixon responded, "Even Lindsay is beginning to learn what issues have appeal."[83] Solidifying its program of environmental restraint as Nixon ordered, the White House mandated that EPA take part in "an early warning system with regard to possible economic dislocations." Before instigating any enforcement actions, EPA would have to notify the Department of Labor, which then would advise the White House. The constraints burdened EPA, most notably when it filed suit against Armco Steel for pollution in Houston's ship channel. William Verity, the president of Armco and a powerful influence in Ohio's Republican Party, complained to Nixon directly, with his complaints ultimately raining down on Ruckelshaus. Ruckelshaus remained amazingly stalwart under the pressure, but his independence was not always easy to maintain. When EPA released its specific emission standards for sulfur oxide from stationary sources of pollution, the last mandated by the Clean Air Act, they were noticeably weaker than the ambient standards released earlier in the year. This made sense according to Stans; the economy was more important than clean air, a "dumb" conclusion in the view of an obviously irritated Whitaker.[84]

Working to shore up its relationship with farmers as well as with industry, the White House announced at the same time that it no longer advocated the abolition of the Department of Agriculture in its reorganization proposal. The farm lobby, now openly hostile to many environmental initiatives, promised to block Nixon's Department of Natural Resources, forcing the White House to relent. Ignoring both this political reality and the fact that Nixon still proposed the Forest Service within the DNR, several environmental groups protested, with the administration's retreat on the pesticides bill still foremost on their minds. Nixon, they claimed, cared more about the farm vote than environmental protection. While this was certainly an accurate claim, it was not necessarily the best example. A better illustration was Nixon's new choice for Secretary of Agriculture, announced in mid-November. The existing secretary, Clifford Hardin, resigned to take a position with the pet-food manufacturer Ralston Purina. To replace him, Nixon chose Earl Butz, who, William Reilly later recalled, "was never on our side," a man "not a friend to [CEQ]." The sixty-one-year-old Butz held a doctorate in agricultural economics from Purdue University and a long record of farm advocacy. He also held strong connections with industry, most noticeably significant stock in chemical corporations. In short, he appeared to offer little help in bridging the divide that existed between the agricultural and environmental communities and their respective advocates within the administration.[85]

The decision to appoint Butz was obviously one that Nixon made directly, but in the waning weeks of the year Congress remained the focus of most significant developments. Muskie led an unsuccessful attempt to derail Butz's nomination, but assisted in the passage of an Alaska native-lands bill that most environmentalists applauded. The final bill presented for Nixon's approval two weeks before Christmas included in most respects provisions that the White House supported. It provided the Alaskan natives with forty-four million acres, a 500-million-dollar payment, and an additional 500 million dollars from a 2 percent royalty on mineral rights. It also, however, added one more critical provision that the administration did not propose: the right for the Department of Interior to withdraw up to eighty million acres for one of the various federal preservation systems before native or state withdrawals. This was, of course, a hotly contested point; all parties recognized that it was not simply a matter of how much land they received as much as it was its quality, whether one found such quality in the land's ecological significance or in its potential for profit. The administration did not insist upon the Interior Department's right of first selection, but with this provision included nevertheless, areas of environmental importance were sure to emerge as a priority.[86]

Nixon had no intention of vetoing the bill and signed the Alaska Native Claims Settlement Act of 1971 on December 18. For Nixon, the bill's attraction came not with its promise of environmental protection, but with the very provisions that most concerned environmentalists. The bill officially ended the "land freeze" that Stewart Udall had issued three years before and explicitly provided for a federal oil pipeline corridor. In essence, the bill eliminated a major obstacle to the pipeline and brought it one step closer to reality. Questions, of course, still remained—Alyeska's ability to meet the Department of Interior's stated stipulations and the adequacy of the department's impact statement—but at the same time the pipeline's fate now rested on these issues and no other. In the words of the Wilderness Society, Alaska was in its "eleventh hour."[87]

If Nixon did not actively resist the native-claims bill that Congress offered him, he promised a battle royal over the water pollution bill that it was debating at the same time. Here, it appeared, Congress might truly force Nixon's hand, a fitting conclusion to a contentious year. Debate over exemptions to endangered-species law, revision of mining law, the impact of NEPA, and the structure and function of the federal bureaucracy had largely set the tone for the waning months of the year. Now, with Muskie and Nixon firm in their respective positions, the struggle over water pollution threatened to produce a new level of animosity.

"We are in trouble on the water quality legislation," Whitaker reported to Ehrlichman in October, the first indication of the dispute to come. It was an ominous prediction, but, unfortunately for the administration, a correct one. A month later the Senate passed unanimously a bill stronger than Muskie's twenty-five-billion-dollar proposal. The bill called for fourteen billion dollars in federal expenditures, half of a twenty-eight-billion-dollar program to build waste-treatment centers and more than double the six billion dollars proposed by Nixon in February. The bill kept both the administration's and Muskie's provisions for tougher enforcement and for extension of federal jurisdiction to all navigable waters. It sided with Muskie, however, in mandating the "best technology available" by 1981, not the best "practical" as the administration's proposal read. To please environmentalists, the bill also called for a national policy to achieve a zero discharge of pollutants by 1985 and for water quality that sustained fish and wildlife by 1981. To attain quality of this level, it provided for a permit program similar to that of the Refuse Act, but at the expense of the states, with more implementation power to EPA.[88]

The Refuse Act program itself, the U.S. District Court for the District of Columbia ruled, required individual impact statements for each permit, effectively terminating the program and leaving the White House little room to maneuver.[89] Nixon, Whitaker argued, had to sign the Senate bill if it were to pass the House intact, an action that Nixon rejected out of hand. The solution, Ehrlichman decided, was to work with allies in Congress to weaken the definition of the term *pollutant* in the bill. In this manner it might mitigate the zero-discharge provision. At the same time, spokesmen should argue that the bill did not consider costs in relation to results. The nation would have to pay twice as much to remove the last 1 percent of pollutants as it did to remove the previous 99 percent. If the White House could convince members of the House that the bill simply did not display an understanding of the technical aspects of pollution control, the question of a veto would never arise.[90]

With Nixon's opposition as firm as Muskie's support, the White House launched a massive lobbying campaign. For over two years Nixon had simply acquiesced when faced with an environmental bill that he thought excessive, but no longer. "Unfortunately," Muskie mocked the White House's position, "it appears that the administration has undergone an environmental metamorphosis, emerging from the cocoon not as a butterfly but as a moth." The administration's implementation of the Refuse Act program was only an indication that Nixon cared nothing about clean water; now voters had proof. It was, all acknowledged, an uphill battle, especially given the vote in the Senate. Resistance made no sense, according to Spencer Smith of the Citizen's Committee on Natural Resources, an amalgam of many environmental groups. Nixon had no reason to make it "such a cause celebre."[91]

If it was an uphill battle, the terrain only became steeper. Just before Christmas, the House Public Works Committee reported out its version of the bill. The committee obviously did not share Nixon's cause célèbre. In spite of the White House's aggressive lobbying campaign, the report provided the administration with relatively little consolation. In place of the no-discharge provision and fish and wildlife deadlines, a national commission was to work with the National Academy of Sciences to ascertain the deadlines' economic ramifications, with its report due in three years. In the interim, the deadlines stood as "national goals" rather than as "national policy." The report pushed back the requirement that industries use the best available technology from 1981 to 1983 and added the phrase "not to exceed" in front of the contract authority provisions. More importantly, however, the report increased this authority to eighteen billion dollars. This was four billion dollars more than Muskie's Senate bill and triple the amount in Nixon's original proposal. Administration lobbying had worked to cast the bill as excessive; the committee obviously did not agree.[92]

Nixon remained undaunted. Rather than perceiving the committee report as further evidence that Whitaker was correct and that continued resistance was futile, Nixon wanted the battle joined when the full House reconvened after its Christmas recess. It was a clear indication of just how far Nixon had evolved over the year. Twelve months earlier, Nixon still sought the political initiative and actively worked to enhance his image with environmentalists. Now he could care less, persisting in a fight that not only appeared hopeless but was sure to wreck his reputation with the very voters he had earlier courted. The new year, an election year, portended new conflict; both environmental decay and those committed to solving it persisted. The Alaska pipeline and the House debate on water pollution alone promised to begin the year just as the previous one had ended.

Free from his desire to win the environmental vote, Nixon was also free from the frustrations that accompanied it. His political stature arguably greater than ever before, Nixon was not about to let the environmental issue spoil his Christmas. Problems obviously existed—a potential war between India and Pakistan, an economy that remained annoyingly sluggish, and, of course, Vietnam. These might keep Nixon awake at night, fueling his anger and political paranoia. The environmental issue would not. It had never been foremost in Nixon's mind, but was now a virtual non-issue, important only to the extent that it hindered solutions to more pressing problems. Leaving for New York to visit his daughters and then settling in for a quiet Christmas at the White House, Nixon had much for which to be thankful. With the successes of the administration's first two years, environmentalists did as well. Given developments of the past year, however, neither was sure to give thanks for the other.[93]

5

"This Political Year" 1972

"I will engage in no public partisan activities until after the Republican Convention," Nixon confidently declared to CBS newsman Dan Rather on the second day of the new year. With all the problems facing the nation, "it will not be possible to take time off for partisan politics." It was obviously an astounding claim. For Nixon to forgo politics was to deny the very core of his professional existence and to recant his greatest strength. The political ramifications of his every move had always been, and would undoubtedly remain, tantamount. Indeed, in the heightened intensity of an election year, where the actions and motivations of all candidates were subject to scrutiny, their popularity constantly gauged and critiqued, success demanded a certain political acumen. Nixon might seek to project himself above the fray much as his mentor Eisenhower, but he had no intention of ignoring the politics of every issue that the new year brought.[1]

In fact, as Nixon sought to cast himself as a statesman concerned solely with the national interest—a role itself that offered political dividends—his staff was already engaged in the arduous task of reelection. Considerable debate existed over whether the campaign should stress themes with broad public appeal or directly cultivate specific voting blocs. With the first polls of the new year indicating a drop in his popularity and with the first primary in New Hampshire looming, Nixon moved quickly to give his campaign the focus that it sorely needed. This focus, of course, reflected the strategy on which Nixon had come to rely—not the "bring us together" theme of his first two years, but the image of a strong conservative leader willing to stand up for what was right. While, on one hand, moving to increase federal spending—a time-honored practice in election years—his campaign would continue to attack government bureaucracy. It would stress deregulation, lower taxes, and zero tolerance for the drug-addicted, unpatriotic, welfare-loving liberals that Nixon insisted threatened the very fabric of the nation. Most importantly, it would build on Nixon's initial success in foreign policy, cultivating his image as a man strong enough to stand up to the communists but smart enough to ensure peace. It would, predictably, have little to do with the environment.[2]

One could hardly blame Nixon. The nation remained riveted on Vietnam, the year beginning with a massive North Vietnamese assault that threatened the survival of the southern regime. Nixon had laid the groundwork for détente with the Soviet Union and formal diplomacy with the People's Republic of China, both of which had historic potential, and, as the previous year indicated, the potential for political gold. Nixon sensed that beyond the bright glare of these momentous events, the environment had begun to fade in public concern. The government, Nixon gauged public sentiment, had begun to address the issue with the successes of his first two years. Problems still existed, but to many voters the matter was less pressing, for solutions were at hand. In the very least, the administration had a record to which it could point, accomplishments that could stand as a defense against the attacks of its environmental-minded critics.[3]

As Nixon denied any political motivation, his Domestic Council met to discuss "selling the President's domestic program in the upcoming election." Outside of the economy, the council agreed, the only issue with any importance was school busing. In the South, a major focus of Nixon's campaign, resistance to forced busing was "virtually the only issue." Nixon should stress his support for equal education, but his solidarity with busing critics. In regard to the environment, the administration should tone down its anti-environmental rhetoric and take what actions it could, those without negative economic ramifications. When pressed, Nixon should stress his earlier accomplishments and always couch the issue in terms of its economic impact. He should deny any animus and at all cost avoid specifics. "Short of major pollution catastrophes," one aide concluded, "the environment will begin to wane."[4]

It was vintage Nixon—keeping the focus on foreign policy, recasting debate to his advantage, and attacking his opponents with a well-financed, dirty campaign. Leading the effort to fill the campaign's coffers was none other than Maurice Stans, the environmentalists' old nemesis. Exploiting his close relationship with industry, Stans did his job well. Raising a record sixty million dollars, Nixon's campaign far outstripped the Democrats, with or without the help of environmentalists. At the same time, the Committee to Reelect the President—CREEP—unleashed its attack dogs on all potential enemies. Authorizing a program of political espionage that eventually included bugging the

Democratic National Headquarters at the Watergate complex in Washington, Nixon demanded that his aides give special attention to his adversary Muskie. Muskie "may have an emotional problem," Nixon told Haldeman; get Agnew and others to go after him. Not only did Nixon's henchmen illegally wiretap the phones of the Senate Subcommittee on Air and Water Pollution, they spread false rumors about Muskie's wife. As for the senator himself, the campaign implied that he had made racist remarks about "Canucks," thus insulting the large Franco-American population of New Hampshire.[5]

A Democratic front-runner, Muskie had his own problems, his staff as divided as Nixon's on the best strategy to employ. In one sense, stressing the environment appeared to be an obvious tactic. Whether it was the sounds of Marvin Gaye bemoaning pollution in his hit song "Mercy, Mercy Me, the Ecology," or the simple fact that membership in environmental organizations continued to grow, one could conclude that the public remained enthusiastic. On the other hand, however, Muskie had hammered away at Nixon's environmental record for over three years with little to show for his efforts. Even as the White House backed away from the issue the previous year, Nixon's poll numbers rose. Perhaps the public cared about the environment just as in 1968, but once again other prominent events overshadowed it. Sensing that the North Vietnamese offensive of the new year clinched the war as the overriding issue of the presidential election, Muskie made a strategic decision not to make the environment central to his campaign. It was, aide Billings later recalled, a mistake. Despite his stellar credentials, Muskie "lost the issue by not stressing it." The environment would play a role in the election, but, with its most forceful congressional advocate deliberately turning his attention elsewhere, obviously not the central role that the problem arguably warranted.[6]

Whether he still anticipated the environment critical to the campaign or simply recognized the election as an opportunity to advance an environmental agenda, Whitaker continued his dogged advocacy. Election or not, however, the results were the same. The White House had struck an initial agreement with Canada eight months before to clean up the Great Lakes, Whitaker noted. With its resistance to banning phosphates firm and with negotiations to formalize the agreement continuing, the White House should consider an "accelerated program" to clean up existing pollution, just as Ruckelshaus recommended. The administration had to do something; a dispute with Canada had the potential to embarrass the administration only months before the election.[7] Also, with Muskie reportedly preparing an election-year bill "to sock us with a huge new [solid-waste] construction grant program," the White House should consider a recycling initiative, either a tax credit as Train and CEQ recommended or a direct subsidy as Secretary of Treasury John Connally advised. To do nothing gave the Democrats more political ammunition.[8]

It did not matter, Ehrlichman concluded. OMB insisted that any "accelerated program" would cost millions and a new tax was out of the question in an election year. Tax credits and subsidies were poor tools to encourage economic behavior, with private industry experts, not federal accountants, better able to determine demand. After Connally had a change of heart and supported the status quo, the matter was effectively dead, any political ramifications with environmentalists notwithstanding. The proposals did not even warrant Nixon's attention, with the president more interested in the Commerce Department's study of the economic impact of environmental initiatives than in more initiatives themselves. Nixon, in short, wanted his own ammunition.[9]

"I have been on the hook a long time to give the President a finite estimate of job losses versus the environment," Whitaker complained as he too waited for the study that Nixon had ordered the year before. When the report finally arrived, it provided the White House with an excellent response to any critic who complained about a lack of new initiatives. The study projected environmental regulations costing through 1976 a rise of one-quarter of 1 percent in unemployment, a rise of half a percent in prices, and a loss of half a percent in the GNP. This translated into four hundred to seven hundred plant closings and the loss of more than 135,000 jobs. While these figures were in one sense nominal, the report concluded that the effects would center on certain key geographical areas, including the Great Lakes. Small businesses, unable to afford the high cost of pollution abatement equipment, would suffer the most, with the negative economic impact sure to increase tremendously beyond four years. The conclusions immediately struck Nixon—the Great Lakes, key to the Electoral College, and the small businessman, arguably the most important constituency of all. To Whitaker, the report was predictable given its authorship and warranted no publicity; to Nixon, it was an affirmation of the correctness of his position.[10]

When it came time to deliver his third environmental message to Congress in early February, Nixon appeared to follow closely the campaign strategy his Domestic Council advocated. He noted the accomplishments of his first term and reiterated his commitment to environmental protection, without mentioning his true reservations. As Train warned that "our opponents will be quick in this political year to seize upon any evidence of backing off or slacking up in interest," Nixon offered few new proposals, preferring instead to stress that the federal government could not do everything. Washington "must provide leadership," but state and local governments were just as critical.[11]

The few specifics Nixon added paled in comparison to the broad agenda he had unveiled two years earlier. In repeating his call for land-use legislation, Nixon included a sanctions provision for noncompliant states, which he had dropped from his previous year's message. He once again announced his support for federal purchase of the Big Cypress Swamp and recommended the addition of 1.3 million acres to the National Wilderness Preservation System. He proposed expanding the endangered-species list and, in the international realm, the creation of a United Nations environmental trust fund. To back up his rhetoric, he issued two executive orders relative to public lands, with one banning poisons for predator control and the other requiring federal agencies to issue regulations for off-road vehicles. Predictably, the message said almost nothing about the issues of air and water pollution, with legislation in regard to the latter set to explode into a contentious election-year showdown.[12]

In essence, the endangered-species proposal was the only addition of any real significance. Nixon's land-use bill remained weaker than Jackson's, which mandated more comprehensive statewide plans. In only requesting plans for areas important environmentally, the administration's bill still begged the question of what land qualified under this criteria, raising doubts about the plan's feasibility. The addition of over one million acres of wilderness was notable, but, when taken in context, Nixon deserved little credit. Just as its predecessor, the administration remained far behind schedule in recommending additions according to the Wilderness Act, with Congress's record of approving those proposed even worse. Nixon's proposal for the international trust fund had potential, but the message included no specific financial commitment, once again raising doubts. In a similar fashion, legislation to purchase Big Cypress remained only a promise; the administration still had not introduced a specific proposal. The executive orders were helpful, but obviously limited given the scope of the environmental problems that remained.[13]

Predictably, the reaction from both environmentalists and Democrats reflected this view. According to Gaylord Nelson, Nixon offered "nothing new" and his record did not support his rhetoric. Accustomed to such criticism, Nixon did not give it a thought.[14] In fact, any personal interest on the part of the president struck his environmental staff as sensational. Just before unveiling his message, Nixon met with Train, Ruckelshaus, and other top officials in the Oval Office. It was a photo session that Train expected, especially in light of the election. "My relationship with Nixon had become ninety percent ceremonial, just window dressing," Train later recalled.[15] However, an offhand substantive comment from the president shocked the CEQ chairman. "Russ, I have something I want you to tell the people," Nixon began. "Last weekend at Key

Biscayne the roads were all clogged, and we've got to do something, perhaps more mass transit. Three-fourths of the cars had only one driver." Train was, in the words of another staffer present, "excited." Proceeding to relay the story in his press conference, Train remained unnerved. "Three-fourths of the cars," Train quoted Nixon, "had a driver."[16]

If enlivened by Train's faux pas, Nixon's message was hardly memorable. "Can your memory bank retrieve the gist of a single major speech on the environment?" the Sierra Club hypothetically asked its members only weeks after the message. "The best evidence of the dilution of environmental problems is revealed in the campaigns of the leading presidential contenders." In short, they ignored the environment; as a political issue, it had suddenly "evaporated."[17]

As a major issue in the presidential campaign it certainly had; as an important issue in its own right it definitely had not. Though the environment was no longer on the front page and absent from most presidential campaign fliers and advertisements, considerable developments continued to unfold. The environment's apparent diminished ability to captivate the public in no way meant that Washington had solved all problems, as Nixon gauged public opinion. In fact, the first few months of the new year brought the most significant developments to date in a number of long-running disputes, developments that previously might have ironically received the press they deserved. Here, behind what election-year rhetoric it offered, the White House's true attitude toward environmentalists remained evident.

In mid-March, the Department of Interior released its long-awaited final impact statement on the Alaska pipeline. Environmentalists had quietly done all they could to delay the statement, first suggesting that too much time had passed since the public hearings mandated by NEPA and then insisting that the Interior Department had not adequately investigated alternative routes. These tactics delayed the statement's release, but did little to blunt criticism. As expected, the statement endorsed the project, noting the years of study and the stipulations placed on construction. While it did not gloss over the environmental concerns that remained—an oil spill in Prince William Sound, for example—it concluded that a raised pipeline on platforms solved most of the problems from unstable permafrost and allowed for the unimpeded passage of wildlife. The statement stressed the economic importance of America's energy supply and concluded that a route through Canada was not in the national interest. It was, according to the leaders of sixteen major environmental groups, a disaster. In a joint letter to Nixon, the group protested that the statement still did not adequately consider alternatives, most notably the Canadian route.

Aware that native claims no longer impeded construction, environmentalists once again sought to extend the court-ordered injunction.[18]

Still locked in battle over the pipeline, the White House took a different tact to meet the nation's energy needs, supporting legislation to exempt nuclear power plants from the impact-statement requirement of NEPA. It was, in the words of one environmental lawyer from North Carolina, "a return to the Dark Ages."[19] Obviously a response to the previous year's debate over the Calvert Cliffs plant on the Chesapeake Bay, and in fear of a "brown out" as several energy experts predicted for the summer, the White House's position struck many environmentalists as opportunistic. Rather than stressing conservation or alternative fuels, Nixon recognized a strong argument to weaken NEPA. Indeed, when the Senate Public Works and Interior committees held hearings throughout the spring, members heard testimony about an array of alleged NEPA horrors, far beyond nuclear facilities. Washington should exempt a number of programs, critics demanded, from proposed highways to water development projects. According to the Sierra Club, "It appears that NEPA may be working a bit too well for its own good," spawning a "crippling backlash." When Congress passed amendments exempting the Atomic Energy Commission, Nixon signed the bill in early June. One proponent of the bill surely reflected the view of the White House: "An American coming home to a blank TV screen and a luke-warm can of beer will care nothing about the reproductive habits of fish in the Mississippi River. He will want the plant on." As the first significant retreat from a cornerstone of environmental law, the amendments appeared to be a manifestation of changing national priorities, for environmentalists an ugly precursor of the future.[20]

A priority for all, of course, was a sufficient energy supply. No one—certainly not a Congress facing reelection—wanted to be blamed for a shortage, which by early 1972 appeared a distinct possibility. Pundits already spoke of a possible "energy crisis." Natural gas posed the most immediate concern, with the Office of Emergency Preparedness warning of possible rationing and rate increases. Ominous signs existed elsewhere. According to the *New York Times*, studies predicted a rise in oil consumption over the decade from 14.7 million to 22.5 million barrels a day, a rate that far outstripped domestic production. American reliance upon Middle Eastern oil posed problems, especially given the strained relations between American oil companies and the Organization of Petroleum Exporting Countries (OPEC). Egypt, reflecting the opinion of many Arab nations, threatened an oil boycott, protesting new American Phantom jet fighter sales to Israel.[21]

In this context one can understand the passage of amendments weakening NEPA and, in a broader sense, Nixon's strong support for greater domestic production. The administration's record in the development of alternative fuels, public transit, and conservation was mixed at best, but to criticize Nixon unduly for his efforts to forestall the predicted "crisis" is to take him out of context. Nixon was not the only reason the nation faced this predicament, and the economical and political ramifications of a shortage in any energy source were real, whatever the cause. Whether the Alaska pipeline or exemptions to environmental law, Nixon's policy carried an environmental cost. At the same time, however, the alternative carried a price as well, one that Nixon had no intention of paying. In an election year, given the same scenario, few politicians would have done otherwise.

Thankfully for all, the "energy crisis" had not grown into the quandary that it became a few years later. It barely garnered more public attention than did the myriad of other environmental issues debated simultaneously. In the House, members wisely cast aside the Harris-Pryor proposal to ban the killing and importation of ocean mammals, the infamous "baby seals legislation" no longer front-page news. To replace it, they favored the permit system recommended by the administration. The White House pressed for Commerce Department jurisdiction, however, angering many environmentalists who advocated the Department of Interior. When the House reported back a bill that split jurisdiction between the two, the issue fell to the Senate.[22] In the Senate, land-use legislation was the issue at hand. Applying considerable pressure, the White House convinced Jackson to drop his own bill in favor of the administration's weaker version. Without Nixon's support, Jackson realized his bill's inevitable demise. Supporting an insufficient program was a bitter pill for the would-be Democratic nominee for president, but it was better than nothing. To gain Jackson's support, the administration promised an advisory board to ensure interagency cooperation. It was little consolation for the environment, however, with the administration's position arguably insufficient to the threat of suburban sprawl.[23]

In mid-April, Nixon signed the Great Lakes Water Quality Agreement with Canada. Predictably, given the administration's position on phosphates, it was not the same agreement promised the previous year. It spoke only of "water quality objectives," relegating specific requirements, at the administration's insistence, to the appendix. These requirements no longer promised an 80 percent phosphate reduction by 1975, but one of only 60 percent.[24] It was, the White House decided, an agreement best downplayed. In a similar fashion, with its strategy in hand, the White House sought to obscure the final report of its own Domestic Council committee on national growth. Unveiling his environmental agenda two years before, Nixon had promised a vigorous, well-planned program. Now, however, the Domestic Council report told the undeniable truth: national growth policy remained mired in questions of jurisdiction and strategy, no closer to reality than at the outset. Despite a year of work, Whitaker lamented, the report offered "no new initiatives." The White House should "announce it in the middle of the other routine announcements of the day, shading it by making it technical." If pressed, spokesmen should dodge the question by referring it to the Department of Housing and Urban Development.[25]

Wisconsin Democratic congressman Henry Reuss, a longtime hawk in the phosphate wars, described the Great Lakes Water Quality Agreement as a victory for Proctor and Gamble and a disaster for Lake Erie. To Muskie, it was a "blatant failure." To a more sarcastic Jackson, it was a "washout." Such sentiments were overly harsh given that the agreement still promised significant improvement.[26] Regardless, outside of the immediate Great Lakes region, few Americans took much notice. Canadians, who had done much to solve the problem from their end, complained about a lack of cooperation, but the technicalities of a bilateral water quality agreement hardly competed with other, more riveting international developments. Quietly, in line with the administration's election-year strategy, the retrenchment in administration environmental policy continued—with little apparent political consequence. Minnesota Democratic senator Walter Mondale wrote that administration intransigence "outraged many of my constituents," but the White House assumed such outrage, if real, would be politically insignificant.[27]

From problems in the water to those on land, environmental criticism obviously was of little concern to Nixon, convinced both of its political inconsequence and the effectiveness of his campaign strategy. In Senate pesticide hearings, the administration pressed for weaker legislative provisions than it had originally introduced, a retreat that Whitaker alone worried might "embarrass" the White House. Although the Tennessee-Tombigbee Waterway remained in limbo pending an adequate court-approved impact statement, the White House still proposed twelve million dollars for construction in its 1973 budget, an obvious slap at critics. In addition, Ehrlichman rejected a CEQ proposal for a White House conference on land use, reflecting once again a strategy to minimize environmental concerns. Nixon might say otherwise in a campaign speech but in private he continued to describe environmentalists as "hopeless softheads" and a lobby best ignored.[28]

One might forget in the spring of 1972 that environmental degradation remained a potent threat. Earth Day, for one, lacked its earlier enthusiasm. Now in its third year, with the celebration officially extended to a week, it naturally attracted less attention than the inaugural. Emotional appeals and bitter diatribes remained expected fare, but somehow the event appeared more routine and less intense. The White House predictably took its share of lumps. Two years before, Muskie reminded his audience, Nixon remarked that it was "now or never" for the environment. With his record since, however, "the President seems to be saying not now and maybe never."[29] Earth Day had, according to the *New York Times*, "incurred the danger inherent in all anniversaries . . . that pious observance may replace inspiration." With demonstrations limited and low key compared to the transcontinental welter two years before, the movement suffered from complacency. Environmentalist David Brower had a different take: "Earth Day started out as an orgasm, and then they couldn't quite repeat that kind of success."[30]

The apparent depreciation of Earth Day hardly signaled the end of the environmental movement. One might conclude—as the White House undoubtedly did—that the diminished stature of the event represented the issue's political impotence. Another might presume that Americans were satisfied or even apathetic. In this way environmentalism appears as a flash in the pan or the dying gasp of 1960s radicalism. More appropriately, however, Earth Day simply proved that the struggle to protect the environment found itself in a new phase. It was not the end but, in a sense, another beginning. Congress continued to advance quietly but assuredly the initial wave of Earth Day–era legislation, changing the nature of the debate. It was arguably a new arena as dependent upon bureaucrats and lawyers as on the grass-roots volunteer. It revolved around legal implementation, the intricacies of interpretation, and the complex minutiae of science. With debate increasingly narrow and technical, and rarely in the national headlines, there existed a "tendency to go to sleep on implementation," according to environmentalist Brent Blackwelder.[31] In addition, the movement had always enjoyed convenient enemies—greedy corporations or ignorant governments. Increasingly, all recognized, solutions revolved around the individual sacrifices of the everyday citizen. In the famous words of Admiral Oliver Perry, "We have met the enemy and they are us." On Earth Day, author Barry Commoner charged that many common conveniences, the same enjoyed by the average housewife, were "ecological idiocy." The car, air conditioning, a large family—all staples of suburban life and all a threat. Clearly, sustaining enthusiasm was no simple task.[32]

Reflecting upon Earth Week, NBC's Chet Huntley concluded, "Celebrants have good reason to fear that the ecological honeymoon is over." The honeymoon, perhaps, but not the marriage. Membership in most major environmental groups continued to climb. New groups, such as Zero Population Growth, dotted the landscape. Politically, if not the most critical issue in presidential elections, the environment remained important in a number of individual congressional contests and at the state and local level. Organizations increased their legal staff, recognizing the battleground of the future. Perpetual fundraising, litigation, and lobbying assumed even greater importance now that the movement faced a more vocal opposition. The initial wave of enthusiasm apparently waning, the movement appeared as just one of many potent special-interest lobbies, facing the eternal competition for the public's attention. In a sense, the era of modern environmental politics had just begun.[33]

Public attention remained riveted on Vietnam and stunning developments in world affairs, of course, dwarfing in political discourse virtually every issue, not simply the environment. In mid-February Nixon left with a large entourage and hundreds of reporters for his historic trip to China. The pictures remain etched in American history—of Nixon meeting with a dying Mao Tse-tung, the famous hero of the Chinese Revolution and a communist of historic proportions, or of walking the Great Wall of China with friendly officials in tow. The summit was important geopolitically and remains one of Nixon's greatest legacies. It was the stuff of history, which Nixon well knew. The fact that it made great television was only icing on the cake. Upon arrival in Peking, Nixon ordered Kissinger and others to wait on the plane until he had completely descended the gangway and greeted Chairman Chou En-lai. A Secret Service agent was to block passage to assure Nixon his moment.[34]

In early May, Nixon went before a nationally televised audience to announce his response to the North Vietnamese offensive, which continued with success. It was a critical moment for Nixon, with his efforts to extricate America on the one hand but his genuine anger and instinctive desire to retaliate on the other. The attack demanded a reaction, but to do so risked renewed domestic upheaval and a disruption of arms negotiations with the Soviets. To retaliate angered the peace lobby, but to do nothing represented surrender. It was, understandably, another moment sure to captivate, history in the making. In the end, Nixon handled the situation well. Reflecting the anger of many Americans, he promised greater bombing and the mining of North Vietnamese ports. At the same time he held out a carrot, promising to stop both upon a cease-fire and a prisoner exchange. The address avoided a call for additional troops and stressed détente with the Soviets, but still sent a blunt, forceful message to the enemy.[35]

Most importantly, Nixon's reaction did not disrupt nuclear-arms talks with the Soviets or preparations for a historic summit. In late May, Air Force One set off for Moscow with an exuberant Nixon inside. "This has to be one of the great diplomatic coups of all time," an equally enthusiastic Kissinger concurred. In reality, the Strategic Arms Limitation Talks—SALT I, as it became known—

was more significant in its symbolism and the future cooperation it foretold than in the specifics of the missile systems it limited. In fact, given the plans of both nations for development and modernization, the narrow confines of the agreement made it almost meaningless in practical terms. Still, for the first time, both nations clearly recognized the wisdom of mutual deterrence and acknowledged the possibility of limits on their destructive capability. In this respect, the agreement warranted the press it received.[36] Once again, only months removed from Peking, Nixon stood before the nation as a great statesman. He had met Soviet leader Leonid Brezhnev, toured the Grand Palace, enjoyed a series of formal banquets, and, upon his return, addressed a joint session of Congress. It all made great press.

By the summer, with the election still months away, the year had already proved memorable. It had been for Nixon a year to savor, as if it all fit in with his grand scheme. Great diplomacy—Nixon's first true love, where he held his greatest expertise and where he saw his most important legacy—dominated the news. The public almost universally welcomed détente, with polls taken after his decision on Vietnam encouraging. A Harris poll found 55 percent supported heavy bombing of North Vietnam, 64 percent the mining of northern ports, and a surprising 74 percent still thought it important that South Vietnam not fall into the hands of the communists.[37] Vietnam remained a political landmine, but everywhere Nixon turned fate smiled upon him. In July, President Anwar al-Sadat of Egypt expelled twenty thousand Soviet military advisors and technicians. A major Cold War triumph, but the United States had barely dreamt it possible.

Announcing a proposal to restrict the busing of students, Nixon stuck to his campaign script. Craftily working with George Wallace to ensure that the renegade Alabama governor stayed within the Democratic Party and did not mount a potentially devastating third-party challenge, Nixon once again positioned himself as a man for the times. The economy, for a change, was an ally. Inflation was down to 2.7 percent; the GNP grew at 6.3 percent; and real income rose to 4.0 percent. For an average family, taxes had dropped almost 20 percent since Nixon's inauguration, while the stock market flirted with an all-time high of a thousand points. The polls proved it was Nixon's year. By early summer, a Gallup poll placed Nixon's approval rating at 61 percent, the highest in almost three years.[38]

As the summer broke, only one major development posed cause for concern politically. In mid-June, Nixon was in Key Biscayne when he learned of the arrests at the Democratic National Headquarters in the Watergate complex. The cover-up began almost immediately, helped by the tremendous media coverage afforded the other momentous events of the day, the same events that obscured the environment. No one, least of all Nixon, thought the incident was the beginning of an infamous national tragedy, and only the *Washington Post* persisted with any degree of investigation. For the most part, the dirty politics inherent in Nixon's strategy worked as well as other aspects of his campaign, that is, quite effectively. Muskie proved to be a case in point. His campaign lagging, Muskie stumped incessantly, with the daily grind of travel and speeches, questions and pressure, slowly taking their toll on the man. Just as a number of crucial primaries approached, disaster struck. Faced with continued allegations of racist remarks and attacks on his wife—most emanating from Nixon allies—Muskie broke down and cried. Standing on a flat-bed truck before a crowd of people and television cameras, Muskie's emotions overcame him. It was, effectively, the end of his campaign. In the following weeks, each successive primary carried disappointment, and by early summer the once front-runner had officially dropped out of the race.[39]

If Nixon needed further proof of the environment's diminished importance in the presidential election, the sad tale of Muskie offered it. The stunning events of the year completely obscured a legislative record unsurpassed in the field. Jackson's campaign was little better, with its candidate mired in his hawkish support for the war. The environment's two leading proponents, unwilling or unable to tout their credentials, were political roadkill only weeks into the official campaign season. No stronger evidence was necessary.[40]

The Democrats were in disarray. South Dakota senator George McGovern and former vice president Hubert Humphrey shredded each other with vicious attacks prior to the Democratic National Convention, the war apparently more divisive to Democrats than to their opponents. When the convention convened in mid-July, new rules allowed representation based not on traditional power blocs or, for that matter, according to any manageable scheme, but according to race, age, gender, and minority interest. The intention was to ensure inclusion; the result was a political sideshow, or in the words of one Nixon biographer, "an undisciplined filibuster, heavily biased towards the radical and the ridiculous."[41] Environmental quality was not forgotten, but it faded nevertheless in the potpourri of specific issues that enjoyed unprecedented attention: women's liberation, homosexual equality, special rights for Mexican farmworkers, compensation for Native American tribes, among numerous others. It was as effective a way to diminish the environment as the White House's conscious efforts to do the same.

McGovern, bloodied, emerged the eventual victor. In essence the zenith of the New Left, the champion of a quick exit from Indochina, McGovern's nomination assured Nixon the vote of many conservative Democrats. He represented to Nixon the perfect liberal foil, the product of a split in the Democratic Party and a man easy to characterize as an uninformed, misguided radical. When, only days after the convention, reports emerged that McGovern's running mate, Missouri senator Thomas Eagleton, had undergone electroshock therapy for depression, Nixon's campaign made the most of the moment.[42] Everything— short of what appeared the relatively minor irritant of Watergate—seemed to go Nixon's way. Stories of electroshock therapy, nuclear warfare, pain in Vietnam and glory in China. Who had time for the environment?

The Republicans were quite the contrast. Convening in Miami in August, they remained cool nevertheless. Focused, optimistic, and moderate to many turned off by the Democrat's spectacle the month before, the GOP appeared as united as a high school pep rally. In accepting the nomination, Nixon stuck to his key themes: the economy, lower taxes, and the importance of negotiating through strength. Absent was the environment, although the omission carried little apparent cost. The first postconvention polls placed Nixon ahead of McGovern by a 64 to 30 percent margin.[43]

The GOP platform largely reflected the White House's policies, the product of a strong administration presence at platform meetings. Just as the Democrats, the Republicans included a statement supporting environmental protection, a plank that administration officials recommended to praise Nixon. Testifying before the platform committee, Train ignored the growing disagreements with his boss: "The President's record is not one of speeches and promises; it is one of action." To Morton, Nixon had offered "spirited and imaginative leadership in the nation's environmental awakening." When it came to the convention, in short, it appeared that even Nixon's disgruntled environmental staff was on the same page.[44]

Ruckelshaus and Train were perfect White House spokesmen, Whitaker insisted as the convention approached. With his growing stature in the environmental movement, Ruckelshaus could "help gain the maximum positive media coverage." Showering his younger colleague Train with praise, Whitaker wrote, "There is no one within the administration who can take your place as the leading advocate on the environmental issue."[45] Whitaker, of course, recognized the reality that went underappreciated in the Oval Office: Ruckelshaus and Train, committed to environmental protection, were a credit to the administration. They might appear 100 percent behind Nixon at the Republican National Convention, but in private they continued their lonely but important efforts to strengthen his policy.

Ruckelshaus, Sierra Club's Berry recalled, was a "gutsy guy."[46] Even as Nixon's campaign sought to downplay the environment, EPA remained its foremost champion. In the weeks before the Republican convention, Ruckelshaus announced a ban on the interstate shipment of pesticides to control predatory animals. More significantly, he announced that EPA denied the request of five major automobile companies for a one-year extension of the Clean Air Act's 1975 hydrocarbon and carbon monoxide standards. The companies, EPA ruled, had to prove that the necessary technology was unavailable. They could not use the cost of technology as an excuse for failure to meet the standards, a decision that in effect locked the manufacturers into catalyst technology, the leading hope for reduced emissions. Technology was sure to emerge as an issue given the law's rigid standards, Whitaker concluded, but Ruckelshaus's decision "puts us on the side of the angels in the minds of the general public."[47] CEQ staffer Alvin Alm was more circumspect. Aware of Nixon's antagonism toward environmentalists and the litigation that would surely follow, Alm warned of possible White House pressure to reverse course. After the five companies sued, generating their own pressure, Alm was blunt: "I believe we can get into real trouble in taking credit for clean air."[48]

Ruckelshaus, meanwhile, continued his efforts. In mid-June, he announced that after a year of court-mandated hearings, EPA planned a complete phase-out of all domestic uses of DDT by the end of the year. The matter was academic to Ruckelshaus, for he assumed that some version of a pesticide permit program would pass Congress. Nixon, however, was furious. "I completely disagree with this decision," Nixon wrote. With farmers an important voting bloc sure to challenge the order in court, Nixon declared, "I want plenty of effort to get it reversed."[49]

Ruckelshaus announced his DDT decision at the United Nations Conference on the Environment, held from June 5 to 16 in Stockholm. The administration hoped for positive publicity and for the United States to take the lead in world environmental affairs. In most ways it succeeded. The conference was a success, for despite ideological, religious, economic, and political differences, delegates from 114 countries attended and agreed on a declaration of principles and an "action plan" to implement them. The delegates adopted a number of American proposals: a ten-year moratorium on whale hunting; an agreement for worldwide monitoring and exchange of information; an ocean-dumping agreement modeled on the legislation still before Congress; and the establishment of an environmental trust fund, first recommended by Train and mentioned in Nixon's February address.[50]

The United States, however, did not completely win over all environmentalists. When developing countries, who perceived environmental regulations as a drain on their growth, demanded compensation, the U.S. delegation objected. The trust fund provided for only forty million dollars in American aid, less than what Train argued was necessary. In addition, several countries objected to the use of defoliants to protect troops in South Vietnam. Together with its bombing, they claimed, America destroyed the region's unique ecosystem. In the words of Swedish prime minister Olaf Palme, "The immense destruction brought about by indiscriminate bombing, by large scale use of bulldozers and herbicides, is an outrage sometimes described as ecocide, which requires urgent international attention."[51]

Despite the conference's obvious success, it was not easy for administration officials to attend. Environmentalist Barry Commoner, who earlier had warned of the threat posed by daily American life, sponsored an "alternative conference" at the same time. When he invited someone from the administration to speak, Ruckelshaus later recalled, "I got the job." It was "a wild group, a mix of anti-war people and environmentalists . . . a super-charged meeting." As Ruckelshaus argued that foreign policy should not dominate an environmental agenda, heckles greeted him. "The vast majority of the audience were expatriate Americans trying to avoid the war," he recalled. "There was some question whether violence would take place and my wife was genuinely scared." Only when famous anthropologist Margaret Mead noted Ruckelshaus's record did the crowd finally calm.[52]

Although worried about efforts to "politicize the conference," Whitaker still recognized its public relations value near the Republican convention. Train did as well, adding that a White House press conference would allow Nixon to "capitalize on the momentum developed at Stockholm." Ehrlichman agreed and, on June 20, Nixon praised the conference as a success to a room packed with reporters. "I am proud," Nixon declared, "that the United States is taking the leading role in international environmental relations."[53]

It was a statement undeniably true. Despite criticism, Ruckelshaus and Train ensured a strong American impact. As Muskie bemoaned what he described as "the limits on free discussion imposed on the American delegation," the delegation itself encouraged less sympathetic nations to comply with international efforts.[54] Cooperation between nations was, and will always remain, critical; pollution knows no boundaries. Criticism on such issues as defoliants in Vietnam or the lack of compensation for regulation could not, therefore, obscure the real gains that the conference achieved nor the credit Ruckelshaus and Train deserved. Just prior to the conference, Train led negotiations on a bilateral agreement with the Soviets to exchange environmental research and information, a direct product of Nixon's efforts at détente. The administration—

including to the extent he participated, the president—was indeed a driving force for reform. Nixon, Train remembered, "was regarded as a very pro-environmental leader in the international community." He "put environmental considerations at a fairly high level around the world."[55]

As long as Nixon maintained his environmental staff, he had a stronger re-tort to critics of his record. Even as Ruckelshaus and Train turned their attention overseas, Secretary Morton announced the addition of eight species of spotted cats to the endangered-species list, including leopards and tigers. Working to protect the environment, Morton and his colleagues shielded Nixon's political flank and mitigated the administration's retreat on the issue. They took what opportunities they could. When just after the conventions the National Wildlife Federation wrote an open letter to both Nixon and McGovern requesting their position on the environment, Whitaker assistant Richard Fairbanks noted the opposition's brief, one-page reply as "weak." The White House, he insisted, should submit a long and detailed response by comparison. When, at the end of the summer, McGovern released a "White Paper" on pollution, raising the matter for the first time, Nixon's staff replied quickly. The administration's record was "one of steady retreat," McGovern's paper claimed. "The only thing Mr. Nixon seems able to recycle is his rhetoric." This was absolutely false, came the response, declaring that the attack was based on "sloppy homework." The administration's record "was unparalleled." It was another example of a well-organized campaign that appeared by the end of the summer well on its way to victory in November.[56]

As the summer slowly ended, the campaigns of both candidates intensified and the environment began to receive greater scrutiny. Whether it was the Stockholm conference, the first salvos by the new nominee McGovern, or simply the fact that Nixon's whirlwind diplomacy had slowed, pundits began at least to acknowledge the issue as a potential factor. A month before the election, the *New York Times* reported that pollution was likely "pivotal" in a number of state and local contests. The League of Conservation Voters, gearing up for its first presidential election, issued a report that chastised most congressional incumbents. Over the past two years, the LCV claimed, the Senate voted "correctly" only 40.5 percent of the time. Nothing suggested that the environment was suddenly a key to the presidential race—it remained "obscured" according to the *Times*—but neither was it an issue that Nixon or any candidate could completely ignore.[57]

One problem for the White House was the final report of the Commission on Population Growth and the American Future, the commission created by the population bill Nixon signed in 1970. The report, in short, endorsed zero population growth, which Nixon had angrily rejected in his confrontation with the Sierra Club's Berry the previous year. Unlike many other environmental pronouncements, Nixon aide Patrick Buchanan warned, this report was sure to attract "generally page one coverage." Not only did many environmentalists argue that overpopulation contributed to all other threats, the report endorsed liberalized abortion laws and was sure to divide the nation. To make matters worse, the Roman Catholic New York Archdiocese released a private Nixon letter opposing the policy that the report endorsed. "Sloppy staff work," Ehrlichman complained. With the report available at low cost in paperback and with extensive television coverage, Ehrlichman recognized that an official White House reception was necessary. This thrust Nixon in the uncomfortable position of publicly thanking the commission while rejecting its conclusions.[58]

Another problem was the negative publicity afforded the annual CEQ report. The *Washington Star* reported that the White House had deleted several chapters that "alienated the energy industry which traditionally supports the Republican Party." With the campaign in full swing, the administration did not want to "stir controversy" with key supporters. The *New York Times* then followed with its own front-page story that the White House planned to delay the controversial chapters until after the election. Recognizing an opportunity, McGovern pounced. Nixon was in "the absurd position of not wanting to receive completed studies that one of its own agencies was trying to submit." It was for the White House a difficult charge to ignore because the reports were in part true. Written by William Reilly, the chapters in question pertained to local zoning and land use and, on first glance, offered nothing incriminating. Whitaker, however, recognized that criticism of local officials, many of whom were Republicans, was not smart as the campaign simultaneously denounced heavy-handed federal mandates. "The trick," Whitaker had first suggested months before, "is to snuff off some of the chapters which are causing problems early in the game."[59]

The White House could not snuff out all problems, although most issues did not so directly involve the presidential candidates. The Corps of Engineers submitted its revised impact statement on the Tennessee-Tombigbee Waterway, which, unlike the partial statement of the previous year, passed judicial scrutiny. Angered by the administration's successful efforts to move the case to the U.S. District Court for the Northern District of Mississippi, a more friendly venue, critics could no longer block construction, which began immediately.[60] Construction had not yet begun on the Alaska pipeline, but the federal court in Washington offered environmentalists no more hope than its counterpart in

Mississippi. The court held that the final impact statement issued by the Department of Interior in March satisfied NEPA, a decision that environmentalists promised to appeal. Litigation had dragged on for much of Nixon's term and the persistence of the pipeline's detractors annoyed Vice President Agnew. Refusing to build the pipeline because of possible environmental damage was "inconsistent with the adventurous spirit of the frontier," Agnew claimed. "Pessimism," in short, guided such "antigrowth" attitudes. Reminiscent of the administration's public hostility the previous year, the statement accurately reflected the White House's continued antipathy toward the environmental community, despite the campaign rhetoric.[61]

The election was too close for Nixon to make such provocative statements, and when he raised the environment in public, it was according to his campaign script. In early September, Ehrlichman arranged a meeting for Nixon with his Citizen's Advisory Committee on Environmental Quality, which Nixon had appointed two years earlier. Although the White House had virtually ignored the group, Ehrlichman thought that positive publicity might counter criticism that the president had abandoned his environmental advisors. "The overriding purpose of this meeting is political," Ehrlichman explained, "to defend our environmental record." It would cover no specific or substantive issues.[62] At the same time, Ehrlichman agreed with Whitaker that the departure of an American environmental delegation to the Soviet Union, part of the bilateral pact recently negotiated, offered another opportunity. Just following this meeting, photographed for the media, Nixon attended the centennial celebration of the National Park System, held at Yellowstone National Park. It too offered positive press free from the constraints of specifics. In private, however, Nixon remained committed to restraining the very cause that he publicly lauded. Even as he visited Yellowstone, Nixon complained to his staff that wilderness areas "are only for rich backpackers who have several weeks vacation."[63]

The campaign script could not cover all contingencies, of course, nor soothe the resentment of Nixon's environmental advisors, who were aware of the private attitudes behind the carefully crafted media events. The situation was bound to produce a public rift despite the election-year loyalty of Ruckelshaus and Train. Only two months before the election, Robert Cahn and Gordon MacDonald, Train's colleagues at CEQ, announced their resignations, much to the dismay of most environmentalists. Cahn avoided direct criticism of Nixon, but acknowledged that "contact between the Council and the White House has at times been less than ideal." The bureaucracy, Cahn complained, had grown slow "in giving weight to environmental factors in decision-making."[64] Obviously more annoyed than MacDonald, who wanted to return to his academic career, Cahn left the exact opposite image of the one that the campaign labored to present. "It was clear," environmentalist Brent Blackwelder recalled, "that the White House was forcing them to do things they didn't want to do." In the words of the *Washington Post*, the resignations "coincide with an increase in political pressures on the CEQ." They were a "setback for environmental quality."[65]

Predictably, Nixon sought more compliant replacements, within weeks settling on Beatrice Willard, a Colorado ecologist, and John Busterud, a former high-ranking Defense Department official. Willard was a lifelong Republican and an avid supporter of the administration. She had a strong relationship with the business community, White House aide Daniel Kingsley wrote, and "is reasonable in her approach to the environment." Her gender was also an advantage in an election year, a fact that Nixon wanted publicized. "Be sure she gets a good ride in the press," Nixon instructed Ehrlichman. Busterud, Kingsley added, "also has a moderate approach on environmental affairs." Both would cause few problems.[66]

"We should force the candidates to face up to the environment," the Sierra Club continued to complain only weeks before the election.[67] It was a lament that by the fall carried less weight than only months before. Nixon, for one, had not been able to ignore completely the environment, which remained a thorn in his side despite the administration's best efforts to couch the issue in its own terms. McGovern, on the other side, succeeded in lobbing several volleys at the White House that solidified his advantage on the issue. Neither candidate, however, pressed the environmental agenda that the Sierra Club thought was essential. The environment remained a skirmish in the war for the presidency as both candidates assumed one political reality: the election turned on other issues. A photograph of a young Vietnamese girl shrieking in terror, her clothes burned off by an American napalm attack, put it all into a different perspective for much of the public. When it came to choosing a chief executive, the environment remained a secondary consideration.

By the fall, the outcome of the presidential election was a foregone conclusion. A desperate McGovern viciously attacked the administration as "the worst leadership in our history," but Nixon appeared unbeatable. In Congress it was different. Pundits predicted a number of close contests turning as much on a broad spectrum of domestic issues as on Vietnam and foreign policy. Nixon could afford to dismiss the environment, dealing with it only when forced or in superficial terms. Congressional incumbents assumed otherwise, assuring that the final weeks before the election were productive despite the momentous events that dominated the national agenda. The Sierra Club might bemoan the lackadaisical attitudes of Nixon and McGovern, but in Congress the competition for votes unleashed a surprising wave of environmental legislation that made such complaints ring hollow. In this contest, the environment won despite its apparently diminished stature.[68]

The first legislation to reach Nixon's desk was the Federal Environmental Pesticide Control Act of 1972, the pesticide legislation that had provoked so much controversy for two years. The bill established a permit system under EPA jurisdiction as the administration first proposed, but included the administration's controversial concessions to farmers. The final bill maintained House Agriculture Committee oversight and required EPA to dispose of canceled pesticides and pay an indemnity for farmers' financial losses. Signing the bill on October 21, Nixon predictably avoided these specifics and portrayed it as a victory for both agriculture and the environment. "We will now be able to ensure that we can continue to reap the benefits which these substances can contribute," Nixon declared, "without risking unwanted hazards to our environment."[69]

Only a week later, on October 27, Nixon signed another bill offered by a Congress anxious over reelection: the Marine Protection, Research and Sanctuaries Act of 1972, the ocean-dumping legislation debated for over a year. A jurisdictional dispute had delayed passage and the final bill was a compromise. It created an EPA permit system, as in both Nixon and Muskie's duplicate bills, but allowed the Corps of Engineers to control the dumping of dredge spoils, traditionally its realm of responsibility. While this and NOAA jurisdiction over future research annoyed most environmentalists, the final bill listed specific types of wastes automatically banned, not originally proposed by Nixon or Muskie. The list included the dumping of chemical and biological warfare agents as well as all radiological wastes. It did not include municipal solid wastes, however—the bill's principal flaw and a long-standing demand of environmentalists. Signing the bill, Nixon once again focused on its strengths and not its weaknesses. The new law was "farsighted," Nixon stated. "Our actions are part of what we hope and trust will be a global commitment to protecting the glory and majesty and life of the shining seas."[70]

With the election only weeks away, Congress was still not finished and presented Nixon with two more bills. The Marine Mammal Protection Act of 1972 emerged nothing like the "baby seals" moratorium originally introduced the previous year. Indeed, the final bill significantly strengthened the permit system that Nixon advocated and which had passed the House in March. It placed a permanent moratorium on the killing and importation of ocean mammals, but allowed for exceptions through a permit system to encourage adequate scientific management. At the administration's insistence, the bill gave the Department of Commerce primary jurisdiction, but mitigated this weakness by codifying the exceptions themselves. In this manner, it ensured that the Commerce Department could not give undue weight to economic considerations at the expense of the environment.[71]

Jurisdictional problems had complicated coastal zone legislation since Hickel's first proposal in 1969, and similar to the ocean mammal debate, the final resolution did not completely please environmentalists. The Coastal Zone Management Act of 1972 created a program of state grants run through the Department of Commerce. The grants were to cover two-thirds of the cost of developing management plans and half the cost of acquiring new estuarine sanctuaries. The bill appropriated for development grants nine million dollars annually for five years, and, for administrative grants, up to thirty million dollars annually for four years. Each state plan was subject to Commerce Department approval, although the Interior Department held the power of veto. The administration's original bill had granted the Interior Department primary jurisdiction over the Commerce Department, but the House Merchant Marine and Fisheries Committee insisted on the opposite and the White House eventually acquiesced. Nixon strongly considered vetoing the legislation, but not because of environmental objections. The bill, Nixon worried, carried too heavy a price tag and might endanger passage of land-use legislation, which Congress had not yet reported. Nevertheless, with the election only days away, Nixon signed the bill and used the occasion as another opportunity to note his concern for the environment.[72]

Environmentalists had little reason to complain, at least with regard to this surprising wave of legislation. Congress had grown more accustomed to debating the battle against communism than the battle against pollution, and the nation had not witnessed such productivity since the early days of 1970. The legislation was clearly not perfect, for the Commerce Department was sure to slight environmental protection when it meant tough economic sacrifices. The end result did not always live up to the potential of Nixon's original proposals. Neither, however, did it represent a complete surrender on the part of the administration, with the final legislation often the best option given the strength of the farm and business lobbies on Capitol Hill. Nixon might have fought harder for stronger environmental provisions, but, given his true disdain for environmentalists, he might as well have simply ignored or vetoed the legislation presented him.

The election, after all, was not enough to encourage Nixon to accept the one bill that arguably surpassed the others in importance, the monumental water pollution legislation that arrived on Nixon's desk with the campaign in its final weeks. It was for Nixon a worst-case scenario, a bill that he viewed as excessive but that Congress correctly recognized as essential. Building in the months before the election, the struggle garnered greater media coverage with each passing week, with both sides refusing to budge. This ensured a political fracas that overshadowed the other bills, exposing both the true limitations of Nixon's policy and the certitude of his assumptions about its political inconsequence.

Water pollution remained a grave dilemma for the nation and, to most environmentalists, the cornerstone of their political agenda. Not only did CEQ estimate the cost of a cleanup at more than eighty billion dollars, one did not have to look far to note the severity of the problem. In the months before the election, Massachusetts banned the sale of shellfish due to deterioration of its water quality, with Governor F. W. Sargent requesting that Nixon declare a state of emergency. Only six weeks before the election, New Jersey warned a number of citizens to boil their drinking water due to high levels of contamination. An EPA study claimed that the water was drinkable, but acknowledged troublesome levels of various chemicals. Water commissioners in New York City estimated their costs alone at almost one billion dollars. Public health officials in many large cities feared an outbreak of disease without similar allocations, which many environmental organizations stressed.[73] In a letter to Edmund Muskie, the leaders of seven leading environmental groups, including the Sierra Club, the National Wildlife Federation, and the Izaak Walton League, described water pollution as the "major conservation and environmental issue before the 92nd Congress." Congressmen on both sides of the aisle felt the pressure. "I am sure," Republican senator Robert Packwood wrote Muskie, "that you have been approached by representatives of the many environmental groups, just as I have been, emphasizing the urgency of a good strong bill."[74]

It was obviously an uphill struggle for Nixon. In March, the full House passed the bill that its Public Works Committee had reported out at the end of December. The bill kept federal appropriations for the construction of waste-treatment centers at eighteen billion dollars, triple the amount that Nixon advocated and four billion dollars more than in Muskie's Senate version. With a conference committee set to resolve the differences between the Senate and House versions—both of which Nixon thought exorbitant—the White House worked to deadlock the committee and prevent any bill. "The environmentalists are going crazy," an exasperated Nixon complained to Republicans who noted that the possibility of a deadlock was unlikely. "The trouble with environmentalists is that everything they do is for the rich."[75] Crucial to Nixon's plan was Tennessee Democratic senator Howard Baker, whom Nixon saw as his most likely ally on the committee. Meeting with Baker in July, Nixon explained that he planned to veto any bill that emerged and that the best option was starting over with the new Congress in January. Baker, recognizing both that the problem necessitated the greater allocations and that the matter had import for his own reelection, refused and implored Nixon not to go through with his veto.[76]

In mid-September, less than two months before the election, the conference committee reported the Water Pollution Control Act Amendments of 1972, which predictably included almost all the provisions Nixon deemed unacceptable. The final bill kept at the expense of the states strong federal jurisdiction over water quality standards and a permit system to achieve them. While it retained the House requirement that industry use the "best available technology" by 1983, not the "best practical" as the White House hoped, it strengthened the House version with regard to the other provisions. Similar to what passed the Senate, the final bill called for water quality that sustained fish and wildlife by 1981 and for zero discharge of pollutants by 1985. It eliminated the House requirement that a national commission study the issue and that Congress pass legislation before EPA implemented the deadlines. Most importantly, the final bill maintained the House's larger federal contract authority, promising eighteen billion dollars in federal assistance to states for the construction of waste-treatment facilities, five billion dollars, six billion dollars, and seven billion dollars in fiscal years 1973, 1974, and 1975, respectively. The only bright spot for the administration was several key phrases. The bill referred to the deadlines as "goals" rather than as policy and added the stipulation "not to exceed" before the contract authority figures.[77]

With the conferee's report sure to pass Congress, Ruckelshaus urged Nixon to sign the bill. When his thirty-three-page "executive communication" leaked to the press, it represented a break in his election-eve public support for his boss and reignited complaints that Nixon ignored his environmental advisors. Nixon had no intention of following Ruckelshaus's advice, of course, perceiving in the new wording of the bill a way out of his dilemma. The phrase "not to exceed," Nixon assumed, might imply that the president did not have to spend the total allocation, only that he not surpass that amount. Because this tactic was sure to face legal challenges, Nixon instructed counsel John Dean to inquire about its legality. When Dean reported that the Department of Justice and OMB agreed that the phrase did allow the president to withhold portions of the money, Nixon felt confident that he could thwart the thrust of the legislation if the full Congress approved the conferee's report.[78]

It did not take long for this to happen. In early October, only weeks before the election, the Senate voted in favor of the report 74–0 and the House followed by a vote of 366–11. Within days, prominent Republicans pleaded with Nixon not to veto the bill as he had threatened. New York congressman Jack Kemp wrote Ehrlichman that McGovern planned to use the pending veto as fodder for a new wave of attacks. "A large portion of the electorate may very well agree with him," Kemp warned. Aware of all the election-eve legislation that Congress then approved, Illinois congressman John Anderson argued that a veto "would endanger the sense of national purpose which has surrounded consensus pollution control."[79]

Within the administration, much disagreement existed. While OMB, the Council of Economic Advisors, and the Department of Treasury recommended a veto, EPA, CEQ, and the departments of State and Interior recommended approval. The remaining departments either deferred to EPA, reported "no objection," or offered "no recommendation."[80] Nixon wanted to pocket veto the bill in order to lessen the political repercussions, but Congress planned to stay in session until he acted. Late on the evening of October 17, therefore, an angry Nixon issued his veto, but only after what he viewed as one final indignity. The Senate that night considered a House report on a separate debt-ceiling bill that Nixon supported, a bill that authorized the president to restrict budget expenditures to 250 billion dollars in fiscal year 1973. When the Senate rejected this, Ehrlichman, who watched from the gallery, quickly announced Nixon's intention to veto the water bill. Nixon planned a veto in any event, but doing so that night sent a message that if the president could not obtain the authority to limit federal expenditures, he would not sign legislation that cost so much and over which he had so little control.[81]

Nixon's veto message focused on the bill's costs. While the bill's intention was "laudable," its total price tag, twenty-four billion dollars, including eighteen billion dollars in federal contracting authority, was "unconscionable." With his "responsibility to protect the working men and women in America against tax increases and inflation," he had no choice. The defeat of the debt-ceiling bill and the passage of the water bill "showed that senators and congressmen are simply AWOL in our fight against higher taxes."[82]

The congressional override was swift, the next day. In the House not one congressman rose in Nixon's defense and the override overwhelmingly passed. In the Senate the result was the same. Environmentalists, joined by the media, understandably lashed out at Nixon. The *New York Times* correctly described the new law as a "critical step towards improving our environment" while questioning Nixon's true commitment. Critics knew that with expenditures spread out over a period of years, inflation was not necessarily a direct by-product. They knew that the severity of the problem demanded strong and immediate action and that no solution was cost-free. In the end, Congress, not Nixon, provided the necessary leadership, adding water pollution control to the wave of its accomplishments just before the election. Congress prepared itself for the election even as Nixon felt confident enough to dismiss the most important environmental legislation in almost two years.[83]

Nixon's campaign strategy, of course, remained intact. Working to mold popular legislation to his policy objectives, Nixon accepted those bills that he thought the nation could afford and rejected the one that he assumed the nation could not. Striving to couch his objections in the best possible light, Nixon attempted to turn debate back to his advantage. The water bill, Nixon insisted, meant more large government, taxes, and regulation—the very thing he opposed, the strength of his campaign. He cared about the environment, but acted only out of economic prudence. "Let's set up the Congress to take the blame for a tax increase," Nixon told Ehrlichman just before the vote to override. "Let them go home and explain that to the folks."[84] Nixon did not succeed in blocking passage of the water bill, but he recognized in it an avenue to continue the struggle. He also recognized that the strength of his campaign lay with other issues, and in this respect he felt supremely confident.

Even as his position on the water bill crumbled, Nixon knew what few in Congress did—that secret negotiations with the North Vietnamese neared a critical juncture, and that, possibly, all sides might reach an agreement before the election. True to form, this occupied Nixon; a peace accord would surely make history, with criticism of Nixon's environmental policy or any domestic issue long forgotten. Throughout October, Kissinger and the North Vietnamese met, ultimately hammering out an accord that provided for an end to the fighting, the withdrawal of American troops, the return of prisoners, and a coalition government in South Vietnam. The problem lay in convincing South Vietnam's president Nguyen Van Thieu, who protested a provision that allowed North Vietnamese troops to remain in his country. With North Vietnam threatening to make the accord public—and thus the American ally the culprit for continued fighting—Kissinger announced on October 26 that "peace was at hand." Only a week after the contentious water pollution debate and two weeks before the election, the statement sent shock waves around the world and reverberated in the homes of every American voter. In fact, Thieu's resistance was understandable, given the threat that the remaining North Vietnamese troops posed, and real peace was not imminent. Nevertheless, the announcement stood as a political coup, another apparent diplomatic triumph for the incumbent that paled all other issues by comparison.[85]

The election was almost anticlimactic, with the result a foregone conclusion. On November 7, Nixon won forty-seven million votes or 60.7 percent of the total, compared to McGovern's twenty-nine million or 35.5 percent. In a stunning triumph and a true landslide, Nixon carried every state but Massachusetts. He earned his victory as much as McGovern self-destructed, but out of the campaign one conclusion was inescapable: Nixon, as always, remained a man for his time, an outstanding politician attuned to the national pulse. He knew early how important environmental quality was to his reelection and his campaign structured its strategy accordingly.[86]

Election day 1972 was not completely rosy for Nixon, however, nor was the scenario so bleak for environmentalists as it might appear. The congressional returns told a different story. Nixon enjoyed no coattails; Republicans lost two seats in the Senate, stretching the Democratic advantage to fifty-eight to forty-two. Although they gained twelve seats in the House, they still remained fifty short of a majority.[87] More specifically, champions of environmental quality—whether Democrats or Republicans—performed well, proving that despite the apparent inconsequence of the issue to the presidential returns, the environment remained a potent political force. The public recognized that despite the recent gains, the threat remained.

From New York to Washington state, the proof was at the ballot box. New Yorkers overwhelmingly approved an astounding 1.15-billion-dollar environmental bond issue. In Florida, it was 240 million dollars; in Washington, 340 million dollars. North Carolina voters passed an "environmental bill of rights," while New Jersey residents rejected a transportation bond issue primarily because of its emphasis on highway construction. All were states that returned Nixon to the White House—two of them by 70 percent or more—and yet they clearly broke with the administration's environmental agenda. It was hardly a mandate to stop "coming up with huge bundles of money to throw at problems," as Nixon described it. Marion Edey, president of the League of Conservation Voters, was ecstatic despite Nixon's triumph. Of the fifty-seven gubernatorial and congressional candidates directly endorsed by her organization, forty-three won. Particularly encouraging were the victories of three candidates in races highlighted by the LCV: the reelection of Montana Democratic senator Lee Metcalf, and the victories in the House of Texas Republican Alan Steelman and Utah Democrat Wayne Owens. A typical environmental clash occurred in Wisconsin's revamped seventh district, where Democrat David Obey defeated Republican Alvin O'Konski. Obey, who strongly opposed a huge underground electronic-communications network, scored ninety of one hundred points in a LCV rating. O'Konski, who favored the project, scored forty. When it came to issues close to home, priorities were obviously different. "The races we won were mostly where opponents were willing to campaign on environmental issues," Edey concluded. "We lost where opponents fogged up their environmental records or managed to divert the argument off the subject"—a tactic that Nixon could appreciate.[88]

Nixon had won his last campaign; the consummate politician would, it appeared, end his career at the top. He might have been happy, but was not. The political resilience of environmentalism played no role in the president's surprisingly sullen mood; inconsequential in his own election, it did not enter his mind. It was, however, the larger issue of which the environment was only a part that made Nixon, in his words, "melancholy."[89] Whether it was the water pollution bill or his frequent inability to block a number of other spending proposals, the conservative revolution that he had come to champion was clearly suffering. For two years he had enjoyed some limited success, but Congress, confident in what it perceived as its own mandate, stood once again in opposition. This annoyed Nixon, with his anger fueling a desire to redouble his efforts. Free from the constraints of the campaign, Nixon planned a new assault, a no-holds-barred effort to take what independent actions he could. Anger was joined with conflict—Nixon remained as persistent as he was consistent.

His loyal cabinet and staff were first to feel the brunt. The day after the election, Nixon left them all dumbfounded with one short demand: their resignations. It was more than the pro-forma requests for resignations that had characterized earlier presidents at the beginning of their second terms. Nixon wanted many of them out, despite the long hours they had labored for his reelection. It was "political butchery," communications director Herbert Klein concluded, and demonstrated "total vindictiveness and insensitivity." Nixon wanted a new team, fresh blood to reinvigorate the revolution he had thus far failed to consummate. New staff and new organization were essential. Congress had never passed his grand scheme for executive reorganization, but Nixon recognized a way to accomplish the same thing without congressional approval. His plan called for four "super-secretaries," four of his closest advisors who would funnel information from the others. Each would hold the title of "counselor" and have jurisdiction over one of four areas: human resources, community development, economic affairs, and natural resources. Technically each existing department would remain, and thus Congress would have no say. He would, however, finally have the tighter management that he deemed essential for the battles to come.[90]

The battle, as Nixon termed it in one interview with the *Washington Star,* was to "shuck off" and "trim down" domestic programs. The man who two years earlier had created EPA now plotted another offensive against a government "too big and too expensive."[91] Predictably, with the election a memory, it did not bode well for the environment. Selected for the position of natural resources counselor was Earl Butz, the champion of farmers nationwide. From now on, Morton, Train, and Ruckelshaus would first have to take their case to a man who obviously did not share their concern. None of the administration's environmental staff had ever enjoyed a close relationship with the president, especially in light of his growing exasperation with their cause. Still, the new order meant a new layer of bureaucracy between the problems they recognized and the ultimate decision makers. If Nixon wanted to ignore the environment completely, his new management made it easy.

The fate of Whitaker, however, was most indicative. For four years he had served as the White House's point man on the environmental issue, first directing an unprecedented agenda that greatly advanced environmental protection and then mitigating his superior's unfortunate policy reversals. The result assured him his fate as a casualty of Nixon's reorganization. "It was pretty clear I was going to get pushed out," Whitaker later recalled. Offered the position of Undersecretary of Interior, Whitaker accepted his new assignment as a good soldier. The pay was only several thousand dollars less, and with his background in geology the position was a natural fit. He still enjoyed government service, and the new assignment allowed him to remain active in a cause he held close. Turning down an offer to join his friend Gordon MacDonald in teaching at Dartmouth, Whitaker did not perceive his new role as a demotion.[92]

Most environmentalists certainly did. Whitaker was not perfect, but he was a proven ally. His new assignment underscored Nixon's intention to abandon the issue, for although Whitaker was still a valued member of the administration, he was no longer privy to the inner circle at the White House. The transfer, Whitaker acknowledged, underscored among environmentalists the sense of administration retreat. This was despite of—or, perhaps, because of—the man Ehrlichman chose as Whitaker's replacement: Richard Fairbanks. Fairbanks was not new to the administration; for over a year he had pushed an environmentalist agenda as one of Whitaker's assistants on the Domestic Council. Like Whitaker, he recognized the environmental threat that remained, and arrived with considerable enthusiasm. He was, however, no Whitaker. A Columbia Law School graduate, he was only thirty-one years old. He lacked his predecessor's environmental experience as well as his personal connections to Nixon. Given Nixon's new intention to limit access to the Oval Office to all but his closest advisors, Fairbanks appeared an unlikely candidate to break through, a thought that perhaps occurred to Ehrlichman as well.[93]

A policy paper submitted just after the election neatly summarized Nixon's second-term goals. The administration, the paper concluded, "should steer clear of heavy federal spending" and address "the difficulties resulting from the present high degree of federal regulation." With regard to the environment, the administration "should encourage rapid development of domestic natural resources" and, specifically, "phase out entirely the federal program addressed to solid wastes." Most importantly, it "should be better attuned to the costs of environmental programs" and allow the state and local governments to take charge.[94]

Clearly, not all was lost. As the year drew to a close, the Forest Service agreed to site-specific impact statements whenever it planned to harvest timber in "de facto wilderness," the virgin forests that environmentalists insisted deserved protection although they were not specifically included in the Wilderness Act. EPA announced a new policy requiring retailers who sold more than two hundred thousand gallons of gasoline annually to offer the alternative of unleaded fuel. A new Congress offered hope for restraint even as the White House redoubled its efforts.[95] Nevertheless, with the election over, Nixon needed no encouragement from like-minded policy experts or strategists. He knew what he wanted and assumed that he knew how to achieve it. As if to give notice of his anger and determination, Nixon ordered EPA to withhold funds from the water bill's contract authority. "I stated," a defiant Nixon proclaimed, "that even if Congress were to default its obligation to the taxpayers through enactment of this legislation, I would not default mine." Citing the phrase "not to exceed" in the new law, Nixon ordered EPA to spend only nine billion dollars, exactly half of that authorized.[96]

If Nixon longed for a fight, he got it. "This is a flagrant disregard of congressional intent," an equally angry Muskie protested, that "demonstrates [Nixon's] half-hearted commitment to the cause of clean water." The executive directors of the U.S. Conference of Mayors complained, as did the National League of Cities. Governors from states set to receive the funds were particularly harsh, and, of course, thousands of letters poured in from around the nation. Predictably, just before Christmas, New York City sued in the U.S. District Court for the District of Columbia. Nixon's order violated the law, the city argued, joined by environmentalists. The court should force the administration to release the full funding authorized.[97]

With a new term before him and his last election behind him, nothing intimidated Nixon. Certainly not the North Vietnamese, who, in the wake of the election, waffled in their commitment to the terms of the agreement tentatively reached. Even as Thieu continued to protest, North Vietnam appeared ready to raise the ante, which outraged an already indignant Nixon. Ordering twelve days of bombing to close out the year, Nixon feared the peace movement as little as he did environmentalists. It was an unprecedented assault, nonstop B-52 carpet bombing of shipyards, docks, radio transmitters, power stations, factories, communications facilities, and, of course, military bases. A wave of terror launched in a season of peace, the "Christmas bombing" was another defiant challenge to all those who stood in his way. Critics pounded him even as he pounded the enemy. "Shame," wrote journalist Tom Wicker. The president "has taken leave of his senses," claimed one senator. He was a "maddened tyrant" concluded another.[98]

The election was over; nothing was going to stop Nixon from achieving his goals. North Vietnam had to reach an acceptable peace or face Nixon's wrath. Congress had to comply with his conservative revolution or he would simply outmaneuver it. Damn the critics and full steam ahead. At the beginning of his first term four years before, Nixon had promised to bring people together. Now, at the beginning of his second, his actions promised to drive them apart. You were either for him or against him; for Nixon, it was us against them. He had long since recognized environmentalists in the latter group, and, with his last campaign now a memory, he had no more reason to hold back. Nixon was bitter and resolute. The lines were drawn.

6

"Get Off the Environmental Kick" 1973–1974

It was great news, so long in coming that it was hard to believe. The Vietnam War would end within days, Nixon proudly announced to a national television audience three weeks into the new year. All parties had agreed to a formal cease-fire on January 27, ending what had become America's longest war. There appeared no better way to begin a new year or a new term. The fighting and divisiveness that had rocked the nation might end and, as Nixon predicted, a "new era of world peace and understanding" might emerge. Nixon's poll numbers soared to an all-time high. Almost seven out of ten Americans approved of the president's job performance. Great news for Nixon indeed.[1]

Of course none of it would last. Not the peace; the accord remained essentially that concluded the previous October, a cease-fire that allowed for a respectable American withdrawal but also for North Vietnamese troops to remain in the south. Nixon had convinced Thieu to agree, but the South Vietnamese leader knew what the future boded. Just over two years later the Americans were gone, the fighting had resumed, and Thieu's regime faced imminent destruction. It was the real end to the Vietnam War.

Nor would Nixon's popularity last; the divisiveness that had come to characterize the Nixon administration grew from more than simply Vietnam. There was a new war brewing, of course, a war between the president and Congress. An angry Nixon had fired the first salvo only weeks after his reelection. His reorganization plans, together with his budget and controversial impoundment of funds, promised to exacerbate an already tense relationship. In time, of course, Watergate would add to the tension and take the nation to new depths, ultimately costing Nixon his presidency.

In late January 1973, however, Nixon was ready for the battle to begin. Confident following the cessation of hostilities in Vietnam and with approval ratings for Congress at an appalling 26 percent, Nixon moved swiftly to drive his conservative revolution home. The *New York Times* predicted an end to forty years of liberalism, a goal that Nixon undoubtedly thought was within his reach. At the end of the previous year, Nixon had impounded 10 billion dollars of a 260-billion-dollar budget. For the new fiscal year, he proposed spending only 268 billion dollars. The cornerstone of the Great Society, the Office of Economic Opportunity, faced complete emasculation. With no tax increase, Nixon promised drastic cuts in health, housing, education, and an array of established social programs.[2]

The environment predictably stood as a major Nixon target. Butz, now operating in his new capacity as natural resources counselor, made this point clear in a policy paper submitted just after the new year. "There are many more important things than the environment," Butz wrote. The issue had not hurt the president in the election and he had no reason to champion the cause now. "In all likelihood environmental problems will be solved by science," Butz continued. Nixon should place environmental protection "in the correct order of priorities."[3] It was, arguably, an ironic statement. The administration's budget—one that Butz supported—called for the elimination of the White House's Office of Science and Technology. For four years the OST had provided valuable data on environmental problems, but now was no longer necessary.[4]

The environment offered millions in savings. With solid wastes a "local problem," the administration proposed slashing the federal waste-disposal program to one-fifth of its current budget, from over thirty million dollars to less than six million dollars. This cut mandated the termination of three-quarters of the staff in the Office of Solid Waste Management. Nixon had just signed coastal zone management legislation before the election, but his new budget provided no additional money for the grants stipulated. It took the persistent lobbying of South Carolina senator Ernest Hollings to prevail upon the White House finally to add just five million dollars in supplemental funds.[5] The administration proposed no additional money for the NIPCC, but not because the White House rejected its staunch pro-industry lobbying. "With the President now so open to the input of the business community into environmental decision-making," Fairbanks explained, "the NIPCC has outlived its usefulness."[6]

Adding insult to injury were those projects that the White House deemed worthy of additional funds. Now that the courts had cleared the way for the Tennessee-Tombigbee Waterway, the administration proposed twenty-five million dollars for construction, more than a 100 percent increase. Although Congress had defeated the SST, Ehrlichman argued that the time was ripe for a new offensive. Rather than propose additional money for the same plane, the administration should simply call it the "experimental ecological transport," or

XXT. The project was exactly the same, Ehrlichman slyly acknowledged. "The name change was only for public relations and political benefits."[7]

With his budget before Congress, Nixon's annual environmental address surprised no one. The message, Fairbanks acknowledged beforehand, "will replay our triumphs of the past" and add "general rhetoric and exhortation." Ehrlichman, terming the Clean Air Act a "complete failure," advised an aggressive defense of the administration's position.[8] Nixon did not disappoint him and essentially declared the environmental crisis over: "When we came to office in 1969, we tackled this problem with all the power at our command. Now there is encouraging evidence that the United States has moved away from the environmental crisis that could have been and toward a new era of restoration and renewal. Today, in 1973, I can report to Congress that we are well on our way to winning the war with environmental degradation, well on our way to making peace with nature." Nixon went on to outline "principles that guide us," explicitly stressing a "balance between economic growth and environmental protection." State and local governments had to take the lead, with costs "more fully met in the marketplace, not in the Federal budget."[9]

The environmental community and many in Congress were in no mood to entertain either Nixon's rhetoric or budget proposals. EPA's budget, according to Muskie aide Billings, was "woefully inadequate."[10] In the words of the Wilderness Society, "There is a current effort to crank up a new anti-environment campaign in the name of jobs, industry, the economy and other motherhood issues." The administration's budget, the Sierra Club added, "raises profound questions about continuing the voyage without paying the fare." If Nixon succeeded, "there will be hard times for programs dear to environmentalists." Clearly not all shared Nixon's declaration of victory and his demobilization of the troops.[11]

Nixon's opponents, of course, had their own agenda and, as the year unfolded, their own questions. Watergate was no longer a scandal that the White House could easily dismiss as a "third-rate burglary." By the time of Nixon's environmental address in mid-February, the trial of the Watergate burglars had ended in convictions and Nixon actively worked to ensure their silence. As the Senate Democratic caucus voted unanimously to establish a special committee chaired by North Carolina senator Sam Ervin to investigate the White House's involvement, the growing cover-up consumed Nixon. Ehrlichman suggested enlisting Whitaker, who as an environmental advisor had never been privy to the dirty politics of his superiors. Nixon thought better of it, however, concerned that Whitaker's loyalties lay as much with the environment as with the administration's political future.[12]

"We've got everybody worrying at this point," Haldeman wrote in his diary. Fear of the web of lies untangling "deeply shook me," Ehrlichman added in his memoirs.[13] Congress had Nixon on the defensive with Watergate, even as Nixon's aggressive policies challenged the status quo on Capitol Hill. The Vietnam War was over as far as America was concerned, but the new war between the president and Congress continued. The nation's environment arguably lay in the balance.

The stage was set for another round of battles over the condition of the nation's land, air, and water, the pillars of environmental degradation whose controversies continued to simmer. The latter two ignited early in the year with court decisions, neither one pleasing the White House. Just as Nixon delivered his environmental address, the U.S. Court of Appeals for the District of Columbia Circuit ruled on the automobile companies' suit for an extension of the Clean Air Act's hydrocarbon and carbon monoxide emission deadlines, the suit filed the previous year. The court upheld Ruckelshaus's denial, but remanded the question back to EPA to determine definitively if adequate technology was available. Butz made it clear where the White House stood, providing Ruckelshaus with "guidance on the implications" of EPA's ultimate decision. Ehrlichman notified Nixon that he had advised EPA "to say a number of things designed to sock the consumer into a realization that the cost of the environment will be very high and that the air quality laws are very impractical."[14]

Within weeks, EPA hearings began. In the year since the original denial, science had developed adequate catalyst technology on prototype cars. Because the cost of expanding this technology to mass-produced models was extensive, the companies argued that the necessary technology was unavailable, a conclusion that environmentalists vigorously challenged. General Motors Corporation, anxious to curry favor with the administration and improve its image with the public, offered a solution: interim standards establishing a two-tier system. California, GM suggested, would have to meet the rigid EPA standards and thus require catalysts on all models. The rest of the nation would only have to meet 50 percent of the standards. This allowed more time for study while making the effort feasible for the companies. The proposal constituted a significant weakening of the law, but Nixon insisted that EPA accept. "Pull Ruckelshaus in when he goes too far," Nixon wrote an aide upon hearing of the offer. "I want sympathetic consideration of this request." Under pressure, Ruckelshaus announced in early April that EPA agreed. The issue was "terribly complex," Ruckelshaus tried to explain. It was inexcusable, the National Resources Defense Council replied. The administration had "sold out to big business."[15]

Both, in retrospect, were true. In one sense pressure to meet the deadlines quickly on mass-produced models led manufacturers to focus almost entirely on catalysts for the traditional internal combustion engine when, in fact, more experimental technology offered the promise of even greater benefits. Both a rotary engine without a catalyst and a carbureted version of a stratified charge engine had shown under initial tests that they could meet the EPA standards, although no hope existed for rapid implementation in mass-produced models. In time, new studies indicated that catalyst technology itself produced its own dangerous emission, sulfuric acid. On the other hand, however, these emissions were nominal at best. In order to reduce them further, EPA later dropped its requirement that cars carry fuel pumps. This and other technological advances prevented the environmental calamity from sulfuric acid that the Ford Motor Company predicted.[16] The relatively minor sulfuric acid issue aside, therefore, no study could deny the law's obvious overall benefits. The rigid EPA standards without a doubt significantly reduced hydrocarbons and carbon monoxide pollution, which constituted one of the greatest threats to the nation's air. It was for the companies only a matter of the bottom line; had EPA not forced them to spend the necessary money, the nation would have paid the price in its air quality. It was indeed complex, but Nixon's order to compromise was more in the interest of the auto industry than the nation's air.

It was also, the White House calculated, in its own political interest. The companies unleashed a furious public relations campaign to convince Americans that the rigid standards necessitated a dramatic increase in the price of a new car. Company engineers insisted that the cost would rise by an average of almost one thousand dollars, a figure outrageously high. They also maintained that fuel efficiency would suffer, that cars with catalysts would consume more gas and thus cost consumers an additional two hundred dollars annually.[17] Environmentalists and their champions on Capitol Hill did their best to counter such claims. "I strenuously disagree with those who would suggest that we must choose between protecting public health and providing a viable transportation system," Muskie argued. "By applying equal amounts of ingenuity, productivity, and activity, we can cope with it." The Sierra Club was more emphatic: "The health of the whole nation is at stake. We fought too hard and too long for a good clean air law to see it destroyed now."[18] It was, however, a tough argument to debunk, as the White House knew. Well-known social and political pundit Paul Harvey asked, "Did we go too fast in demanding depollution? Looking at the mathematics of this subject, we've made a very costly boo-boo." In Ohio, several entrepreneurial mechanics recognized an opportunity to turn public fears into profit. Noting that nothing in the EPA regulations prevented the removal of the equipment, they offered to do the job for less than one hundred dollars, a cost they maintained the customer would recoup after just a year of filling up their tanks.[19]

Nixon, under assault as the noose of Watergate tightened, could ill afford to alienate potential supporters. Indeed, while the public demanded clean air, the elections suggested that support for environmental restrictions had limits. It was a political decision for the White House, but one not based in reality. Not only did catalyst technology fail to drive up the price of a new car to the extent predicted, but it increased rather than decreased fuel efficiency. Models with catalysts proved over 10 percent more efficient, exactly the opposite result of the auto companies' predictions. Industry studies, to the contrary, did not consider the role of automatic transmissions, air conditioning, and, most importantly, auto weight in drawing their conclusions.[20]

The court decision on water pollution was less complex, but no less controversial. In early May the U.S. District Court for the District of Columbia agreed with New York City that the administration's impoundment of water pollution funds violated the Water Pollution Control Act and ordered the full allocation released. The court rejected administration arguments that the phrase "not to exceed" gave Nixon authority for impoundment and that the funding levels were so high that the construction industry could not meet the demand. It was a welcome decision; given the fact that urban growth far outstripped the construction of waste-treatment centers, the nation needed every penny. Some truth existed in administration arguments that the law placed so many requirements on states for them to receive the cash that dispersal of the funds according to schedule was in doubt. Nevertheless, it was not this that bothered the administration, but simply the level of federal spending for a problem that Nixon now thought would be best addressed at the state level.[21]

A broader question remained, however. Did a president have the right to refuse to spend money allocated by Congress? To Nixon the answer was clear, and not just a matter for the environment. While appealing the water pollution decision, the administration began impounding funds allocated in an array of spending bills, which predictably spawned a new wave of litigation. To Congress the answer was just as clear, but obviously not the same. It was surprising given two centuries of the republic, but no clear answer existed, with the matter left to the courts and Congress. As debate over budget reform therefore began, Nixon and his opposition found their initial disagreement over water pollution expanded into an acrimonious struggle over the balance of power. The battle between Nixon and Congress continued to rage.

The slow atrophy of adequate land-use legislation was no less frustrating than the roadblocks to clean air and water, and in this case the culprit was as much Congress as Nixon. Over three years earlier Jackson had introduced a strong bill mandating comprehensive statewide land-use plans, a proposal the White House defeated in favor of its own weaker version. Nixon's bill provided for state plans covering all areas of critical environmental importance, with its principal flaw its failure to define definitively exactly what land qualified under this criterion. With the new year came new proposals, unfortunately ones that made the White House version appear strong by comparison. First, Wayne Aspinall, the father of the Public Land Law Review Commission, introduced legislation combining land use with the question of public lands. Aspinall's bill required federal agencies to review all public lands, which environmentalists recognized might lead to multiple-use designations on land already protected as wilderness or wildlife refuges. Next came a proposal by Arizona Republican Sam Steiger. Steiger's bill omitted all requirements that states regulate areas of ecological importance, the central element of the administration's bill. It simply called on states to develop their own plans with little or no federal guidelines. It was, as Whitaker would later term it, "a no strings attached categorical grant of $200 million." Despite the funds, Washington had no way to determine if the plans were adequate or even if the money went to land use in the first place.[22]

The White House offered little hope. A central tenet of Nixon's conservative revolution was state autonomy, and one could argue that even his weak version was at odds with his own recent rhetoric. With his political opponents on the attack, Nixon's hopes rested on solidifying his conservative base, the same constituency that Steiger represented. It was a vocal constituency, as Jackson, the foremost advocate of land-use planning, knew. "I have cast my last vote for you," one man wrote Jackson. "Evidently you think the government should have control over every facet of our lives, and that is fascism."[23] Jackson did his best both to defend his position and persuade Nixon to remain firm in support of his own bill. It was a frustrating endeavor. "I am concerned that the President's failure to stand by his position represents more than an abdication of leadership on one crucial legislative measure," Jackson lamented. "If there's been a presidential change of heart, the Congress and the American people have a right to know."[24]

Jackson had good company in the early months of the new year. At almost every turn, environmentalists met frustration. Train recommended a renewed effort to establish a national growth policy only to have Ehrlichman cite an article by University of Pennsylvania professor Edward Banfield as a refusal.

Banfield wrote that congestion was decreasing, not increasing, and that the problem arose from "changes in the state of the public mind." Banfield was correct, Ehrlichman noted; the only solution was a change in public values, not new government programs. Undaunted, Train then suggested a renewed effort in family planning, only to face rejection again. "There is little to be gained," one White House aide cryptically concluded.[25]

Fairbanks, still settling into his new position, complained that Morton, Train, and, most importantly, Ruckelshaus ignored him as he attempted to quell their protests. Butz replied with a letter to the trio reminding them that he was their "liaison" to Nixon and that while they could recommend topics for "the agenda," he was their only avenue of dissent and the final arbiter of their objections. Ehrlichman was blunt with Fairbanks, telling him not to worry, that "Ruckelshaus is off base."[26] As this unfolded, Laurance Rockefeller resigned as chair of Nixon's Citizen's Advisory Committee on Environmental Quality. For three years the White House had largely ignored the committee, but in resigning Rockefeller offered only muted criticism. Nixon's first term had accomplished much, Rockefeller declared, but "progress must continue in the second." Rockefeller's replacement, Henry L. Diamond, was not so restrained. "While we understand your responsibility for safeguarding the economy as a whole," Diamond wrote after only weeks on the job, "you should not neglect environmental protection."[27]

Reflecting the protests of Nixon's environmental staff, Canada blasted American compliance with the Great Lakes Water Quality Agreement signed the previous year. The administration, the Canadians complained, had fallen behind in its promised construction of waste-treatment centers and had reduced its contribution to the International Joint Commission, necessitating cuts in its Great Lakes field office. It had also failed to deliver the necessary monitoring and surveillance equipment required in the agreement.[28]

Equally troubling was the administration's insistence upon an increase in the timber harvest from the national forests, which the White House's Cost of Living Council said the public should expect for the next several years. Currying favor with key congressmen and bowing to the intense lobbying of the Weyerhauser Corporation, the administration cited a 17 percent increase in lumber prices over the previous year. The administration, Butz announced, planned to sell 11.8 billion board feet of timber in calendar 1973 and fiscal 1974, an increase of approximately 10 percent over previous estimates. At the same time, the Department of Agriculture issued a policy directive requiring the Forest Service to prioritize its programs. In light of the lumber situation, the timber harvest would receive the greatest attention and, more importantly, the greatest share of Forest Service funds.[29]

It was an easy position to take, especially given the famine rhetoric of the timber industry. Just as in the past, Nixon's position won the bipartisan support of politicians from timber-producing states, including Jackson, thus muting the criticism that Nixon's position arguably deserved. In any event, Nixon could point to his support for new wilderness areas in the eastern part of the country as proof that he had not forgotten the environmental amenities of the nation's forests. The Wilderness Act prescribed that all potential wilderness "be untrammeled by man," but with high population density east of the Mississippi and with 87 percent of the 187 million acres of national forest land in the West, few eastern forests qualified. The legislation that Nixon supported allowed for the Wilderness System to include not only virgin forests, but land restored to its primitive character. With such a criterion, the administration proposed 184,000 acres of new eastern wilderness. Following this, the White House proposed the addition of another million acres for the Wilderness System drawn from throughout the nation.[30]

Nixon was no environmentalist, however. The administration remained behind schedule in proposing new wilderness according to the statutory requirements of the Wilderness Act, and legislation for new eastern wilderness was set to pass Congress with or without White House support. Given his many disagreements with Congress, resistance made no political sense. As if to remind critics that his position on this bill did not dampen his support for the timber harvest, Nixon leveled a broadside against wilderness advocates. Their claims that the harvest threatened wilderness were "unfounded, misleading or exaggerated." The Forest Service added that environmental concerns exacerbated an already troubled timber industry, potentially raising prices by 60 percent, an outlandish prediction by almost all accounts. More to the point, Nixon's second wilderness proposal included no national forest land. Just as in the past, the administration relied on the Department of Interior, not the Forest Service, for its wilderness designations. This ensured that many of the nation's most notable primitive areas remained open for the timber harvest.[31]

The conclusion of the Forest Service's Roadless Area Review and Evaluation (RARE), initiated in late 1970 as an attempt to reconcile which primitive forests deserved wilderness protection, only compounded environmentalists' disappointment and anger. In total, the Forest Service identified approximately fifty-six million "de facto wilderness" acres throughout eleven western states. For further wilderness study it recommended just over twelve million acres, with the remainder, more than three times as much acreage, released for "multiple use" development. The areas identified for possible protection were, predictably, those with the least feasibly marketable timber. The outcome obviously owed more to trepidation over the timber market than to the objective criteria of the Wilderness Act.[32] Angered, the Izaak Walton League filed suit to block the Forest Service from clear-cutting on the Monongahela National Forest in West Virginia. Unlike their unsuccessful 1970 clear-cutting suit, the plaintiffs did not base their objections on NEPA or the Wilderness Act but on the seventy-six-year-old Forest Management Act of 1897. This legislation allowed harvesting on mature trees previously marked. Clear-cutting, the new suit maintained, harvested more than just these trees, an argument that won a temporary court injunction and thus once again found environmentalists attempting to halt administration momentum.[33]

In the White House protests from environmental groups fell on deaf ears. Just after Nixon's environmental address, the leaders of several prominent organizations asked to meet with Nixon. The White House did not reply for almost three months, and then issued a curt denial. Environmental lobbyists, Fairbanks later acknowledged, "very seldom had contact with the White House." CEQ remained "the lightening rod for dealing with environmentalists" even as its influence with its superiors waned.[34] When CEQ revised its guidelines for agency implementation of NEPA, making its standards more stringent and thus provoking protests from throughout the executive branch, the White House ordered most of the new guidelines removed.[35] When CEQ issued its annual report, Nixon ignored that it still placed the annual cost of cleaning up pollution at over 250 dollars per family. The report, Nixon proclaimed instead, illustrated what progress had taken place. "In place of organizational disorder and fragmentation, we have developed institutions capable of dealing with environmental problems in a systematic and effective way," Nixon replied. With new laws, "we have made substantial progress in defining problems, establishing goals, and designing strategies for abating pollution and preserving our natural heritage."[36]

There was, of course, some truth in Nixon's statement, although the thrust of his remarks completely distorted the report's conclusions as well as the reality of the environmental threat that remained. When at the end of his comments Nixon briefly acknowledged that "the job still remains," he stressed private initiative rather than government action. "In the final analysis, the struggle for environmental quality rests with the citizens of our nation." It was by all appearances another presidential statement of victory in a battle far from concluded.[37]

Having dismissed the environment, Nixon saw a better use for Ruckelshaus. Ruckelshaus's independence had frequently annoyed his superiors, but Nixon recognized that it was exactly this trait that made his EPA administrator so popular. His stellar reputation, especially among the growing number of administration foes, offered an opportunity for political advantage. L. Patrick

Gray, the existing director of the Federal Bureau of Investigation, had become embroiled in the expanding Watergate probe and a replacement was necessary. The White House needed someone with connections to the administration, but one whose appointment would not raise the eyebrows of critics. "Our old friend Mr. Clean," as Nixon somewhat sarcastically referred to Ruckelshaus, was the perfect selection. "I think the rest of the country respects him," Nixon said, and no one could accuse the White House of appointing a political lackey.[38] Ruckelshaus welcomed the opportunity for all the obvious reasons. The new job offered more responsibility and authority, not to mention money and status. It was, of course, a new challenge. "There was no sense of frustration when I moved," Ruckelshaus later recalled, although the growing constraints he faced at EPA surely made his decision easier.[39]

It was without a doubt a blow to all those who looked to EPA to stem the tide of administration retreat. Ruckelshaus had established a fledgling agency with questionable authority as a major force in domestic policy; he arguably remains to this day the agency's most accomplished administrator. It was, thankfully, a blow softened somewhat by Nixon's selection as Ruckelshaus's replacement: Russell Train. Train's decision to take the EPA post was as easy as Ruckleshaus's decision to move to the FBI. "The action had really moved from CEQ and its policy focus to EPA and implementation," Train explained, understating the poor standing of CEQ within the administration. "It made sense," William Reilly, a later EPA administrator, agreed. "CEQ had a very fast start, but when the president became wary, the handwriting was on the wall." EPA's legislative mandate assured it a vital role as the struggle over environmental policy continued, making it an agency not so easily ignored.[40]

Ignoring EPA, of course, was exactly what Nixon had in mind. Nixon's appointment of Train in no way signaled a renewed commitment to environmental protection, but just the opposite. Anticipating criticism if he were to appoint someone overtly hostile to the environmental agenda—criticism he could ill afford with each passing day of the Watergate saga—Nixon recognized Train as a popular choice. He did not intend, however, to give Train free reign. Even as Train insisted upon written confirmation that he would have final authority over the substance of all EPA regulations, the White House made it clear that it wanted no more Ruckleshaus-like independence. In Train's initial discussions about the job with General Alexander Haig, who had risen quickly to the top levels of the White House staff, Haig stressed the need to place environmental protection in the broader context of administration policy. Later, just before the official announcement of the appointment, Nixon met with Train and reiterated the same marching orders. Environmental policy, Nixon told Train, "was moving into a new and difficult period of maturity." The "earlier first blush of emotion and commitment" had passed and, as the new EPA administrator, his job was to "balance environmental protection with other pressing needs."[41]

Train was sure to test this mandate, but the realignment of Nixon's environmental staff, coming so soon following the transfer of Whitaker, underscored the difficult road ahead. To replace Train at CEQ, Nixon settled on the former governor of Delaware, Russell W. Peterson. Although Republican Party chairman George Bush warned that Peterson might prove too forceful an environmental advocate, the White House assured Bush that Peterson understood his assignment. Peterson's first name was all he had in common with his predecessor; without Train's reputation, he could not exert the same influence. After Peterson's selection, many agencies did not even know of his appointment; the White House sent no memorandum announcing the choice. One agency head spoke with Peterson several times before realizing that he was not just bantering with a former governor.[42]

Peterson knew CEQ's bleak future just as well as Train, for the White House had predictably targeted the council for major budget cuts. An OMB study recommended "reducing [CEQ's] size, role and impact," only narrowly rejecting complete abolition. "This reduces environmental advocacy," OMB wrote, "which is in keeping with the policy of reducing the size of the Executive Office." All recognized that CEQ, without the forceful Train at the helm and the money that it needed, would exist as a pale shadow of its former self. The years that followed were, in the understatement of one observer, "not very distinguished."[43] To this extent at least, Nixon had accomplished his goal.

Much more, of course, hindered completion of the environmentalists' agenda. Vietnam no longer overshadowed the issue, but the nation's attention remained riveted elsewhere nevertheless. By the summer of 1973, this meant, of course, Watergate and the apparently dire status of the nation's energy supply. To an extent, these two issues defined the remaining months of the Nixon presidency, forming the backdrop not only for environmental policy but for all important issues for national debate. In the growing glare of presidential scandal and, to a lesser degree, the nagging threat of an energy shortage, nothing could compete. The momentous first months of the year did not unfold well for the environment, or for Nixon and the nation.

Nixon knew his conservative revolution, his entire presidency, indeed his very legacy was on the line. With Ervin's Senate committee beginning its investigation, he moved quickly to put out the fires that threatened to consume him. After one of the original defendants agreed to tell prosecutors all he knew, a flood of confessions followed. Resignations and plea bargains, one by one creeping ever closer to Nixon's inner circle, threw light on White House complicity. Maintaining both his innocence and his determination to uncover the whole truth, Nixon appointed Elliot Richardson, his Defense Department secretary and, like Ruckelshaus, a man of unassailable integrity, as his new attorney general. After the Senate demanded a special prosecutor for further investigation, Richardson appointed Archibald Cox, a Harvard law professor, to the task. By summer, the Senate had begun its own nationally televised public hearings and the nation faced a drama delivered straight into its living rooms.

All the issues then unfolding, from the budget and pollution debates to the timber harvest to the fate of CEQ, registered barely a blip on the national radar. Rather, the sensational charges that Vice President Spiro Agnew accepted kickbacks as governor of Maryland captivated the public. By the summer the astounding Watergate resignations of Haldeman and Ehrlichman, with the latter obviously tremendously important for the environment, dominated the news. For four years no one on Nixon's staff had wielded more power on environmental policy than Ehrlichman, now just another casualty sacrificed to protect the president. He had led the administration's retreat on the issue, but in Nixon's first term his presence as a reformer was hard to deny. In retrospect, many environmentalists were willing to overlook his later years in favor of his earlier accomplishments. "Overall, he seemed fairly sympathetic to the issue," recalled Laurence Moss, then director of the Sierra Club. "I liked him as a person," added Train. "He was extremely helpful to me on a number of occasions."[44] Ehrlichman's political demise was not necessarily good news to those who continued to wage the forgotten struggle for the nation's environment.

Increasingly isolated, with his congressional foes on the offensive, Nixon knew the scandal ate away at his authority and eroded hopes for his conservative revolution. The year had begun with some hope, but any administration momentum had quickly stalled with each passing week and each new Watergate revelation. If amidst the turmoil he could find common ground with his political enemies, it was not in his continued proclamations of innocence but in his determination to avoid an energy shortage. Just as the Watergate scandal exploded, with environmental policy hanging in the balance, the nation once again flirted with the possibility of an inadequate supply of oil, coal, natural gas, and other valuable energy sources. A familiar scenario in many respects, the situation now appeared even more ominous than before. This time, it appeared, the long anticipated "crisis" might actually prove to be a reality.

The previous year Nixon had reacted quickly and forcibly when facing similar dire predictions, working to weaken NEPA and to expand domestic energy supply. It was not necessarily in the best interest of the environment, but, given the situation, it won support from both sides of the aisle and made political sense. The new year — the new threat — prompted a similar reaction, both from Nixon and from many of his congressional foes. Even as increasing numbers of Democrats denounced the administration's agenda and called for Nixon's political head, many were reticent to stand up for the environment when facing the possibility of "brown outs," rationing, or worse. They sensed, just as the president, that voters were more than willing to accept environmental trade-offs when it came to their cars, their homes, and the many conveniences of their daily lives. Watergate eroded his authority, but on this issue Nixon appeared to enjoy more support than on any other.

America had grown into a superpower on a diet of cheap, plentiful, indigenous energy sources. With 6 percent of the world's population, it accounted for almost 33 percent of the world's energy consumption. From New York to San Francisco, the American public consumed natural resources without a second thought. Homeowners flooded their houses with light, even when not home; many citizens kept their homes as toasty as an oven in winter and as cool as a refrigerator in summer. Driving a gas-guzzling car a block for a pack of cigarettes made sense. Electric toothbrushes, combs, tie racks, and hair dryers helped define American daily life. The problem, of course, was that the indigenous energy sources that the public took for granted were no longer plentiful and thus no longer cheap. Even as the nation careened into the worst political scandal in its history, Jackson spoke for many Americans facing an end to their cherished lifestyle: "The most difficult problem facing the nation today, either internationally or domestically, is the energy crisis."[45]

It was a difficult problem, with no single culprit. Overconsumption certainly played a part, but it was more than simply the public's voracious appetite. After all, experts maintained that the world still contained enough oil, gas, and coal to last for over a century. Simply put, while Americans faced a shortage of supply, there was no physical shortage in overall world reserves. It was as much a problem of poor planning, unfortunate geographic and political considerations, limited technological capabilities, greed for profit, and, yes, federal restrictions, many designed to protect the environment. Since the New Deal, federal energy policy revolved around keeping costs as low as possible to stimulate use and thus the common good. This policy contributed to the postwar economic boom, but exhausted almost all readily available domestic reserves. As national demand expanded, so did American reliance upon foreign imports, most notably from the Middle East and the Organization of Petroleum Exporting Countries. A new unity among OPEC members intent upon driving up prices spelled trouble for Western industrial consumers, not to mention OPEC's anger over the Western alliance with Israel. A number of alternative sources of energy existed, including solar power, geothermal energy, and even the possibility of nuclear fusion, but over the years the nation had never embarked on any coordinated, well-funded program of development. As a result, options such as these remained limited and distant. Without any similar program of conservation, which required sacrifice and thus serious political ramifications, many looked to expand domestic production. This meant, however, more strip mining, more off-shore oil drilling, more exploration into pristine wilderness, and, potentially, more nuclear energy. In many ways it simply meant relaxing environmental standards in one form or another. Energy-related industries pointed to environmental restrictions as the primary culprit, even as they hoped to parlay the situation into increased profits. It was a policy minefield, any action rife with negative consequences and with agreement on only one point: the status quo was clearly unacceptable.

"Dogmatic environmentalists," Ehrlichman told the Economic Club of Detroit just before his resignation, were a major cause of the nation's predicament. "You've got to get it across to them that there's a cost to environmental protection that's very much involved in this whole subject of energy."[46] It was a sentiment reflected in two special energy messages that Nixon delivered to Congress in response to the unfolding situation. In April, Nixon ordered Morton to triple the acreage leased for oil drilling on the outer-continental shelf. He also ordered an end to the Mandatory Oil Import Program (MOIP), which placed a quota on oil imports to increase domestic production. Environmentalists complained that an end to the program might lead to increased use of oil at the expense of other cleaner fuels and that the order meant more oil vessels on the seas and inevitably more spills. While encouraging conservation and calling for deregulation of natural gas—a clean fuel—Nixon also stressed the need for nuclear power and more deepwater ports capable of handling supertankers. The former increased the problem of radioactive wastes, while the latter raised the specter of a major oil spill. The administration argued that since deepwater ports were usually miles off shore, the risk to the mainland was minimal. Environmentalists countered that the ports necessitated the transfer of oil to smaller vessels for the trip ashore, as well as encouraging the construction of more refineries and petrochemical plants nearby. Nixon concluded by lambasting critics of the Alaska pipeline and proposing new leasing of oil shale lands. This involved huge open pits akin to strip mining and complicated the problem of overburden.[47]

In June, Nixon reiterated his call for action. Once again he endorsed the

Alaska pipeline, describing it in letters to key senators as "the highest priority among my legislative initiatives." Although he ordered all federal agencies to reduce energy consumption by 7 percent, the thrust of his message involved government reorganization. In place of his earlier proposal for a Department of Natural Resources, which environmentalists welcomed, Nixon now proposed a Department of Energy and Natural Resources. More than just a name change, the department would deal "exclusively with energy," Nixon declared in his memoirs, ignoring all the department's environmental obligations. Nixon also proposed an Energy Research and Development Administration, a new agency whose primary mandate included nuclear technology more than solar and wind. To coordinate energy policy, Nixon issued an executive order creating an Energy Policy Office headed by former Colorado governor John Love.[48]

It was no coincidence that Nixon stressed the Alaska pipeline. Just as oil shortages appeared imminent, the U.S. Court of Appeals for the District of Columbia Circuit dealt the project a severe blow. Acting on an appeal by environmentalists, the court overturned the lower court's ruling the previous year that the Department of Interior's impact statement satisfied NEPA. Ruling that questions of fact remained, the court placed a new injunction against construction pending additional inquiry. Given the situation, pipeline supporters quickly introduced legislation to exempt the project from NEPA, which gained support and passed the Senate thanks to Agnew's tie-breaking vote. Within weeks, a similar bill passed the House overwhelmingly, and all that remained was for a conference committee to iron out the differences between the two bills.[49]

The Senate version required the owner of a vessel carrying pipeline oil to face personal liability for the first 14 million dollars in damages following an oil spill, with the next 100 million dollars paid from a fund created by taxing oil companies at five cents a barrel. It also exempted from price controls wells that produced less than ten barrels a day. These provisions, Jackson argued, ensured the nation against potential oil spills and encouraged conservation. The administration objected, despite criticism from environmentalists. Because almost 20 percent of American oil came from wells that produced less than ten barrels a day, prices would remain too high, "untenable" in the words of OMB. In addition, strict liability might discourage companies from investing in the project.[50]

Disagreement over the specifics of the pipeline authorization remained, but through it all one fact was obvious: concern for energy was about to turn the tide against environmentalists in a struggle they had waged since before Nixon took office. "When political and economic pressure is applied, NEPA is not worth a damn," an obviously frustrated Wilderness Society concluded. The congressional votes were "an open assault on NEPA," the *Washington Post* added.[51] It was the type of criticism from environmentalists to which the administration had grown accustomed. The only difference was that it was now aimed as much at Congress as the president, a strong indication that energy concerns altered the terrain in the struggle to protect the environment. On this issue at least, Nixon found support even as his authority crumbled elsewhere.

It all came to a head in the fall. The summer Watergate congressional hearings uncovered the existence of a taping system in the White House, which energized both congressional Democrats and special prosecutor Cox. Both demanded access to the tapes, only to have Nixon's claim of executive privilege block them. The potential for an energy shortage, manifested throughout the summer by rising gas prices and periodic brown outs, added to a sense of impending disaster, that events were spiraling out of control and were certain to explode into something big. It was, of course, more premonition than paranoia, for the incredible events of October made the entire summer appear nothing but prelude. The environment was long forgotten, with its fate nevertheless determined by the climactic events of the day.

On Saturday morning, October 6, the holy day of Yom Kippur, Egypt and Syria attacked Israel. Shocked Israeli troops retreated, leaving the matter as much to Washington as Jerusalem. Three days later Agnew announced his intention to resign, having struck a deal with the Justice Department to plead guilty to tax evasion. Once again the public looked to Nixon, everyone aware that with Watergate his selection as vice president might carry additional significance. On both counts Nixon moved swiftly, ordering Israel resupplied and selecting House Minority Leader Gerald Ford of Michigan as the new vice president. Both actions won applause. The public remained staunchly behind Israel, and Ford was amicable and personally popular. He was, most importantly, a moderate at a time when Nixon's conservative agenda alienated so many in Congress. His selection, one could argue, indicated just how concerned Nixon was over the scandal, moving to mend fences rather than advance his agenda.

Both actions came with serious consequences, however. The selection of Ford obviously determined America's next chief executive. The consequences of aiding Israel were more immediate. Waves of C-130 transports arrived daily and Israeli troops slowly pushed back the Arab assault. With Israel the obvious victor and the United States pressing for a cease-fire, OPEC retaliated in the one way it could—ordering a complete oil embargo on America. For the United States it was the proverbial straw that broke the camel's back; the long-predicted and long-feared "energy crisis" had finally arrived in full force.

October carried still more surprise. Amidst the international and domestic turmoil, the U.S. Court of Appeals ruled that Nixon had to surrender the Watergate tapes subpoenaed by prosecutor Cox, and Cox then rejected an administration proposal to release summaries. The situation left him no alternative, Nixon assumed. He had to fire Cox. On October 20, Nixon ordered Attorney General Elliot Richardson to carry out the task. Richardson refused and resigned. The order then fell to Ruckelshaus, who likewise refused and resigned. Finally, Solicitor General Robert Bork fired Cox, but by this point the damage from the "Saturday Night Massacre" was obvious.

NBC news reported, "The country tonight is in the midst of what may be the most serious constitutional crisis in its history." Clearly a gross exaggeration, the report nevertheless summarized the impact of Nixon's order on the public. As Nixon appointed a new prosecutor, Houston lawyer Leon Jaworski, a man he hoped would prove more compliant, his approval ratings fell to an amazing 17 percent.[52] For the first time substantial numbers of congressmen from both parties called for impeachment. It was the beginning of the end.

"It is announced that Saudi Arabia has cut off its oil supplies to the United States," journalist Elizabeth Drew noted in her journal. "Can't think about that now."[53] Drew was not alone, but neither she nor the millions of Americans riveted to the scandal could long ignore the reality that the oil embargo unleashed. By the end of the year gasoline prices in some areas had almost quadrupled. Many filling stations closed on Sundays, after doling out dwindling supplies to long lines of angry motorists during the week. Bribes and fights were common. In one city a struggle for gas led to murder. "Topping off" became a new national neurosis, the attempt to keep one's tank perpetually filled. After one motorist in Pittsburgh purchased eleven cents' worth of gas, the attendant spat in his face and a fight ensued. Boston police reported that the number of automobile arson cases more than doubled. The majority of the torched cars, it turned out, were gas guzzlers attacked in protest.[54]

In cities from coast to coast, local officials worked to limit energy use. The New York City Port Authority announced that unlike previous years no decorative lighting would adorn the city's bridges during the Christmas season. Many merchandisers across the country similarly scaled back their holiday displays. Energy concerns soon prompted layoffs, with economists predicting a dramatic rise in unemployment the longer shortages continued. This came simultaneously with a significant increase in the consumer price index and a drop in the stock market. Oil supply, it appeared, exacerbated an already troublesome inflation rate. Schools closed early; airlines reduced daily schedules; states lowered thermostats on government buildings and speed limits on state

highways. The Woman's Christian Temperance Union suggested limiting production of alcohol to save energy. Pundits predicted the cessation of major
sporting and entertainment events, at least those held in large venues. In Eu-
rope and Japan, more dependent upon Middle Eastern oil, it was worse. Great
Britain ordered a shorter work week; Japan declared a state of emergency; rationing became the order of the day. In only three months, from October to
December, the entire industrial West appeared on its knees, desperate for help.
It was hard to miss.[55]

And it was an opportunity Nixon could not miss. The situation demanded
government action, but for Nixon it also was a welcome diversion from his own
troubles, if not completely. It offered a chance to appear presidential, to stand
before the nation as a leader, and to demonstrate that Watergate did not paralyze his administration. Nixon made the most of it. On November 7, only
weeks after the Saturday Night Massacre, he went on national television to announce "Project Independence," his program to make the nation energy self-
sufficient by 1980. Appearing calm, relaxed, and fit, he likened his proposal to
the Manhattan Project and the Apollo space program. Given his earlier proposals, the thrust of the program was hardly surprising: more use of coal, increased
outer-continental shelf oil drilling and oil shale leasing, more reliance upon
nuclear energy, and final approval of the Alaska pipeline. The address gave cursory attention to conservation measures, urging carpooling, lower office thermostats, and fewer commercial operating hours, among others. His proposals
for a maximum fifty-five-mile-per-hour highway speed limit and continuation
of daylight savings time were significant, but did not change the reality that restraints on consumption were largely limited and voluntary. Nixon noted that
if the crisis remained rationing might prove an unpleasant but necessary measure, but it appeared more a hollow threat than an imminent possibility. The
emphasis remained on increased production, and the address left no doubt that
environmental restrictions were a major problem. For one, Nixon proposed,
Congress should exempt power plants from regulations that inhibited them.[56]

The message emboldened those who had long sought a relaxation of environmental law. "It is apparent that the growing dependence on imported energy must be offset by the development of indigenous energy sources," lobbied
California governor Ronald Reagan. California's own off-shore oil "was estimated at upwards of twenty billion barrels."[57] The coal industry obviously
agreed and attacked as impractical the Clean Air Act's sulfur oxide emission
standards for stationary sources of pollution. This came just as the administration announced another weakening of the law's auto emission standards.
The data used to determine the 1976 nitrogen oxide standard was faulty, EPA

declared in granting the auto companies a one-year extension. It was the truth, but, following so closely the administration's recent compromises with regard to hydrocarbons and carbon monoxide, environmentalists assumed the worse. According to the Natural Resources Defense Council, further relaxing the standards was "a shocking attempt to make American's lungs bear the burden of the administration's failure to take meaningful steps to improve our short-term energy situation."[58]

The NRDC was unduly harsh, for the influence of industry was substantial given the situation. Nixon, weakened by scandal, was in no position to advance painful and undoubtedly unpopular conservation measures. He was, in fact, taking meaningful steps to address the shortages, just not those that the NRDC wanted. He had not completely ignored the demand side of the equation, even as his efforts stressed increasing supply. He had encouraged the development of clean, alternative sources of energy, even if the thrust of his program was to remove the roadblocks to traditional fossil fuels. In any event, it might have been worse. With the coal industry actively lobbying the Department of Interior to lift its 1971 temporary moratorium on new coal leasing, which was still in effect, Secretary Morton announced a continuation of the status quo. He did allow new short-term criteria that made it easier for established companies to expand operations to meet energy demands, but, given the momentum and power of industry, he might have just given them carte blanche. Years later many environmentalists had not forgotten Morton's courageous stance. He was "one of the best Interior Department secretaries ever," recalled Joe Browder.[59]

As if in answer to Nixon's pleas, the conference committee reported out an Alaska pipeline bill within a week of his address. The final bill kept the Senate liability and price-control provisions, which Jackson supported and the administration opposed, but otherwise fulfilled the worst fears of Browder and his allies. With the oil embargo, it was hardly a surprise. "To preserve the 7,680 acres that would be occupied by the pipeline seems an inordinate price to pay for fuel rationing, cold homes, and blackmail by the Arab world," concluded California Republican congressman Craig Hosmer. The report quickly passed both houses of Congress and Nixon signed it into law on November 16. The Federal Land Right-of-Way Act of 1973 explicitly authorized the pipeline and prohibited further environmental review. It provided sixty days in which opponents might mount a constitutional challenge, but given the national uproar over oil shortages, such a challenge appeared futile. The courts lifted the injunction which had blocked construction for so many years and Nixon had finally won a battle he had waged since his first inaugural.[60]

The whole situation frustrated Muskie—the strength of industry, the relative impotence of his environmental allies, and, in his view, the apparent willingness of the public to comply with the administration's proposals. The pipeline had raised a chorus of critics only three years before, but final approval of the project appeared a forgone conclusion and, for much of the public, a welcome development. Protest appeared to flicker out quietly. His colleague Jackson had, for one, emerged as a vocal proponent of the pipeline only to witness his popularity rise. Increasing numbers of polls began to indicate a drop in public concern for the environment. The election had suggested as much, but for the first time a greater percentage of Americans rated a shortage of energy as more important than pollution. Don Nicoll, Muskie's aide, lamented the situation, but questioned the death of the environmental movement that so many now predicted. "To date there has been little effective, public rebuttal or even analysis of the myths about the energy crisis and its relationship to environmental protection programs," Nicoll wrote. The picture was "very gloomy," but Muskie should persevere.[61]

Nicoll was correct, of course. American environmentalism was far from dead; the energy crisis just appeared at the time a blow from which the movement had little hope of recovering. The environment was as much a victim of the energy crisis as its cause, but on this issue at least Nixon appeared to have the momentum. It was Nixon's only taste of success, a fact that he undoubtedly bemoaned.

The end of the year brought little relief. With his instincts telling him to take the offensive, Nixon began a tour of the South in what turned out to be a vain attempt to rally support. Although cheering crowds greeted him at every turn, he could not hide from the reality that only his energy policy had won any degree of support. Hounded by a media in a frenzy from the scent of blood, Nixon felt compelled to deny charges of illegality. "People have got to know if their president is a crook," he emphatically declared, hands clinched, in a press conference in Orlando, Florida. "Well, I am not a crook." Although Nixon had planned to make the statement, it was a rare political blunder. Comedians and late-night talk-show hosts soon mocked the comments, and to this day the quote stands as one of the most famous in American history.[62]

It was easy to mock. In an attempt to defuse criticism, Nixon agreed to hand over to the court the tapes subpoenaed by Cox. The result was an uproar over an eighteen-minute gap in one of the key recorded conversations, an obvious attempt to erase incriminating evidence. Nixon's secretary, Rose Mary Woods, bravely claimed it was an inadvertent mistake on her part, but the public was in no mood to give the president the benefit of the doubt. Nixon's own lawyers now urged him to resign while the House Judiciary Committee began preparations for impeachment hearings.

Angry and defiant, Nixon forged ahead. In private consumed with Watergate just like the rest of the nation, in public he did his best to give the impression of business as usual. This, of course, meant the energy situation — and more bad news for the environment. Under pressure from the White House, the Department of Interior announced its intention to issue a new environmental impact statement on oil leasing and drilling in the Santa Barbara Channel, the scene of the disastrous 1969 spill. Two years earlier the administration had announced that it would not allow drilling to resume on most wells, prompting several oil companies to sue. Regretting its decision, the White House now searched for ways to reverse itself. Assuming that the resumption of drilling would instigate new litigation from environmentalists, the Interior Department calculated that a completed impact statement removed potential roadblocks. In short, it facilitated bringing the oil to market. The administration's intentions were obvious, but, because of the scandal, nary a peep of protest was heard outside of Santa Barbara itself.[63]

Recognizing an opportunity to turn the tables and criticize Congress, Nixon noted that legislators still debated the majority of the administration's energy program, including his proposal for a Department of Energy and Natural Resources. The country could no longer wait, Nixon declared in early December. He would have to act unilaterally once again, announcing the creation of a new Federal Energy Office to replace the Energy Policy Office he had created only months before. The new agency combined more energy-related functions from other departments and would have to suffice until Congress finally moved, Nixon explained. As Nixon appointed Deputy Secretary of Treasury William E. Simon to head the new agency, John Love, who had just arrived in Washington to lead the old EPO, left in a huff, understandably angered by the sudden turn of events.[64]

Although criticism from a weakened president failed to worry Congress, Nixon still had a point; unlike the White House, Congress had yet to take action to address the immediate situation. Thirty-two congressional committees had collectively held over 650 days of hearings on more than a thousand energy-related bills, but there was little to show for the effort. There was another shortage, one could fairly claim, a shortage of action.[65] The result was the Emergency Petroleum Allocation Act of 1973, which complemented Nixon's agenda. It too sought to stimulate domestic production, in this case by raising the controlled price of domestic oil to $5.25 a barrel, a significant dollar-per-barrel increase. It also exempted from controls new wells or existing ones that operated in excess of 1972 volume. Higher prices in one sense promoted consumer conservation, but, at the same time, encouraged companies to expand operations and exploit new reserves. In any event, the law empowered Nixon's new agency with emergency powers to allocate scarce fuel supplies. Simon responded by ordering a cutback in jet-fuel production, directing refineries to make more heating oil and less gasoline for the coming winter months, and providing more fuel to industry to prevent factory shutdowns and layoffs. The law also passed Nixon's fifty-five-mile-per-hour speed limit. Just like Nixon's program, it promised quick relief but came with an environmental cost.[66]

Congress and the courts provided environmentalists with consolation, although they received virtually no press in the crisis-laden days of the end of the year. Just as Nixon signed the emergency energy legislation, the U.S. District Court for the District of West Virginia ruled against the administration in the clear-cutting case that environmentalists had filed only months before. Clear-cutting did illegally harvest young trees, the court held. More significantly, Congress passed the Endangered Species Act of 1973. The new law expanded federal jurisdiction to species "threatened" as well as "endangered," and prohibited harassment as well as simple killing. It also allowed federal jurisdiction over "critical habitats," areas vital for the species survival. Arguably one of the most significant wildlife bills passed during the Nixon years, the new law barely registered with the public.[67]

Engulfed by Watergate, the White House not surprisingly had little to do with the bill. While Nixon signed it, he worried that its appropriations were too high and searched for ways to limit its impact. OMB reassured him that "the normal budget process was a means of control" and, regardless, "Interior and Commerce might implement strict management guidelines to hold down costs."[68] With the Forest Service issuing another scathing report attacking environmentalists, the administration appealed the clear-cutting case only to witness new litigation arise in regard to Alaska. According to the native-claims bill signed two years before as a necessary prelude to pipeline authorization, the Department of Interior was to select land for one of the nation's preservation systems. The department, environmentalists now protested, proposed too much land for national forests and not enough for wildlife or wilderness reserves. This was not the case, the state government and the natives protested simultaneously; the department had not allowed them the best land for development. Construction was set to begin on the pipeline, but the future of Alaska remained as contentious as ever.[69]

No one was happy. Not environmentalists, who, despite the new endangered-species law, remained downcast in the face of the energy crisis. It was an "environmental sellout," in the words of an angry Train. "A country that runs on oil had better run fast," the Sierra Club sarcastically warned.[70] And not consumers, many of whom found adjustment to energy scarcity difficult and lashed out at government despite the lack of more coercive conservation measures. The Thanksgiving and Christmas season were hardly festive, with fewer cars traveling the nation's roads, especially on Sundays. Businesses dependent upon a mobile America—hotels, fast-food restaurants, tourist attractions—suffered. Truckers, angry over the new speed restrictions, blocked highways and prompted in some states a response from the National Guard. Even industry and its political allies complained that Washington had not taken their interests into account. "The solution for this fuel mess," the lieutenant governor of Georgia told one farm organization, "is to ride mules, burros, donkeys, horses and jackasses up and down Pennsylvania Avenue and show those folks what pollution really is."[71]

As the end of the year approached, Nixon struggled to prove at least publicly that Watergate did not paralyze his administration. Despite his obvious troubles, he labored to cast himself as a leader up to the energy crisis. Ordering the lighting on the national Christmas tree dimmed, he traveled to California on a commercial jetliner, not Air Force One. Walking the aisle in the coach section, shaking hands and making small talk with fellow passengers stunned to meet him, Nixon gave every impression that he understood the hardship created by energy shortages. He, too, was willing to sacrifice for conservation. It was all symbolism, of course, which could not erase the black cloud of scandal that followed him. Nixon was no happier than the rest of America.

The gloom carried into the new year, brightened only by the knowledge that the previous year was over. It rained incessantly at Nixon's San Clemente home, reflecting the mood of the first family holed up inside. Although his approval ratings stood at 29 percent, Nixon braced himself for his return to the nation's capital and the war with Congress that would surely resume. Boarding, on January 13, a small government plane for the transcontinental flight—another gesture in response to the energy crisis—Nixon planned a new wave of legislative initiatives, a renewed effort to prove himself undaunted and indispensable.[72]

His proposals ran the gamut, from campaign-finance reform to education to aid for farmers. Although many Democrats found the proposals a pleasant surprise, nothing indicated a shift in environmental policy. In his much-anticipated State of the Union address, Nixon noted his administration's accomplishments, including the environment. He called for land-use planning, if only for a pale imitation of the legislation originally proposed. It was, however, more a matter of what he omitted than what he included. For the first time in four years Nixon sent no environmental message to Congress, a clear indication of both his legislative priorities and his preoccupation with Watergate.[73]

Nixon did deliver another energy message, which better reflected his true view of environmental regulations. Ordering the Department of Interior to increase once again outer-continental shelf oil drilling, he threw all caution to the winds. The department, Nixon ordered, was to lease ten million acres by 1975, a tenfold increase over the present rate. Still frustrated that Congress had not passed his Department of Energy and Natural Resources, Nixon proposed an alternative, the Federal Energy Administration. This new agency, he hoped, stood a better chance of quick passage. If Congress agreed, it would preempt the FEO just created, combining its functions with the energy responsibilities of the Cost of Living Council.[74]

Nixon's instructions, one aide wrote, were to "prepare as soon as possible legislation that would remove all environmental roadblocks to energy production and supply by canceling environmental inhibitions."[75] Nixon was in no mood to consider other contributing factors, namely the complicity of the oil industry in limiting supply and driving up prices. This was exactly the culprit according to a growing number of congressional Democrats, who cited new polls indicating that much of the public questioned corporate innocence. Muskie led the skeptics and viewed the entire crisis as a "phony issue." In the words of aide Billings, the crisis was "just the antagonists using the issue."[76] Pressing the matter, Muskie and his colleagues introduced legislation for a corporate "windfall profits" tax that they insisted would recapture ill-gotten gains. It was a direct assault upon the oil industry, as direct as Nixon's simultaneous order to gut remaining environmental regulations.[77]

Neither Nixon nor Muskie had a monopoly on the truth. The "Seven Sisters," the world's seven leading oil companies, recognized that the gradual influx of minor independent competitors threatened their control of the retail business.[78] Using the Arab oil embargo as an excuse to claim a shortage of oil, they stopped supplying off-brand independent dealers with their surpluses as they had in the past. They simultaneously deactivated a large percentage of their brand stations leased to independent dealers and, in time, planned to reintroduce their own self-service "independent" stations. These stations would sell gas for a few cents less than the major brand, but would not offer credit or extra services. For the present, however, their strategy meant less gas, higher prices, and longer lines. To this extent, the oil industry was complicit. Muskie and his allies had a point, although to suggest that industry was the sole culprit was as patently false as placing the blame entirely on environmental regulations, the unspoken conclusion of Nixon's energy message.[79]

Nixon held the upper hand, vetoing the "windfall profits" tax when it passed Congress and proposing legislation that effectively removed at least one "environmental roadblock," the Clean Air Act that still annoyed industry despite the administration's successful efforts to weaken it. Nixon proposed once again to extend the deadlines for compliance with the carbon monoxide, hydrocarbons, and nitrogen oxide auto emission standards, this time for two more years. Additional proposals included granting EPA the authority to relax more restrictive state standards, exempting coal conversion from NEPA's impact-statement requirement, and allowing air quality to deteriorate in regions cleaner than federal mandates. Once again, the White House threw environmental caution to the winds. No longer could the administration fairly point to questions of technical feasibility; just as Nixon ordered, the new proposals were solely intended to facilitate energy supply and for no other reason. That they might succeed in this endeavor was more than likely, but at a significant cost to the nation's air.[80]

Recognizing all this, Train refused to testify before Congress in support of the administration's bill. This refusal and his public support for the "windfall profit" tax prompted a rebuke from his superiors. "It is particularly important that you continue your efforts to balance our environmental goals with our energy needs," Nixon wrote in a letter surprisingly mild. Before his cabinet, however, Nixon was blunter. "Promote energy developments," he ordered. "Get off the environmental kick."[81]

In late March, thankfully, the Arab countries lifted their oil embargo. The crisis was not completely over, however. Not only did the price of oil remain unbearably high, experts predicted shortages of approximately 435 million barrels of low-sulfur fuel, 200 million tons of low-sulfur coal, and 3.3 trillion cubic feet of natural gas, all critical in meeting the requirements of the Clean Air Act. Without the will to enforce stricter conservation measures, much of the public still welcomed Nixon's energy agenda. Despite the end of the embargo, the White House's blatant assault on the nation's Clean Air Act was not dead.[82]

The result was the Energy Supply and Environmental Coordination Act of 1974, a bill that did not incorporate all of the administration's proposals but still paid a price in environmental quality. It gave automotive companies two additional years of grace "for the development of emission control technology" so that they might "focus attention on improving fuel economy." Equally important, it encouraged power plants to convert from oil to coal, the nation's most abundant energy source but one with its own environmental cost: the smoke, ash, sulfur, and particulate matter that spewed out of smokestacks. With both the shortage in low-sulfur coal and the resistance of industry to using costly "stack scrubbers" to check pollution, the new law granted EPA the authority to suspend sulfur oxide emission limits. At the same time, Congress passed Nixon's Federal Energy Administration, ensuring yet another overhaul of the nation's emergent energy bureaucracy but dooming any hopes for a Department of Energy and Natural Resources. Although it explicitly rejected further assault on NEPA, Congress's priorities were obvious.[83]

With the use of coal critical to lessening the demand for oil, the White House had no intention of extending Morton's moratorium on new coal leasing. Working to develop a program to encourage new leasing, the administration released a draft environmental impact statement that suggested that a dramatic expansion of coal leasing caused little environmental harm, a conclusion obviously open to debate. Although a formal administration proposal was not finalized, the Natural Resources Defense Council filed suit claiming the administration's draft was inadequate. The administration needed to file site-specific statements, the NRDC argued, not an overall statement on the entire program. For the immediate future Morton's moratorium remained in place, but as long as the energy crisis continued the future did not bode well.[84]

In retrospect, neither the administration nor Congress dallied in its response to the nation's shortage of energy. In a sense, both proposed viable solutions to this crisis, but sacrificed hard-earned gains in regard to another, environmental degradation. By focusing primarily on increasing the domestic supply of traditional energy sources, they chose the easy political route and the one most readily accomplished. In many respects, however, they missed an opportunity to advance a more advantageous long-term agenda that stressed America's need for conservation as well as her need for new, environmentally friendly alternative sources of energy. Although Nixon acknowledged the necessity of both goals and agreed with Congress in increasing research appropriations, the thrust of his program was clearly elsewhere. Facing the possibility of impeachment, which loomed greater with each passing day, it is difficult to fault him for taking the most expedient political route. One might argue that given the situation, environmental trade-offs were inevitable and constituted a necessary component of any successful response. Nevertheless, from an environmental standpoint, the result of the energy crisis was unfortunate.

The crisis itself eventually ended, of course. The efforts of Nixon and his successors brought more domestic oil and coal to the market; the unity of OPEC disintegrated; and in time gas prices dropped and the lines at the pump evaporated. The nation bore the environmental cost and moved on. Once again

Americans resumed their wasteful ways, driving bigger cars, consuming more fossil fuels, and quickly forgetting their brief bout with scarcity.

Of course the public could never forget Watergate. Even as the energy crisis slowly dragged on into the new year, the scandal in Washington continued to build to its inevitable climax. First, the House Judiciary Committee subpoenaed an additional forty-two White House tapes, which Nixon tried to avoid by releasing transcripts. Eliminating words, phrases, or passages that were particularly embarrassing, such as curse words or insulting references to senators, Nixon hoped to demonstrate compliance without further weakening his position. Ensuring that the transcripts were as accurate as possible without revealing definitive evidence of a crime was a difficult task. The result was no smoking gun, but hardly a favorable portrait of the president. Out for public consumption was the now infamous "dark side" to Nixon's persona: his vindictiveness, anger, and political ruthlessness. Nixon's language was probably no worse than many of his predecessors, yet the frequent insertion of the phrase "expletives deleted" into the record left much to the imagination and drew attention in a way it might not have otherwise.[85]

Worse for Nixon was the new special prosecutor, Leon Jaworski. Proving just as persistent as his predecessor, Cox, Jaworski issued his own subpoena for sixty-four tapes. In claiming executive privilege once again, Nixon argued that Jaworski, as an employee of the executive branch, could never compel the White House to produce documents. This made a farce of the special prosecutor's charter, Jaworski responded, an argument that carried the day with the court. The stage, therefore, was set for an administration appeal, the famous Supreme Court case *United States of America v. Richard Nixon, President of the United States.* It all seemed somehow surreal—the most powerful nation in the world hobbled by energy shortages; its leader, the most powerful man in the world, self-destructing before everyone's eyes.[86]

Given Nixon's desperate political situation, it was amazing that the White House took the active role in energy policy that it did. By the spring of 1974, official Washington appeared to grind to a halt, the press corps in a deathwatch and the public anxiously waiting for the proverbial shoe to drop. Nixon labored to present the image of business as usual, but in private he spent his days alternatively plotting and brooding over the scandal. Legislation before Congress slowed, and, one way or another, many matters simply had to wait for a resolution of Nixon's fate. To conclude, however, that the federal government accomplished nothing during the dark days of 1974, or at least nothing beyond the energy crisis, would overstate the point. In many respects the wheels of govern-

ment continued to turn, albeit completely out of the public eye and largely beyond the interest of the embattled Nixon.[87]

In the waning weeks of the Nixon presidency, Congress passed the Congressional Budget and Impoundment Control Act of 1974. A compromise over the
administration's controversial impoundment of congressionally allocated
funds, an important matter that infuriated members of Congress the previous
year, the new legislation nevertheless paled in the shadow of Watergate's sensational developments. It established budget committees in both houses of Congress as well as a Congressional Budget Office, staffed with experts to guide but
not bind the appropriation process. The president, the law provided, was to release all funds if one of the budget committees requested it. The process would,
everyone hoped, avoid litigation that threatened to persist indefinitely.[88] For its
part, EPA announced that it would allow exemptions to its bans on DDT and
on poisons to control predatory animals. The announcement annoyed environmentalists, although it was only a minor policy adjustment. The exemption
for DDT use was aimed only at a specific moth that threatened valuable
forests in the Pacific Northwest. More troublesome was the U.S. Fish and
Wildlife's permit to use the M-44, a spring-loading, cyanide-ejecting tube
placed in the ground with a scented bait to lure and kill coyotes. The device,
environmentalists correctly noted, was sure to lure other animals, including
endangered species.[89]

The struggle over the nation's forests continued through Nixon's last days.
The White House proposed several significant additions to the Wilderness System and made considerable progress toward fulfilling the statutory requirements of the Wilderness Act. Once again, however, the proposals included no
national forests and ensured the preeminence of the timber harvest. Working
to block the administration's announced plans to increase this harvest, environmentalists won from the U.S. District Court for the District of Columbia a
temporary court injunction. The court agreed that the Forest Service first had
to complete an impact statement before the additional harvest could commence.[90] Turning to NEPA once again, the Natural Resources Defense Council
filed suit to block a new livestock-grazing program proposed by the Bureau of
Land Management. Insisting that this program allowed overgrazing and damaged the public domain, the NRDC argued that the BLM's impact statement
was inadequate. Each individual grazing district should file its own impact
statement, the NRDC maintained, a questionable interpretation of NEPA obviously intended simply to delay the program's implementation.[91]

The final death of land-use legislation drew as little attention as the timber
or grazing debates. The White House announced that it now supported the

Steiger bill, which omitted all requirements that states regulate areas of ecological importance, only to see this emasculated proposal still provoke conservative resistance. In June, opponents succeeded in blocking all consideration of the issue by rejecting the rule under which Congress was to consider both the administration's original proposal and the Steiger bill that the White House now supported. A potent coalition composed of the timber, livestock, and farm industries, as well as traditional conservative groups such as the John Birch Society and the Liberty Lobby, prevailed upon Nixon not to press the matter. Recognizing that these groups were the constituency upon which his political survival depended, Nixon quickly agreed. The original champion of land-use legislation, Senator Jackson, was understandably irate. "Impeachment politics," Jackson complained. "I am at a total loss to assign any other explanation."[92]

Indeed unfortunately, the nation had lost its best chance to address one of its most pressing environmental problems, urban sprawl. Only local zoning remained, often unable to meet the challenge of protecting fragile environments that stretched across several jurisdictions. And of course the issue played absolutely no role in slowing the speeding train of impeachment that bore down on Nixon. Congress, the press, and, most importantly, the public were little diverted by policy debates of any kind, much less those pertaining to the environment. Land use, timber, grazing, even questions of executive impoundment seemed insignificant compared to the historic culmination of a scandal that captivated the nation, if not the world.

Early on the morning of July 24 the news arrived. The Supreme Court had ruled against the White House in its landmark executive-privilege case. Nixon would have to turn over all the tapes subpoenaed — not edited versions or transcripts, but the full tapes — one of which Nixon knew contained irrefutable evidence of his complicity in the cover-up. It was agonizing for a man who had always prided himself on his ability to fight back. There seemed no way out. That night, the House Judiciary Committee began its debate over Articles of Impeachment. A Harris poll showed that the public favored impeachment 66 to 27 percent, while national television and radio carried the committee proceedings live.[93]

A stunned Nixon performed his duties in an almost robotic fashion, with no feeling or emotion and with everyone waiting for the scandal's anticipated bleak end. Two days after the Supreme Court ruling, Nixon flew to Los Angeles for what the White House bravely touted as a major speech on inflation. With the obvious looming, the content of the speech was almost an afterthought. Still, Nixon found time to launch a volley at environmentalists. Government and corporations spent too much money on environmental control, Nixon proclaimed, which contributed to the nation's inflationary woes. Nixon, it appeared, carried his disdain for environmentalists to the bitter end.[94]

By early August the tapes were public, the Judiciary Committee had voted to send three Articles of Impeachment to the full House, and Nixon had made his decision. He had no choice. He would have to resign. The charges were serious—obstruction of justice and abuse of power—and the "smoking gun" tape had eroded what little support he had left. Gathering his family and friends, he quietly gave them the news. What would history say of him, Nixon wondered. It would, Kissinger replied, record his great accomplishments.[95]

On the evening of Thursday, August 8, Nixon went on national television to announce his decision to the world. The emotion had returned, a combination of pity and anger, and it was all Nixon could do to maintain his composure. He claimed that he had always tried to do what was best for the nation, ignoring his political motivations, which had in fact guided much of his domestic policy, especially with regard to the environment. He noted his lack of support in Congress and his conclusion that resignation was in the best interest of the nation, both beyond dispute. Then came his fateful words: "Therefore, I shall resign the presidency effective at noon tomorrow."[96]

When Nixon boarded a helicopter outside the White House for the last time the next day, turning to the nation and emphatically waving a defiant "V for Victory" sign, he ended a drama that had been too long in the making. His presidency had begun with much hope, a call for unity, and a plea for moderation. He would, he promised, bring the nation together. Now, almost six years later, one was left to wonder where it all went wrong. Nowhere was this more evident than in regard to the environment. As one of his last official acts, Nixon angrily vetoed a seven-billion-dollar budget for EPA, necessary to complete the agency's mandate. It was, in his view, one final blow for fiscal restraint against a government out of control. It was also an action that angered Train, the environmental community, and much of the public that had earlier applauded him for creating the agency.[97] Nixon's veto was, in a sense, symbolic of the administration's drift away from its earlier environmental advocacy and indicative of the anger and divisiveness that had come to characterize his term. It symbolized the chasm that had grown between the administration and those who realized that the struggle against environment degradation must continue without pause. Environmentalists played no role in the events that finally toppled the Nixon administration, but as Nixon's helicopter vanished into the horizon, they undoubtedly joined the rest of the nation relieved that the drama had finally ended.

Epilogue
"Our Day Will Come Again"

Several years after Nixon's resignation, Whitaker visited the former president at his San Clemente home. It had not been easy for Nixon, then languishing in political exile. Although President Ford had issued an unconditional pardon, a new struggle over control of Nixon's presidential papers loomed. Critics alleged that the pardon was part of a quid pro quo with Ford and complained that Nixon's memoirs and interviews allowed him to profit from his illegal acts. Nixon had fought off a serious bout with phlebitis and a blood clot that threatened his life, only to have his beloved wife, Pat, suffer a stroke. Whitaker, researching his own memoirs, hoped to discuss the specifics of natural resources and environmental policy. He also recognized, however, the need to cheer up his old boss. Years from now, Whitaker remarked, it would not be Vietnam or foreign policy that people remembered about the Nixon administration, but rather its tremendous successes in domestic policy, most notably with regard to the environment. "For God's sake, John," Nixon replied, "I hope that's not true."[1]

With Vietnam and Watergate still fresh in the nation's memory, Nixon could not imagine environmental policy as a defining characteristic of his administration, much less as a point of pride. Sitting in his California estate, Nixon recalled his diplomatic accomplishments with great satisfaction. Foreign policy had always been his first love and the area of his greatest expertise, in his mind the realm of his most significant accomplishments. To think that domestic policy—so often an afterthought to him—would overshadow all of this somehow diminished his historical importance. Nixon had no plans to go quietly into the night. He had one final task to accomplish: resurrecting his historical legacy from the sewer of scandal and resignation. "Our day will come again," he vowed to friends.[2] Nixon undoubtedly appreciated Whitaker's comments, but in planning his comeback he saw opportunity only in the role of elder statesman.

History would surely place his presidency into context, Nixon believed, recalling first and foremost his great accomplishments on the world stage.

The reality, of course, was that neither Nixon nor Whitaker had a monopoly on the truth. While often controversial, Nixon's efforts to extricate America from Vietnam, to open diplomatic ties with the People's Republic of China, and to seek disarmament with the Soviet Union were historic by all accounts. While Nixon could never erase the stain of Watergate, the years that followed indeed brought perspective and cooled tensions, paving the way for Nixon's well-planned political rehabilitation. Focusing always on his agenda, politics and foreign policy, and never shy about reminding the public of his achievements, Nixon slowly proved himself to be a political phoenix. First with a handful of interviews and articles, then with a number of well-publicized trips, and, finally, with a series of best-selling books, Nixon became the elder statesman he envisioned. By the early 1990s, his public rehabilitation was virtually complete; his day had indeed come. He appeared on the most prestigious television programs and his face covered the weekly newsmagazines. Everywhere he went cameras followed and provided a constant stage to enhance his image. Most importantly, presidents and leaders throughout the world called on him, and quick to play the role of diplomatic sage, he readily dispensed advice and words of wisdom.[3]

Not once did Nixon raise the environment, not in his books, speeches, or interviews. Nothing suggested that Nixon had changed his conclusions about the environmental movement that he had formed during his presidency. For Nixon, environmentalism remained largely a temporary phenomenon, a movement guided by radicals who neither appreciated his efforts nor other pressing realities. His early efforts had paid little political dividends, destroyed the budget, alienated conservative allies, and hampered economic recovery. His extensive program had addressed the matter, overblown as it was, but had not received the credit it deserved. The public may continue to care, Nixon assumed, but other bread-and-butter issues—the constant effort to make ends meet and the life-and-death issues of war and peace—would forever overshadow environmental protection. In any event, his ultimate retreat had cost him little. He had no reason to raise the environment now.

Indeed, the environmental movement had entered a new, more mature phase. The era of abundance that the nation had enjoyed since the conclusion of the Second World War had begun to end, a new reality portended by the energy crisis and a fact painfully evident throughout the remainder of the decade and the administrations of Ford and his successor, Jimmy Carter. The accomplishments of the Nixon era certainly diminished the sense of crisis that had surrounded the first Earth Day, turning much of the debate off the front page and into the legal and technical arena. Lawyers with briefcases replaced protesters with signs, while debate often centered on the minutia of science. The struggles remained tremendously important, but the media frequently recognized other headlines as more gripping. In addition, industry, armed with considerable clout and money, had begun an effective counterattack, restless under new regulations. In essence, a more developed environmental movement now stood as one of many special-interest lobbies, struggling to maintain public momentum and often facing a chief executive that did not always share its agenda.

Most importantly, however, for many Americans the economic, political, and international turmoil of the 1970s challenged their assumptions of eternal plenty, an ever-expanding economy that allowed for the perpetual removal of natural resources from potential production. As the decade progressed, unemployment approached 10 percent and inflation 13 percent; energy shortages lingered, forcing a shocked American public to pay more than a dollar for a gallon of gasoline.[4] Environmentalism spoke for the spiritual and nonutilitarian values of natural resources, contrary to historic patterns of economic endeavor. In times of prosperity, the nation could easily cherish these values as signs of a compassionate and rational culture that understood its technical limitations. However, in times of economic strain—indicative of the Ford and Carter years—they became to many a luxury that the nation could no longer afford. The goals of environmentalism increasingly appeared class-based and insensitive to more basic concerns of economic survival, a difficult obstacle for environmentalists to overcome.[5]

If the nation worried over its economic future, it remained no less preoccupied with foreign affairs. During the Nixon era, stunning developments on the world stage had dominated the news, diverting attention from environmental degradation and ensuring that, on the national level at least, elections primarily turned on other matters. The Vietnam War was now over, but developments around the world were no less momentous nor was their political impact less significant. Whether it was friction in the Middle East, the Soviet takeover of Afghanistan, or the rise of Islamic fundamentalism in Iran, international turmoil fueled Nixon's rehabilitation. Diplomatic expertise, it appeared, was a valued commodity in an increasingly troubled world. It enhanced Nixon's stage, but did nothing to help environmentalists struggling to keep their agenda before the public.[6]

By the end of the 1970s, a number of polls suggested a decline in public support for environmental protection. The polls hardly, however, told the whole story. Public concern for the nation's environment had indeed begun to wane, but just as Whitaker assumed in the dark days after Watergate, neither the nation's economic woes nor its preoccupation with international developments meant that the public had forgotten that eternal vigilance was necessary. Americans still cared and would forever respect leaders who took their obligation to the natural world seriously.[7]

One did not have to look far in the 1970s to realize that an environmental threat remained. In 1976 officials discovered the hazardous chemical kepone in Virginia's James River. That same year New Yorkers learned of polychlorinated biphenyls (PCBs) contamination in the Hudson River, while in Michigan polybrominated biphenyls (PBBs) accidentally poisoned hundreds of cows, raising the ugly specter of tainted human food. In 1978, residents living near Love Canal in upstate New York discovered that their neighborhood sat upon an industrial waste dump. With the carcinogen benzene permeating the air in local homes, a complete evacuation was necessary, drawing the attention of the nation's media in a way not seen since early in Nixon's first term. Most shocking was the infamous 1979 Three-Mile Island nuclear-power plant accident in Pennsylvania, the worst such incident in the nation's history. A partial meltdown of the core of one of the reactors resulted in the release of radioactive steam, which panicked the local citizenry. In a case of life imitating art, the accident occurred just after Hollywood had released a film, *The China Syndrome*, which dramatized exactly such a scenario. An environmental disaster, it appeared, could occur anywhere and at any time.[8]

Such sensational disasters jarred public complacency from coast to coast, but for many environmental activism had simply shifted from the national to the local level. Perhaps made public only on the regional news, efforts to remove blight from neighborhoods or to improve a city's drinking water were still important to local citizens. Local grass-roots campaigns flourished, often short-lived but equally often effective—a new venue and a new challenge perhaps, but far from the demise of environmentalism.[9]

The dawn of the Reagan era early in 1981 marked a greater challenge to environmental values, but, in a sense, it was one that environmentalists met. The "Reagan antienvironmental revolution," in the words of historian Samuel Hays, represented the culmination of the backlash to environmentalism that had been growing since Nixon's initial retreat. Setting out to undo the accomplishments of the preceding two decades of Republican and Democratic leadership, Reagan assumed that there was no serious threat to the environment and no genuine support among the public. It was all a facade perpetuated by a small minority, easily swept aside by vigorous presidential leadership.[10] He was, Philip Berry disdainfully concluded, "totally uninformed."[11]

Maintaining that government bureaucracy stifled America, Reagan used the

Office of Management and Budget to drain power from regulatory agencies. EPA was hit particularly hard, deprived of 29 percent of its budget and a quarter of its staff in the first two years of the administration. Innovative programs in such areas as solar energy and alternative fuels faced complete emasculation. To assist industries such as timber, mining, and oil, the administration virtually ignored existing regulations and often invited industry trade groups to assist in drafting new ones on terms they thought satisfactory. Using his power of appointment, Reagan installed critics of regulation as the heads of the regulatory agencies themselves. Anne Gorsuch, named as new EPA administrator, was a Colorado lawyer whose clients included many extractive and agricultural interests openly opposed to federal mandates. Of the fifteen subordinates she named, eleven had connections to industries regulated by EPA. The most notable Reagan appointment was Secretary of Interior James Watt. As director of the Mountain States Legal Foundation, Watt had brought lawsuits challenging federal environmental authority. Comparing environmentalists to Nazis and Bolsheviks, he worked diligently to return the public domain to private interests. One incident, however, epitomized the extent to which Reagan and his appointees opposed the environmental movement. A 1982 United Nations "World Charter for Nature" declared that "nature shall be respected and its essential processes not impaired." Only one member nation failed to sign the document—the United States, under orders from Ronald Reagan.[12]

Projecting optimism and confidence that had been lacking in the White House for years, Reagan was undeniably popular. Not even the withering attacks of a popular president, however, completely undercut the public's allegiance to environmental values. As the 1970s progressed, many national organizations had struggled to maintain membership. Although the Sierra Club prospered over the decade, membership in the Wilderness Society and the Izaak Walton League declined, suggesting that popular enthusiasm waned. Ironically, however, the Reagan assault proved just the antidote to complacency. Far from ending the environmental movement, Reagan provided an opportunity "to demonstrate the breadth of concern in the broader society," in the words of Hays. "In being forced to recognize that environmental affairs were not momentary, limited, and superficial, the [Reagan] administration, in fact, more firmly rooted their legitimacy on American politics."[13]

By the mid-1980s, total membership in environmental organizations approached a record five million. In only five years, from 1980 to 1985, the Sierra Club's membership doubled. The Wilderness Society and the Izaak Walton League reversed their decline in spectacular fashion, while membership in groups such as the National Wildlife Federation and the Friends of the Earth skyrocketed as well. Perhaps as a response to the militancy of the Reagan on-slaught, a number of new, more radical organizations formed. For example, the group Earth First! proudly proclaimed its motto: "No compromise in defense of Mother Earth." A movement called "Deep Ecology" stressed ecological equality and the need for extreme measures to protect wildlife. Frustrated rad-icals were a clear challenge to the traditional mainstream organizations, but, in their own way, demonstrated public resistance to the Reagan agenda.[14]

It all culminated with the twentieth anniversary of Earth Day in 1990, an event in which the nation seemed to declare its interest in the environment everlasting. A middle-aged Denis Hayes returned to coordinate the day's festiv-ities, this time aided by a huge staff in offices across the country. With corpo-rate sponsorship and high-profile Hollywood stars to attract attention, the number of participants approached that of the inaugural. More celebration than protest, the event spawned no major legislation; indeed, organizers had no official legislative agenda. It was simply a statement of the nation's renewed in-terest and a promise never to concede defeat.[15]

Throughout it all, therefore, from slowly waning public enthusiasm in the 1970s to the enmity of the Reaganites in the 1980s, environmentalism perse-vered. Whether a response to specific incidences of ecological disaster or, in a sense, a backlash to a backlash, the environmental movement proved itself to be no passing phenomenon, as Nixon assumed, but an enduring fabric in American life. Nixon correctly recognized that the public would eventually put his presidency into perspective, valuing his accomplishments and allowing his final renewal. Whitaker was correct as well, however, in recognizing that envi-ronmental protection would play an integral part in this perspective, as impor-tant as the stain of scandal or the fame of diplomatic success. Nixon's maternal grandmother, Almira Milhous, once inspired the young Nixon to leave behind "footprints in the sands of time."[16] Nixon clearly succeeded in this regard, a man as contentious in history as he was in life. Nevertheless, as the wheels of time continue to turn and the environment persists as an issue, perhaps the footprints Nixon left are not just those that he envisioned.

Nixon had no reason to fear the verdict of history. His presidency was, in a sense, a window of opportunity for the nation's environment. The problems were tremendous and complex, but never before or since has public enthusi-asm been so great or the political climate so accommodating for progress. The window was short, perhaps, beginning to shut before Nixon left office, but one still cannot deny the long list of accomplishments that remain.

For one, the National Environmental Policy Act stands out. NEPA remains in many respects the cornerstone of American environmental policy, a clear and concise statement of American environmental values. Thirty years later it is essentially unchanged, emulated by over half the states, eighty other nations, and by economic institutions such as the European Union, the World Bank, and the Asian Development Bank. Although underappreciated at the time of passage, its impact-statement requirement transformed the balance of power in the environmental struggles that followed, with the Nixon administration only the beginning. By 1980, agencies had filed over eleven thousand statements, almost 10 percent ending in litigation. Of this total, the courts blocked action in almost 20 percent. By 1990, the number of statements had stabilized at almost five hundred a year, and showed no sign of abating. In effect, NEPA ended the era of large-scale federal development projects; the Cross-Florida Barge Canal, it appears, was the last of a dying breed.[17]

NEPA's Council on Environmental Quality was, arguably, at its strongest early during the Nixon years. Nixon initially staffed it with competent environmental advocates who helped institutionalize the impact-statement review process and made important policy recommendations. In the years since, however, CEQ's influence has declined considerably, beginning with Nixon's second term and culminating with Reagan, who fired its entire staff, drastically reduced its budget, and in essence destroyed it in all but name only. In addition, a post-Watergate Congress passed legislation intended to make executive agencies more accountable to the public, but, in regard to CEQ, the effect was to inhibit its advisory role. The council remains, however, having defeated repeated attempts to abolish it.[18]

The Environmental Protection Agency remains as well, of course, a bulwark against pollution for thirty years. It has performed admirably overall, despite shifts in public opinion. By 1980 its staff had grown to thirteen thousand people and its budget expanded to 5.6 billion dollars, not including the power to distribute an additional 1.6 billion dollars in toxic-waste cleanup funds. By 1990 most states had adopted similar agencies, with imitation again proving to be the sincerest form of flattery. EPA stands as one of the largest federal agencies, surpassed only by the Veteran's Administration and the Office of Personnel Management, an indication of its importance as well as of its relative success. At the center of federal environmental regulation, EPA has endured criticism from all sides, but few would suggest that it had not accomplished the goal Nixon declared for it early in 1970. It has eliminated much of the redundancy and overlap characteristic of the nation's pollution-fighting bureaucracy and proved to be a strong regulatory force on behalf of the environment.[19]

Many of the regulations themselves, of course, emerged from the Nixon era in a spate of legislation unsurpassed in the years since. Endangered species, pesticide control, ocean dumping, coastal zone management, marine mammals — the breadth of legislation was matched only by the rapidity with which Congress passed it. Russell Train was correct in concluding that the Nixon era "put into place the basic principles and framework of environmental law."[20] If amended in later years, for example, the water and air pollution legislation of the period still provides the basic outline for national standards and thus the parameters for debate, the pillars on which the quality of the nation's environment depends. In these and other ways, one could conclude that the nation had indeed made the most of its window of opportunity and that Nixon, to the extent of his contributions, deserves credit.

This credit is not exclusively Nixon's, of course, and this is not to deny his policy reversal or to suggest that nothing more was possible. It was Nixon who often fought to limit, both in terms of budget and extent, the very legislation that is now so impressive. While he signed NEPA and assisted in its initial implementation, he also later chafed under its restrictions. After proposing EPA, he worked to limit its effectiveness. Whether attempting to weaken legislative provisions or simply accepting stronger versions with reluctance, Nixon and his second-term conservative revolution helped break a bipartisan consensus in favor of the strongest protections possible. His emerging budget priorities increasingly antagonized his environmental staff and energized the environmental opposition. When it was all over, the nation had gained a stronger defense against pollution, but had accomplished little to stop urban sprawl, with Nixon a major culprit.

Nevertheless, in the end, whatever his motivation, Nixon signed each of the bills passed by Congress, with water pollution legislation the major exception. The reality is that another conservative president might not have done so. Early in his administration, if solely to gain the political initiative, Nixon lent the full weight of the presidency, the prestige and aura of his office, to the environmental cause. His speeches, if not his heart, were unequivocal. If, at the outset, his program was insufficient to meet the challenge and sure to engender criticism in Congress, it still significantly improved upon the existing state of affairs. Many of his proposals were themselves revolutionary and were ultimately incorporated into law. Nixon, in short, helped build the momentum for environmental protection that he later found so troublesome.

There is certainly enough credit to go around. Congress, obviously, was vital in two respects. First, when Nixon sought to seize the environmental initiative, the competition it unleashed in Congress ensured stronger provisions. Democrats, led by Senators Edmund Muskie and Henry Jackson, had no intention of relinquishing their advantage on the issue, especially with the first Earth Day looming and the public, apparently, in an environmental frenzy. They responded with tougher proposals, which, on occasion, spurred Nixon on further. Second, after Nixon concluded that this competition was in neither his own political interest nor in the nation's economic interest, Congress mitigated Nixon's retreat. It was not just Congress, however. Nixon's own environmental staff played a major role throughout Nixon's term and, as such, also deserves considerable credit. The task for John Whitaker, Russell Train, William Ruckelshaus, and others was never easy and, later in Nixon's presidency, often frustrating. Still, one must acknowledge the role each played in crafting an administration legacy worthy of respect.

It is easy to fault Nixon for his political motivation. One must remember, however, that no president operates in a vacuum. Despite the gravity of environmental degradation, other pressing matters competed for Nixon's attention. The administration's stance on such issues as timber, mining, oil, and other economic interests reflected powerful constituencies that no president could ignore. The energy crisis was real, whatever its cause, and Nixon faced strong political pressure as a result. To expect a weakened president in the midst of a scandal to press forward with any energy program other than the most politically expedient was, perhaps, to entertain unreasonable hopes. Too often, one could argue, the environmental movement failed to consider adequately Nixon's predicament. He could not afford the perspective of a single-minded lobby, however legitimate, but had to consider the broader context, constantly weighing costs, both financial and political. Politics, as the old adage goes, is the art of compromise. Reflecting on the Nixon years, David Brower, the patriarch of the modern environmental movement, acknowledged as much. With Nixon's shifting policy, Brower concluded, environmentalists had reason for complaint. Nevertheless, he added, "we did not know how to say thank you." Had environmentalists courted, not chastised, the White House as it retreated, Brower said, "we could have advanced our cause." Nixon "had great promise and did great things, but we deserted him."[21]

Nixon was correct, after all, in recognizing that the climate for environmental activism had begun to change, that growing economic worries, first manifested in the energy crisis, had begun to narrow environmentalists' window of opportunity. Indeed, one could argue that every president since has demonstrated that no matter what one's motivation—political or altruistic—growing limits existed to what was possible politically. Ford, for example, inherited a number of Nixon's advisors, including Whitaker, but also the troubled state of the economy. The result was a continuation of Nixon's retreat. "I pursue the goal of clean air and pure water, but I must also pursue the objective of maximum jobs and continued economic progress," Ford declared, apparently assuming, like Nixon, that the two were mutually exclusive.[22] Angering environmentalists, Ford never attempted to resurrect land-use legislation or Nixon's proposal for a Department of Natural Resources. Just as his predecessor, he weakened auto emission requirements and proposed legislation to exploit quickly natural resources reserves. When Congress passed legislation to restrict surface mining, Ford vetoed it. Legislation to strengthen the Clean Air Act never emerged from Congress. The only significant environmental legislation that Ford signed was the Federal Lands Policy and Management Act of 1976. This legislation did not end the debate that had raged throughout the Nixon years on the proper use of the public domain, but confirmed federal management in perpetuity and challenged the Sagebrush Rebellion, which demanded state and private control. In addition, it strengthened the hand of environmentalists in protecting land governed by the Bureau of Land Management.[23]

Carter, by contrast, arrived intent upon carrying out an environmental agenda, and his concern was genuine. The result was a record that surpassed Ford's, but still bowed to the reality of other pressing demands, disappointing environmentalists who had placed such hope in his election.[24] Carter signed the Surface Mining Control and Reclamation Act, the legislation that Ford vetoed, and amendments strengthening the Clean Air Act and Clean Water Act.[25] The Alaska National Interest Lands Act, which Carter signed in 1980, settled much of the dispute over the disposition of Alaskan lands and placed 104 million acres in wildlife refuges or national parks.[26] In response to the threat from toxic substances, Congress passed and Carter signed the Resource Conservation and Recovery Act and the Toxic Substances Control Act. The former regulated the disposal and treatment of hazardous wastes from "cradle to grave," while the latter required that all chemicals imported into the country face strict testing and regulations.[27] Most significantly, Congress, working in conjunction with Carter, passed the Comprehensive Environmental Response, Compensation, and Liability Act of 1980, better known as Superfund. Creating a 1.6-billion-dollar trust fund financed primarily by a tax on industrial feedstock chemicals, Superfund empowered EPA to respond to emergencies caused by abandoned hazardous-waste dumps. If it could locate those liable, EPA could sue to recover cleanup costs. Perhaps the most significant environmental legislation since the Nixon years, even Superfund could not erase a sense among environmentalists that Carter had let them down.[28]

For one thing, Carter was unsuccessful in blocking construction of the Tellico Dam in Tennessee, ultimately capitulating to the power of entrenched political interests despite the project's controversial destruction of an endangered-species habitat. With energy concerns worsening, Carter backed away from his commitment to stress conservation, solar power, and rigorous air quality standards in favor of relaxing certain environmental regulations, a move that both Nixon and Ford could appreciate. Preoccupied by the stagnant economy and several world crises that made him appear impotent, Carter had precious little time to devote to a cause that he still held dear. He was, Philip Berry concluded, "too distracted by events that were hurting him." He was "well intended but stumbled around a lot." In a sense, therefore, environmentalists still expected too much, not fully appreciating the pressures that Carter, like Nixon before him, faced.[29]

Even the popular Reagan learned that when it came to the environment, he could not always have his way. Surprised by the persistence of public support for the environment, the Reagan White House belatedly curtailed its assault. Both EPA Administrator Gorsuch and Secretary of Interior Watt were forced to resign, a clear victory for moderation. In battles reminiscent of Nixon's second term, legislators successfully mitigated at least some of the Reagan budget cuts, stifling a number of administration initiatives. Congress even succeeded in passing amendments strengthening both Superfund and the Clean Water Act.[30] By the time George Bush and Bill Clinton arrived in the Oval Office, both men had learned to master the rhetoric of environmentalism but to steer a middle course in an attempt to pacify all powerful interests. The result was an occasional victory for the environment. Bush, for example, signed the Clean Air Act of 1990, and Clinton, several years later, signed legislation to protect millions of acres of California desert.[31] Neither, however, attempted a more forceful agenda in any direction, with both, apparently, fully cognizant of the powerful forces at play.

In retrospect, Nixon's record compares favorably with all his successors, his growing animosity to a degree less significant and his retreat more indicative of changing social, economic, and political circumstances, the type of inevitable compromises all presidents are forced to make in balancing legitimate but competing interests. It was, arguably, the "politics of the pendulum," as one historian has termed it.[32] Nixon, of course, might have accomplished more; his record remains incomplete if understandable. Nevertheless, taken in context, Nixon had little for which to be ashamed.

Americans today recognize that the threat to the natural world remains; public attention and activism may ebb and flow, the window of political opportunity may open and shut, but America has never repudiated the central tenets

of environmentalism. The American environmental movement has proved re-
silient. It has persevered. This reality will undoubtedly shape America's view of
the past—of Nixon, for one—but will also mold her future.

The challenge for the future is truly significant. Depletion of the earth's
ozone layer and global warming paints as bleak a scenario as that envisioned by
the worst doomsday prognosticators of the Nixon era. Destruction of the world's
rainforests and, indeed, the multi-faceted threats facing the underdeveloped
third-world—of which overpopulation is only the most obvious—necessitates
renewed activism. In the United States, the environmental movement must
continue its rejuvenation far beyond the Reagan years, for the problems facing
the nation's air, water, and land, while perhaps diminished, persist nevertheless.
In many respects, the nation still needs an era of public and government activism—an era as productive as the Nixon administration.

In 1991 Nixon gave a speech at the Plaza Hotel in New York City. Afterwards,
he ran into William Reilly, a Nixon veteran but then Bush's EPA administrator.
"I know you," Nixon volunteered. "You're at EPA, and I founded EPA. I'm an
environmentalist too."[33] It was, most likely, small talk or a bit of flattery. Nevertheless, without mentioning it otherwise, perhaps Nixon had finally come to
realize the true magnitude of environmental issues, and, as such, the importance of his own administration. Despite Watergate and the foreign policy in
which he took so much pride, perhaps, in the wisdom of old age, he had come
to appreciate the significance of his administration's own environmental accomplishments. Three years later, Nixon quietly passed away—on April 22,
1994, the twenty-fourth anniversary of the first Earth Day. It seemed, somehow,
appropriate.

Notes

Introduction

1. *New York Times*, Apr. 23, 1970, 1; *Washington Post*, Apr. 23, 1970, 1; Steve Cotton, "What Happened," *Audubon* 72, no. 4 (July 1970): 112–15.

2. Samuel Hays, "From Conservation to Environment," *Environmental Review* 6 (Fall 1982): 14–41; Donald Fleming, "Roots of the New Conservation Movements," *Perspectives in American History* 6 (1972): 7–91; Carrol Pursell, ed., *From Conservation to Ecology* (New York: Crowell, 1973). The best overview of environmental politics in the post–World War II era is Samuel Hays, *Beauty, Health and Permanence: Environmental Politics in the United States, 1955–1985* (New York: Cambridge University Press, 1987).

3. John Kenneth Galbraith, *The Affluent Society* (Boston: Houghton Mifflin, 1958); William H. Chafe, *The Unfinished Journey* (New York: Oxford University Press, 1986), 123; Arthur S. Link and William B. Catton, *American Epoch*, (New York: Alfred A. Knopf, 1980), 562, 566–67.

4. Hays, *Beauty, Health and Permanence*, 22–24; Chafe, *Unfinished Journey*, 118–19; Link and Catton, *American Epoch*, 581, 610.

5. Eric F. Goldman, *The Crucial Decade and After* (New York: Random House, 1960), 296, 303.

6. Chafe, *Unfinished Journey*, 117; Link and Catton, *American Epoch*, 608–9.

7. Hays, *Beauty, Health and Permanence*, 90–91; Daniel J. Boorstin, *The Americans: The Democratic Experience* (New York: Vintage Books, 1974), 270.

8. Joseph M. Petulla, *American Environmental History* (San Francisco: Boyd and Fraser, 1977), 375; Victor B. Scheffer, *The Shaping of Environmentalism in America* (Seattle: University of Washington Press, 1991), 152.

9. Richard H. K. Vietor, *Environmental Politics and the Coal Coalition* (College Station: Texas A&M University Press, 1980), 127–37; Walter A. Rosenbaum, *The Politics of Environmental Concern* (New York: Praeger, 1974), 147–53.

10. Rachel Carson, *Silent Spring* (Boston: Houghton Mifflin, 1962). For a review of Carson's life and impact, see Linda Lear, *Rachel Carson: Witness for Nature* (New York: Henry Holt, 1997).

11. Interview, Author with Brent Blackwelder, Mar. 23, 1998.

12. James McEvoy, "The American Concern for the Environment," in William Burch, et al., eds., *Social Behavior, Natural Resources, and the Environment* (New York: Harper and Row, 1972), 214–36; John Whitaker, *Striking a Balance: Environment and Natural Resources Policy in the Nixon-Ford Years* (Washington, D.C.: American Enterprise Institute, 1976), 7–9.

13. Interview, Author with Joe Browder, Mar. 24, 1998.

14. Interview, Author with David Brower, Apr. 7, 1998; *New York Times*, Mar. 14, 1969.

15. *Living Wilderness* 32, no. 101 (Spring 1968): 2.

16. Ibid; Benjamin Kline, *First Along the River: A Brief History of the U.S. Environmental Movement* (San Francisco: Acada Books, 1997), 81–85; Hays, *Beauty, Health and Permanence*, 53, 55, 62–66; Scheffer, *Shaping of Environmentalism*, 113–14; See Philip Shabecoff, *A Fierce Green Fire: The American Environmental Movement* (New York: Hill and Wang, 1993).

17. Interview, Author with Philip Berry, June 19, 1998; Interview, Author with David Brower, Apr. 7, 1998; Interview, Author with Laurence Moss, Mar. 25, 1998.

18. See Mark Harvey, *A Symbol of Wilderness: Echo Park and the American Conservation Movement* (Albuquerque: University of New Mexico Press, 1994); David R. Long, "Pipe Dreams, Hetch Hetchy, the Urban West, and the Hydraulic Society Revisited," *Journal of the American West* (July 1995): 22; Michael Cohen, *The Pathless Way: John Muir and the American Wilderness* (Madison: University of Wisconsin Press, 1984).

19. Respectively, the Air Quality Act of 1967, the Water Quality Act of 1965, the Wilderness Act of 1964, the Land and Water Conservation Act of 1965, the Solid Waste Disposal Act of 1965, and the Endangered Species Preservation Act of 1966, all of which are discussed in later chapters; Johnson also signed the Motor Vehicle Pollution Control Act of 1965, the National Trails Act of 1968, and the National Wild and Scenic Rivers Act of 1968. For an overview of the Johnson administration, see Doris Kearns, *Lyndon Johnson and the American Dream* (New York: Harper and Row, 1976).

20. *Sierra Club Bulletin* 53, no. 1 (January 1968): 7. See Udall's text on the environmental crisis, published as *The Quiet Crisis* (New York: Holt, Rinehart and Winston, 1963); Thomas G. Smith, "John Kennedy, Stewart Udall and the New Frontier Conservation," *Pacific Historical Review* 64, no. 3 (August 1995): 329.

21. Highway Beautification Act of 1965; Link and Catton, *American Epoch*, 854; Scheffer, *Shaping of Environmentalism*, 154.

22. Interview, Author with Don Nicoll, Apr. 1, 1998; Charles O. Jones, *Clean Air: The Policies and Politics of Pollution Control* (Pittsburgh: University of Pittsburgh Press, 1975), 56. For additional information on Muskie's career, see David Nevin, *Muskie of Maine* (New York: Random House, 1972); and Theo Lippman, Jr., and Donald C. Hansen, *Muskie* (New York: W. W. Norton, 1971).

23. Cotton, "What Happened," 112; Tom Wicker, *One of Us* (New York: Random House, 1991), 508.

24. Cotton, "What Happened," 113–14.

25. *Portland Press Herald*, Jan. 20, 1970, A1.

26. Memo, Eliot Cutler to Sheppie Abramowitz, Apr. 2, 1970, Folder 8, "1969–1970 Po-

litical File, Speech Materials," Box 1525, U.S. Senate, Senate Office Series (hereafter cited as USSSO), Edmund S. Muskie Papers, Edmund S. Muskie Archives (hereafter cited as EMA), Bates College, Lewiston, Maine.

27. Interview, Author with Leon Billings, June 26, 1998.

28. Quoted in Cotton, "What Happened," 113.

29. Interview, Author with Richard Fairbanks, Mar. 24, 1998.

30. Memo, Christopher DeMuth to John Ehrlichman and John Whitaker, Dec. 4, 1969, Folder "485-OA#2977, Environment," Box 63, Egil Krogh Files, White House Special Files (hereafter cited as WHSF), Richard Nixon White House Papers, Richard Nixon Presidential Materials Project (hereafter cited as RNPMP), National Archives II, College Park, Maryland; Whitaker, *Striking a Balance*, 29.

31. Interview, Author with John Whitaker, July 23, 1996; Whitaker, *Striking A Balance*, xi.

32. Interview, Author with Gaylord Nelson, Sept. 4, 1996.

33. Memo, John Ehrlichman to Richard Nixon, Dec. 5, 1969, Folder "EX NR Natural Resources, 1 of 3, 1969–1970," Box 1, Natural Resources Files, White House Central Files (hereafter cited as WHCF), RNPMP.

34. Nelson quoted in *Seattle Post-Intelligencer*, Sept. 21, 1969, A3.

35. Interview, Author with Walter Hickel, Mar. 27, 1998; Memo, Walter Hickel to Richard Nixon, Dec. 16, 1969, Folder "485-OA#2977, Environment," Box 63, Egil Krogh Files, WHCF, RNPMP; Memo, John Whitaker to Russell Train, Dec. 11, 1969, Folder "June–December, 1969, 6 of 6, December, 1969," Box 1, John Whitaker Files, WHCF.

36. Ibid; Interview, Author with Mike Leavitt, June 22, 1998; Walter Hickel, *Who Owns America?* (Englewood Cliffs, N.J.: Prentice-Hall, 1971), 230–31.

37. Whitaker, *Striking A Balance*, 6; Memo, John Whitaker to John Ehrlichman, Jan. 7, 1970, Folder "Misc., 1969–1970, 2 of 2," Box 21, John Ehrlichman Files, WHSF, RNPMP.

38. Memo, John Whitaker to Secs. Hardin, Hickel, Finch, et. al., Jan. 8, 1970, Folder "White House, Environment, 1970," Box 9, Edward David Files, WHCF, RNPMP; Memo, John Whitaker to Christopher DeMuth, Jan. 16, 1970, Folder "January–April, 1970, 1 of 4, January, 1970," Box 2, John Whitaker Files, WHCF, RNPMP; Memo, Christopher DeMuth to Patrick Buchanan, Jan. 29, 1970, Folder "Environmental Briefing, January–February, 1970," Box 13, Patrick Buchanan Files, WHCF, RNPMP; Memo, John Whitaker to Christopher DeMuth, Feb. 2, 1970, Folder "January–April, 1970, 2 of 4, February, 1970," Box 2, John Whitaker, WHCF, RNPMP.

39. Stephen E. Ambrose, *Nixon: The Triumph of a Politician, 1962–1972* (New York: Simon and Schuster, 1989), 333.

40. Hickel, *Who Owns America?*, 231–32.

41. Ibid., 239; Ambrose, *Nixon, Triumph*, 334, 338; Cotton, "What Happened," 114.

42. See Ambrose, *Nixon, Triumph*, chap. 15.

43. Interview, Author with Russell Train, July 8, 1998.

44. Interview, Author with William Reilly, June 26, 1998.

45. Cotton, "What Happened," 112–13; Scheffer, *Shaping of Environmentalism*, 125.

46. Interview, Author with John Whitaker, July 23, 1996; Hickel, *Who Owns America?*, 239–240; Whitaker, *Striking a Balance*, 4, 6.

47. Cronkite, Schorr, and Rather quoted in Whitaker, *Striking A Balance*, 7; Vonnegut and Hayes quoted in Cotton, "What Happened," 113–14.

48. Letter, John Whitaker to Donald S. Heintzelman, May 4, 1970, Folder "May–August, 1971, 1 of 4, May, 1970," Box 2, John Whitaker Files, WHCF, RNPMP; *Washington Post*, Apr. 26, 1970, B1.

49. *Public Papers of the Presidents, Richard Nixon, 1970* (Washington, D.C.: U.S. Government Printing Office, 1971), 405–10; Nixon quoted in Ambrose, *Nixon, Triumph*, 345, 348.

50. Ambrose, *Nixon, Triumph*, 355–56.

51. Interview, Author with Philip Berry, June 19, 1998.

Chapter 1

1. Richard Nixon, *RN: The Memoirs of Richard Nixon* (New York: Grosset and Dunlap, 1978), 1, 4; Stephen E. Ambrose, *Nixon: The Education of a Politician, 1913–1962* (New York: Simon and Schuster, 1987), 27.

2. Letter, Harry March to Richard Nixon, June 9, 1953, General Correspondence (hereafter cited as GC), Series 320, Box 757, Folder 7, Richard Nixon Vice Presidential Papers (hereafter cited as RNVPP), National Archives, Southwest Region, Laguna Hills, California; Letter, Robert Irvin to Richard Nixon, June 8, 1953, GC, Series 320, Box 757, Folder 7, RNVPP; Letter, Richard Nixon to Sam Mosher, Jan. 2, 1959, GC, Series 320, Box 534, Folder 17, RNVPP; Letter, Sam Mosher to Paul Smith, Dec. 22, 1958, GC, Series 320, Box 534, Folder 17, RNVPP; *Congressional Record*, 80th Cong., 2d sess., Vol. 94, pt. 1 (January 26, 1948), 579. Standard Oil, Richfield Oil, and Union Oil companies contributed to Nixon's 1946 campaign. Roger Morris, *Richard Milhous Nixon: The Rise of An American Politician* (New York: Holt and Company, 1990), 308; Gerald Mangrove, *Marine Policy for America* (New York: Taylor and Francis, 1988), 187.

3. *Sierra Club Bulletin* 39, no. 6 (June 1954): 6, 10; *Congressional Record*, 84th Cong., 1st sess., Vol. 101, pt. 7 (June 23, 1955), 9140–41; Elmo Richardson, *Dams, Parks, and Politics: Resource Development and Preservation in the Truman-Eisenhower Era* (Lexington: University of Kentucky Press, 1973), 155; Joseph M. Petulla, *American Environmentalism: Values, Tactics and Priorities* (College Station: Texas A&M University Press, 1980), 52–53; Robert L. Sansom, *The New American Dream Machine: Towards a Simpler Lifestyle in an Environmental Age* (Garden City, N.Y.: Anchor Press, 1976), 204.

4. *Congressional Record*, 81st Cong., 1st sess., Vol. 95, pt. 1 (Jan. 3, 1949), 26. Nixon was also a forceful advocate of California's rights to Colorado river water; see John Upton Terrell, *War for the Colorado River* (Glendale, Ariz.: Arthur H. Clark, 1965).

5. *Business Week Magazine* (Nov. 17, 1956): 47.

6. Letter, Francis Kovalcik to Dwight Eisenhower, Nov. 23, 1956, GC, Series 320, Box 613, Folder 21, RNVPP; see also Final Draft of Remarks, Richard Nixon Speech, National Rivers and Harbors Conference, Washington, D.C., May 17, 1957, Appearances, Series 207, Box 64, Folder 12, RNVPP.

7. Samuel Kirkpatrick and Melvin Jones, "Vote Direction and Issue Cleavage in 1968," *Social Science Quarterly* 51 (December 1970): 689–705; Philip Converse et al., "Continu-

ity and Change in American Politics: Parties and Issues in the 1968 Election," *American Political Science Review* 63 (December, 1969): 1083–1105. For a discussion of 1968, see David Caute, *The Year of the Barricades* (New York: Harper and Row, 1988).

8. *Sierra Club Bulletin* 43, no. 3 (April 1958): 9–12; Donald Johnson and Kirk Porter, *National Party Platforms* (Urbana: University of Illinois Press, 1973), 591–93, 612, 739, 758; Press Release, Senator Edmund Muskie, Oct. 18, 1968, Folder 8, "1969 Political Files, 1000 Politics, Conservation," Box SE1467, USSSO, EMA.

9. Humphrey quoted in Carl Solberg, *Hubert Humphrey* (New York: W. W. Norton, 1984), 419; Whitaker, *Striking a Balance*, 1–2.

10. Whitaker, *Striking a Balance*, 1–2. For a discussion of the 1968 campaign, see Ambrose, *Nixon, Triumph*, chap. 10; see also Douglas T. Miller, *On Our Own: America in the Sixties* (Lexington, Mass.: D. C. Heath and Company, 1996), 327–30.

11. Nixon quoted in Herbert S. Parmet, *Richard Nixon and His America* (Boston: Little, Brown and Company, 1990), 529.

12. Interview, Author with Don Nicoll, Apr. 1, 1998.

13. *Sierra Club Bulletin* 54, no. 1 (January 1969): 2.

14. For the best overview of Nixon's domestic record, see Joan Hoff, *Nixon Reconsidered* (New York: Basicbooks, 1994).

15. Quoted in Julie Nixon Eisenhower, *Pat Nixon: The Untold Story* (New York: Simon and Schuster, 1986), 252. For overviews of the Eisenhower administration, see Herbert Parmet, *Eisenhower and the American Crusades* (New York: Macmillan, 1972); and Stephen E. Ambrose, *Eisenhower the President* (New York: Simon and Schuster, 1984).

16. Ambrose, *Nixon, Triumph*, 224.

17. Membership List, Natural Resources and Environment Transitional Task Force, November 1969, Folder "Task Force Reports, Transition Period, 1968–1969," Box 1, Transition Task Force Reports, WHCF, RNPMP.

18. Interview, Author with Russell Train, July 8, 1998; Report, Natural Resources and Environment Transitional Task Force, Dec. 5, 1968, Folder "Task Force Reports, Transition Period, 1968–1969," Box 1, Transition Task Force Reports, WHCF, RNPMP.

19. Ibid.

20. Memo, John Whitaker to John Ehrlichman, June 25, 1969, Folder "182, Domestic Program Coordination," Box 31, John Ehrlichman Files, WHSF, RNPMP.

21. Other candidates who held varying responsibilities for the environment included Clifford Hardin as Secretary of Agriculture, George Romney as Secretary of Housing and Urban Development, John Volpe as Secretary of Transportation, Maurice Stans as Secretary of Commerce, and Robert Finch as Secretary of Health, Education and Welfare; *New York Times*, Dec. 12, 1968, 1.

22. For a detailed discussion of Hickel's background and gubernatorial record, see J. Brooks Flippen, "Mr. Hickel Goes to Washington," *Alaska History* 12, no. 2 (Fall 1998): 1–22. *Anchorage Daily News*, Jan. 29, 1991, B5; Aug. 26, 1991, D1; Dec. 6, 1994, B1; Nov. 23, 1994, B8; Oct. 19, 1997, F3. See also Malcolm Roberts, *The Wit and Wisdom of Wally Hickel* (Anchorage: Searchers Press, 1994); Campaign Flier, Harnessing Alaska's Potential, Hickel for Governor Campaign, 1990, Vertical File, Alaska Collection, Z. J. Loussac Public Library, Anchorage, Alaska.

23. See *Hearings Before the Committee on Interior and Insular Affairs on the Nomination of Walter Hickel to be Secretary of Interior*, 91st Cong., 1st sess., Jan. 15–18, 1969 (Washington, D.C.: U.S. Government Printing Office, 1969). For Hickel's perspective, see his memoirs, *Who Owns America?*, 1–11.

24. Hickel quoted in *New York Times*, Dec. 19, 1968, 26; Hickel, *Who Owns America?*, 11; *New York Times*, Dec. 20, 1968, 46; see also Dec. 28, 1968, 26; Jan. 14, 1969, 44.

25. Letter, E. J. Powers to Gaylord Nelson et al., Jan. 4, 1969, Folder 14, "1969 Correspondence, 100 Interior and Insular Affairs, Secretary of Interior, Hickel Letters, Robo," Box SE1369, USSSO, EMA.

26. *Hearings, Hickel*, 9–12; *Boston Globe*, Jan. 16, 1969, 1, 11.

27. Interview, Author with Walter Hickel, Mar. 27, 1998; Memo, Leon Billings to Edmund Muskie, Jan. 14, 1969, Folder 5, "1966–1976 Miscellaneous Memos," Box 1961, USSSO, EMA.

28. *Sierra Club Bulletin* 54, no. 2 (February 1969): 2; Muskie quoted in *Boston Globe*, Jan. 16, 1969, 44.

29. Interview, Author with David Parker, July 6, 1998.

30. *Public Papers of the Presidents: Richard Nixon, 1969* (Washington, D.C.: U.S. Government Printing Office, 1971), 1–4.

31. *Sierra Club Bulletin* 54, no. 3 (March 1969): 9; Stahr quoted in *The Santa Barbara News Press*, Mar. 19, 1969, A8; Hartzog quoted in Ross MacDonald and Robert Easton, "Santa Barbarans Cite an Eleventh Commandment: 'Thou Shalt Not Abuse the Earth,'" in Amos H. Hawley, ed., *Man and Environment* (New York: New York Times Company, 1975), 136; *New York Times*, Feb. 1, 1969, 32; Feb. 2, 1969, 1.

32. Interview, Author with Walter Hickel, Mar. 27, 1998; Memo, Rose Mary Woods to Bryce Harlow, Feb. 6, 1969, Folder "EX NR 6 Oil-Natural Gas (1 of 10)," Box 10, Natural Resources Files, WHCF, RNPMP; Memorandum for the President's File, Feb. 6, 1969, Folder "Meetings File, Beginning February 2, 1969," Box 77, President's Office Files, WHSF, RNPMP; Robert Easton, *Black Tide: The Santa Barbara Oil Spill and Its Consequences* (New York: Delacorte Press, 1972), 51–52.

33. *Public Papers, 1969*, 93–94; Memo, Patrick Buchanan to Richard Nixon, Feb. 11, 1969, Folder "Meetings File, Beginning February 11, 1969," Box 77, President's Office Files, WHSF, RNPMP; Nixon quoted in Transcript, Press Conference, Richard Nixon, Folder "Meetings File, Beginning February 9, 1969," Box 77, President's Office Files, WHSF, RNPMP.

34. Memo, Walter Hickel to Richard Nixon, Mar. 17, 1969, Folder "OA 3247—Environment—Santa Barbara Oil Pollution—Union Oil," Box 67, Egil Krogh Files, WHSF, RNPMP; Memo, John Ehrlichman to Ken Cole, Mar. 19, 1969, Folder "OA 3247—Environment—Santa Barbara Oil Pollution—Union Oil," Box 67, Egil Krogh Files, WHSF, RNPMP; Easton, *Black Tide*, 136.

35. Letter, Ralph E. Hallock to Walter Hickel, Feb. 6, 1969, Folder 3, "1969 Correspondence, 500 Public Works, Santa Barbara Materials," Box 1560, USSSO, EMA.

36. Transcript, Opening Statement by Senator Edmund Muskie, Hearings of the Subcommittee on Air and Water Pollution, Senate Committee on Public Works, Feb. 5, 1969, Folder 6, "1969 Correspondence, 500 Public Works, Santa Barbara Materials," Box 1560, USSSO, EMA; *New York Times*, Feb. 6, 1969, 22.

37. Press Release, Office of Senator Alan Cranston, Feb. 26, 1969, Folder 2, "1969 Correspondence, 500 Public Works, Santa Barbara Materials," Box 1560, USSSO, EMA.

38. Resolution, The Sierra Club, Feb. 26, 1969, Folder 5, "1969 Correspondence, 500 Public Works, Santa Barbara Materials," Box 1560, USSSO, EMA.

39. Interview, Author with Russell Train, July 8, 1998.

40. Press Release, Department of Interior, Mar. 21, 1969, Folder "OA 3247 — Environment — Santa Barbara Oil Pollution — Union Oil," Box 67, Egil Krogh Files, WHSF, RNPMP; Transcript, President's Remarks, Mar. 21, 1969, Folder "OA 3247 — Environment — Santa Barbara Oil Pollution — Union Oil," Box 67, Egil Krogh Files, WHSF, RNPMP; *New York Times*, Aug. 22, 1969, 1; Easton, *Black Tide*, 173.

41. *New York Times*, Apr. 2, 1969; Easton, *Black Tide*, 142.

42. Memo, John Whitaker to John Ehrlichman, Dec. 22, 1969, Folder "Santa Barbara, 1970, 2 of 3," Box 103, John Whitaker Files, WHCF, RNPMP; Whitaker, *Striking a Balance*, 269.

43. Memo, Richard Nixon to John Ehrlichman, Mar. 13, 1969, Folder "355, Domestic Policy, 2 of 2," Box 31, John Ehrlichman Files, WHSF, RNPMP; Memo, Alexander Butterfield to H. R. Haldeman, Apr. 7, 1969, Folder "355, Domestic Policy, 2 of 2," Box 31, John Ehrlichman Files, WHSF, RNPMP.

44. Interview, Author with David Parker, July 6, 1998; Memo, John Ehrlichman to Richard Nixon, Mar. 14, 1969, Folder "355, Domestic Policy, 2 of 2," Box 31, John Ehrlichman Files, WHSF, RNPMP; Memo, Daniel Moynihan to Walter Hickel, Mar. 14, 1969, Folder "355, Domestic Policy, 2 of 2," Box 31, John Ehrlichman Files, WHSF, RNPMP; Memo, John McClaughry to Len Garmet and Bryce Harlow, Apr. 2, 1969, Folder "355, Domestic Policy, 2 of 2," Box 31, John Ehrlichman Files, WHSF, RNPMP.

45. Introduced as S. 1075; Jackson was Chair of the Senate Interior and Insular Affairs Committee. Although he previously had called for a stated national policy for the environment, S. 1075 pertained solely to the creation of CEQ, primarily to forestall any controversy over committee jurisdiction with Muskie's Subcommittee on Air and Water Pollution, whose jurisdiction included nearly all previous environmental legislation; Richard Andrews, *Environmental Policy and Administrative Change* (Lexington, Mass..: D. C. Heath, 1976), 8–9.

46. Letter, Stewart Udall to Henry Jackson, July 31, 1969, Folder 20, "Legislation-HMJ-91, S.1075, 1969–1970," Box 213, Accession No. 3560–4, Papers of Henry Jackson (hereafter cited as PHJ), Manuscripts and University Archives Division, University of Washington Libraries; Letter, Patricia Ernst to Henry Jackson, Aug. 1, 1969, Folder 20, "Legislation-HMJ-91, S.1075, 1969–1970," Box 213, Accession No. 3560–4, PHJ.

47. Introduced as S. 7; Muskie quoted in *Los Angeles Times*, May 21, 1969, A12.

48. A transitional task force on executive reorganization chaired by Nixon's former law partner Franklin Lindsay had recommended the creation of PACEO; *New York Times*, Apr. 6, 1969, 1; Chronology of Reorganization Proposals, March 1971, Folder "Chronology of Reorganization Proposals," Box 22, PACEO Files, WHCF, RNPMP; Stanley Kutler, *The Wars of Watergate* (New York: Alfred A. Knopf, 1990), 137.

49. Executive Order 11472; Robert A. Shanley, "Presidential Executive Orders and Environmental Policy," *Presidential Studies Quarterly* 13, no. 1 (Summer, 1983): 405–16.

50. Interview, Author with Laurence Moss, Mar. 25, 1998; Joel Primack and Frank Von

Hippel, "Scientists, Politics and the SST: A Critical Review," *Science and Public Affairs* 28, no. 4 (April 1972): 24–30. Science advisor DuBridge appointed the members, many from the president's Science Advisory Committee; an additional committee of high-ranking departmental officials, the "Ad Hoc SST Review Committee," simultaneously investigated the matter. For a full discussion of the SST controversy, see Melvin Horwitch, *Clipped Wings: The American SST Conflict* (Cambridge, Mass.: MIT Press, 1982).

51. See Thomas Dunlap, *DDT, Scientists, Citizens, and Public Policy* (Princeton, N.J.: Princeton University Press, 1981).

52. *Report of the Secretary's Commission on Pesticides and their Relationship to Environmental Health* (Washington, D.C.: U.S. Government Printing Office, 1969); Memo, Robert Finch to Members, EQC, Aug. 26, 1969, Folder "Pesticides, 1970 (1969–1970), 3 of 3," Box 90, John Whitaker Files, WHCF, RNPMP.

53. Interview, Author with Joe Browder, Mar. 24, 1998; *Living Wilderness* 33, no. 103 (Spring 1969): 3; Howard Bloomfield, "The Everglades: Pregnant with Risks," *American Forests* 78 (May 1970): 27; Gary A. Soucie, "The Everglades Jetport: One Hell of an Uproar," *Sierra Club Bulletin* 54 (July 1969): 23; *BioScience* 19, no. 7 (July 1969): 64.

54. Dennis LeMaster, *Decade of Change: The Remaking of Forest Service Statutory Authority in the 1970s* (Westport, Conn.: Greenwood Press, 1984), 19–20; Michael Frome, *Battle for the Wilderness* (Boulder, Colo.: Westview Press, 1984), 129–40.; Rapid new home construction led to overcutting on many private forests. The clamor for wood-based products slowed the Forest Service's existing program of "primitive" land classification, prompting it to protect only those forests with the least timber value.

55. By Nixon's election, Congress had added only four new wilderness units for a total of 800,000 acres, a small percentage of that covered in the Wilderness Act; Kevin Haight, "The Wilderness Act: Ten Years After," *Environmental Affairs* 3 (1974): 279.

56. *Parker v. United States*, 309 F. Supp. 593 (1970); see Dennis Murrow Roth, *The Wilderness Movement and the National Forests* (College Station, Tex.: Intaglio Press, 1988), 1–5, 7, 10.

57. H.R. 10344, later reintroduced as H.R. 12025, popularly known as Timber Supply Act; *Sierra Club Bulletin* 54, no. 5 (May 1969): 6, 10; Hardy L. Shirley, "Timber and the Environment," *BioScience* 24 (August 1974): 473; *New York Times*, May 13, 1969, 46; Nixon quoted in Report on Meeting of Cabinet Committee on Economic Policy, Mar. 7, 1969, Folder "Meetings File, Beginning March 2, 1969," Box 77, President's Office Files, WHSF, RNPMP; Train quoted in Memo, John Whitaker to Russell Train, Dec. 4, 1969, Folder "June–December, 1969, 6 of 6, December, 1969," Box 1, John Whitaker Files, WHCF, RNPMP.

58. *Living Wilderness* 33. no. 106 (Summer 1969): 38.

59. Interview, Author with David Parker, July 6, 1998; Craig W. Allin, *The Politics of Wilderness Preservation* (Westport, Conn.: Greenwood Press, 1982), 209; Alaska Pipeline, Chronology of Events, 1968–1970, Folder "Alaska Pipeline, 1969–1970, 2 of 4," Box 25, John Whitaker Files, WHCF, RNPMP. See Peter Coates, *The Trans-Alaska Pipeline Controversy* (Bethlehem, Pa.: Lehigh University Press, 1991).

60. Memo, Richard Nixon to Walter Hickel, May 9, 1969, Folder "EX FG 221–25, Protection of Alaska's Artic Environment, 1969–1970," Box 5, Presidential Task Forces, WHCF, RNPMP.

61. Memo, Jack Caulfield to John Ehrlichman, June 11, 1969, Folder "357-OA #4295, Pollution Control," Box 73, Egil Krogh Files, WHSF, RNPMP.

62. See Ambrose, *Nixon, Triumph*, chap. 12. Nixon's proposal for welfare reform, the Family Assistance Plan, promised to diminish the AFDC bureaucracy, but initially required an increase in federal expenditures, anathema to conservatives. Illegal 1969 wiretaps included columnist Joseph Kraft, four other journalists, and Nixon's own brother, Don Nixon.

63. Memo, John Ehrlichman to Lee DuBridge, June 16, 1969, Folder "357-OA #4295, Pollution Control," Box 73, Egil Krogh Files, WHSF, RNPMP.

64. Whitaker, *Striking a Balance*, 29.

65. *Sierra Club Bulletin* 54, no. 8 (August 1969): 16.

66. Andrews, *Environmental Policy*, 9–10.

67. *Seattle Post Intelligencer*, Mar. 16, 1969, 27.

68. Jackson quoted in *Hearings on S.1075 Before the Senate Committee on Interior and Insular Affairs*, 91st Cong., 1st sess., June 1969 (Washington, D.C.: U.S. Government Printing Office, 1969), 137.

69. Memo, Lee DuBridge to Richard Nixon, July 9, 1969, Folder "White House-President-Vol. II, 1969, 1 of 2," Box 26, Edward David Files, WHCF, RNPMP.

70. Nixon quoted in Memorandum for the President's File, Lee Dubridge, Aug. 26, 1969, Folder "Meetings File, Beginning August 24, 1969," Box 79, President's Office Files, WHSF, RNPMP.

71. Memo, Arthur Burns to Richard Nixon, Mar. 19, 1969, Folder "Presidential Handwriting, March 16–31, 1969," Box 1, President's Office File, WHSF, RNPMP; Parmet, *Richard Nixon and His America*, 543–44; Paul Ehrlich, *The Population Bomb: Population Control or Race to Oblivion?* (New York: Ballantine Books, 1968), xi.

72. Press Release, House Republican Task Force on Earth Resources and Population, July 11, 1969, Folder Population," Box 57, Edwin Harper Files, WHSF, RNPMP; Agenda, Cabinet Meeting, July 10, 1969, Folder "Memos—Cabinet Members, July, 1969," Box 51, H. R. Haldeman Files, WHSF, RNPMP; See *Congressional Record*, 91st Cong., 1st sess., Vol. 115, pt. 3 (June 18, 1969).

73. *New York Times*, July 19, 1969, 1; Final Draft, Population Message to Congress, undated, Folder "White House-Environment, 1969," Box 9, Edward David Files, WHCF, RNPMP.

74. *New York Times*, Sept. 22, 1969, 31; *Atlanta Constitution*, Sept. 24, 1969, B5.

75. Nixon quoted in Ambrose, *Nixon, Triumph*, 284, 285.

76. *Living Wilderness* 33, no. 106 (Summer 1969): 35; *Sierra Club Bulletin* 54, no. 9 (September 1969): 2.

77. Interview, Author with Walter Hickel, Mar. 27, 1998; Memo, Walter Hickel to Director, National Park Service, June 18, 1969, Folder "President's Handwriting, June, 1969," Box 2, President's Office Files, WHSF, RNPMP; Memo, Walter Hickel to Richard Nixon, June 20, 1969, Folder "President's Handwriting, June, 1969," Box 2, President's Office Files, WHSF, RNPMP; Memo, Alexander Butterfield to Richard Nixon, July 28, 1969, Folder "Memos, John Ehrlichman, June, 1969," Box 50, H. R. Haldeman Files, WHSF, RNPMP; Memo, Egil Krogh to Herb Klein, July 1, 1969, Folder "Memo, July, 1969," Box 1, Egil Krogh Files, WHSF, RNPMP; Whitaker, *Striking a Balance*, 185.

78. Letter, Edmund Muskie to Ernest Malter, Aug. 8, 1970, Folder 3, "1970 Resource, 500 — Public Works — Pollution General," Box 1093, USSSO, EMA.

79. Stewart quoted in *Seattle Post Intelligencer*, July 20, 1969, A1.

80. Rosenbaum, *Politics of Environmental Concern*, 168–69.

81. Memo, Walter Hickel to John Ehrlichman, Sept. 14, 1969, Folder "Dade County Jetport, 1970 (1969–1970), 3 of 3," Box 46, John Whitaker Files, WHCF, RNPMP; Memo, John Whitaker to John Ehrlichman, Nov. 5, 1969, Folder "Dade County Jetport, 1970 (1969–1970), 3 of 3," Box 46, John Whitaker Files, WHCF, RNPMP; Memo, Egil Krogh to John Whitaker, Nov. 18, 1969, Folder "Dade County Jetport, 1970 (1969–1970), 3 of 3," Box 46, John Whitaker Files, WHCF, RNPMP.

82. Memo, John Whitaker to John Ehrlichman, Dec. 12, 1969, Folder "June–December, 1969, 6 of 6, December, 1969," Box 1, John Whitaker Files, WHCF, RNPMP; Memo, John Whitaker to Russell Train and James Beggs, Dec. 12, 1969, Folder "Dade County Jetport, 1970 (1969–1970), 2 of 3," Box 46, John Whitaker Files, WHCF, RNPMP; *Christian Science Monitor*, Dec. 15, 1969, 6–7.

83. Clean Water Restoration Act of 1966.

84. Commission on Marine Science, Engineering and Resources, *Our Nation and the Sea: Report of the Commission on Marine Science, Engineering and Resources* (Washington, D.C.: U.S. Government Printing Office, 1969), vi, 57; Mangrove, *Marine Policy*, 260; Jeffrey K. Stine, "Regulating Wetlands in the 1970s: U.S. Army Corps of Engineers and the Environmental Organizations," *Journal of Forest History* 27 (April 1983): 60–65. For a broader discussion of wetlands, see Ann Vileisis, *Discovering the Unknown Landscape: A History of America's Wetlands* (Washington, D.C.: Island Press, 1997).

85. Whitaker, *Striking a Balance*, 151.

86. The bill provided for a maximum grant of 200,000 dollars in each phase; introduced as H.R. 14845; David Adams, "Management Systems Under Consideration at the Federal-State Level," in James C. Hite and James M. Stepp, *Coastal Zone Resource Management* (New York: Praeger, 1971), 23–28.

87. Memo, Walter Hickel to Richard Nixon, Aug. 13, 1969, Folder "White House-President, Vol. II, 1969, 1 of 2," Box 26, Edward David Files, WHCF, RNPMP.

88. *Christian Science Monitor*, June 23, 1969, 13; Nixon Handwritten Comments, Daily News Summary, June 24, 1969, Folder "Annotated News Summaries, June, 1969," Box 30, President's Office Files, WHSF, RNPMP; Memo, Alexander Butterfield to John Ehrlichman, June 30, 1969, Folder "Memos — John Ehrlichman, June, 1969," Box 50, H. R. Haldeman Files, WHSF, RNPMP.

89. Memo, John Ehrlichman to H. R. Haldeman, Oct. 22, 1969, Folder "Memos — John Ehrlichman, October, 1969," Box 53, H. R. Haldeman Files, WHSF, RNPMP; Memo, H. R. Haldeman to John Ehrlichman, Oct. 22, 1969, Folder "Memos — John Ehrlichman, October, 1969," Box 53, H. R. Haldeman Files, WHSF, RNPMP.

90. *Tacoma News Tribune*, Dec. 14, 1969, A8.

91. *Public Papers, 1969*, 737–38; Final Report of the SST Ad Hoc Review Committee, 1969, Folder "OST — White House, Supersonic Transport, Oversized Materials, 1969," Box 38, Edward David Files, WHCF, RNPMP.

92. Memo, Richard Nixon to John Volpe, Jan. 24, 1969, Folder "EX CA 8, Aircraft Development, 1969–1970, 1 of 3," Box 28, Civil Aviation Files, WHCF, RNPMP.

93. Memorandum for the File, Agenda, Staff Meeting, H. R. Haldeman, Sept. 24, 1969, Folder "Meetings, Part II, Summary," Box 737, H. R. Haldeman Files, WHSF, RNPMP.

94. Primack and Von Hippel, "Scientists, Politics, and the SST"; Memo, John Ehrlichman to Richard Nixon, Apr. 3, 1969, Folder "EX CA 8, Aircraft Development, 1969–1970, 1 of 3," Box 28, Civil Aviation Files, WHCF, RNPMP.

95. Final Draft, Edmund Muskie Article for *Trial Magazine*, submitted Dec. 3, 1969, Folder 4, "1969 Press Files, Speeches, December," Box 1532, USSSO, EMA; Letter, Gladys Kessler to John Volpe, Dec. 10, 1969, Folder "White House — SST Litigation, 1969–1970," Box 38, Edward David Files, WHCF, RNPMP; Letter, Lee DuBridge to Gladys Kessler, Apr. 8, 1970, Folder "White House — SST Litigation, 1969–1970," Box 38, Edward David Files, WHCF, RNPMP.

96. Report of the Secretary's Commission on Pesticides and Their Relationship to Environmental Health, Folder "Pesticides — 1970 (1969–1970), 3 of 3," Box 90, John Whitaker Files, WHCF, RNPMP; Press Release, Ban on DDT, Nov. 20, 1969, Folder "Conservation Foundation," Box 52, Charles Colson Files, WHSF, RNPMP; Memo, John Whitaker to Charles Colson, Nov. 24, 1969, Folder "Pesticides — 1970 (1969–1970), 3 of 3," Box 90, John Whitaker Files, WHCF, RNPMP.

97. Whitaker, *Striking a Balance*, 133; Harrison Wellford, "Pesticides" in James Rathlesberger, editor, *Nixon and the Environment: The Politics of Devastation* (New York: Village Voice, 1972), 152.

98. The companies included Allied Chemical and Stauffer Chemical of New York City, Lebanon Chemical of Pennsylvania, Diamond Shamrock Corp. of Ohio, Black Leaf Products of Illinois, and Carolina Chemical of North Carolina; *Congressional Quarterly Almanac*, 91st Cong., 1st sess. (June 23, 1970), 229.

99. Coates, *Trans-Alaska Pipeline*, 180–82; Alaska Pipeline, Chronology of Events, 1968–1970, Folder "Alaska Pipeline, 1969–1970, 2 of 4," Box 25, John Whitaker Files, WHCF, RNPMP; Hickel, *Who Owns America?*, 123–24.

100. Report of the Federal Task Force on Alaskan Oil Development, Sept. 15, 1969, Folder "White House — Oceanography, 1969–1970," Box 15, Edward David Files, WHCF, RNPMP.

101. Memo, John Whitaker to Walter Hickel, Dec. 16, 1969, Folder "Alaska Land Selection, 1969–1970," Box 25, John Whitaker Files, WHCF, RNPMP.

102. Coates, *Trans-Alaska Pipeline*, 184–85.

103. Jackson quoted in Memo, John Ehrlichman to John Whitaker, Dec. 8, 1969, Folder "Alaska Pipeline, 1969–1970, 1 of 4," Box 25, John Whitaker Files, WHCF, RNPMP.

104. Alaska Pipeline Chronology of Events, 1968–1970, Folder "Alaska Pipeline, 1969–1970, 2 of 4," Box 25, John Whitaker Files, WHCF, RNPMP.

105. Memo, John Ehrlichman to John Whitaker, Dec. 8, 1969, Folder "Alaska Pipeline, 1969–1970, 1 of 4," Box 25, John Whitaker Files, WHCF, RNPMP.

106. Andrews, *Environmental Policy*, 12.

107. Interview, Author with Leon Billings, June 26, 1998.

108. Memo, John Whitaker to John Ehrlichman, Nov. 18, 1969, Folder "440 — OA 2975, Conservation," Box 63, Egil Krogh Files, WHSF, RNPMP; Memo, Russell Train to John Ehrlichman, Nov. 3, 1969, Folder "485 — OA 2977, Environment," Box 63, Egil Krogh Files, WHSF, RNPMP.

109. Whitaker, *Striking a Balance*, 31.

110. Memo, John Whitaker to Ken Cole, undated, Folder "Endangered Species Act," Box 60, Charles Colson Files, WHSF, RNPMP; Memo, Dwight Chapin to Richard Nixon, Dec. 2, 1969, Folder "EX NR Fish-Wildlife, 1 of 7, 1969–1970," Box 3, Natural Resources File, WHCF, RNPMP; Memo, Russell Train to John Whitaker, Aug. 26, 1969, Folder "EX NR Fish-Wildlife, 1 of 7, 1969–1970," Box 3, Natural Resources Files, WHCF, RNPMP; Scheffer, *Shaping of Environmentalism*, 158–59.

111. Presidential Statement on Signing of Wildlife Bill, Dec. 5, 1969, Folder "Endangered Species Act," Box 60, Charles Colson Files, WHSF, RNPMP; *New York Times*, Dec. 6, 1969, 1.

112. Interview, Author with John Whitaker, July 23, 1996. For a full discussion of NEPA and its implementation, see Lynton Caldwell, *The National Environmental Policy Act: An Agenda for the Future* (Bloomington: Indiana University Press, 1998); and Lynton Caldwell, *Science and the National Environmental Policy Act: Redirecting Policy through Procedural Reform* (University, Ala.: University of Alabama Press, 1982).

113. Memo, John Whitaker to John Ehrlichman, Dec. 24, 1969, Folder "EX FG 251, EQC; FG 251, CCE, Terminated July 1, 1970, 2 of 2," Box 1, Cabinet Committee on the Environment Files, WHCF, RNPMP; Memo, John Whitaker to Lee DuBridge, Dec. 17, 1969, Folder "June–December, 1969, 6 of 6, December, 1969," Box 1, John Whitaker Files, WHCF, RNPMP; Memo, Wilfred Rommel to Richard Nixon, Dec. 30, 1969, Folder "EX FG 251, EQC, FG 251, CCE, Terminated July 1, 1970, 2 of 2," Box 1, Cabinet Committee on the Environment Files, WHCF, RNPMP; Kent Portney, *Controversial Issues in Environmental Policy* (Newbury Park, Calif..: Sage, 1992), 41; Andrews, *Environmental Policy*, 13.

114. See Ambrose, *Nixon, Triumph*, 308–10.

Chapter 2

1. *New York Times*, Jan. 2, 1970, 1, 20.

2. Interview, Author with John Whitaker, July 23, 1996; Whitaker, *Striking a Balance*, 49–50.

3. *Public Papers, 1970*, 2–3.

4. *New York Times*, Jan. 2, 1970, 1, 12.

5. *Public Papers, 1970*, 3.

6. Letter, Harold LeVonder to Richard Nixon, Jan. 2, 1970, Folder "EX FG 251, EQC; FG 251, CCE, Terminated July 1, 1970, 2 of 2," Box 1, Cabinet Committee on Environment Files, WHCF, RNPMP; Letter, John Nanna to Richard Nixon, Jan. 12, 1970, Folder "White House-President-Public Mail, Environmental Council, 2 of 3," Box 28, Edward David Files, WHCF, RNPMP; *New York Times*, Jan. 4, 1970, IV, 12; Jan. 23, 1970, 46.

7. Interview, Author with Mike Leavitt, July 22, 1998; Interview, Author with David Parker, July 6, 1998; Interview, Author with John Whitaker, July 23, 1996.

8. Memo, John Whitaker to Richard Nixon, Jan. 28, 1970, Folder "January–April, 1 of 4, January, January, 1970," Box 2, John Whitaker Files, WHCF, RNPMP; *New York Times*, Jan. 30, 1970, 31; Whitaker, *Striking a Balance*, 51.

9. Executive Order no. 11514; Shanley, "Presidential Executive Orders"; Robert Shan-

ley, *Presidential Influence and Environmental Policy* (Westport, Conn.: Greenwood Press, 1992), 53; Press Release, Executive Order, Protection and Enhancement of Environmental Quality, Mar. 5, 1970, Folder "The Environmental Coalition, 1 of 2," Box 61, Charles Colson Files, WHSF, RNPMP; Memo, John Ehrlichman to Richard Nixon, Feb. 27, 1970, Folder "January-April, 1970, 2 of 4, February, 1970," Box 2, John Whitaker Files, WHCF, RNPMP.

10. *Public Papers, 1970,* 13.

11. *New York Times,* Jan. 4, 1970, 2; Jan. 4, 1970, IV, 5; Feb. 15, 1970, 36; Feb. 1, 1970, 1; Feb. 21, 1970, 12.

12. Ibid., Jan. 2, 1970, 14. The restructuring included more representation for members east of the Mississippi River, the area of its most rapidly growing membership.

13. *The Arizona Republic,* Jan. 16, 1970, 21.

14. Ambrose, *Nixon, Triumph,* 333. See Miller, *On Our Own;* William Tulio Divale, *I Lived Inside the Campus Revolution* (New York: College Notes, 1970).

15. Memo, John Ehrlichman to Richard Nixon, Jan. 14, 1970, Folder "January–April, 1970, 1 of 4, January, 1970," Box 2, John Whitaker Files, WHCF, RNPMP.

16. Memo, John Whitaker to John Ehrlichman, Jan. 20, 1970, Folder "January–April, 1970, 1 of 4, January, 1970," Box 2, John Whitaker Files, WHCF, RNPMP; Memo, Charles Clapp to Patrick Moynihan, Jan. 20, 1970, Folder "HE 9–1, Air Pollution, Begin-January 31, 1970," Box 30, Health Files, WHCF, RNPMP; Letter, Lee DuBridge to Leigh H. Frederickson, Jan. 21, 1970, Folder "White House-President-Environmental Council, 1970, 2 of 3," Box 28, Edward David Files, WHCF, RNPMP; Letter, Lee DuBridge to William Haney, Jan. 23, 1970, Folder "White House-President-Environmental Council, 2 of 3," Box 28, Edward David Files, WHCF, RNPMP.

17. Memo, John Whitaker to Christopher DeMuth, Feb. 2, 1979, "January–April, 1970, 2 of 4, February, 1970," Box 2, John Whitaker Files, WHCF, RNPMP; Memo, Christopher DeMuth to Patrick Buchanan, Jan. 29, 1970, Folder "Environmental Briefing, January-February, 1970," Box 13, Patrick Buchanan Files, WHSF, RNPMP.

18. Articles of Agreement, The Everglades-Jetport Pact, January 1970, Folder "Dade County Jetport, 1970 (1969–70), 1 of 3" Box 46, John Whitaker Files, WHCF, RNPMP.

19. Memo, John Ehrlichman to Richard Nixon, Jan. 14, 1970, Folder "January–April, 1970, 1 of 4, January, 1970," Box 2, John Whitaker Files, WHCF, RNPMP; Press Release, Statement by the President, Everglades Jetport Pact, Jan. 15, 1970, Folder "Jetport, 1970–72," Box 76, John Whitaker Files, WHCF, RNPMP.

20. Transcript, Press Conference, Walter Hickel and John Volpe, Jan. 15, 1970, Folder "Jetport, 1970–72," Box 76, John Whitaker Files, WHCF, RNPMP.

21. Letter, Anthony Wayne Smith to Richard Nixon, Jan. 14, 1970, Folder "Conservation-Miami Jetport," Box 52, Charles Colson Files, WHSF, RNPMP; Letter, Anthony Wayne Smith to Russell Train, Jan. 14, 1970, Folder "Conservation-Miami Jetport," Box 52, Charles Colson Files, WHSF, RNPMP; Letter, John Whitaker to Anthony Wayne Smith, Jan. 16, 1970, Folder "Dade County Jetport, 1970 (1969–70), 1 of 3," Box 46, John Whitaker Files, WHCF, RNPMP.

22. Tim Palmer, *Endangered Rivers and the Conservation Movement* (Berkeley: University of California Press, 1986), 97; Scheffer, *Shaping of Environmentalism,* 136; Resolution,

City of Palatka, Florida, Feb. 13, 1969, Folder "GEN NR 7–1, A-Z Projects, 3 of 50, 1969–1970, CFBC, 1969–70," Box 20, Natural Resources Files, WHCF, RNPMP; Letter, Charles E. Bennett to Richard Nixon, Oct. 15, 1969, Folder "GEN NR 7–1, A-Z Projects, 3 of 50, 1969–70, CFBC, 1969–70," Box 20, Natural Resources Files, WHCF, RNPMP; Letter, L. C. Ringhaver to Richard Nixon, Dec. 15, 1969, Folder "June-December, 1969, 6 of 6, December, 1969," Box 1, John Whitaker Files, WHCF, RNPMP.

23. Jeffrey K. Stine, *Mixing the Waters: Environment, Politics, and the Building of the Tennessee-Tombigbee Waterway* (Akron, Ohio: University of Akron Press, 1993), 28–32; Jeffrey K. Stine, "Environmental Politics in the American South: The Fight over the Tennessee-Tombigbee Waterway," *Environmental History Review* 15, no. 1 (Spring 1991): 5–7; William H. Stewart, Jr., *The Tennessee-Tombigbee Waterway: A Case Study in the Politics of Water Transportation* (University, Ala.: Bureau of Public Administration, University of Alabama, 1971), 1–2; 101.

24. Summary of Environmental Considerations, CEQ Report, 1970, Folder "Cross Florida Barge Canal," Box 25, John Dean Files, WHSF, RNPMP; List of Studies and Reports on the Cross Florida Barge Canal, 1970, Folder "Cross Florida Barge Canal," Box 25, John Dean Files, WHSF, RNPMP; Palmer, *Endangered Rivers*, 99.

25. Stine, "Environmental Politics," 5–7.

26. Jackson quoted in *The Sacramento Union*, Jan. 23, 1970, 1; Muskie quoted in *The Arizona Republic*, Jan. 16, 1970, 23; Mansfield quoted in *Washington Post*, Jan. 22, 1970, 2.

27. *New York Times*, Jan. 4, 1970, 53; Jan. 18, 1970, 51.

28. Interview, Author with John Whitaker, July 23, 1996.

29. Memo, John Whitaker to Russell Train, Mar. 16, 1970, Folder "485-Z-Environment," Box 63, Egil Krogh Files, WHSF, RNPMP.

30. *Environmental Defense Fund v. Corps of Engineers*, 324 F. Supp. 878; Frederick R. Anderson and Robert H, Daniels, *NEPA in the Courts* (Baltimore: Johns Hopkins University Press, 1973): 147–48.

31. Letter, Albert P. Brewer to Richard Nixon, Nov. 6, 1969, Folder "GEN NR 7–1, A-Z Projects, 10 of 50, 1969–70, T-Z," Box 22, Natural Resources Files, WHCF, RNPMP; Stewart, *Tennessee-Tombigbee Waterway*, 101; Stine, *Mixing the Waters*, 29.

32. *U.S. News and World Report*, Jan. 19, 1970, 48–50; Memo, John Whitaker to James Krogh, Jan. 22, 1970, Folder "January-April, 1970, 1 of 4, January, 1970," Box 2, John Whitaker Files, WHCF, RNPMP; Memo, John Whitaker to Ronald Ziegler, Jan. 21, 1970, Folder "January-April, 1970, 1 of 4, January, 1970," Box 2, John Whitaker Files, WHCF, RNPMP; Memo, John Whitaker to Russell Train and Walter Hickel, Feb. 9, 1970, Folder "January–April, 2 of 4, February, 1970," Box 2, John Whitaker Files, WHCF, RNPMP.

33. Executive Order 11752; Transcript, Press Conference, Russell Train and James Schlesinger, Feb. 4, 1970, Folder "HE 9–1, Air Pollution, February 1, 1970–February 28, 1970," Box 30, Health Files, WHCF, RNPMP.

34. Memorandum for the President's File, unsigned, Feb. 6, 1970, Folder "Meetings File, Beginning February 1, 1970," Box 80, President's Office Files, WHSF, RNPMP.

35. S. 3354; Jackson quoted in *Congressional Record*, 91st Cong., 2d sess., Vol. 116, pt. 1 (Jan. 29, 1970), 5836.

36. Letter, Henry Jackson to James Findlay, May 5, 1970, Folder 38, "Legislation-HMJ-

91," Box 214, Accession No. 3560–4, PHJ; Transcript, Address of Henry Jackson to 25th Annual National Conference on Higher Education, Mar. 2, 1970, Folder 42, "Speeches and Writings-The Environmental Crisis: Issues and Answers, National Conference on Higher Education, Chicago, March 2, 1970," Box 234, Accession No. 3560–4, PHJ.

37. *Public Papers, 1970,* 95–108; Press Release, Environmental Message, Feb. 10, 1970, Folder "Environmental Message, February 10, 1970," Box 58, John Whitaker Files, WHCF, RNPMP; *New York Times,* Feb. 11, 1970, 1.

38. Vietor, *Environmental Politics,* 127–37; Rosenbaum, *Politics of Environmental Concern,* 147–53.

39. *New York Times,* Jan. 15, 1970, 30; Jan. 28, 1970, 90; Mar. 19, 1970, 95.

40. P.L. 88–206; John E. Heer, Jr., and D. Joseph Hagerty, *Environmental Assessments and Statements* (New York: Van Nostrand Reinhold, 1977), 41–42; American Enterprise Institute for Public Policy Research, *The Clean Air Act: Proposals for Revisions* (Washington, D.C.: American Enterprise Institute, 1981), 2.

41. American Enterprise Institute, *Clean Air Act,* 2; P.L. 89–272.

42. P.L. 90–148; Vietor, *Environmental Politics,* 150–54; Heer and Hagerty, *Environmental Assessments,* 42–43.

43. Nixon quoted in Memorandum for the File, John R. Price, Oct. 29, 1969, Folder "HE 9–1, Air Pollution, Begin-January 31, 1970," Box 30, Health Files, WHCF, RNPMP.

44. Memo, Lee DuBridge to Richard Nixon, Sept. 12, 1969, Folder "White House-President-Vol. II (1969), 2 of 2," Box 26, Edward David Files, WHCF, RNPMP; Memo, John Ehrlichman to Lee DuBridge, Nov. 21, 1969, Folder "291-OA#3053-Environmental Quality Council," Box 65, Egil Krogh Files, WHCF, RNPMP; Memo, John Ehrlichman to Richard Nixon, Dec. 22, 1969, Folder "HE 9–1, Air Pollution, Begin-January 31, 1970," Box 30, Health Files, WHCF, RNPMP; Memo, James Schlesinger to John Whitaker, Dec. 12, 1969, Folder "Auto-Unconventional, 1969–71, 2 of 2," Box 30, John Whitaker Files, WHCF, RNPMP.

45. *Public Papers, 1970,* 101–4; *New York Times,* Feb. 11, 1970, 1.

46. Hays, *Beauty, Health and Permanence,* 77; Petulla, *American Environmental History,* 340, 375.

47. Water Pollution Control Act of 1948, P.L. 80–845; Water Pollution Control Amendments of 1956, P.L. 84–660; Robert F. Durant, *When Government Regulates Itself* (Knoxville: University of Tennessee Press, 1985), 20; J. Clarence Davies, *The Politics of Pollution* (New York: Pegasus, 1970), 40.

48. Water Quality Act of 1965, P.L. 89–234; Clean Water Restoration Act of 1966, P.L. 89–753; Harvey Lieber, *Federalism and Clean Waters: The 1972 Water Pollution Control Act* (Lexington, Mass.: Lexington Books, D. C. Heath and Co., 1975), 12.

49. *Public Papers, 1970,* 100.

50. Memorandum for the File, Mar. 17, 1969, Folder "Meetings File, Beginning March 16, 1969," Box 77, President's Office Files, WHSF, RNPMP; Whitaker, *Striking a Balance,* 76–77.

51. Memo, David Kennedy to Richard Nixon, Dec. 22, 1969, Folder "President's Handwriting, December 16–31, 1969," Box 4, President's Office Files, WHSF, RNPMP; Memo, John Whitaker to John Ehrlichman, Dec. 23, 1969, Folder "Park Acquisition, Recreation,

1969–70," Box 90, John Whitaker Files, WHCF, RNPMP; Memo, Edwin Harper to John Whitaker et al., Dec. 16, 1969, Folder "Water, 1969–71, 4 of 5," Box 117, John Whitaker Files, WHCF, RNPMP; Memo, Paul McCracken to Ken Cole, Nov. 4, 1969, Folder "Pollution," Box 56, Edwin Harper Files, WHSF, RNPMP; Whitaker, *Striking a Balance*, 77–78; *New York Times*, Dec. 18, 1969, 31.

52. Memo, Maurice Stans to Richard Nixon, Feb. 4, 1970, Folder "White House-Issues, 1970, 1 of 2," Box 11, Edward David Files, WHCF, RNPMP; Memo, Maurice Stans to Richard Nixon, Feb. 4, 1970, Folder "NIPCC, 1970–71, 5 of 5," Box 84, John Whitaker Files, WHCF, RNPMP.

53. Memo, John Whitaker to Maurice Stans, Feb. 5, 1970, Folder "NIPCC, 1970–71, 5 of 5," Box 84, John Whitaker Files, WHCF, RNPMP.

54. Memorandum for the President's File, John Whitaker, Feb. 4, 1970, Folder "Meetings File, Beginning February 1, 1970," Box 80, President's Office File, WHSF, RNPMP.

55. *Feedstuffs* 4, no. 41 (Oct. 2, 1972): 28; Press Release, "Muskie Asks for Support for Water Pollution Programs," Folder 44, "1970 Press File, December 11; Statement by ESM, Water Pollution Support," Box SE 1536, USSSO, EMA.

56. P.L. 89–272; Whitaker, *Striking a Balance*, 111–13; Scheffer, *Shaping of Environmentalism*, 152; Kent E. Portney, *Controversial Issues*, 62; Rosenbaum, *Politics of Environmental Concern*, 251.

57. Muskie named his legislation the Resource Recovery Act; *Public Papers, 1970*, 104–5.

58. Janet Schaeffer, "Solid Wastes," in Rathlesberger, *Nixon and the Environment*, 239–41; Scheffer, *Shaping of Environmentalism*, 152.

59. Executive Order 11508; Press Release, Identification of Unneeded Federal Real Property, Feb. 10, 1970, Folder "Parklands," Box 56, Edwin Harper Files, WHSF, RNPMP; Memorandum for the President's File, Darrell Trent, July 15, 1970, Folder "Meetings File, Beginning July 12, 1970," Box 81, President's Office Files, WHSF, RNPMP; *Public Papers, 1970*, 103.

60. Interview, Author with Ronald Walker, Nov. 29, 1998; Whitaker quoted in Jonathan Aitken, *Nixon: A Life* (Washington, D.C.: Regnery Publishing, 1993), 398.

61. *Public Papers, 1970*, 109.

62. See Whitaker, *Striking a Balance*, 40.

63. *Washington Post*, Feb. 11, 1970, 20; *New York Times*, Feb. 11, 1970, 46.

64. Letter, Jack Urich to Richard Nixon, June 4, 1970, Folder "Auto-Leaded Gas Tax, 1970–71," Box 30, John Whitaker Files, WHCF, RNPMP.

65. Interview, Author with Maurice Stans, Aug. 11, 1996.

66. Transcript, Interview, Edmund Muskie with WMAL-TV, Washington, D.C., Apr. 19, 1970, Folder 5, "1970 Press File, April, Speeches," Box 1534, USSSO, EMA; Memo, Leon Billings to Edmund Muskie, Feb. 9, 1970, Folder 6, "1970 Correspondence—500 Public Works—Environmental Pollution," Box 1053, USSSO, EMA.

67. Transcript, Interview, Edmund Muskie, CBS News Special on the Environment, Feb. 18, 1970, Folder 6, "1970 Correspondence—500 Public Works—Environmental Pollution," Box 1053, USSSO, EMA.

68. *Sierra Club Bulletin* 55, no. 2 (February 1970): 23.

69. Memo, Charles Colson to John Whitaker, Feb. 23, 1970, Folder "Water, 1969–1971, 3 of 5," Box 117, John Whitaker Files, WHCF, RNPMP; Letter, R. A. Kotria to Richard Nixon, Feb. 11, 1970, Folder "Water, 1969–1971, 3 of 5," Box 117, John Whitaker Files, WHCF, RNPMP; President's Handwriting, Daily News Summaries, February, 1970, Box 31, President's Office Files, WHSF, RNPMP.

70. Interview, Author with John Whitaker, July 23, 1996; *New York Times*, Feb. 12, 1970, 27; Feb. 13, 1970, 20; Feb. 15, 1970, 23.

71. *New York Times*, Feb. 21, 1970, 64; Feb. 24, 1970, 51; Mar. 7, 1970, 3.

72. P.L. 91–213; *Public Papers, 1970*, 266–67.

73. P.L. 91–224; *BioScience* 20, no.8 (Apr. 15, 1970): 501; Memo, John Whitaker to Walter Hickel, Apr. 20, 1970, Folder "January-April, 1970, 4 of 4, April, 1970," Box 2, John Whitaker Files, WHCF, RNPMP; *New York Times*, Apr. 4, 1970, 30.

74. Nixon quoted in Ambrose, *Nixon, Triumph*, 339.

75. Aitken, *Nixon*, 385.

76. Ibid., 392–393; Ambrose, *Nixon, Triumph*, 335–39.

77. *New York Times*, Apr. 12, 1970, 30.

78. Nixon quoted in Parmet, *Richard Nixon and His America*, 4.

Chapter 3

1. Interview, Author with Walter Hickel, Mar. 27, 1998.

2. Hickel, *Who Owns America?*, 241–49; *New York Times*, May 7, 1970, 18.

3. Interview, Author with Walter Hickel, Mar. 27, 1998; Interview, Author with David Parker, July 6, 1998; Interview, Author with Mike Leavitt, June 22, 1998.

4. Ibid; John Ehrlichman, *Witness to Power* (New York: Pocket Books, 1982), 79; Nixon quoted in Haldeman Personal Notes, May 7, 1970, Folder "Haldeman Notes, April–June, 1970 (May 6-June 30, 1970), Part II, Box 41, H. R. Haldeman Files, WHSF, RNPMP.

5. Interview, Author with Hickel, Mar. 27, 1998; Ehrlichman, *Witness to Power*, 79.

6. Nixon quoted in Haldeman Personal Notes, May 8, 1970, Folder "Haldeman Notes, April–June, 1970 (May 6–June 30, 1970), Part II," Box 41, H. R. Haldeman Files, WHSF, RNPMP; Memo, John Ehrlichman to Richard Nixon, Nov. 24, 1970, Folder "Hickel Resignation," Box 20, John Ehrlichman Files, RNPMP; *New York Times*, May 22, 1970, 35.

7. Nixon quoted in Haldeman Personal Notes, May 10, 1970, Folder "Haldeman Notes, April–June, 1970 (May 6–June 30, 1970), Part II," Box 41, H. R. Haldeman Notes, WHSF, RNPMP.

8. Letter, Anthony Wayne Smith to Richard Nixon, June 26, 1970, Folder "GEN FG 19/A, Department of Interior/Appointments, 1 of 3, January–June, 1969," Box 3, Interior Files, WHCF, RNPMP.

9. Interview, Author with David Brower, Apr. 7, 1998.

10. Interview, Author with Joseph B. Browder, Mar. 24, 1998; Hickel, *Who Owns America?*, 250.

11. Nixon, *RN*, 457; *New York Times*, May 17, 1970, IV, 1.

12. Parmet, *Richard Nixon and His America*, 589.

13. Ambrose, *Nixon, Triumph*, 359–60.

14. Interview, Author with Hickel, Mar. 27, 1998.

15. H. R. Haldeman, *Ends of Power* (New York: New York Times Books, 1978), 107.

16. At various times assisting Whitaker were Christopher DeMuth, James Hyde, Glenn Schledee, Alvin Alm, Roger Strelow, John Quarles, Charles Elkins, Daniel Kingsley, James Schlesinger, Darrell Trent, Raymond Price, and James Lynn.

17. Interview, Author with William Ruckelshaus, Apr. 2, 1998; Interview, Author with Richard Fairbanks, Mar. 24, 1998.

18. Memorandum for the President's File, Roy Ash, Apr. 29, 1969, Folder "EX 250, PACEO, 1 of 6, April-August, 1969," Box 1, PACEO Files, WHSF, RNPMP.

19. Marc K. Landy, Marc J. Roberts, and Stephen R. Thomas, *The Environmental Protection Agency: Asking the Wrong Questions, from Nixon to Clinton* (New York: Oxford University Press, 1994), 30–33; Whitaker, *Striking a Balance*, 59–60; Memo, Roy Ash to Richard Nixon, Apr. 29, 1970, Folder "April 29, 1970, EPA Memorandum for the President on Environmental Protection," Box 2, PACEO Files, WHCF, RNPMP.

20. The Atomic Energy Commission lost the Division of Radiation Standards, and the Department of Agriculture the Pesticides Regulation Division. Interior also lost the Office of Research on Effects of Pesticides on Wildlife and Fish, while HEW also lost the Office of Pesticides Research. EPA finally gained the Interagency Federal Radiation Council.

21. Memo, John Whitaker to Bryce Harlow, Nov. 28, 1969, Folder "Department of Natural Resources, 1969–1971, 1 of 4," Box 47, John Whitaker Files, WHCF, RNPMP; Landy et al., *Environmental Protection Agency*, 31–32.

22. Letter, Maurice Stans to Richard Nixon, Feb. 4, 1970, Folder "White House-Issues, 1970, 1 of 2," Box 11, Edward David Files, WHCF, RNPMP.

23. Interview, Author with Maurice Stans, Aug. 11, 1996; Letter, Thomas Kimball to Charles Colson, June 29, 1970, Folder "Izaak Walton League of America, Etc.," Box 74, Charles Colson Files, WHSF, RNPMP.

24. Chronology of Ash Council-Natural Resources, December, 1971, Folder "Chronology of Reorganization Proposals," Box 22, PACEO Files, WHCF, RNPMP; Whitaker, *Striking a Balance*, 54.

25. Transcript, Press Conference, Russell Train and Rocco Siciliano, July 9, 1970, Folder "EPA, Creation of by Reorganization Plan #3 of 1970, 1 of 3," Box 64, John Whitaker Files, WHCF, RNPMP; Whitaker, *Striking a Balance*, 57–58.

26. Whitaker, *Striking a Balance*, 55–56, 66.

27. Letter, Edmund Muskie to Donald Songer, Aug. 6, 1970, Folder 2, "1970 Correspondence, 500 Public Works, Environment Correspondence," Box 1052, USSSO, EMA; Press Release, Muskie Calls for New Environmental Protection Agency, Office of Senator Edmund M. Muskie, Dec. 29, 1969, Folder 4, "1969 Press File-Speeches, December," Box 1532, USSSO, EMA.

28. Letter, John Whitaker to Roy Ash, July 9, 1970, Folder "May–August, 1970, 3 of 4, July, 1970," Box 2, John Whitaker Files, WHCF, RNPMP.

29. Memo, John Whitaker to John Ehrlichman, July 31, 1970, Folder "EPA, Creation of by Reorganization Plan #3 of 1970, 2 of 3," Box 64, John Whitaker Files, WHCF, RNPMP.

30. *The Izaak Walton League of America, Washington Newsletter,* Special Edition (Aug. 14, 1970): 1.

31. Senate Resolution 433, *Congressional Record,* 91st Cong., 2d sess., Vol. 116, pt. 4 (July 28, 1970), 8636; Statement by Senator Gaylord Nelson to Subcommittee on Executive Reorganization of the Senate Government Operations Committee, July 28, 1970, Folder 1, "1970 Correspondence, 100 Commerce, National Oceanic and Atmospheric Administration, EPA," Box 1232, USSSO, EMA; Memo, Eliot Cutler to Edmund Muskie, July 28, 1970, Folder 1, "1970 Correspondence, 100 Commerce, National Oceanic and Atmospheric Administration, EPA," Box 1232, USSSO, EMA; "Udall on the Environment," *Newsday,* Special Edition (June 29, 1970): 23.

32. Interview, Author with Whitaker, July 23, 1996.

33. Memo, John Whitaker to John Ehrlichman, Sept. 8, 1970, Folder "September–December, 1970, 1 of 4, September, 1970," Box 2, John Whitaker Files, WHCF, RNPMP.

34. Interview, Author with Hickel, Mar. 27, 1998.

35. Memo, John Whitaker to John Ehrlichman, Sept. 30, 1970, Folder "September–December, 1970, 2 of 4, October, 1970," Box 2, John Whitaker Files, WHCF, RNPMP; Memo, John Whitaker to John Ehrlichman, Oct. 14, 1970, Folder "September-December, 1970, 2 of 4, October, 1970," Box 2, John Whitaker Files, WHCF, RNPMP.

36. Interview, Author with William Ruckelshaus, Apr. 2, 1998; Landy et al., *Environmental Protection Agency,* 34.

37. Memo, John Whitaker to John Ehrlichman, Sept. 10, 1970, Folder "September–December, 1970, 1 of 4, September, 1970," Box 2, John Whitaker Files, WHCF, RNPMP; Memo, Tod Hullin to John Whitaker, Sept. 12, 1970, Folder "EX FG 999–23, EPA," Box 13, Proposed Departments File, WHCF, RNPMP; Memo, John Whitaker to John Ehrlichman, Feb. 23, 1971, Folder "January–March, 1971, 2 of 3, February, 1971," Box 3, John Whitaker Files, WHCF, RNPMP.

38. Memo, Leon Billings to Edmund Muskie, Nov. 13, 1970, Folder 2, "1970 Correspondence, 500 Public Works, Environment Correspondence," Box 1052, USSSO, EMA. Contending for the right to confirm the EPA administrator were the Senate committees on Commerce, Interior, and Public Works.

39. Memo, Eliot Cutler to Edmund Muskie, July 28, 1970, Folder 2, "1970 Resource, 200 Joint Committee on the Environment," Box 1064, USSSO, EMA; Memo, Eliot Cutler to Edmund Muskie, Oct. 7, 1970, Folder 2, "1970 Resource, 200 Joint Committee on the Environment," Box 1064, USSSO, EMA; Memo, Eliot Cutler to Edmund Muskie, Nov. 19, 1970, Folder 2, "1970 Resource, 200 Joint Committee on the Environment," Box 1064, USSSO, EMA.

40. *New York Times,* June 26, 1970, 1.

41. Press Release, Edmund S. Muskie, Apr. 23, 1970, Folder 3, "1970 Press File-Speeches-April," Box 1534, USSSO, EMA.

42. Coates, *Trans-Alaska Pipeline,* 189–90, 193; Mary Clay Berry, *The Alaska Pipeline* (Bloomington: Indiana University Press, 1975), 124–30; Allin, *Politics of Wilderness Preservation,* 212–13; Hickel, *Who Owns America?,* 126. The native claims bill that passed the Senate in mid-July provided the natives a ten-million-acre land grant, a cash payment of 500 million dollars, and a 2 percent royalty until profits totaled 500 million dol-

lars. The environmentalists' lawsuit was *Wilderness Society, et al. v. Hickel,* 325 F. Supp. 422–41. Memo, John Whitaker to Jack Horton, Mar. 12, 1970, Folder "Alaska Pipeline, 1969–1970, 3 of 4," Box 25, John Whitaker Files, WHCF, RNPMP; Memo, Walter Hickel to Richard Nixon, Mar. 20, 1970, Folder "EX NR 4, Land, 1 of 3, 1969–1970," Box 8, Natural Resources File, WHCF, RNPMP.

43. Transcript, Speech Before the American Association for Health, Physical Education and Recreation, June 3, 1970, Folder 30, "Speeches and Writings, Conservation, American Association for Health, Physical Education and Recreation, Seattle," Box 234, Accession No. 3560–4, PHJ.

44. *New York Times,* Mar. 17, 1970, 35; Sept. 28, 1970, 41, Aug. 23, 1970, 59; Nov. 18, 1970, 3.

45. Memo, Caspar Weinberger to John Ehrlichman, Aug. 3, 1970, Folder "Nixon Legacy of Parks, 1970–1972, 1 of 2," Box 87, John Whitaker Files, WHCF, RNPMP; Memo, John Whitaker to John Campbell, July 31, 1970, Folder "Nixon Legacy of Parks, 1970–1972, 1 of 2," Box 87, John Whitaker Files, WHCF, RNPMP; Memo, Ken Cole to John Whitaker, Aug. 24, 1970, Folder "Nixon Legacy of Parks, 1970–1972, 1 of 2" Box 87, John Whitaker Files, WHCF, RNPMP.

46. See Paul J. Culhane, *Public Lands Politics* (Baltimore: Johns Hopkins University Press, 1981); Marion Clawson, *The Federal Lands Revisited* (Baltimore: Johns Hopkins University Press, 1983); Hays, *Beauty, Health and Permanence,* chap. 4.

47. 16 U.S.C. 528. Initially, the Forest Management Act of 1897 established the continual supply of timber as the Forest Service's primary mandate, 16 U.S.C. 475. See Hal K. Rothman, *The Greening of a Nation?* (Orlando, Fla.: Harcourt Brace, 1998), 58–73; LeMaster, *Decade of Change*; Perry Hagenstein, "The Federal Lands Today: Uses and Limits," in Sterling Brubaker, ed., *Rethinking the Federal Lands* (Baltimore: Johns Hopkins University Press, 1984), 77–78, 83–86.

48. Richard Jordan, *Trees and People* (Washington, D.C.: Regnery Publishing, 1994), 3.

49. *New York Times,* June 3, 1970, X, 1; Nov. 19, 1970, 25.

50. See James Muhn and Hanson R. Stuart, *Opportunity and Challenge: The Story of the BLM* (Washington, D.C.: U.S. Government Printing Office, 1988).

51. Rothman, *Greening of a Nation?,* 69–73. For a discussion of the Sagebrush Rebellion, see *Environmental Forum* 2 (May 1983): 32–33; La Varr Webb, "The Sagebrush Rebellion: Coming on Strong," *State Legislatures* 6 (1980): 18–21.

52. Jackson also pushed, however, for stronger environmental provisions in the bill; Letter, Henry Jackson to Roger Woods, Mar. 13, 1970, Folder 1, "Legislation-HMJ-91, S. 1832-Timber Supply, 1969–1970," Box 214, Accession No. 3560–4, PHJ.

53. Transcript, George Romney Statement, Feb. 10, 1970, Folder "Timber Act," Box 117, Charles Colson Files, WHSF, RNPMP; Letter, Clifford Hardin to W. R. Poage, Feb. 12, 1970, Folder "Timber Act," Box 117, Charles Colson Files, WHSF, RNPMP.

54. Memo, Don Nicoll to Eliot Cutler, Feb. 21, 1970, Folder 9, "1970 Resource, 100 Agriculture, S.1832, National Timber Supply," Box 1072, USSSO, EMA; Muskie quoted in *New York Times,* Feb. 22, 1970, 44.

55. *Congressional Quarterly Almanac,* 91st Cong., 2d sess., 26 (1970), 334.

56. *Sierra Club v. Hardin*, 325 F. Supp.99 (D. Alaska, 1971); David Clary, *Timber and the Forest Service* (Lawrence: University of Kansas Press, 1986), 180–81; LeMaster, *Decade of Change*, 18; Memo, Russell Train to John Whitaker, Apr. 7, 1971, Folder "Wilderness Areas-1971, 3 of 4," Box 118, John Whitaker Files, WHCF, RNPMP.

57. National Forest Products Association White Paper, Apr. 17, 1970, Folder "Timber Act," Box 117, Charles Colson Files, WHSF, RNPMP; Memo, Russell Train to John Whitaker, Apr. 7, 1971, Folder "Wilderness Areas, 1971," Box 118, John Whitaker Files, WHCF, RNPMP.

58. Memo, Charles Colson to Robert Mayo, Apr. 17, 1970, Folder "Timber Act," Box 117, Charles Colson Files, WHSF, RNPMP.

59. Transcript, Press Conference, Staff, Council of Economic Advisors, June 19, 1970, Folder "EX FG 221–24, Lumber 1969–1970," Box 5, Presidential Task Forces, WHCF, RNPMP; Memo, John Whitaker to John Campbell, undated, Folder "EX FG 221–24, Lumber 1969–1970," Box 5, Presidential Task Forces, WHCF, RNPMP.

60. Letter, James Turnbill to Richard Nixon, July 1, 1970, Folder "GEN FG 221–24, Lumber 1969–1970," Box 5, Presidential Task Forces, WHCF, RNPMP; McCloskey quoted in *Sierra Club Bulletin* 55, no. 11 (November 1970): 4; Saylor quoted in *Congressional Record*, 91st Cong., 2d sess., Vol. 16, pt. 27 (Oct. 14, 1970), 36758.

61. See Clary, *Timber and the Forest Service*; George Alderson, "Public Lands," in Rathlesberger, *Nixon and the Environment*, 117.

62. Public Land Law Review Commission, *One Third of the Nation's Land: A Report to the President and to the Congress* (Washington, D.C.: U.S. Government Printing Office, 1970), x; Carl J. Mayer and George A. Riley, *Public Domain, Private Dominion: A History of Public Mineral Policy in the United States* (San Francisco, CA.: Sierra Club Books, 1985), 11–12.

63. Memo, Thomas P. Holley to John Whitaker, Mar. 23, 1970, Folder "Public Land Law Review, Grazing, 1969–1970, 2 of 2," Box 96, John Whitaker Files, WHCF, RNPMP.

64. Memo, John Whitaker to Bob Haldeman, June 17, 1970, Folder "May–August, 1970, 2 of 4, June, 1970," Box 2, John Whitaker Files, WHCF, RNPMP.

65. *Public Papers, 1970*, 515; *New York Times*, June 24, 1970, 1.

66. Public Land Law Review Commission, *One Third of the Nation's Lands*, Recommendations no. 3, 4, 13, 28, 30, 32–33, 36, 43, 56–59; Clawson, *Federal Lands Revisited*, 165.

67. *New York Times*, June 24, 1970, 1; Sept. 20, 1970, 61; Harold Peterson, "Moving in for a Land Grab," *Sports Illustrated* (June 20, 1970): 22–27; William K. Wyatt, *Westward in Eden: The Public Lands and the Conservation Movement* (Berkeley: University of California Press, 1982), 127.

68. William D. Rowley, *U.S. Forest Service Grazing and Rangelands* (College Station: Texas A&M University Press, 1985), 164–65; Muhn and Stuart, *Opportunity and Challenge*, 137; *Wildlife Management Institute Outdoor News Bulletin* 23, no. 22 (Nov. 7, 1969); *Washington Post*, Dec. 3, 1969, F11; Memo, John Whitaker to John Ehrlichman, Nov. 20, 1969, Folder "Public Land Law Review, Grazing, 1969–1970, 2 of 2," Box 96, John Whitaker Files, WHCF, RNPMP.

69. Public Land Law Review Commission, *One Third of the Nation's Lands*,

Recommendation no. 44; Press Release, Department of Interior, Grazing Fees, Dec. 22, 1970, Folder "Grazing Fees, Department of Interior, 1970–1971," Box 70, John Whitaker Files, WHCF, RNPMP.

70. The federal government had amended mineral policy only twice since 1872. The Mineral Leasing Act of 1920 placed coal, oil, and gas as well as several bedded minerals, such as phosphates, sodium, and sulfur under a leasing system. In 1955 Congress allowed competitive bidding of common building materials, such as sand, stone, and gravel. For a discussion of the Mining Law of 1872, 17 Stat. 91, see George Riley, "The Mining Law of 1872," *Amicus Journal* 2, no. 4 (1981): 17–21; Whitaker, *Striking a Balance*, 219–20; Alderson, "Public Lands," in Rathlesberger, *Nixon and the Environment*, 113.

71. Gibson quoted in Harry Caudill, *My Land Is Dying* (New York: E. P. Dutton, 1971), 17–18; *New York Times*, Apr. 23, 1970, 75; May 10, 1970, 63, June 8, 1970, 21.

72. Caudill, *My Land Is Dying*, 45. See John F. Stacks, *Stripping: The Surface Mining of America* (San Francisco: Sierra Club Books, 1972); Hays, *Beauty, Health and Permanence*, 144–45.

73. Transcript, Muskie Interview with Mitchell Krause, Channel 13, New York City, May 11, 1970, Folder 9, "1970 Press File, Speeches, May," Box 1533, USSSO, EMA.

74. *New York Times*, June 2, 1970, 79; Aug. 30, 1970, VII, 3; July 6, 1970, 27: July 5, 1970, 24; Nov. 19, 1970, 24; Kirkpatrick Sale, *The Green Revolution: The American Environmental Movement, 1962–1992* (New York: Hill and Wang, 1993), 23.

75. Robert Cameron Mitchell et al., "Twenty Years of Environmental Mobilization: Trends among National Environmental Organizations," in Riley Dunlap and Angela Mertig, *American Environmentalism: The U.S. Environmental Movement, 1970–1990* (Washington, D.C.: Taylor and Francis, 1992), 15.

76. Interview, Author with Browder, Mar. 24, 1970; Kline, *First Along the River*, 85; *New York Times*, Apr. 22, 1970, 35.

77. Primack and Von Hippel, "Scientists, Politics and the SST," 28; Memo, Russell Train to Richard Nixon, Aug. 12, 1970, Folder "Supersonic Transport, 1969–1971, 2 of 6," Box 109, John Whitaker Files, WHCF, RNPMP.

78. Letter, Edmund Muskie to Roy Daly, Aug. 9, 1970, Folder 5, "1970 Resource, 100 Appropriations, Supersonic Transport," Box 1974, USSSO, EMA; Order, United States District Court for the District of Columbia, *Gary A. Soucie, et al., v. Lee DuBridge*, Civil Action no. 1571-70, Aug. 21, 1970; *The Columbian Vancouver*, Dec. 10, 1970, 1; Memo, William Ruckelshaus to Frank Pagnolta, Aug. 25, 1970, Folder "White House-SST Litigation, 1969–1970," Box 38, Edward David Files, WHCF, RNPMP.

79. Helen M. Ingram, *Public Policy and the Natural Environment* (Greenwich, Conn.: JAI Press, 1985), 206; Letter, John Whitaker to Parke Brinkley, Aug. 5, 1970, Folder "May–August, 1970, 4 of 4, August, 1970," Box 2, John Whitaker Files, WHCF, RNPMP; Letter, John Whitaker to George Blair, Aug. 5, 1970, Folder "May–August, 1970, 4 of 4, August, 1970," Box 2, John Whitaker Files, WHCF, RNPMP; Memo, John Whitaker to John Ehrlichman, July 3, 1970, Folder "Pesticides-General, DDT, 3 Materials (1971)," Box 91, John Whitaker Files, WHCF, RNPMP; Whitaker, *Striking a Balance*, 127–28, 133.

80. Press Release, Department of Interior, Ban on Pesticides on Interior Land, June 18, 1970, Folder "Environment," Box 60, Charles Colson Files, WHSF, RNPMP; Memo,

Charles Colson to John Whitaker, June 19, 1970, Folder "Environment," Box 60, Charles Colson Files, WHSF, RNPMP; Memo, John Whitaker to Gerry Warren, Feb. 27, 1970, Folder "Pesticides, 1970 (1969–1970), 2 of 3," Box 90, John Whitaker Files, WHCF, RNPMP; Memo, Lee DuBridge to John Ehrlichman, July 3, 1970, Folder "Pesticides, 1970 (1969–1970), 3 of 3," Box 90, John Whitaker Files, WHCF, RNPMP.

81. Interview, Author with William Ruckelshaus, Apr. 2, 1998.

82. Interview, Author with Richard Fairbanks, Mar. 24, 1998; Memo, John Quarles to Daniel Patrick Moynihan, May 1, 1970, Folder "EX MC 26, National Growth Policy Conference," Box 7, Meetings and Conferences File, WHCF, RMPMP; Memo, Richard J. Barber to Bud Krogh, Nov. 18, 1970, Folder "National Growth Policy, 1970," Box 16, Egil Krogh Files, WHSF, RNPMP; Memo, John Whitaker to John Ehrlichman, Dec. 4, 1970, Folder "September–December, 1970, 4 of 4, December, 1970," Box 3, John Whitaker Files, WHCF, RNPMP.

83. Transcript, Speech Before the National Wildlife Federation, Henry Jackson, Chicago, Illinois, June 21, 1970, Folder 44, "Speeches and Writings, Environmental Quality in the Decade of the Seventies, NWF, Chicago, June 21, 1970," Box 234, Accession No. 3560–4, PHJ.

84. Letter, Philip Berry to Richard Nixon, Apr. 9, 1970, Folder "Population, 1970," Box 92, John Whitaker Files, WHCF, RNPMP; Memo, John Whitaker to Patrick Moynihan, Apr. 29, 1970, Folder "January–April, 1970, 4 of 4, April, 1970," Box 2, John Whitaker Files, WHCF, RNPMP.

85. Interview, Author with Philip Berry, June 19, 1998.

86. Kissinger quoted in Interview, Author with David Brower, Apr. 7, 1998.

87. Tydings's bill, S. 2108, was titled the Family Planning and Population Research Act of 1970; Transcript, Press Conference, Daniel P. Moynihan, June 4, 1970, Folder "Population," Box 57, Edwin Harper Files, WHCF, RNPMP; Carl Pope, "Population," in Rathlesberger, *Nixon and the Environment*, 172.

88. Quoted in David Zwick, "Water Pollution," in Rathlesberger, *Nixon and the Environment*, 46.

89. Terence Kehoe, *Cleaning Up the Great Lakes: From Cooperation to Confrontation* (Dekalb: Northern Illinois University Press, 1997), 110; Memo, John Ehrlichman to Richard Nixon, Mar. 9, 1970, Folder "January–April, 1970, 3 of 4, March, 1970," Box 2, John Whitaker Files, WHCF, RNPMP.

90. Nixon quoted in Memo, Timothy Atkeson to Wilfred Rommel, Sept. 11, 1970, Folder "Ocean Dumping, 1970, 2 of 2," Box 88, John Whitaker Files, WHCF, RNPMP; Memo, John Whitaker to Charles Colson, Sept. 8, 1970, Folder "Ocean Dumping, 1970, 1 of 2," Box 88, John Whitaker Files, WHCF, RNPMP.

91. Memo, John Whitaker to John Ehrlichman, Sept. 3, 1970, Folder "September–December, 1970, 1 of 4, September, 1970," Box 2, John Whitaker Files, WHCF, RNPMP.

92. The International Joint Commission, established under the 1909 Boundary Waters Treaty, appointed the "U.S.-Canada Joint Working Group" in 1964 to investigate and report on the condition of the waters.

93. Philip Abelson, "Excessive Emotion about Detergents," *Science* 169, no. 3950 (Sept. 11, 1970): 31; Memo, John Ehrlichman to Richard Nixon, Apr. 6, 1970, Folder "357-OA

#4295, Pollution Control," Box 73, Egil Krogh Files, WHSF, RNPMP; Memo, Paul McCracken to Richard Nixon, June 9, 1970, Folder "Detergents–1970, 2 of 2" Box 48, John Whitaker Files, WHCF, RNPMP; Memo, Maurice Stans to Ken Cole, June 10, 1970, Folder "Detergents, 1970, 2 of 2," Box 48, John Whitaker Files, WHCF, RNPMP; Memo, Russell Train to Richard Nixon, May 22, 1970, Folder "Detergents–1970, 2 of 2," Box 48, John Whitaker Files, WHCF, RNPMP.

94. CEQ Decision Document, Automobile Cycle: Environmental and Resource Conservation Problems, June, 1970, Folder "White House-Environment, Oversized, 1969–1970," Box 9, Edward David Files, WHCF, RNPMP; Memo, Russell Train to Richard Nixon, June 4, 1970, Folder "White House-Environment, Vol. III, 1971," Box 9, Edward David Files, WHCF, RNPMP.

95. Council on Environmental Quality, *First Annual Report of the President's Council on Environmental Quality* (Washington, D.C.: U.S. Government Printing Office, 1970); Memo, John Whitaker to John Ehrlichman, July 29, 1970, Folder "May–August, 1970, 3 of 4, July, 1970," Box 2, John Whitaker Files, WHCF, RNPMP; First Report of the National Industrial Pollution Control Council, July, 1970, Folder "EX FG 278, NIPCC, 1970," Box 1, NIPCC Files, WHCF, RNPMP; Memo, John Whitaker to John Campbell, July 23, 1970, Folder "EX FG 278, NIPCC, 1970," Box 1, NIPCC Files, WHCF, RNPMP.

96. Memo, Russell Train to John Whitaker, Nov. 24, 1970, Folder "EX FG 251, EQC; FG 251, CCE, Terminated July 1, 1970, 2 of 2,' Box 1, Cabinet Committee on the Environment Files, WHCF, RNPMP; Memo, Timothy Atkeson to Federal Agency Liaison Officials," Dec. 1, 1970, Folder "Section 102, EIS, 1970–1972, 2 of 2," Box 60, John Whitaker Files, WHCF, RNPMP.

97. Thomas Dunlap, *Saving America's Wildlife* (Princeton, N.J.: Princeton University Press, 1988), 139; Memo, John Whitaker to Walter Hickel, July 2, 1970, Folder "EX FG 19–7–1, Bureau of Commercial Fisheries, 1970," Box 5, Interior Department Files, WHCF, RNPMP.

98. Palmer, *Endangered Rivers*, 99; Letter, Walter Hickel to Claude Kirk, June 5, 1970, Folder "Cross Florida Barge Canal, 1970–1971," Box 44, John Whitaker Files, WHCF, RNPMP; Letter, Walter Hickel to Donald Maughan, June 5, 1970, Folder "Cross Florida Barge Canal, 1970–1971," Box 44, John Whitaker Files, WHCF, RNPMP.

99. S. 3516, Santa Barbara Channel Preservation Act of 1970; Transcript, Message to Congress, Santa Barbara Channel Oil, June 11, 1970, Folder "EX NR 6, Oil-Natural Gas, 3 of 10, June–July, 1970," Box 10, Natural Resources Files, WHCF, RNPMP; Memo, John Whitaker to Dwight Chapin, June 9, 1970, Folder "EX NR 6, Oil-Natural Gas, 3 of 10, June–July, 1970," Box 10, Natural Resources Files, WHCF, RNPMP.

100. 84 Stat. 794 (Aug. 13, 1970).

101. Memo, W. M. Magruder to Walter Hickel et al., Sept. 14, 1970, Folder "SCOPE," Box 65, John Dean Files, WHSF, RNPMP; Memo, Tom Charles Huston to John Dean, Sept. 21, 1970, Folder "SCOPE," Box 65, John Dean Files, WHSF, RNPMP; Memo, Mitchell Melich to John Dean, Oct. 6, 1970, Folder "SCOPE," Box 65, John Dean Files, WHSF, RNPMP.

102. *New York Times*, Oct. 15, 1970, 40; Oct. 18, 1970, E6; Letter, Walter Hamilton to John Oakes, Oct. 24, 1970, Folder "NIPCC, 1970–1971, 3 of 5," Box 83, John Whitaker

Files, WHCF, RNPMP; Memo, Russell Train to John Ehrlichman, Oct. 23, 1970, Folder "NIPCC, 1970–1971, 3 of 5," Box 83, John Whitaker Files, WHCF, RNPMP.

103. Ambrose, *Nixon, Triumph*, 387, 391.

104. Ibid., 394.

105. *New York Times*, Sept. 27, 1970, 1; Sept. 28, 1970, 44; June 2, 1970, 30.

106. Press Release, Air Pollution, Backing Words with Action, Edmund Muskie, Aug. 16, 1970, Folder 3, "1970 Press File-Ledger Syndicate Columns, 1970-So Goes the Nation," Box 1533, USSSO, EMA.

107. Interview, Author with Don Nicoll, Apr. 1, 1998; John Esposito, *The Ralph Nader Study Group Report on Air Pollution: Vanishing Air* (New York: Grossman Publishers, 1970), 290; Press Release, Air Pollution, Sept. 25, 1970, Folder 27, "1970 Press Files, September 25, 1970, Muskie Asks Nixon," Box 1021, USSSO, EMA.

108. Hays, *Beauty, Health and Permanence*, 75–76, 250–51.

109. Letter, E. N. Cole to Edmund Muskie, Sept. 17, 1970, Folder "Air Pollution-Automobile Exhaust Problem," Box 30, Charles Colson Files, WHSF, RNPMP; Memo, Peter Flanigan to Hugh Sloan, Aug. 26, 1970, Folder "HE 9–1, Air Pollution, September 1–30, 1970," Box 30, Health Files, WHCF, RNPMP; Memo, High Sloan to Charles Colson, Sept. 14, 1970, Folder "HE 9–1, Air Pollution, September 1–30, 1970," Box 30, Health Files, WHCF, RNPMP; Memo, John Whitaker to Ken Cole, Sept. 1, 1970, Folder "September–December, 1970, 1 of 4, September, 1970," Box 2, John Whitaker Files, WHCF, RNPMP.

110. Interview, Author with Richard Fairbanks, Mar. 24, 1998.

111. Interview, Author with Don Nicoll, Apr. 1, 1998.

112. S. S. Monroe, "Air Pollution Control Hits Red Tape," *Environmental Science and Technology* 4, no. 10 (October 1970): 802–4; Option Paper, Air Pollution Conference Committee, October, 1970, Folder "Air Pollution Bill, 2 of 4," Box 24, John Whitaker Files, WHCF, RNPMP; Memo, Maurice Stans to John Ehrlichman, Oct. 2, 1970, Folder "Air Pollution Bill, 2 of 4," Box 24, John Whitaker Files, WHCF, RNPMP; Memo, Ken Cole to John Whitaker, Oct. 3, 1970, Folder "Air Pollution Bill, 2 of 4," Box 24, John Whitaker Files, WHCF, RNPMP; Press Release, GSA Regulations on Government Vehicles, Oct. 26, 1970, Folder "Auto Emissions, Government Vehicles, 1970–1971," Box 30, John Whitaker Files, WHCF, RNPMP.

113. Memo, John Whitaker to Russell Train, July 31, 1970, Folder "May–August, 1970, 4 of 4, August, 1970," Box 2, John Whitaker Files, WHCF, RNPMP; Schaeffer, "Solid Wastes," 243; Whitaker, *Striking a Balance*, 112–13.

114. Schaeffer, "Solid Wastes," 243; P.L. 91–512.

115. 30 Stat. 1151; Memo, John Whitaker to John Ehrlichman, Oct. 6, 1970, Folder September–December, 1970, 2 of 4, October, 1970, Box 2, John Whitaker Files, WHCF, RNPMP; Memo, Alvin Alm to John Whitaker, Sept. 7, 1970, Folder "Water, 1969–1971, 1 of 5," Box 116, John Whitaker Files, WHCF, RNPMP; Lieber, *Federalism and Clean Waters*, 24; Whitaker, *Striking a Balance*, 79.

116. *New York Times*, Nov. 1, 1970, 1; Ambrose, *Nixon, Triumph*, 396.

117. Price quoted in Ambrose, *Nixon, Triumph*, 397; *New York Times*, Nov. 5, 1970. 37; Nov. 6, 1970, 40.

118. *New York Times*, Nov. 9, 1970, 1, 27.

119. Species included Blue, Finback, Sei, Sperm, Humpback, Right, Grey and Bowhead. Hickel, *Who Owns America?*, 145; Scheffer, *Shaping of Environmentalism*, 159; Nixon quoted in Memorandum for the President's File, John Ehrlichman, Dec. 16, 1970, Folder "Hickel Resignation," Box 20, John Ehrlichman Files, WHSF, RNPMP; and in Haldeman Personal Notes, Dec. 2, 1970, Folder "Haldeman Notes, October–December, 1970, Part II," Box 42, H. R. Haldeman Files, WHSF, RNPMP.

120. Hickel quotes himself in Letter, Walter Hickel to John Ehrlichman, Feb. 1, 1970, Folder "Ehrlichman Scrapbook, Items, 2 of 2," Box 18, John Ehrlichman Files, WHSF, RNPMP; Memo, Maurice Stans to Richard Nixon, June 4, 1971, Folder "Fred Malek, June, 1971," Box 81, H. R. Haldeman Files, WHSF, RNPMP; Memo, Fred Malek to H. R. Haldeman, August 11, 1971, Folder "Fred Malek, September, 1971," Box 85, H. R. Haldeman Files, WHSF, RNPMP.

121. Interview, Author with Richard Fairbanks, Mar. 24, 1998.

122. Interview, Author with Joe Browder, Mar. 24, 1998. Morton won confirmation easily on Jan. 28, 1971; *New York Times*, Jan. 29, 1971, 7.

123. Interview, Author with Leon Billings, June 26, 1998; *New York Times*, Nov. 18, 1970, 28; Memo, John Whitaker to Ken Cole, Nov. 18, 1970, Folder "Ocean Dumping, 1970, 1 of 2," Box 88, John Whitaker Files, WHCF, RNPMP.

124. *Chicago Daily News*, Dec. 4, 1970, 5; Memo, W. E. Timmons to Richard Nixon, Dec. 19, 1970, Folder "EX CA 8, Aircraft Development, 1969–1970, 3 of 3," Box 28, Civil Aviation Files, WHCF, RNPMP; Robert Waldrop, "Transportation,' in Rathlesberger, *Nixon and the Environment*, 190–91.

125. Memo, John Whitaker to John Ehrlichman, Nov. 18, 1970, Folder "EX CA Aircraft Development, 1969–1970, 3 of 3," Box 28, Civil Aviation Files, WHCF, RNPMP; Memo, John Whitaker to Patrick Buchanan, Dec. 10, 1970, Folder "Supersonic Transport, 1969–1971, 2 of 6," Box 109, John Whitaker Files, WHCF, RNPMP; *New York Times*, Nov. 26, 1970, 31.

126. Interview, Author with Brent Blackwelder, Mar. 23, 1998; Executive Order 311574; *New York Times*, Dec. 24, 1970, 1; Zwick, "Water Pollution," 40.

127. Clary, *Timber and the Forest Service*, 176; LeMaster, *Decade of Change*, 14; Memo, John Ehrlichman to Russell Train, Jan. 3, 1971, Folder "Wilderness Areas, 1971,' Box 118. John Whitaker Files, WHCF, RNPMP; Memo, Russell Train to John Whitaker, Apr. 7, 1971, Folder "Wilderness Areas, 1971," Box 118, John Whitaker Files, WHCF, RNPMP.

128. Richard Liroff, *A National Policy for the Environment* (Bloomington: Indiana University Press, 1976), 65–69; Thomas B. Allen, *Guardian of the Wild* (Bloomington: Indiana University Press, 1987), 152, 198.

129. P.L. 91–572; *New York Times*, Dec. 27, 1970, 1; Pope, "Population," 172.

130. Congressional Research Service, *A Legislative History of the Clean Air Act Amendments of 1970* (Washington, D.C.: U.S. Government Printing Office, 1974), 3, 151.

131. Memo, Ken Cole to Dwight Chapin, Dec. 18, 1970, Folder "Clean Air Act, 1970, 1 of 2," Box 34, John Whitaker Files, WHCF, RNPMP; Memo, John Whitaker to Russell Train, Dec. 21, 1970, Folder "Clean Air Act, 1970, 1 of 2," Box 34, John Whitaker Files, WHCF, RNPMP.

132. Interview, Author with Leon Billings, June 26, 1998; P.L. 91–604; Transcript, Press Conference, Russell Train and William Ruckelshaus, Dec. 31, 1970, Folder "Environment," Box 44, Edwin Harper Files, WHSF, RNPMP; Memo, Dwight Chapin to H. R. Haldeman, Dec. 31, 1970, Folder "Air Pollution, December 1–31, 1970," Box 30, Health Files, WHCF, RNPMP; *New York Times*, Jan. 1, 1971, 1.

133. Press Release, Muskie Commends President for Signing Air Bill, Dec. 31, 1970, Folder 14, "1970 Press File, December 31, 1970, Muskie Commends President, Air Bill," Box SE1537, USSO, EMA.

134. Interview, Author with Don Nicoll, Apr. 1, 1998; Interview, Author with Leon Billings, June 26, 1998.

135. Memo, Charles Colson to Dwight Chapin, Jan. 12, 1971, Folder "Air Pollution-General, 1 of 2," Box 30, Charles Colson Files, WHSF, RNPMP; Memo, Jeb Magruder to Ed Morgan, Feb. 25, 1971, Folder "February, 1971, 1 of 2," Box 271, H. R. Haldeman Files, WHSF, RNPMP.

Chapter 4

1. Memo, John Whitaker to Ed Morgan, Jan. 8, 1971, Folder "OA #5713–25, Department of Natural Resources," Box 79, Egil Krogh Files, WHSF, RNPMP.

2. Memo, Leon Billings to Edmund Muskie, Feb. 6, 1971, Folder 11, "1971 Correspondence, 500 Public Works, S.3286, Water Quality Improvement Act," Box 1840, USSSO, EMA.

3. *New York Times*, Jan. 5, 1971, 1; Jan. 7, 1971, 1; Nixon quoted in Ambrose, *Nixon, Triumph*, 404–5.

4. Stine, *Mixing the Waters*, 30; Scheffer, *Shaping of Environmentalism*, 136; Memo, John Whitaker to John Ehrlichman, Jan. 20, 1971, Folder "Cross Florida Barge Canal, 1970–1971, 2 of 4," Box 44, John Whitaker Files, WHCF, RNPMP.

5. *Public Papers of the Presidents, Richard Nixon, 1971* (Washington, D.C.: U.S. Government Printing Office, 1972), 125–42.

6. Council on Environmental Quality, *The President's 1971 Environmental Program* (Washington, D.C.: U.S. Government Printing Office, 1971), 25–52; Transcript, Press Conference, William Ruckelshaus and Rogers Morton, Feb. 8, 1971, Folder "Environmental Press Conference, February 8, 1971," Box 58, John Whitaker Files, WHCF, RNPMP.

7. Council on Environmental Quality, *The President's 1971 Environmental Program*, 207–22; Whitaker, *Striking a Balance*, 158–59; CEQ Draft Bill, National Land Use Policy, October 1970, Folder "Land Use Policy, 1970," Box 15, Egil Krogh Files, WHSF, RNPMP; Memorandum for the President's File, John Whitaker, Dec. 23, 1970, Folder "Meetings File, Beginning December 20, 1970," Box 83, President's Office Files, WHSF, RNPMP; Memo, John Ehrlichman to Richard Nixon, Jan. 18, 1971, Folder "President's Meeting with Nat Owings, December 23, 1970," Box 6, John Whitaker Files, WHCF, RNPMP.

8. 61 Stat. 163; Sansom, *New American Dream Machine*, 59; Whitaker, *Striking a Balance*, 127; Harrison Wellford, "Pesticides," 148–49.

9. Whitaker, *Striking a Balance*, 128, 132; Chronology of DDT Events, June 30, 1971,

Folder "Pesticides-General, DDT, 3 Materials, 1971," Box 91, John Whitaker Files, WHCF, RNPMP; Memo, Alvin Alm to John Whitaker, Nov. 23, 1970, Folder "Pesticides–1970. 3 of 3," Box 90, John Whitaker Files, WHCF, RNPMP.

10. Council on Environmental Quality, *The President's 1971 Environmental Program*, 163–82; *New York Times*, Feb. 9, 1971, 77; Feb. 10, 1971, 42; Transcript, Press Conference, William Ruckelshaus and Rogers Morton, Feb. 8, 1971, Folder "Environmental Press Conference, February 8, 1971," Box 58, John Whitaker Files, WHCF, RNPMP.

11. *Boston Globe*, May 23, 1971, 3; *New York Times*, Apr. 1, 1971, 1; Feb. 11, 1971, 42; Mar. 4, 1971, 24; Ambrose, *Nixon, Triumph*, 413; Press Release, Edmund Muskie, 1970 Congressional Conservationist of the Year, Folder 44, "1971 Press Files, February, 1971, 1970 Congressional Conservationist of the Year," Box 1898, USSSO, EMA.

12. Nixon quoted in Haldeman Personal Notes, Jan. 14, 1971, Folder "Notes, January–March, 1971 (January 1–February 15, 1971), Part I," Box 43, H. R. Haldeman Files, WHSF, RNPMP.

13. Transcript, Remarks by Senator Edmund Muskie, St. Regis College, Nov. 6, 1971, Folder 9, "1971–1972 Press File-Muskie Position Statements-Environment," Box 1597, USSSO, EMA.

14. Proponents of the canal also sued, claiming that Nixon did not have the authority to order construction halted; Letter, Wallace Duncan to John Dean, Feb. 3, 1971, Folder "Cross Florida Barge Canal, 1970–1971, 1 of 4," Box 44, John Whitaker Files, WHCF, RNPMP; Memo, Timothy Atkeson to Clark MacGregor, Feb. 3, 1971, Folder "Cross Florida Barge Canal, 1970–1971, 1 of 4," Box 44, John Whitaker Files, WHCF, RNPMP.

15. Environmentalists also complained about the number of permits granted; Lieber, *Federalism and Clean Waters*, 24–25; Shanley, "Presidential Executive Orders," 407; Zwick, "Water Pollution," 41, 43.

16. Memo, Alvin Alm to John Whitaker, Jan. 14, 1971, Folder "Ocean Dumping, 1971," Box 88, John Whitaker Files, WHCF, RNPMP; Letter, Howard Pollock to Russell Train, July 28, 1971, Folder "Legislation-Ocean Dumping, 1971–1972," Box 141, John Whitaker Files, WHCF, RNPMP; Memo, John Whitaker to Ed Coate, Apr. 5, 1971, Folder "April–June, 1971, 1 of 3, April, 1971," Box 4, John Whitaker Files, WHCF, RNPMP. CEQ hired two land-use attorneys to study the issue, and claimed that their report supported the administration's position; see Fred Busselman and David Callies, *The Quiet Revolution in Land Use Control* (Washington, D.C.: U.S. Government Printing Office, 1971).

17. Lieber, *Federalism and Clean Waters*, 38–39; Memo, John Whitaker to John Ehrlichman, June 24, 1971, Folder "April–June, 1971, 3 of 3, June, 1971," Box 4, John Whitaker Files, WHCF, RNPMP.

18. Interview, Author with William Ruckelshaus, Apr. 2, 1998; Interview, Author with Ronald Walker, Nov. 29, 1998; Memo, William Ruckelshaus to John Whitaker, Jan. 11, 1971, Folder "Great Lakes Agreement, U.S.-Canada, 1972, 2 of 2," Box 135, John Whitaker Files, WHCF, RNPMP.

19. Nixon quoted in Haldeman Personal Notes, Feb. 9, 1971, Folder "Notes, January–March, 1971 (January 1–February 15, 1971), Part I," Box 43, H. R. Haldeman Files, WHSF, RNPMP.

20. See Ambrose, *Nixon, Triumph*, 431–36.

21. Buchanan quoted in ibid, 405.

22. Nixon quoted in edited compilation of White House tapes, Stanley I. Kutler, ed., *Abuse of Power* (New York: The Free Press, 1997), 8, 26, 37.

23. Buchanan and Nixon quoted in Ambrose, *Nixon, Triumph*, 414.

24. Nixon quoted in Memorandum for the President's File, Charles Colson, Mar. 9, 1971, Folder "Meetings File, Beginning March 7, 1971," Box 84, President's Office Files, WHSF, RNPMP.

25. The final SST vote was 51–46; *New York Times*, Mar. 25, 1971, 1; Nixon quoted in Ambrose, *Nixon, Triumph*, 433; Draft, EIS, Alaska Pipeline. January 1971, Folder "Trans-Alaska Pipeline, 1970–1971, 2 of 3," Box 26. John Whitaker Files, WHCF, RNPMP; Memo, John Whitaker to John Ehrlichman, Jan. 14, 1971, Folder "EX TN 3, Pipelines, January 1-," Box 5, Transportation Files, WHCF, RNPMP.

26. Stine's *Mixing the Waters* is the definitive work on the Tennessee-Tombigbee Waterway. Stine, "Environmental Politics," 13–14; Memo, Russell Train to John Whitaker, Apr. 25, 1971, Folder "Presidential Events File-Tennessee-Tombigbee Dedication, May 25, 1971, Box 6, John Whitaker Files, WHCF, RNPMP; Memo, Russell Train to Richard Nixon, May 10, 1971, Folder "Presidential Events File-Tennessee-Tombigbee Dedication, May 25, 1971," Box 6, John Whitaker Files, WHCF, RNPMP; Memo, John Whitaker to John Ehrlichman, May 18, 1971, Folder "April–June, 1971, 2 of 3, May, 1971," Box 4, John Whitaker Files, WHCF, RNPMP.

27. Interview, Author with Richard Fairbanks, Mar. 24, 1998.

28. Interview, Author with David Brower, Apr. 7, 1998.

29. Interview, Author with Joe Browder, Mar. 24, 1998; *New York Times*, June 21, 1970, 23; July 12, 1969, III, 7.

30. Interview, Author with William Ruckelshaus, Apr. 2, 1998.

31. Interview, Author with Philip Berry, June 19, 1998.

32. Interview, Author with William Ruckelshaus, Apr. 2, 1998.

33. Edward Abbey, *The Monkey Wrench Gang* (Philadelphia: Lippincott, 1975).

34. Kline, *First Along the River*, 90–93; Shabecoff, *Fierce Green Fire*, 123. For additional information on radical environmentalism, see Rik Scarce, *Eco-Warriors: Understanding the Alternative Environmental Movement* (Chicago: The Noble Press, 1990); Bill Devall, "Deep Ecology and Radical Environmentalism," in Dunlap and Mertig, *American Environmentalism*, 51–62.

35. *Living Wilderness* 35, no. 114 (Summer 1971): 2; Hays, *Beauty, Health and Permanence*, 307–13. For additional information on the environmental opposition, see Jacqueline Switzer, *Green Backlash: The History and Politics of Environmental Opposition in the U.S.* (New York: Lynne Reinner Publishers, 1997).

36. Hays, *Beauty, Health and Permanence*, 311–12; *Los Angeles Times*, Jan. 9, 1979, 29; *New York Times*, May 25, 1970, 32.

37. *New York Times*, May 2, 1971, III, 3; June 7, 1971, 1; Haldeman Personal Notes, June 9, 1971, Folder "Notes, April–June, 1971 (May 20–June 30, 1971), Part II," Box 43, H. R. Haldeman Files, WHSF, RNPMP; Memo, John Whitaker to John Ehrlichman, June 4, 1971, Folder "April–June, 1971, 3 of 3, June, 1971," Box 4, John Whitaker Files, WHCF, RNPMP.

38. Memo, William Lestor to Peter Flanigan, May 24, 1971, Folder "Confidential Files,

HE-9, Sanitary Services Pollution Control," Box 34, WHSF, RNPMP; Letter, Maurice Stans to Richard Nixon, Apr. 12, 1971, Folder "Meetings File, Beginning April 11, 1971," Box 84, President's Office Files, WHSF, RNPMP; Press Release, Commerce Department, Remarks of Harold Passer Before Business Economists Conference, Apr. 26, 1971, Folder "The Environmental Coalition, 1 of 2," Box 61, Charles Colson Files, WHSF, RNPMP; Lowry Wyatt, "Economy and the Environment: The Need for Integrity," *Vital Speeches of the Day* 37, no. 16 (June 1, 1971): 509–12.

39. Interview, Author with Gaylord Nelson, Sept. 4, 1996; Memo, John Whitaker to Richard Nixon, June 6, 1971, Folder "Environment," Box 44, Edwin Harper Files, WHSF, RNPMP; Memo, John Whitaker to John Ehrlichman, July 9, 1971, Folder "Polls, 1970–1972, 2 of 4," Box 92, John Whitaker Files, WHCF, RNPMP; Memo, John Whitaker to John Ehrlichman, Feb. 11, 1971, Folder "Earth Week, 1970–1971," Box 51, John Whitaker Files, WHCF, RNPMP; Memo, John Whitaker to John Ehrlichman, Feb. 27, 1971, Folder "January–March, 1971, 2 of 3, February, 1971," Box 3, John Whitaker Files, WHCF, RNPMP; Memo, John Whitaker to Richard Nixon, Mar. 12, 1971, Folder "President's Handwriting, March 1–15, 1971," Box 9, President's Office Files, WHSF, RNPMP.

40. *Public Papers, 1971,* 146–47; Report of the National Industrial Pollution Control Council, Feb. 10, 1971, Folder "EX FG 278, NIPCC, January 1, 1971–1972," Box 1, NIPCC Files, WHCF, RNPMP.

41. Letter, J. W. Penfold to Richard Nixon, Feb. 11, 1971, Folder "GEN FG 278, NIPCC, January 1, 1971–1972," Box 1, NIPCC Files, WHCF, RNPMP; Memo, Charles Colson to John Ehrlichman, Feb. 27, 1971, Folder "EPA, 1971, 1 of 4," Box 64, John Whitaker Files, WHCF, RNPMP.

42. Memo, John Whitaker to John Ehrlichman, Feb. 20, 1971, Folder "Supersonic Transport, 1969–1971, 1 of 6," Box 109, John Whitaker Files, WHCF, RNPMP; *Washington Post,* Mar. 19, 1971, 22: Chronology of DDT Events, June 30, 1971, Folder "Pesticides-General, DDT, 3 Materials (1971)," Box 91, John Whitaker Files, WHCF, RNPMP; Memo, John Whitaker to Russell Train, Mar. 29, 1971, Folder "Pesticides–1971 (1970–1972), 2 of 3," Box 91, John Whitaker Files, WHCF, RNPMP; Memo, Russell Train to Richard Nixon, Apr. 25, 1971, Folder "Presidential Events File-Tennessee-Tombigbee Dedication, May 25, 1971, Box 6, John Whitaker Files, WHCF, RNPMP; Memo, John Ehrlichman to Russell Train, May 18, 1971, Folder "April–June, 1971, 2 of 3, May, 1971," Box 4, John Ehrlichman Files, WHCF, RNPMP.

43. Letter, John Whitaker to Laurence Rockefeller, Jan. 15, 1971, Folder "EX FG CACEQ, January 15, 1971–December 8, 1972," Box 1, CCE/CACEQ Files, WHCF, RNPMP; Memo, Harrison Loesch to John Whitaker, June 15, 1971, Folder "CACEQ, 1969–1973, 1 of 2," Box 34, John Whitaker Files, WHCF, RNPMP.

44. Press Release, CEQ Revised Guidelines, Jan. 25, 1971, Folder "Section 102, Environmental Impact Statements, 1970–1972, 1 of 2," Box 60, John Whitaker Files, WHCF, RNPMP; Andrews, *Environmental Policy,* 31–32; Transcript, Henry Jackson Speech, "Law, Lawyers, and the Environment," ABA, Jan. 28, 1971, Folder "NEPA, 1971–1973, 3 of 3," Box 142, John Whitaker Files, WHCF, RNPMP.

45. Standards included sulphur oxides at .8 micrograms per cubic meter, nitrogen oxide at .05 parts per million as annual mean, carbon monoxide at 9 parts per million

as maximum eight-hour concentration, and hydrocarbons at.24 parts as maximum three-hour average concentration; Press Release, National Air Quality Standards, Apr. 30, 1971, Folder "Air Quality-General. 3 Memorandum, 1971–1972, 4 of 5," Box 123, John Whitaker Files, WHCF, RNPMP; *New York Times*, May 1, 1971, 1.

46. Interview, Author with Russell Train, July 8, 1998; Press Release, Administration of the Clean Air Act, June 30, 1971, Folder "Clean Air Act, 1971," Box 34, John Whitaker Files, WHCF, RNPMP; Whitaker, *Striking a Balance*, 190–91; Memo, John Whitaker to John Ehrlichman, May 26, 1971, Folder "Strip Mining, 1971–1972," Box 108, John Whitaker Files, WHCF, RNPMP.

47. Interview, Author with William Ruckelshaus, Apr. 2, 1998.

48. Interview, Author with Laurence Moss, Mar. 25, 1998; Nixon Written Comments on News Summary, June 6, 1971, Folder "News Summaries-June, 1971," Box 32, President's Office Files, WHSF, RNPMP; Nixon quoted in Wicker, *One of Us*, 515–16; Memo, Peter Flanigan to Richard Nixon, Apr. 27, 1971, Folder "President's Handwriting, April 16–30, 1971," Box 10, President's Office Files, WHSF, RNPMP.

49. Interview, Author with William Reilly, June 26, 1998.

50. Interview, Author with William Ruckelshaus, Apr. 2, 1998.

51. Memo, Will Kriegsman to John Whitaker, Mar. 29, 1971, Folder "January–March, 1971, 3 of 3, March, 1971," Box 3, John Whitaker Files, WHCF, RNPMP.

52. Nixon quoted in Haldeman Personal Notes, June 9, 1971, Folder "Notes, April–June, 1971 (May 20–June 30, 1971), Part II," Box 43, H. R. Haldeman Files, WHSF, RNPMP.

53. Press Release, Department of State, Report of U.S.-Canada Joint Working Group, June 10, 1971, Folder "Great Lakes, 1971–1972, 2 of 2," Box 70, John Whitaker Files, WHCF, RNPMP; Zwick, "Water Pollution," 50; Executive Order 11738.

54. *Public Papers, 1971*, 472–89; Raymond Price, *With Nixon* (New York: Viking Press, 1977), 195–97; Richard P. Nathan, *The Plot that Failed: Nixon and the Administrative Presidency* (New York: John Wiley and Sons, 1975), 60; Memo, Egil Krogh to Andrew Rouse, Jan. 1, 1971, Folder "Memos, January, 1971," Box 4, Egil Krogh Files, WHSF, RNPMP.

55. S. 1315 and H.R. 6558; *Washington Post*, Mar. 24, 1971, 1; Memo, David Wilson to John Dean, June 4, 1971, Folder "Legislation-Ocean Mammal Protection Act, 1971–1972, 1 of 2," Box 141, John Whitaker Files, WHCF, RNPMP; Letter, William Towell to Richard Nixon, June 9, 1971, Folder "Legislation-Ocean Mammal Protection Act, 1971–1972, 1 of 2," Box 141, John Whitaker Files, WHCF, RNPMP.

56. North Pacific Fur Seal Convention; John Dean quoted in Memo, Bobbie Kilberg to Ken Cole, June 11, 1971, Folder "EX NR Fish-Wildlife, 2 of 7, 1971," Natural Resources File, WHCF, RNPMP.

57. The administration largely supported legislation introduced by California Democrat Glenn Anderson and Washington Republican Thomas Pelly, introduced as H.R. 10420 and S. 2871, the Marine Mammal Protection Act of 1971; See *Congressional Quarterly Almanac*, 92d Cong., 2d sess., Vol. 28 (1972), 62; *BioScience* 22 (March 1972): 171; Letter, William Towell to Richard Nixon, June 9, 1971, Folder "Legislation-Ocean Mammal Protection Act, 1971–1972, 1 of 2,' Box 141, John Whitaker Files, WHCF, RNPMP.

58. Scheffer, *Shaping of Environmentalism*, 151; Hays, *Beauty, Health and Permanence*,

295; Whitaker, *Striking a Balance*, 128; Memo, John Whitaker to Russell Train, May 14, 1971, Folder "April–June, 1971, 2 of 3, May, 1971," Box 4, John Whitaker Files, WHCF, RNPMP; Memo, John Whitaker to John Campbell, Sept. 11, 1971, Folder "July–October, 1971, 3 of 4, September, 1971," Box 4, John Whitaker Files, WHCF, RNPMP; Letter, Richard Nixon to Page Belcher, Sept. 22, 1971, Folder "Pesticides–1971 (1970–1972), 1 of 3," Box 91, John Whitaker Files, WHCF, RNPMP.

59. Fact Sheet, Energy Message, June 4, 1971, Folder "Energy," Box 44, Edwin Harper Files, WHSF, RNPMP; Press Release, Energy Message, June 4, 1971, Folder "Energy," Box 44, Edwin Harper Files, WHSF, RNPMP; William Barber and James Cochrane, "Energy: From John F. Kennedy to Jimmy Carter," *Wilson Quarterly* 5, no. 2 (1981): 70–90; Philip Micklin, "The Environmental Hazards of Nuclear Wastes," *Science and Public Affairs* 30, no. 4 (April 1974): 36–44; Russell Train, "Energy Problems and Environmental Concern," *Science and Public Affairs* 29, no. 9 (November 1973): 43–47.

60. *Public Papers, 1971,* 500; Udall quoted in *Washington Post*, Apr. 15, 1971, 12; Pope, "Population," 172–73.

61. Interview, Author with Russell Train, July 8, 1998; Landy et al., *Environmental Protection Agency*, 37; Domestic Council Study Memorandum no. 15, June 26, 1971, Folder "EX FG 298, EPA, January 1, 1971–1972, 1 of 3," Box 1, EPA Files, WHCF, RNPMP; Memo, Edward David to Members, Domestic Council Committee on Quality of Life, June 28, 1971, Folder "Quality of Life, 1971 (1970–1972), 3 of 4," Box 96, John Whitaker Files, WHCF, RNPMP.

62. Memo, John Whitaker to Alexander Butterfield, July 2, 1971, Folder "July–October, 1971, 1 of 4, July, 1971," Box 4, John Whitaker Files, WHCF, RNPMP; Memo, John Whitaker to Dwight Chapin, June 29, 1971, Folder "April–June, 1971, 3 of 3, June, 1971," Box 4, John Whitaker Files, WHCF, RNPMP; *Environmental Defense Fund v. Corps of Engineers*, 331 F. Supp. 925 (D.D.C., 1971); Stine, "Environmental Politics," 16–18; Brent Blackwelder, "Water Resources," in Rathlesberger, *Nixon and the Environment*, 64–65; Allen, *Guardian of the Wild*, 152, 198; Liroff, *National Policy*, 40.

63. Memo, John Whitaker to John Ehrlichman, Aug. 4, 1971, Folder "July–October, 1971, 2 of 4, August, 1971," Box 4, John Whitaker Files, WHCF, RNPMP; Memo, H. R. Haldeman to John Ehrlichman, July 30, 1971, Folder "Presidential Speech-Environmental Speech, 1971–1972, 3 of 3," Box 13, John Whitaker Files, WHCF, RNPMP.

64. Press Release, Muskie Opening Statement, Senate Subcommittee on Air and Water Pollution Hearings on Economic Dislocation, May 17, 1971, Folder 8, "1971 Press File, May 17, 1971, Opening Remarks for Hearings on Economic Dislocations," Box 1901, USSA, EMA; Memo, John Ehrlichman to John Whitaker, Aug. 20, 1971, Folder "July–October, 1971, 2 of 4, August, 1971," Box 4, John Whitaker Files, WHCF, RNPMP.

65. Press Release, Muskie Opening Statement, Senate Subcommittee on Air and Water Pollution Hearings on Economic Dislocation, May 17, 1971, Folder 8, "1971 Press File, May 17, 1971, Opening Remarks for Hearings on Economic Dislocations," Box 1901, USSA, EMA; Memo, John Ehrlichman to John Whitaker, Aug. 20, 1971, Folder "July–October, 1971, 2 of 4, August, 1971," Box 4, John Whitaker Files, WHCF, RNPMP; President's Handwriting on Memo, John Ehrlichman to Richard Nixon, Aug. 5, 1971, Folder "President's Handwriting, August 1–15, 1971," Box 13, President's Office Files, WHSF, RNPMP.

66. *Public Papers, 1971,* 868–73; Transcript, Secretary Stans Speech Before the National Petroleum Council, July 15, 1971, Folder "Quality of Life–1971 (1970–1972), 3 of 4," Box 96, John Whitaker Files, WHCF, RNPMP; Summary, Second Annual Report, Council on Environmental Quality, August 1971, Folder "CEQ, 1971–1972, 2 of 3," Box 123, John Whitaker Files, WHCF, RNPMP.

67. *New York Times,* July 16, 1971, 62; Memo, John Whitaker to Donald Rice, Nov. 3, 1971, Folder "November–December, 1971, 1 of 2, November, 1971," Box 4, John Whitaker Files, WHCF, RNPMP; Memo, John Ehrlichman to Peter Flanigan, Aug. 25, 1971, Folder "John Ehrlichman, August, 1971," Box 83, H. R. Haldeman Files, WHSF, RNPMP.

68. *New York Times,* Aug. 11, 1971, 36; Memo, Russell Train to Richard Nixon, July 23, 1971, Folder "Quality of Life–1971 (1970–1972), 3 of 4," Box 96, John Whitaker Files, WHCF, RNPMP; Memo, John Whitaker to Peter Flanigan, Sept. 12, 1971, Folder "EPA, 1971, 3 of 4," Box 64, John Whitaker Files, WHCF, RNPMP; Memo, John Whitaker to John Ehrlichman, Sept. 1, 1971, Folder "July–October, 1971, 3 of 4, September, 1971," Box 4, John Whitaker Files, WHCF, RNPMP.

69. *Public Papers, 1971,* 819–20; See Henry Kissinger's memoirs, *White House Years* (Boston: Little, Brown, 1979) and *Years of Upheaval* (Boston: Little, Brown, 1982).

70. Quoted in Aitken, *Nixon,* 429.

71. For a full discussion of Nixon's economic and domestic policies, see Ehrlichman, *Witness to Power;* and Hoff, *Nixon Reconsidered.*

72. *New York Times,* Oct. 17, 1971, 38; Oct. 24, 1971, 64; Nov. 7, 1971, 1; Nov. 10, 1971, 1; Ambrose, *Nixon, Triumph,* 477.

73. Interview, Author with William Ruckelshaus, Apr. 2, 1998.

74. Nixon quoted in Wicker, *One of Us,* 514.

75. *Kalur v. Resor,* 325 F. Supp. 1 (D.D.C., 1971): Memo, John Whitaker to John Ehrlichman, Sept. 1, 1971, Folder "July–October, 1971, 3 of 4, September, 1971," Box 4, John Whitaker Files, WHCF, RNPMP; Stine, "Environmental Politics," 18; Memo, John Ehrlichman to John Mitchell, Sept. 24, 1971, Folder "EX NR 7–1, A-Z Projects, 7 of 10, 1971–1972, T-Z," Box 19, Natural Resources Files, WHCF, RNPMP.

76. Transcript, Henry Jackson Speech Before the American Law Institute, Sept. 28, 1971, Folder 2, "Speeches and Writings, 'Law, Lawyers and the Environment,' ABA, ALI, Smithsonian," Box 236, Accession No. 3560–4, PHJ; Interview, Author with William Reilly, June 26, 1998. For a full explanation on the evolution of the interpretation of NEPA, see Roger W. Findley and Daniel A. Farber, *Environmental Law* (St. Paul: West Publishing, 1988), 22–55.

77. *New York Times,* Nov. 8, 1971, 28; Nov. 18, 1971, 22.

78. Interview, Author with Leon Billings, June 26, 1998; Jackson quoted in *Berlin New Hampshire Reporter,* Aug. 12, 1971, 1; *Seattle Post Intelligencer,* Sept. 3, 1971, 31; Press Release, Henry Jackson, Announcement of Presidential Candidacy, Nov. 19, 1971, Folder 7, "Speeches and Writings-Black Books-Democratic Speeches, I, 1948–1973," Box 237, Accession No. 3560–4, PHJ.

79. Memo, John Whitaker to Richard Nixon, Dec. 1, 1971, Folder "HE 9–1, Air Pollution, August 1-," Box 31, Health Files, WHCF, RNPMP; Nixon quoted in Memo, John Ehrlichman to John Connally, Dec. 8, 1971, Folder "Recycling, 1971–1972, 3 of 3," Box 98, John Whitaker Files, WHCF, RNPMP.

80. Nixon quoted in Ambrose, *Nixon, Triumph*, 478, 480.

81. Hays, *Beauty, Health and Permanence*, 220–21; Alderson, "Public Lands," 114–15; Mayer and Riley, *Public Domain*, 82–83; Whitaker, *Striking a Balance*, 221; Memo, Donald Rice to Rogers Morton, Sept. 13, 1971, Folder "Strip Mining, 1971–1972," Box 108, John Whitaker Files, WHCF, RNPMP; Muhn and Stuart, *Opportunity and Challenge*, 207; Letter, Richard Fairbanks to Thomas Kimball, Jan. 16, 1973, Folder "USDA-Forest Service, 1971–1973, 4 of 4," Box 21, John Whitaker Files, WHCF, RNPMP.

82. Tom Garrett, "Wildlife, in Rathlesberger, *Nixon and the Environment*" 135; Scheffer, *Shaping of Environmentalism*, 162; *New York Times*, Dec. 3, 1971, 24; Memo, Fred Malek to H. R. Haldeman, Dec. 15, 1971, Folder "Fred Malek, December, 1971," Box 87, H. R. Haldeman Files, WHSF, RNPMP; Memo, John Whitaker to John Ehrlichman, Nov. 19, 1971, Folder "Presidential Meeting-Secretary Morton, Big Cypress, November 23, 1971," Box 6, John Whitaker Files, WHCF, RNPMP; Press Release, Statement by the President, Big Cypress National Fresh Water Reserve, Nov. 23, 1971, Folder "Big Cypress, 1971–1973," Box 123, John Whitaker Files, WHCF, RNPMP.

83. The Wild, Free-Roaming Horses and Burros Act of 1971, P.L. 92–195; Nixon quoted in Memo, Alexander Butterfield to John Ehrlichman, Nov. 1, 1971, Folder "Environment, General, 3 of 3," Box 59, John Whitaker Files, WHCF, RNPMP.

84. Memorandum of Understanding, Administrator of EPA and Secretary of Labor, October 1971, Folder "Environmental Economics, 3 Materials (1971–1972), 2 of 3," Box 132, John Whitaker Files, WHCF; Landy et al., *Environmental Protection Agency*, 37; Elizabeth Haskell, *The Politics of Clean Air* (New York: Praeger, 1982), 9–11; Memo, John Whitaker to John Ehrlichman, Nov. 1, 1971, Folder "Confidential Files, HE 9–1, Air Pollution, 1971–1974," Box 34, White House Special Files, Central Files, WHSF, RNPMP.

85. Interview, Author with William Reilly, June 26, 1998; *New York Times*, Nov. 12, 1971, 33; Nov. 28, 1971, IV, 4; Nov. 30, 1971, 39; Whitaker, *Striking a Balance*, 129; Fact Sheet, Decision to Retain the Department of Agriculture, Nov. 11, 1971, Folder "Government Reorganization, 1971–1973, 2 of 2," Box 69, John Whitaker Files, WHCF, RNPMP; Memo, John Whitaker to John Ehrlichman, Nov. 10, 1971, Folder "November–December, 1971, 1 of 2, November, 1971," Box 4, John Whitaker Files, WHCF, RNPMP; Memo, John Whitaker to Richard Nixon, Oct. 29, 1971, Folder "July–October, 1971, 4 of 4, October, 1971," Box 4, John Whitaker Files, WHCF, RNPMP.

86. Press Release, Edmund Muskie Opposition to Nomination of Earl Butz as Secretary of Agriculture, Nov. 22, 1971, Folder 6, "1971 Press File, November 22, 1971-Against Nomination of Earl Butz," Box 1895, USSSO, EMA; Allin, *Politics of Wilderness Preservation*, 215; Culhane, *Public Lands Politics*, 96–97. See Julis Discha, "How the Alaska Act Was Won," in *Living Wilderness* 44, no. 152 (Autumn 1981): 4–9.

87. P.L. 92–203; *Living Wilderness* 35, no. 113 (Spring 1971): 2.

88. Memo, John Whitaker to John Ehrlichman, Oct. 5, 1971, Folder "July–October, 1971, 4 of 4, October, 1971," Box 4, John Whitaker Files, WHCF, RNPMP: S.2770; Lieber, *Federalism and Clean Waters*, 41–50.

89. Stine, "Regulating Wetlands," 63–64.

90. Whitaker, *Striking a Balance*, 79; Zwick, "Water Pollution," 43; Sansom, *New American Dream Machine*, 85; Memo, Richard Fairbanks to Donald Rice et al., Oct. 7,

1971, Folder "Legislation-water, 1971, 1 of 2," Box 117, John Whitaker Files, WHCF, RNPMP.

91. Press Release, Edmund Muskie, Water Pollution Bill, Nov. 17, 1971, Folder "Water Bill, I, 1971–1972, 2 of 3," Box 113, John Whitaker Files, WHCF, RNPMP; Smith quoted in *Washington Post*, Nov. 18, 1971, 20; *New York Times*, Nov. 8, 1971, 28.

92. H.R. 11896; Press Release, U.S. House of Representatives, Committee on Public Works, Dec. 16, 1971, Folder "Water Bill, I, 1971–1972, 3 of 3," Box 113, John Whitaker Files, WHCF, RNPMP; Lieber, *Federalism and Clean Waters*, 68–70; Whitaker, *Striking a Balance*, 82–83.

93. *New York Times*, Dec. 20, 1971, 1; Ambrose, *Nixon, Triumph, 482–91*.

Chapter 5

1. Nixon quoted in *New York Times*, Jan. 3, 1972, 1, 20.

2. Ambrose, *Nixon, Triumph*, 542, 572; 604–5; Aitken, *Nixon*, 441–50.

3. Interview, Author with William Ruckelshaus, Apr. 2, 1998; Interview, Author with Brent Blackwelder, Mar. 23, 1998.

4. Domestic Council Agenda, Apr. 19, 1972; Folder "Selling the Domestic Programs, 1972," Box 19, Egil Krogh Files, WHSF, RNPMP; Memo, John Whitaker to John Ehrlichman, Apr. 20, 1972, Folder "Selling the Domestic Programs, 1972," Box 19, Egil Krogh Files, WHSF, RNPMP; Memo, Ray Waldmann to Ed Harper, June 9, 1971, Folder "Budget Review," Box 15, John Ehrlichman Files, WHCF, RNPMP; Ambrose, *Nixon, Triumph*, 542.

5. Nixon quoted in Ambrose, *Nixon, Triumph*, 500; Interview, Author with Leon Billings, June 26, 1998; Aitken, *Nixon*, 443.

6. Interview, Author with Leon Billings, June 26, 1998.

7. Memo, John Whitaker to John Ehrlichman, Jan. 13, 1972, Folder "Great Lakes Agreement, U.S.-Canada, 1972, 2 of 2," Box 135, John Whitaker Files, WHCF, RNPMP.

8. Memo, John Whitaker to John Ehrlichman, Jan. 5, 1972, Folder "Recycling, 1971–1972, 2 of 3," Box 97, John Whitaker Files, WHCF, RNPMP; Memo, John Whitaker to John Ehrlichman, Jan. 29, 1972, Folder "Recycling, 1971–1972, 2 of 3," Box 97, John Whitaker Files, WHCF, RNPMP; Whitaker, *Striking a Balance*, 114.

9. Whitaker, *Striking a Balance*, 115; Memo, John Whitaker to John Ehrlichman, Feb. 1, 1971, Folder "Recycling, 1971–1972, 2 of 3," Box 97, John Whitaker Files, WHCF, RNPMP; Memo, Russell Train to William Morrill, July 19, 1972, Folder "Recycling, 1971–1972, 1 of 3," Box 97, John Whitaker Files, WHCF, RNPMP.

10. Memo, John Whitaker to John Ehrlichman, Jan. 7, 1972, Folder "Quality of Life, 1971 (1970–1972), 1 of 4," Box 96, John Whitaker Files, WHCF, RNPMP; "The Economic Impact of Pollution Control: A Report Prepared for the President by the Department of Commerce," Mar. 3, 1972, Folder "Environmental Economics, Materials-Vol. II, 1971–1972, 1 of 4," Box 132, John Whitaker Files, WHCF, RNPMP; Memo, John Whitaker to Herbert Stein, Mar. 6, 1972, Folder "Quality of Life, 1971 (1970–1972), 1 of 4," Box 96, John Whitaker Files, WHCF, RNPMP.

11. *Public Papers of the Presidents, Richard Nixon, 1972* (Washington, D.C.: U.S. Government Printing Office, 1974), 174; Memo, Russell Train to John Ehrlichman, Jan. 17,

1972, Folder "Environmental Message, 3 of 3," Box 62, John Whitaker Files, WHCF, RNPMP.

12. *Public Papers, 1972*, 174; Council on Environmental Quality, *The President's 1972 Environmental Program* (Washington, D.C.: U.S. Government Printing Office, 1972), 3, 79–94, 213–214, 143–55, 159–78; Executive Orders 11643 and 11644, respectively.

13. Letter, Herman Kerst to Richard Nixon, Feb. 22, 1972, Folder "EX NR, Fish-Wildlife, 4 of 7, April–December, 1972," Box 3, Natural Resources Files, WHCF, RNPMP; Letter, John Keynes to Richard Nixon, Feb. 25, 1972, Folder "Environment, General, 1971, 3 of 3," Box 59, John Whitaker Files, WHCF, RNPMP; Memo, John Whitaker to David Parker, Feb. 18, 1972, Folder "EX NR 3, Forests, 3 of 5, September, 1971–February, 1972," Box 6, Natural Resources Files, WHCF, RNPMP; *American Motorcycle Association News* (March 1972): 26–27.

14. Nelson quoted in President's Handwriting on Daily Annotated News Summary, Feb. 9, 1972, Folder "Annotated News Summaries, February 8–10, 1972," Box 38, President's Office Files, WHSF, RNPMP.

15. Interview, Author with Russell Train, July 8, 1998.

16. Nixon and Train quoted in Interview, Author with Richard Fairbanks, Mar. 24, 1998.

17. *Sierra Club Bulletin* 57, no. 6 (June 1972): 20.

18. Coates, *Trans-Alaska Pipeline Controversy*, 226–28; Memo, Robert Hill to John Ehrlichman, Jan. 26, 1972, Folder "Trans-Alaska Pipeline, 3 of 4," Box 26, John Whitaker Files, WHCF, RNPMP; Letter, Russell Train to Anthony Wayne Smith, Jan. 6, 1972, Folder "Trans-Alaska Pipeline, 3 of 4," Box 26, John Whitaker Files, WHCF, RNPMP; Press Release, Department of Interior, Final Environmental Impact Statement on the Trans-Alaska Pipeline, Mar. 20, 1972, Folder "Trans-Alaska Pipeline, 1971–1973, 2 of 4," Box 26, John Whitaker Files, WHCF, RNPMP; Letter, Sidney Howe et al. to Richard Nixon, Apr. 4, 1972, Folder "Trans-Alaska Pipeline, 1971–1973, 2 of 4," Box 26, John Whitaker Files, WHCF, RNPMP.

19. Letter, Edmund Adams to Everett Jordan, Feb. 25, 1972, Folder 2, "1972 Correspondence, LEG/Public Works Committee," Box SE1704, USSSO, EMA.

20. P.L. 92–307; *Sierra Club Bulletin* 57, no. 4 (April 1972): 12; vol. 57, no. 5 (May 1972): 31; Anderson and Daniels, *NEPA in the Courts*, x; Rosenbaum, *Politics of Environmental Concern*, 270; Memo, John Whitaker to Clark Macgregor, Mar. 23, 1972, Folder "NEPA Amendments, 1972, 2 of 2," Box 143, John Whitaker Files, WHCF, RNPMP; Memo, Russell Train to John Whitaker, Mar. 14, 1974, Folder "Section 102, Environmental Impact Statements, 1979–1972, 1 of 2," Box 60, John Whitaker Files, WHCF, RNPMP.

21. *New York Times*, Jan. 1, 1972, 36; Jan. 24, 1972, 10; Mar. 3, 1972, 10; Apr. 26, 1972, 65; May 1, 1972, 26; June 20, 1972, 51.

22. Garrett, "Wildlife," 132; Dunlap, *Saving America's Wildlife*, 140; Whitaker, *Striking a Balance*, 141.

23. Letter, Richard Nixon to Henry Jackson, Apr. 24, 1972, Folder "EX NR Natural Resources Files, WHCF, RNPMP; Memo, Frank Turner to John Whitaker, Mar. 21, 1972, Folder "Land Use, Council on Environmental Quality, 1970–1972," Box 77, John Whitaker Files, WHCF, RNPMP; Memo, John Whitaker to John Ehrlichman, May 11,

1972, Folder "Land Use, Council on Environmental Quality, 1970–1972," Box 77, John Whitaker Files, WHCF, RNPMP; *National Journal* (July 22, 1972): 1193.

24. Kehoe, *Cleaning Up the Great Lakes*, 149, 164–65.

25. Domestic Council Subcommittee on National Growth, *Report on National Growth, 1972* (Washington, D.C. U.S. Government Printing Office, 1972); Memo, John Whitaker to John Ehrlichman, Jan. 25, 1972, Folder "Earth Week, 1972," Box 51, John Whitaker Files, WHCF, RNPMP; Memo, John Whitaker to John Ehrlichman, Feb. 11, 1972, Folder "National Growth Policy Message, 1972," Box 81, John Whitaker Files, WHCF, RNPMP.

26. Ruess quoted in Kehoe, *Cleaning Up the Great Lakes*, 149; Letter, Edmund Muskie to William P. Rogers, Apr. 7, 1972, Folder 9, "1971–1972 Press File-Muskie Position Statements-Environment," Box 1597, USSSO, EMA; Press Release, Senator Jackson Urges New Programs to Save Lake Erie, Apr. 18, 1972, Folder "Speeches and Writings-Black Books-Environment," Box 4, Accession No. 3560, PHJ.

27. Letter, Walter Mondale to Richard Nixon, May 1, 1972, Folder "Legislation-Ocean Mammal Protection Act, 1971–1973, 1 of 2," Box 141, John Whitaker Files, WHCF, RNPMP.

28. Letter, John Whitaker to J. Philip Campbell, Jan. 7, 1972, Folder "Pesticides–1971 (1970–1972)," Box 91, John Whitaker Files, WHCF, RNPMP; Stine, "Environmental Politics," 18; Blackwelder, "Water Resources," 65; Memo, John Ehrlichman to John Mitchell, Sept. 24, 1971, Folder "NR 7–1, A-Z Projects, 7 of 10, 1971–1972, T-Z," Box 19, Natural Resources Files, WHCF, RNPMP; Memo, Boyd Gibbons to Richard Fairbanks, June 14, 1972, Folder "Council on Environmental Quality, 1971–1972, 1 of 3," Box 126, John Whitaker Files, WHCF, RNPMP; Memo, John Whitaker to John Ehrlichman, June 19, 1972, Folder "Council on Environmental Quality, 1971–1972, 1 of 3," Box 126, John Whitaker Files, WHCF, RNPMP; President's Handwritten Comments on Daily News Summaries, Jan. 25, 1972, Folder "Annotated News Summaries, January 25–31, 1972," Box 38, President's Office Files, WHSF, RNPMP.

29. Press Release, Muskie Statement on Earth Day, 1972, Folder 34, "1972 Press Files, On Earth Day," Box 1573, USSSO, EMA.

30. Interview, Author with David Brower, Apr. 7, 1998; *New York Times*, Apr. 19, 1972, 46.

31. Interview, Author with Brent Blackwelder, Mar. 23, 1998. See Hays, *Beauty, Health and Permanence*, 315.

32. Commoner quoted in *New York Times*, Apr. 18, 1972, 31.

33. Huntley quoted in *Living Wilderness* 35, no. 116 (Winter, 1971–1972): 4.

34. Ambrose, *Nixon, Triumph*, 512–16.

35. Ibid., 536–41; *Public Papers, 1972*, 583–87.

36. Ibid., 544–48; Kissinger quoted, ibid., 544.

37. Aitken, *Nixon*, 442.

38. Ibid., 441; *New York Times*, June 4, 1972, 60.

39. The 1973 Watergate investigations uncovered the unethical campaign against Muskie; *New York Times*, Mar 5, 1972, IV, 1; Apr. 28, 1972, 1.

40. Interview, Author with Leon Billings, June 26, 1998.

41. Aitken, *Nixon*, 442–43.

42. Theodore White, *The Making of the President, 1972* (New York: Atheneum, 1973), 202; *New York Times*, July 26, 1972, 1; Aug. 1, 1972, 1.

43. Ambrose, *Nixon, Triumph*, 601.

44. Transcript, Remarks of Honorable Russell E. Train Before Platform Committee of the Republican National Convention, Aug. 17, 1972, Folder "1972 Campaign, II, 1 of 2," Box 124, John Whitaker Files, WHCF, RNPMP; Transcript, Remarks of Honorable Rogers C. B. Morton Before the Platform Committee of the Republican National Convention, Aug. 17, 1972, Folder "1972 Campaign, II, 1 of 2," Box 124, John Whitaker Files, WHCF, RNPMP.

45. Memo, John Whitaker to James Barnes, Mar. 1, 1972, Folder "1972 Campaign, 3 of 3," Box 33, John Whitaker Files, WHCF, RNPMP; Memo, John Whitaker to Russell Train, Mar. 3, 1972, Folder "1972 Campaign, I, 2 of 5," Box 123, John Whitaker Files, WHCF, RNPMP.

46. Interview, Author with Philip Berry, June 19, 1998.

47. *New York Times*, May 13, 1972, 1; Memo, Nathaniel Reed to John Whitaker, Feb. 7, 1972, Folder "National Wildlife Week," Box 143, John Whitaker Files, WHCF, RNPMP; John Whitaker to Ken Cole, May 24, 1972, Folder "EPA-1971 (1972), 3 of 3," Box 63, John Whitaker Files, WHCF, RNPMP.

48. The five companies were Ford, General Motors, Chrysler, International Harvester, and Volvo. *International Harvester, et al. v. Ruckelshaus*; Memo, Alvin Alm to Richard Fairbanks, May 26, 1972, Folder "President-Vice President-Appearances and Statements By, Concerning the Environment, 1971–1972," Box 16, John Whitaker Files, WHCF, RNPMP.

49. Ingram, *Public Policy*, 209–14; Whitaker, *Striking a Balance*, 135; Ambrose, *Nixon, Triumph*, 553; Nixon's Handwritten Comments on Daily News Summaries, June 15, 1972, Folder "Annotated News Summaries, June 7–23, 1972, 1 of 2," Box 40, President's Office Files, WHSF, RNPMP; Memo, John Whitaker to Richard Nixon, June 20, 1972, Folder "EX FG 298, EPA, January 1, 1972-(1972), 2 of 3," Box 1, EPA Files, WHCF, RNPMP.

50. R. Stephen Berry, "What Happened at Stockholm," *Science and Public Affairs* 28, no. 7 (September 1972): 16–58; Petulla, *American Environmentalism*, 168; Rosenbaum, *Politics of Environmental Concern*, 260.

51. Palme quoted in Berry, "What Happened at Stockholm," 47.

52. Interview, Author with William Ruckelshaus, Apr. 2, 1998.

53. *Public Papers, 1972*, 689; Transcript, Telephone Conversation, John Whitaker to John Ehrlichman, June 13, 1972, Folder "CEQ, 1971–1972, 1 of 3," Box 126, John Whitaker Files, WHCF, RNPMP; Memo, Russell Train to Richard Nixon, June 19, 1972, Folder "EX FG 6–17, CEQ, September 1, 1971–December 27, 1972," Box 1, CEQ Files, WHCF, RNPMP.

54. Press Release, Muskie Blasts Administration Restraints in Stockholm Conference, May 25, 1972, Folder 20, "1972 Press Files, May 25th, On Stockholm Conference," Box 1584, USSSO, EMA.

55. Interview, Author with Russell Train, July 8, 1998; *BioScience* 22, no. 7 (July 1972): 424; Memo, Edwin Coate to John Whitaker, May 26, 1972, Folder "CEQ, 1972–1973, 1 of 2," Box 43, John Whitaker Files, WHCF, RNPMP.

56. Garrett, "Wildlife," 132; Dunlap, *Saving America's Wildlife*, 140; Memo, Nathaniel Reed to John Whitaker, Feb. 7, 1972, Folder "National Wildlife Week," Box 143, John Whitaker Files, WHCF, RNPMP; Memo, Richard Fairbanks to John Ehrlichman, July 31, 1972, Folder "1972 Campaign, I, 5 of 5," Box 124, John Whitaker Files, WHCF, RNPMP; Letter, Richard Nixon to Thomas Kimball, Aug. 3, 1972, Folder "1972 Campaign, I, 5 of 5," Box 124, John Whitaker Files, WHCF, RNPMP; Press Release, McGovern for President, Environmental White Paper, Aug. 13, 1972, Folder "McGovern White Paper, McGovern's Environmental Proposals, 1972, 1 of 3," Box 79, John Whitaker Files, WHCF, RNPMP; Memo, John Whitaker to H. R. Haldeman, Aug. 8, 1972, Folder "1972 Campaign, I, 5 of 5," Box 124, John Whitaker Files, WHCF, RNPMP.

57. *New York Times*, Oct. 1, 1972, 46; Oct. 2, 1972, 17; Oct. 22, 1972, 27; Nov. 12, 1972, 41.

58. *Public Papers, 1972*, 576–77; Hays, *Beauty, Health and Permanence*, 213–14; Pope, "Population," 176; Ehrlichman quoted in Memorandum for the President's File, Ken Cole, May 5, 1972.

59. Interview, Author with William Reilly, June 26, 1998; *Washington Evening Star*, Aug. 7, 1972, 1; *New York Times*, Aug. 8, 1972, 1; Aug. 9, 1972, 36; Aug. 10, 1972, 24; *Washington Post*, Aug. 10, 1972, 2; Joseph Browder, "Decision-Making in the White House" in Rathlesberger, *Nixon and the Environment*, 267; Memo, John Whitaker to William Morrill, May 23, 1972, Folder "Annual Report, 1972, CEQ," Box 43, John Whitaker Files, WHCF, RNPMP.

60. Stine, *Mixing the Waters*, 120; Stine, "Environmental Politics," 18; Blackwelder, "Water Resources," 65.

61. Coates, *Trans-Alaska Pipeline Controversy*, 234; Allin, *Politics of Wilderness Preservation*, 218–19; *Washington Post*, Aug. 3, 1972, 26.

62. Memo, John Ehrlichman to Richard Nixon, Sept. 4, 1972, Folder "EX FG 251, CACEQ, January 15, 1971–December 8, 1972," Box 1, CCE/CACEQ Files, WHCF, RNPMP.

63. Memo, John Whitaker to Richard Nixon, Sept. 9, 1972, Folder "EX FG 6–17, CEQ, September 1, 1971–December 27, 1972," Box 1, CEQ Files, WHCF, RNPMP; President's Daily News Summary, Sept. 18, 1972, Folder "Annotated News Summaries, September 1–18, 1972, 3 of 3," Box 43, President's Office Files, WHSF, RNPMP; Nixon quoted in Memorandum for the President's File, John Whitaker, Sept. 14, 1972, Folder "Meetings File, Beginning September 10, 1972," Box 89, President's Office Files, WHSF, RNPMP.

64. Cahn quoted in *New York Times*, Sept. 6, 1972, 12; Memo, Richard Fairbanks to Neal Ball, Sept. 1, 1972, Folder "CEQ, 1972, 1 of 2," Box 126, John Whitaker Files, WHCF, RNPMP.

65. Interview, Author with Brent Blackwelder, Mar. 23, 1998; Interview, Author with Richard Fairbanks, Mar. 24, 1998; Interview, Author with William Reilly, June 26, 1998; *Washington Post*, Sept. 6, 1972, 31.

66. Memo, Daniel Kingsley to Richard Nixon, Sept. 22, 1972, Folder "Presidential Handwriting, September 15–30, 1972," Box 18, President's Office Files, WHSF, RNPMP; Handwritten Note, Richard Nixon to John Ehrlichman, Sept. 22, 1972, Folder "Presidential Handwriting, September 15–30, 1972," Box 18, President's Office Files, WHSF, RNPMP; Press Release, CEQ Appointments, Sept. 29, 1972, Folder "CEQ, 1972, 1 of 2," Box 126, John Whitaker Files, WHCF, RNPMP; *New York Times*, Sept. 30, 1972, 13.

67. *Sierra Club Bulletin* 57, no. 8 (September 1972): 30.

68. McGovern quoted in *New York Times*, Oct. 3, 1972, 1.

69. P.L. 92–516; *Public Papers, 1972*, 1005.

70. P.L. 92–532; *Public Papers, 1972*, 1050–51; Mangrove, *Marine Policy*, 256–59; Memo, Russell Train to Richard Nixon, Nov. 20, 1972, Folder "CEQ, 1972, 1 of 2," Box 126, John Whitaker Files, WHCF, RNPMP.

71. P.L. 92–522; *Public Papers, 1972*, 1051; Dunlap, *Saving America's Wildlife*, 152; Fact Sheet, Marine Mammal Protection Act, Oct. 26, 1972, Folder "Legislation-Ocean Mammal Protection Act, 1971–1973, 1 of 2," Box 141, WHCF, RNPMP.

72. P.L. 92–583; *Public Papers, 1972*, 1051–52; Robert B. Abel, "The History of the United States Ocean Policy Program," in Francis Hoole, Robert Friedheim, and Timothy Hennessey, eds., *Making Ocean Policy* (Boulder, Colo.: Westview Press, 1981), 27; Mangrove, *Marine Policy*, 260–61; Whitaker, *Striking a Balance*, 153–54.

73. *New York Times*, Aug. 8, 1972, 1; Sept. 16, 1972, 15; Sept. 24, 1972, 1; Sept. 27, 1972, 33; Sept. 28, 1972, 98; Oct. 9, 1972, 86.

74. Letter, Thomas Kimball et al. to Edmund Muskie, July 11, 1972, Folder 7, "1972 Correspondence, Public Works Committee, S2770, Federal Water Pollution Control," Box SE1703, USSSO, EMA; Letter, Robert Packwood to Edmund Muskie, July 19, 1972, Folder 7, "1972 Correspondence, Public Works Committee, S2770, Federal Water Pollution Control," Box Se1703, USSSO, EMA.

75. Nixon quoted in Memorandum for the President's File, Herbert Stein, June 26, 1972, Folder "Meetings File, Beginning June 18, 1972," Box 89, President's Office File, WHSF, RNPMP.

76. Memo, John Whitaker to Harry Dent, July 24, 1972, Folder "Water Bill, III, 1972, 2 of 3," Box 114, John Whitaker Files, WHCF, RNPMP; Memorandum for the President's File, Tom Korologos, June 27, 1972, Folder "Meetings File, Beginning June 25, 1972," Box 89, President's Office Files, WHSF, RNPMP; Memo, Caspar Weinberger to Ken Cole, July 31, 1972, Folder "Water Bill, I, 1971–1972, 2 of 3," Box 113, John Whitaker Files, WHCF, RNPMP; Memo, John Ehrlichman to Richard Nixon, Aug. 2, 1972, Folder "EX HE 9–4, Water Pollution-Purification, January 1, 1971-, 2 of 3," Box 36, Health Files, WHCF, RNPMP; Letter, Howard Baker to Richard Nixon, Aug. 4, 1972, Folder "EX HE 9–4, Water Pollution-Purification, January 1, 1971-, 2 of 3," Box 36, Health Files, WHCF, RNPMP.

77. Congressional Research Service, *A Legislative History of the Water Pollution Control Act Amendments of 1972* (Washington, D.C.: U.S. Government Printing Office, 1973), 281–339; *BioScience* 22, no. 12 (December 1972): 728; Lieber, *Federalism and Clean Waters*, 80–82.

78. Lieber, *Federalism and Clean Waters*, 80–82.; John Dean to Roger Cramton, Sept. 19, 1972, Folder "Water Quality Bill," Box 76, John Dean Files, WHSF, RNPMP; Memo, Roger Cramton to John Dean, Sept. 20, 1972, Folder "Water Quality Bill," Box 76, John Dean Files, WHSF, RNPMP; Memo, Roger Cramton to John Ehrlichman, Oct. 5, 1972, Folder "Water Bill, I, 1972, 1 of 3," Box 114, John Whitaker Files, WHCF, RNPMP.

79. Lieber, *Federalism and Clean Waters*, 82; *New York Times*, Oct. 19, 1972, 1; Letter, Jack Kemp to John Ehrlichman, Oct. 10, 1972, Folder "EX HE 9–4, Water Pollution-

Purification, January 1, 1971-, 3 of 3," Box 36, Health Files, WHCF, RNPMP; Letter, John Anderson et al. to Richard Nixon, Oct. 13, 1972, Folder "EX HE 9–4, Water Pollution-Purification, January 1, 1971-, 3 of 3," Box 36, Health Files, WHCF, RNPMP; Letter, John Anderson to Richard Nixon, Oct. 16, 1972, Folder "EX HE 9–4, Water Pollution-Purification, January 1, 1971-, 3 of 3," Box 36, Health Files, WHCF, RNPMP.

80. Memo, Caspar Weinberger to Richard Nixon, Oct. 13, 1972, Folder "The Aged, Water Pollution Control," Box 1, Ronald Ziegler Files, WHSF, RNPMP.

81. Ehrlichman, *Witness to Power*, 330; Lieber, *Federalism and Clean Waters*, 82. Congress labeled the debt-ceiling bill 16810. Memo, Ken Cole to John Ehrlichman, Oct. 17, 1972, Folder "EX HE 9–4, Water Pollution Control-Purification, January 1, 1971-, 3 of 3," Box 36, Health Files, WHCF, RNPMP.

82. *Public Papers, 1972*, 992.

83. *New York Times*, Oct. 19, 1972, 1, 46; Kutler, *Wars of Watergate*, 135–36; Memo, William Timmons to Richard Nixon, Oct. 18, 1972, Folder "EX HE 9–1, Water Pollution-Purification, January 1, 1971-, 3 of 3," Health Files, WHCF, RNPMP.

84. Nixon quoted in Ehrlichman, *Witness to Power*, 297.

85. Parmet, *Richard Nixon and His America*, 625; Aitken, *Nixon*, 453; Ambrose, *Nixon, Triumph*, 641–46.

86. *Washington Post*, Nov. 8, 1972, 1; *New York Times*, Nov. 8, 1972, 1.

87. Ibid; Ambrose, *Nixon, Triumph*, 651–52.

88. Nixon quoted in *New York Times*, Nov. 13, 1972, 37; Edey quoted in *New York Times*, Nov. 11, 1972, 41.

89. Nixon, *RN*, 717.

90. H. R. Haldeman, *The Haldeman Diaries: Inside the Nixon White House* (New York: G.P. Putnam's Sons, 1994), 532; Nathan, *Plot that Failed*, 61–65; Price, *With Nixon*, 197–98; Klein quoted in Stephen Ambrose, *Nixon: Ruin and Recovery, 1972–1990* (New York: Simon and Schuster, 1991), 15, 22–24.

91. *Washington Star*, Nov. 9, 1972, 1; *Public Papers, 1972*, 1147–52.

92. Interview, Author with John Whitaker, July 23, 1996.

93. Ibid; Interview, Author with Joe Browder, Mar. 24, 1998; Memo, John Ehrlichman to Richard Nixon, Dec. 6, 1972, Folder "President's Handwriting, December 16–31, 1972," Box 20, President's Office Files, WHSF, RNPMP.

94. Position Paper, Domestic Policy, Second Term, Ken Cole, December 1972, Folder "President's Handwriting, December 16–31, 1972," Box 20, President's Office Files, WHSF, RNPMP.

95. Clary, *Timber and the Forest Service*, 176, LeMaster, *Decade of Change*, 14; *New York Times*, Dec. 28, 1972, 62; Memo, Edward David to Donald Crabill, Nov. 1, 1972, Folder "EDD, Chronological, November, 1972," Box 45, Edward David Files, WHCF, RNPMP.

96. Nixon quoted in *New York Times*, Nov. 29, 1972, 1; Letter, Richard Nixon to William Ruckelshaus, Nov. 22, 1972, Folder "EX FG 9–4, Water Pollution-Purification, January 1, 1971-, 3 of 3," Box 36, Health Files, WHCF, RNPMP.

97. *New York Times*, Dec. 13, 1972, 1; Letter, Arthur Link to Richard Nixon, Jan. 5, 1973, Folder "EX HE 9–4, Water Pollution-Purification, January 1, 1973–January 31, 1973," Box 36, Health Files, WHCF, RNPMP; Letter, Linwood Holton to Richard Nixon, Jan. 22,

1973, Folder "EX HE 9–4, Water Pollution-Purification, January 1, 1973–January 31, 1973," Box 36, Health Files, WHCF, RNPMP; Letter, Sherman Tribbitt to Richard Nixon, Feb. 6, 1973, Folder "EX HE 9–4, Water Pollution-Purification, February 1, 1973–February 28, 1973," Box 36, Health Files, WHCF, RNPMP; Letter, Allan Pritchard et al. to Richard Nixon, Mar. 30, 1973, Folder "EX HE 9–4, Water Pollution-Purification, March 1, 1973–June 30, 1973," Box 36, Health Files, WHCF, RNPMP.

98. Quoted in Aitken, *Nixon*, 455.

Chapter 6

1. *Public Papers of the Presidents, Richard Nixon, 1973* (Washington, D.C.: U.S. Government Printing Office, 1975), 28; Ambrose, *Nixon: Ruin and Recovery*, 56.

2. *New York Times*, Jan. 15, 1973, 28; Ambrose, *Nixon: Ruin and Recovery*, 61–62.

3. Policy Paper for Natural Resources, 1973, Earl Butz, Jan. 30, 1973, Folder "Environment-General, 1972–1973, 1 of 2," Box 60, John Whitaker Files, WHCF, RNPMP.

4. *Science and Public Affairs* 29, no. 5 (May 1973): 5–42; Press Release, Reorganization Plan no. 1 of 1973, Jan. 26, 1973, Folder "Government Reorganization, 1971–1973, 1 of 2," Box 69, John Whitaker Files, WHCF, RNPMP.

5. Ingram, *Public Policy*, 56; Whitaker, *Striking a Balance*, 115, 154–55.

6. Memo, Richard Fairbanks to Tod Hullin, Jan. 4, 1973, Folder "NIPCC, 1971–1973," Box 143, John Whitaker Files, WHCF, RNPMP; Whitaker, *Striking a Balance*, 40n.

7. Stine, "Environmental Politics," 18, Blackwelder, "Water Resources," 65; Discussion Paper, The Case for an XXT, January 1973, Folder "EX CA 8, Aircraft Development, January 1, 1973-," Box 28, Civil Aviation Files, WHCF, RNPMP; Memo, John Ehrlichman to Tod Hullin, Jan. 18, 1973, Folder "EX CA 8, Aircraft Development, January 1, 1973-," Box 28, Civil Aviation Files, WHCF, RNPMP.

8. Memo, Richard Fairbanks to Ken Cole, Jan. 10, 1973, Folder "Environmental Message, 1973 (1972–1973), 3 of 3," Box 58, John Whitaker Files, WHCF, RNPMP; Memo, John Ehrlichman to Richard Nixon, Nov. 20, 1972, Folder "Environmental Message, 1973 (1972–1973), 3 of 3," Box 58, John Whitaker Files, WHCF, RNPMP.

9. Council on Environmental Quality, *The President's 1973 Environmental Program* (Washington, D.C.: U.S. Government Printing Office, 1973), 3–12.

10. Memo, Leon Billings to Edmund Muskie, Jan. 3, 1973, Folder 6 "1970–1973, Misc., Leon Billings, Other Legislation," Box 1961, USSSO, EMA.

11. *Living Wilderness* 37, no. 121 (Spring 1973): 2; *Sierra Club Bulletin* 58, no. 3 (March 1973): 17.

12. Interview, Author with Richard Fairbanks, Mar. 24, 1998.

13. Haldeman, *Haldeman Diaries*, 582; Ehrlichman, *Witness to Power*, 311.

14. *New York Times*, Feb. 11, 1973, 1; Memo, Earl Butz to John Ehrlichman, Feb. 24, 1973, Folder "HE 9–1, Air Pollution, January 1, 1973–August 31, 1973," Box 31, Health Files, WHCF, RNPMP; Memo, John Ehrlichman to Richard Nixon, Mar. 1, 1973, Folder "President's Handwriting, March 1–10, 1973," Box 21, President's Office Files, WHSF, RNPMP.

15. *Wall Street Journal*, Apr. 12, 1973, 1; Press Release, EPA, Statement by Administrator William Ruckelshaus on Air Quality Standards, Apr. 11, 1973, Folder "Auto Emissions,

1973, 1 of 2," Box 29, John Whitaker Files, WHCF, RNPMP; President's Handwritten Notes, Mar. 13, 1973, Folder "Annotated News Summaries, March 1–7, 1973, 3 of 3," Box 49, President's Office Files, WHSF, RNPMP; President's Handwritten Notes, Mar. 14, 1973, Folder "Annotated News Summaries, March 1–7, 1973, 3 of 3," Box 49, President's Office Files, WHSF, RNPMP.

16. Whitaker, *Striking a Balance*, 100–2.

17. *New York Times*, Jan. 9, 1973, 77; Jan. 10, 1973, 30.

18. *Sierra Club Bulletin* 58, no. 9 (October 1973): 33; Press Release, Statement of Senator Edmund Muskie on EPA Implementation of Air Quality Standards, Jan. 16, 1973, Folder 5, "Leon Billings File," Box 1962, USSSO, EMA.

19. Transcript, Paul Harvey Editorial, undated, Folder 9, "1973–1975 Correspondence," Box 1948, USSSO, EMA.

20. Whitaker, *Striking a Balance*, 101–2: *New York Times*, June 14, 1973, 34.

21. Whitaker, *Striking a Balance*, 87–92; Memo, Geoff Shepard to Ken Cole, May 9, 1973, Folder "EX FG 298, EPA, May 1, 1973–December 31, 1973," Box 2, EPA Files, WHCF, RNPMP; Memo, Richard Fairbanks to John Ehrlichman, May 29, 1973, Folder "EX HE 9–4, Water Pollution-Purification, March 1, 1973–June 30, 1973," Box 36, Health Files, WHCF, RNPMP.

22. Whitaker, *Striking a Balance*, 161–64; *Congressional Quarterly Almanac*, 92d Cong., 2d sess., Vol. 28 (1972), 829; Memo, Ken Cole to John Ehrlichman, Sept. 13, 1973, Folder "Land Use, 1972–1973," Box 77, John Whitaker Files, WHCF, RNPMP.

23. Letter, Steve Crick to Henry Jackson, Apr. 11, 1973, Folder 19, "General Correspondence-Legislation-Land Use Planning Bill," Box 120, Accession No. 3560–5, PHJ.

24. Press Release, Statement of Henry M. Jackson, Mar. 13, 1973, Folder 85, "Letter to the President on Land Use Stuff," Box 260, Accession No. 3560–5, PHJ.

25. Memo, Ken Cole to Russell Train, Oct. 9, 1973, Folder "EX FG 298, EPA," Box 2, EPA Files, WHCF, RNPMP; Unmarked Photocopy, "A Critical View of the Urban Crisis," by Edward Banfield, January 1973, Folder "President's Handwriting, March 11–31, 1973," Box 21, President's Office Files, WHSF, RNPMP; Memo, Bruce Kehrli to John Ehrlichman, Mar. 12, 1973, Folder "President's Handwriting, March 11–31, 1973," Box 21, President's Office Files, WHSF, RNPMP; Memo, Leonard Laster to Kenneth Cole, Jan. 5, 1973, Folder "White House Life Sciences, 1973," Box 12, Edward David Files, WHCF, RNPMP.

26. Memo, Richard Fairbanks to John Ehrlichman, Mar. 3, 1973, Folder "EX NR Natural Resources, 3 of 3, 1973–1974," Box 1, Natural Resources Files, WHCF, RNPMP; Memo and Handwritten Response, Ken Cole to John Ehrlichman, Mar. 3, 1973, Folder "EX FG 298, EPA, January 1–April 30, 1973," Box 2, EPA Files, WHCF, RNPMP; Memo, Earl Butz to Rogers Morton et al., Mar. 12, 1973, Folder "EX FG 999–28, DNR, 1971–1973," Box 14, Proposed Departments, WHCF, RNPMP.

27. Letter, Laurance Rockefeller to Richard Nixon, Jan. 23, 1973, Folder "EX FG 251/A, February 5, 1973–October 9, 1973," Box 1, CCE/CACEQ Files, WHCF, RNPMP; Letter, Henry L. Diamond to Richard Nixon, Apr. 18, 1973, Folder "EX FG 251, CACEQ, January 1, 1973–March 14, 1973," Box 1, CCE/CACEQ Files, WHCF, RNPMP.

28. Kehoe, *Cleaning Up the Great Lakes*, 164–65; Memo, Theodore L. Eliot to Henry

Kissinger, Feb. 9, 1973, Folder "EX NR 7–1, Projects 3 of 3, 1973–1974," Box 17, Natural Resources Files, WHCF, RNPMP.

29. LeMaster, *Decade of* Change, 34; Clary, *Timber and the Forest Service*, 190–92; *Congressional Quarterly Almanac*, 93d Cong., 1st sess., Vol. 29 (1973), 681; *New York Times*, Mar. 27, 1973, 1; Letter, Richard Fairbanks to Steven Symms, Mar. 28, 1973, Folder "EX NR 3, Forests 5 of 5, 1973–1974," Box 7, Natural Resources Files, WHCF, RNPMP.

30. LeMaster, *Decade of Change*, 50–51; *American Forests* 77 (April 1972), 24; *Congressional Quarterly Almanac*, 92d Cong., 2d sess., Vol. 28 (1972), 309; Haight, "Wilderness Act," appendix 1. For a fuller discussion of the eastern wilderness question, see Frome, *Battle for the Wilderness*, chap. 11; and Allin, *Politics of Wilderness Preservation*. Press Release, Henry M. Jackson, Jan. 8, 1973, Folder 5, "Speeches and Writings-Timber-January 8, 1973," Box 244, Accession No. 3560–5, PHJ.

31. President's Advisory Panel on Timber and the Environment, *Report of the President's Advisory Panel on Timber and the Environment* (Washington, D.C. U.S. Government Printing Office, 1973), 12; Haight, "Wilderness Act," appendix 1; Memorandum for the President's File, Richard Fairbanks, Sept. 24, 1973, Folder "Meetings File, Beginning September 23, 1973," Box 92, President's Office Files, WHSF, RNPMP.

32. Frome, *Battle for the Wilderness*, 162–63; Roth, *Wilderness Movement*, chap. 7.

33. *West Virginia Division of Izaak Walton League vs. Butz*; Memo, Geoff Shepard to Ken Cole, May 9, 1973, Folder "EX FG 298, EPA, May 1, 1973–December 31, 1973," Box 2, EPA Files, WHCF, RNPMP.

34. Interview, Author with Richard Fairbanks, Mar. 24, 1998; Memo, David Parker to Richard Fairbanks, Mar. 9, 1973, Folder "EX NR Natural Resources, 3 of 3, 1973–1974," Box 1, Natural Resources Files, WHCF, RNPMP; Memo, Richard Fairbanks to John Ehrlichman, June 3, 1973, Folder "EX NR Natural Resources, 3 of 3, 1973–1974," Box 1, Natural Resources Files, WHCF, RNPMP.

35. Andrews, *Environmental Policy*, 36–38, 43. The guidelines proclaimed CEQ's broad statutory authority to "review and appraise" all federal programs, and required each agency to include a draft EIS as part of its initial OMB clearance.

36. *Public Papers, 1973*, 792–94; Council on Environmental Quality, *Fourth Annual Report of the President's Council on Environmental Quality* (Washington, D.C.: U.S. Government Printing Office, 1973); *New York Times*, Sept. 18, 1973, 26.

37. *Public Papers, 1973*, 792–94.

38. Nixon quoted in Kutler, *Abuse of Power*, 362.

39. Interview, Author with William Ruckelshaus, Apr. 2, 1998.

40. Interview, Author with William Reilly, June 26, 1998; Interview, Author with Russell Train, July 8, 1998; Landy et al., *Environmental Protection Agency*, 38–39.

41. Interview, Author with Russell Train, July 8, 1998; Nixon quoted in Memorandum for the President's File, July 26, 1973, Folder "Meetings File, Beginning July 22, 1973," Box 92, President's Office Files, WHSF, RNPMP; *New York Times*, July 27, 1973, 32; Landy et al., *Environmental Protection Agency*, 38.

42. Sansom, *New American Dream Machine*, 28–29; Memo, Bryce Harlow to Jerry Jones, Sept. 11, 1973, Folder "EX FG 6–17, CEQ, January 1, 1973–July 29, 1974," Box 2, CEQ Files, WHCF, RNPMP.

43. Interview, Author with William Reilly, June 26, 1998; Memo, John Sawhill to Ken Cole, Roy Ash, et al., Sept. 21, 1973, Folder "EX FG 6–17, CEQ, January 1, 1973–July 29, 1974," Box 2, CEQ Files, WHCF, RNPMP.

44. Interview, Author with Laurence Moss, Mar. 25, 1998; Interview, Author with Russell Train, July 8, 1998.

45. Jackson quoted in *New York Times*, Apr. 17, 1973, 1.

46. Transcript, John Ehrlichman Speech before the Economic Club of Detroit, Feb. 26, 1973, Folder "February 26, 1973, Economic Club of Detroit," Box 68, John Ehrlichman Files, WHSF, RNPMP.

47. *Public Papers, 1973*, 302–19; Nixon, *RN*, 983–84; *New York Times*, Apr. 19, 1973, 1, 53; Whitaker, *Striking a Balance*, 69, 228, 274, 312–14.

48. *Public Papers, 1973*, 623–30; Letter, Richard Nixon to Henry Jackson, July 12, 1973, Folder "EX TN 3, Pipelines, January 1, 1973-, 1 of 2," Box 5, Transportation Files, WHCF, RNPMP; Nixon, *RN*, 983; Barber and Cochran, "Energy," 70–90; Henry Strum and Fred Strum, "American Solar Energy Policy," *Environmental* Review 7, no. 2 (Summer 1983): 135–53; New York Times, June 30, 1973, 1; Executive Order 11726.

49. *Congressional Record*, 93d Cong., 1st sess., Vol. 119, pt. 4 (Aug. 2, 1973), 27649; Coates, *Trans-Alaska Pipeline Controversy*, 237; Berry, *Alaska Pipeline*, 272.

50. Berry, *Alaska Pipeline*, 274–75; Memo, Roy Ash to Richard Nixon, Oct. 23, 1973, Folder "EX TN 3, Pipelines, January 1, 1973-, 2 of 2," Box 5, Transportation Files, WHCF, RNPMP.

51. Quoted in Coates, *Trans-Alaska Pipeline Controversy*, 245–47.

52. Quoted in Ambrose, *Nixon: Ruin and Recovery*, 249, 250.

53. Quoted in ibid, 250.

54. David Halberstam, *The Reckoning* (New York: William Morrow, 1986), 458–59.

55. *New York Times*, Nov. 11, 1973, 66; Nov. 13, 1973, 11; Nov. 15, 1973, 59, 70; Nov. 18, 1973, 48; Nov. 20, 1973, 1; Nov. 22, 1973, 1; Link and Catton, *American Epoch*, 987–88.

56. *Public Papers, 1973*, 916–22; *New York Times*, Nov. 8, 1973, 1; *Nation* 28, no. 1 (Jan. 5, 1974): 11–16; *New Republic* 169, no. 26 (Dec. 29, 1973): 5–6.

57. Letter, Ronald Reagan to Richard Nixon, Nov. 12, 1973, Folder "EX FG 999–45, DENR, 1973–1974," Box 16, Proposed Departments Files, WHCF, RNPMP.

58. Whitaker, *Striking a Balance*, 101; Letter, David Hawkins et al. to John Love, Nov. 12, 1973, Folder "EX HE 9–4, Water Pollution-Purification, July 1, 1973–November 12, 1973," Box 36, Health Files, WHCF, RNPMP.

59. Interview, Author with Joe Browder, Mar. 24, 1998; Vietor, *Environmental Politics*, 93.

60. P.L. 93–153; Donald Paul Hodel and Robert Deitz, *Crisis in the Oil Patch* (Washington, D.C.: Regnery Publishing, 1994), 74; Berry, *Alaska Pipeline*, 278; Hosmer quoted in Coates, *Trans-Alaska Pipeline Controversy*, 249; *New York Times*, Nov. 17, 1973, 1.

61. Interview, Author with Don Nicoll, Apr. 1, 1998; R. E. Dunlap, "Trends in Public Opinion Toward Environmental Issues," in Dunlap and Mertig, eds., *American Environmentalism*, 96–102; Memo, Don Nicoll to Edmund Muskie, Oct. 21, 1973, Folder 5, "Leon Billings File," Box 1962, USSSO, EMA.

62. *Public Papers, 1973*, 946–64; Ambrose, *Nixon: Ruin and Recovery*, 271–72.

63. Memo, Ken Cole to Richard Nixon, Nov. 9, 1974, Folder "President's Handwriting, November 1–15, 1973," Box 23, President's Office Files, WHSF, RNPMP.

64. *Public Papers, 1973,* 990–91; Executive Order 11748; *New York Times,* Dec. 4, 1973, 1.

65. Ruth Sheldon Knowles, *America's Energy Famine* (Norman: University of Oklahoma Press, 1980), 60.

66. P.L. 93–159; Kutler, *Wars of Watergate,* 436–37; Link and Catton, *American Epoch,* 994.

67. P.L. 93–205; Dunlap, *Saving America's Wildlife,* 153, Culhane, *Public Lands Politics,* 118; Garrett, "Wildlife," 133.

68. Memo, Roy Ash to Richard Nixon, Dec. 23, 1973, Folder "EX NR Fish-Wildlife, 6 of 7, May–December, 1973," Box 3, Natural Resources Files, WHCF, RNPMP.

69. Allin, *Politics of Wilderness Preservation,* 219.

70. *Sierra Club Bulletin* 58, no. 10 (November–December 1973): 9; *New York Times,* Nov. 24, 1973, IV, 14.

71. *New York Times,* Dec. 8, 1973, 25; Ambrose, *Nixon: Ruin and Recovery,* 279–80.

72. Ambrose, *Nixon: Ruin and Recovery,* 289–91.

73. *Public Papers of the Presidents, Richard Nixon, 1974* (Washington, D.C.: U.S. Government Printing Office, 1975), 47–55; J. Clarence Davies, "The Greening of American Politics," *Wilson Quarterly* 1, no. 4 (Summer 1977): 95.

74. *Public Papers, 1974,* 17–32; Whitaker, *Striking a Balance,* 274.

75. Memo, Ken Cole to Richard Nixon, Feb. 27, 1974, Folder "HE 9–1, Air Pollution, September 1, 1973-, 2 of 2," Box 31, Health Files, WHCF, RNPMP.

76. Interview, Author with Leon Billings, June 26, 1998.

77. Train, "Energy Problems and Environmental Concern"; *New York Times,* Mar. 7, 1974, 1.

78. Standard Oil of New Jersey, Royal Dutch Shell Group, Texaco, Standard Oil of California, Socony Mobil, Gulf, and British Petroleum.

79. Petulla, *American Environmental History,* 345.

80. *New York Times,* Mar. 22, 1974, 62. Proposed as Clean Air Act Amendments of 1974; Fact Sheet, Clean Air Act Proposal, March 1974, Folder "HE 9–1, Air Pollution, September 1, 1973-, 2 of 2," Box 31, Health Files, WHCF, RNPMP.

81. Memo, Richard Nixon to Russell Train, Mar. 22, 1974, Folder "EX FG 298, EPA, January 1, 1974–May 30, 1974," Box 2, EPA Files, WHCF, RNPMP; Memorandum for the President's File, David Parker, Mar. 29, 1974, Folder "Meetings File, Beginning March 24, 1974," Box 94, President's Office Files, WHSF, RNPMP.

82. Whitaker, *Striking a Balance,* 106.

83. Ibid., 110; P.L. 93–319; The Federal Energy Administration Act of 1974, P.L. 93–438; David Howard Davis, *Energy Politics* (New York: St. Martin's Press, 1982), 193, 198; Scheffer, *Shaping of Environmentalism,* 165.

84. *NRDC, et al. v. Kleppe*; Vietor, *Environmental Politics,* 110–11.

85. Aitken, *Nixon,* 510–13; Ambrose, *Nixon: Ruin and Recovery,* 276–78.

86. Ambrose, *Nixon: Ruin and Recovery,* 343.

87. Interview, Author with Ronald Walker, Nov. 29, 1998.

88. P.L. 93–344; Kutler, *Wars of Watergate,* 594–95.

89. Petulla, *American Environmentalism*, 136; Dunlap, *Saving America's Wildlife*, 157; Press Release, Control of Predatory Animals, July 1974, Folder "GEN NR Fish-Wildlife, 17 of 17, June, 1973–July, 1974," Box 6, Natural Resources Files, WHCF, RNPMP.

90. Christine Russell, "President Proposes Doubling Wilderness System," *BioScience* 24 (August 1974): 471; Haight, "Wilderness Act," appendix 1; Memo, Frank Zarb to David Parker, May 21, 1974, Folder "EX NR 3, Forests, 5 of 5, 1973–1974," Box 7, Natural Resources Files, WHCF, RNPMP; Memo, Richard Fairbanks to G. Powell, Apr. 9, 1974, Folder "GEN NR 3, Forests, 9 of 9, 1973–1974," Box 8, Natural Resources Files, WHCF, RNPMP; Memo, Richard Fairbanks to Ken Cole, Feb. 8, 1974, Folder "GEN NR 3, Forests, 9 of 9, 1973–1974," Box 8, Natural Resources Files, WHCF, RNPMP.

91. *Natural Resources Defense Council v. Morton*; Culhane, *Public Lands Politics*, 95; Muhn and Stuart, *Opportunity and Challenge*, 165, 181.

92. *Congressional Record*, 93d Cong., 2d sess., Vol. 120, pt. 10 (June 11, 1974), H5028; *Congressional Quarterly Almanac*, 93d Cong., 2d sess., Vol. 30 (1974), 790; Whitaker, *Striking a Balance*, 164–65; *BioScience* 24, no. 8 (August 1974): 470–71.

93. Ambrose, *Nixon: Ruin and Recovery*, 394–99.

94. Ibid., 398–99; *Public Papers, 1974*, 606–14.

95. Nixon, *RN*, 1076–77; Kissinger, *Years of Upheaval*, 1207–9.

96. *Public Papers, 1974*, 626–29.

97. Kutler, *Wars of Watergate*, 545.

Epilogue

1. Interview, Author with John Whitaker, July 23, 1996; Interview, Author with Richard Fairbanks, Mar. 24, 1998.

2. Quoted in Ambrose, *Nixon: Ruin and Recovery*, 482.

3. Ibid., 550–80; Aitken, *Nixon*, 560–69.

4. Kline, *First Along the River*, 98–99; Link and Catton, *American Epoch*, 993; 1026; 1032–33.

5. Rothman, *Greening of a Nation?*, 132–33.

6. See Timothy P. Maga, *The World of Jimmy Carter: United States Foreign Policy, 1977–1981* (West Haven, Conn.: University of New Haven Press, 1994); and John Robert Greene, *The Presidency of Gerald R. Ford* (Lawrence: University of Kansas Press, 1995).

7. Dunlap, "Trends in Public Opinion," in Dunlap and Mertig, *American Environmentalism*, 98, 100–1.

8. Christopher Bosso, *Pesticides and Politics: The LifeCycle of a Public Issue* (Pittsburgh: University of Pittsburgh Press, 1987), 198–99; Lewis Regenstein, *America the Poisoned* (Washington, D.C.: Acropolis, 1982), 231–33; Richard Andrews, *Managing the Environment, Managing Ourselves: A History of American Environmental Policy* (New Haven, Conn.: Yale University Press, 1999), 185, 247; Sale, *Green Revolution*, 31, 59, 60, 98.

9. *Outside Magazine* 24, no. 4 (April 1999): 65–80.

10. Hays, *Beauty, Health, and Permanence*, 491.

11. Interview, Author with Philip Berry, June 19, 1998.

12. Sale, *Green Revolution*, 50–51; Kline, *First Along the River*, 104–8; Hays, *Beauty*,

Health, and Permanence, 491–526. See Norman Vig and Michael Kraft, *Environmental Policy in the 1980s* (Washington, D.C.: Congressional Quarterly, 1984).

13. Shabecoff, *Fierce Green Fire*, 209–10; Hays, *Beauty, Health, and Permanence*, 491–92; Sale, *Green Revolution*, 33.

14. Devall, "Deep Ecology," 51–61; Sale, *Green Revolution*, 53.

15. *New York Times*, Apr. 22, 1990, 1; Apr. 23, 1990, 1.

16. Quoted in Aitken, *Nixon*, 565.

17. Andrews, *Managing the Environment, Managing Ourselves*, 285–88.

18. Government in the Sunshine Act of 1976, P.L. 94–409; Caldwell, *National Environmental Policy Act*, 72, 100, 159–60.

19. Sale, *Green Revolution*, 36.

20. Interview, Author with Russell Train, July 8, 1998.

21. Interview, Author with David Brower, Apr. 7, 1998.

22. Quoted in Mary H. Cooper, "Environmental Movement at 25," *Congressional Quarterly Researcher* (Mar. 31, 1995): 418; Kline, *First Along the River*, 98.

23. P.L. 94–579.

24. Jeffrey K. Stine, "Environmental Policy during the Carter Presidency," in Gary M. Fink and Hugh Davis Graham, eds., *The Carter Presidency: Policy Choices in the Post-New Deal Era* (Lawrence: University of Kansas Press, 1998), 179–201.

25. P.L. 95–87; P.L. 95–95; P.L. 95–217, respectively.

26. P.L. 96–487.

27. P.L. 94–580 and P.L. 94–469, respectively.

28. P.L. 96–510. See Stine, "Environmental Policy during the Carter Presidency," 179.

29. Interview, Author with Philip Berry, June 19, 1998.

30. P.L. 99–499. See Jonathan Lash, Katherine Gillman, and David Sheridan, *A Season of Spoils: The Story of the Reagan Administration's Attack on the Environment* (New York: Pantheon, 1984).

31. P.L. 101–549 and P.L. 103–433, respectively; *New York Times*, Sept. 1, 1998, II, 9; Sept. 24, 1998, 27; Gary Bryner, *Blue Skies, Green Politics: The Clean Air Act of 1990* (Washington, D.C.: Congressional Quarterly, 1993), 94; Robert Paarlberg, "A Diplomatic Dispute: Clinton, Congress, and International Environmental Policy," *Environment* 38, no. 8 (1996): 16–20, 28–33; Paul Rauber, "The Great Green Hope," *Sierra* 82, no. 4 (1997): 40–43, 60–63; Tom Wicker, "Waiting for an Environmental President," *Audubon* 96, no. 5 (1994): 49–54, 102–3.

32. Andrews, *Managing the Environment, Managing Ourselves*, 255.

33. Interview, Author with William Reilly, June 26, 1998.

Bibliography

Manuscript and Archive Collections

The Richard M. Nixon Presidential Materials Project
National Archives II
College Park, Maryland

White House Special Files

Patrick Buchanan
Charles Colson
John Dean
John Ehrlichman
H. R. Haldeman
David Hoopes
Egil Krogh
Ronald Ziegler

White House Central Files

Citizen's Advisory Committee on Environmental Quality
Civil Aviation and Transportation
Council on Environmental Quality
Department of Agriculture
Department of Health, Education and Welfare
Department of Interior
Department of Transportation
Domestic Council
Energy Policy Office
Environmental Protection Agency
Federal Energy Administration

Federal Energy Office
Natural Resources
National Industrial Pollution Control Council
Office of Science and Technology
President's Advisory Council on Executive Organization
John Whitaker

Richard M. Nixon Vice-Presidential Papers
National Archives, Southwest Region
Laguna Hills, California
Appearance Files and Press Releases
Campaign Files
General Correspondence Files

The Edmund S. Muskie Archives
Bates College
Lewiston, Maine
Senate Office Files
Washington Inner Office Files
U.S. Senate Clippings
Periodicals

The Papers of Henry M. Jackson
Manuscript and Archives Division
Allen Library, University of Washington
Seattle, Washington
Senate Case Files

Washington National Record Center
Suitland, Maryland
U.S. Environmental Protection Agency

Alaska Collection
Z. J. Loussac Library
Anchorage, Alaska
Vertical Files

Interviews

Philip Berry
Leon Billings
Brent Blackwelder

Joe B. Browder
David Brower
Richard Fairbanks
Walter Hickel
Mike Leavitt
Laurence I. Moss
Gaylord Nelson
Don Nicoll
David Parker
William Reilly
William Ruckelshaus
Maurice Stans
Russell Train
Ron Walker
John Whitaker

Government Documents

Commission on Marine Science, Engineering and Resources. *Our Nation and the Sea: Report of the Commission on Marine Science, Engineering and Resources.* Washington, D.C.: U.S. Government Printing Office, 1969.

Commission on Pesticides and their Relationship to Health, Department of Health, Education and Welfare. *Report of the Secretary's Commission on Pesticides and their Relationship to Environmental Health.* Washington, D.C.: U.S. Government Printing Office, 1969.

Council on Environmental Quality. *First Annual Report of the President's Council on Environmental Quality.* Washington, D.C.: U.S. Government Printing Office, 1970.

———. *The President's 1971 Environmental Program.* Washington, D.C.: U.S. Government Printing Office, 1971.

———. *The President's 1972 Environmental Program.* Washington, D.C.: U.S. Government Printing Office, 1972.

———. *The President's 1973 Environmental Program.* Washington, D.C.: U.S. Government Printing Office, 1973.

———. *Fourth Annual Report of the President's Council on Environmental Quality.* Washington, D.C.: U.S. Government Printing Press, 1973.

———. *The Global 2000 Report to the President.* Washington, D.C.: U.S. Government Printing Office, 1981.

———. *Report on Channel Modification.* Washington, D.C.: U.S. Government Printing Office, 1973.

Domestic Council. Subcommittee on National Growth. *Report on National Growth, 1972.* Washington, D.C.: U.S. Government Printing Office, 1972.

President's Advisory Panel on Timber and the Environment. *Report of the President's Advisory Panel on Timber and the Environment.* Washington, D.C.: U.S. Government Printing Office, 1973.

Public Land Law Review Commission. *One Third of the Nation's Land: A Report to the President and to the Congress.* Washington, D.C.: U.S. Government Printing Office, 1970.

Public Papers of the Presidents, Richard Nixon. Volumes 1–6, 1969–1974. Washington, D.C. U.S. Government Printing Office, 1971–1975.

U.S. Bureau of the Census. *Historical Statistics of the United States.* Washington, D.C.: U.S. Government Printing Office, 1974.

U.S. Congress. House Committee on Government Operations. *Phosphates in Detergents and Eutrophication of America's Waters: Hearings Before the Subcommittee on Conservation and Natural Resources.* 91st Cong., 1st sess., Dec. 15–16, 1969.

U.S. Congress. Senate Committee on Interior and Insular Affairs. *Hearings before the Committee on Interior and Insular Affairs on the Nomination of Walter Hickel to be Secretary of Interior.* 91st Cong., 1st sess., Jan. 15–18, 1969.

———. *Hearings on S.1075 before the Senate Committee on Interior and Insular Affairs.* 91st Cong., 1st sess., June, 1969.

U.S. Congress. Senate Committee on Public Works. *Water Pollution 1970 (Part I): Hearings Before the Subcommittee on Air and Water Pollution.* 91st Cong., 2d sess., Apr. 20–21, 27, 1970.

U.S. Environmental Protection Agency. *The First Two Years: A Review of EPA's Enforcement, February, 1973.* Washington, D.C.: U.S. Government Printing Office, 1973.

U.S. Water Resources Council. *Water and Related Land Resources: Establishment of Principles and Standards for Planning.* Washington, D.C.: U.S. Government Printing Office, 1973.

Newspapers

Anchorage Daily News
Arizona Republic
Atlanta Constitution
Berlin New Hampshire Reporter
Boston Globe
Chicago Daily News
Chicago Tribune
Columbian Vancouver
Christian Science Monitor
Los Angeles Times
New York Times
Portland Press Herald
Sacramento Union

Santa Barbara News Press
Seattle Post-Intelligencer
Tacoma News Tribune
Wall Street Journal
Washington Post
Washington Star

Journals-Periodicals

Audubon
Alaska Business Monthly
Alaska Homesteaders Handbook
American Forests
American Motorcycle Association News
BioScience
Business Week Magazine
Congressional Record
Congressional Quarterly Almanac
Environmental Affairs
Environmental Forum
Environmental Review
Environmental Science and Technology
Feedstuffs
Izaak Walton League of America Washington Newsletter
Living Wilderness
Nation
National Journal
New Republic
Oregon Law Review
Outside Magazine
Science
Science and Public Affairs
Sierra Club Bulletin
Sports Illustrated
U.S. News and World Report
Vital Speeches of the Day
Wildlife Management Institute Outdoor News Bulletin

Memoirs

Brower, David. *The Life and Times of David Brower*. Salt Lake City, UT: Peneguine
    Smith Books, 1990.
Ehrlichman, John. *Witness to Power*. New York: Pocket Books, 1982.

Eisenhower, Julie Nixon. *Pat Nixon: The Untold Story*. New York: Simon and Schuster, 1986.

Haldeman, H. R. *The Ends of Power*. New York: New York Times Books, 1978.

———. *The Haldeman Diaries: Inside the Nixon White House*. New York: G. P. Putnam's Sons, 1994.

Hickel, Walter. *Who Owns America?* Englewood Cliffs, N.J.: Prentice Hall, 1971.

Kissinger, Henry. *White House Years*. Boston: Little Brown, 1979.

———. *Years of Upheaval*. Boston: Little Brown, 1982.

Nixon, Richard. *RN: The Memoirs of Richard Nixon*. New York; Grosset and Dunlap, 1978.

Whitaker, John. *Striking A Balance: Environment and Natural Resources Policy in the Nixon-Ford Years*. Washington, D.C.: American Enterprise Institute, 1976.

Secondary Sources

Abbey, Edward. *The Monkey Wrench Gang*. Philadelphia: Lippincott, 1975.

Abel, Robert B. "The History of the United States Ocean Policy Program." In Francis Hoole, Robert Friedman, and Timothy Hennessey, eds., *Making Ocean Policy*. Boulder, Colo.: Westview, 1981.

Adams, David. "Management Systems under Consideration at the Federal-State Level." In James C. Hite and James M. Stepp, eds., *Coastal Zone Management*. New York: Praeger, 1971.

Aitken, Jonathan. *Nixon: A Life*. Washington, D.C.: Regnery Publishing, 1993.

Allen, Thomas B. *Guardian of the Wild*. Bloomington: Indiana University Press, 1987.

Allin, Craig W. *The Politics of Wilderness Preservation*. Westport, Conn.: Greenwood Press, 1982.

Ambrose, Stephen. *Eisenhower, the President*. New York: Simon and Schuster, 1984.

———. *Nixon: The Education of a Politician, 1913–1962*. New York: Simon and Schuster, 1987.

———. *Nixon: The Triumph of a Politician, 1962–1972*. New York: Simon and Schuster, 1989.

———. *Nixon: Ruin and Recovery, 1972–1990*. New York: Simon and Schuster, 1991.

American Enterprise Institute for Public Policy Research. *The Clean Air Act: Proposals for Revisions*. Washington, D.C.: American Enterprise Institute, 1981.

Anderson, Frederick R., and Robert H. Daniels. *NEPA in the Courts*. Baltimore: Johns Hopkins University Press, 1973.

Andrews, Richard. *Environmental Policy and Administrative Change*. Lexington, Mass.: D.C. Heath, 1976.

———. *Managing the Environment, Managing Ourselves: A History of American Environmental Policy*. New Haven, Conn.: Yale University Press, 1999.

Barber, William, and James Cochran. "Energy: From John F. Kennedy to Jimmy Carter." *Wilson Quarterly* 5, no. 2 (1981): 70–90.

Berry, Mary Clay. *The Alaska Pipeline*. Bloomington: Indiana University Press, 1975.

Boorstin, Daniel. *The Americans: The Democratic Experience.* New York: Vintage Books, 1974.

Bosso, Christopher. *Pesticides and Politics: The LifeCycle of a Public Issue.* Pittsburgh: University of Pittsburgh Press, 1987.

Bryner, Gary. *Blue Skies, Green Politics: The Clean Air Act of 1990.* Washington, D.C.: Congressional Quarterly, 1993.

Brown, Theodore L. *Energy and the Environment.* Columbus, Ohio: Charles Merrill Publishing, 1971.

Busselman, Fred, and David Callies. *The Quiet Revolution in Land Use Control.* Washington, D.C.: U.S. Government Printing Office, 1971.

Caldwell, Lynton Keith. *The National Environmental Policy Act: An Agenda for the Future.* Bloomington: Indiana University Press, 1998.

———. *Science and the National Environmental Policy Act: Redirecting Policy through Procedural Reform.* University, Ala.: University of Alabama Press, 1982.

Carson, Rachel. *Silent Spring.* Boston: Houghton Mifflin, 1962.

Caudill, Harry. *My Land is Dying.* New York: E. P. Dutton, 1971.

Caute, David. *The Year of the Barricades.* New York: Harper and Row, 1988.

Chafe, William H. *The Unfinished Journey.* New York: Oxford University Press, 1986.

Clary, David. *Timber and the Forest Service.* Lawrence: University of Kansas Press, 1986.

Clawson, Marion. *The Federal Lands Revisited.* Baltimore: Johns Hopkins University Press, 1983.

Coates, Peter. *The Trans-Alaska Pipeline Controversy.* Bethlehem, Pa.: Lehigh University Press, 1991.

Cohen, Michael. *The Pathless Way: John Muir and the American Wilderness.* Madison: University of Wisconsin Press, 1984.

———. *The History of the Sierra Club, 1892–1970.* San Francisco: Sierra Club Books, 1988.

Congressional Research Service, *A Legislative History of the Water Pollution Control Act Amendments of 1972.* Washington, D.C.: U.S. Government Printing Office, 1973.

———. *A Legislative History of the Clean Air Act Amendments of 1970.* Washington, D.C.: U.S. Government Printing Office, 1974.

Converse, Philip, et al. "Continuity and Change in American Politics: Parties and Issues in the 1968 Election." *American Political Science Review* 63 (December 1969): 1083–1105.

Cooper, Mary H. "Environmental Movement at 25." *Congressional Quarterly Researcher* (Mar. 31, 1995): 418.

Culhane, Paul. *Public Lands Politics.* Baltimore: Johns Hopkins University Press, 1981.

Davies, J. Clarence. *The Politics of Pollution.* New York: Pegasus, 1970.

———. "The Greening of American Politics." *Wilson Quarterly* 1, no. 4 (Summer 1977): 95.

Davis, David Howard. *Energy Politics.* New York: St. Martin's Press, 1982.

Devall, Bill. "Deep Ecology and Radical Environmentalism." In Riley Dunlap and Angela Mertig, eds., *American Environmentalism: The U.S. Environmental Movement, 1970–1990.* New York: Taylor and Francis, 1992.

Discha, Julis. "How the Alaska Act Was Won." *Living Wilderness* 44, no. 152 (Autumn 1981): 4–9.

Divale, William Tulio. *I Lived Inside the Campus Revolution.* New York: College Notes, 1970.

Dunlap, R. E. "Trends in Public Opinion Toward Environmental Issues." In Riley Dunlap and Angela Mertig, eds., *American Environmentalism: The U.S. Environmental Movement, 1970–1990.* New York: Taylor and Francis, 1992.

Dunlap, Thomas. *DDT: Scientists, Citizens, and Public Policy.* Princeton, N.J.: Princeton University Press, 1981.

———. *Saving America's Wildlife.* Princeton, N.J.: Princeton University Press, 1988.

Durant, Robert F. *When Government Regulates Itself.* Knoxville: University of Tennessee Press, 1985.

Easton, Robert. *Black Tide: The Santa Barbara Oil Spill and Its Consequences.* New York: Delacorte Press, 1972.

Ehrlich, Paul. *The Population Bomb: Population Control or Race to Oblivion?* New York: Ballantine Books, 1968.

Esposito, John. *The Ralph Nader Study Group Report on Air Pollution: Vanishing Air.* New York: Grossman Publishers, 1970.

Findley, Roger W., and Daniel A. Farber. *Environmental Law.* St. Paul: West Publishing, 1988.

Fleming, Donald. "Roots of the New Conservation Movements." *Perspectives in American History* 6 (1972): 7–91.

Flippen, J. Brooks. "Mr. Hickel Goes to Washington." *Alaska History* 12, no. 2 (Fall 1998): 1–22.

Frome, Michael. *Battle for the Wilderness.* Boulder, Colo.: Westview Press, 1984.

Galbraith, John Kenneth. *The Affluent Society.* Boston: Houghton Mifflin, 1958.

Goldman, Eric F. *The Crucial Decade and After.* New York: Random House, 1960.

Graham, Frank. *The Audubon Ark: A History of the National Audubon Society.* New York: Knopf, 1990.

Greene, John Robert. *The Presidency of Gerald R. Ford.* Lawrence: University of Kansas Press, 1995.

Hagenstein, Perry. "The Federal Lands Today: Uses and Limits." In Sterling Brubaker, ed., *Rethinking the Federal Lands.* Baltimore: Johns Hopkins University Press, 1984.

Haight, Kevin. "The Wilderness Act: Ten Years After." *Environmental Affairs* 3 (1974): 279.

Halberstam, David. *The Reckoning.* New York: William Morrow, 1986.

Harvey, Mark: *A Symbol of Wilderness: Echo Park and the American Conservation Movement.* Albuquerque: University of New Mexico Press, 1994.

Haskell, Elizabeth H. *The Politics of Clean Air.* New York: Praeger, 1982.

Hays, Samuel. "From Conservation to Environment." *Environmental Review* 6 (Fall 1982): 14–41.

———. *Beauty, Health and Permanence: Environmental Politics in the United States, 1955–1985.* New York: Cambridge University Press, 1987.

Heer, John E., and D. Joseph Hagerty. *Environmental Assessments and Statements.* New York: Van Nostrant Reinhold, 1977.

Hodel, Donald Paul, and Robert Deitz. *Crisis in the Oil Patch.* Washington, D.C.; Regnery Publishing, 1994.

Hoff, Joan. *Nixon Reconsidered.* New York: Basicbooks, 1994.

Horwitch, Melvin. *Clipped Wings: The American SST Conflict.* Cambridge, Mass.: MIT Press, 1982.

Ingram, Helen M. *Public Policy and the Natural Environment.* Greenwich, Conn.: JAI Press, 1985.

Johnson, Donald, and Kirk Porter. *National Party Platforms.* Urbana: University of Illinois Press, 1973.

Jones, Charles O. *Clean Air: The Policies and Politics of Pollution Control.* Pittsburgh: University of Pittsburgh Press, 1975.

Jordan, Richard. *Trees and People.* Washington, D.C.: Regnery Publishing, 1994.

Kearns, Doris. *Lyndon Johnson and the American Dream.* New York: Harper and Row, 1976.

Kehoe, Terence. *Cleaning Up the Great Lakes: From Cooperation to Confrontation.* DeKalb: Northern Illinois University Press, 1997.

Kirkpatrick, Samuel, and Melvin. "Vote Direction and Issue Cleavage in 1968." *Social Science Quarterly* 51 (December 1970): 689–705.

Kline, Benjamin. *First Along the River: A Brief History of the U.S. Environmental Movement.* San Francisco: Acada Books, 1997.

Knowles, Ruth Sheldon. *America's Energy Famine.* Norman: University of Oklahoma Press, 1980.

Kutler, Stanley. *The Wars of Watergate.* New York: Alfred A. Knopf, 1990.

Kutler, Stanley, ed. *Abuse of Power.* New York: The Free Press, 1997.

Landy, Marc K., Marc J. Roberts, and Stephen R. Thomas. *The Environmental Protection Agency: Asking the Wrong Questions, from Nixon to Clinton.* New York: Oxford University Press, 1994.

Lash, Jonathan, Katherine Fillman and David Sheridan. *A Season of Spoils: The Story of the Reagan Administration's Attack on the Environment.* New York: Pantheon, 1984.

Lear, Linda. *Rachel Carson: Witness for Nature.* New York: Henry Holt, 1997.

LeMaster, Dennis. *Decade of Change: The Remaking of Forest Service Statutory Authority in the 1970s.* Westport, Conn.: Greenwood Press, 1984.

Lieber, Harvey. *Federalism and Clean Waters: The 1972 Water Pollution Control Act.* Lexington, Mass.: Lexington Books, D. C. Heath and Co., 1975.

Link, Arthur S., and William B. Catton. *American Epoch.* New York: Alfred A. Knopf, 1980.

Lippman, Theo, Jr., and Donald C. Hansen. *Muskie.* New York: W. W. Norton, 1971.

Liroff, Richard. *A National Policy for the Environment.* Bloomington: Indiana University Press, 1976.

Long, David R. "Pipe Dreams, Hetch Hetchy, the Urban West, and the Hydraulic Society Revisited." *Journal of the American West* (July 1995): 22–34.

MacDonald, Ross, and Robert Easton. "Santa Barbarans Cite an Eleventh Commandment: 'Thou Shall Not Abuse the Earth.'" In Amos H. Hawley, ed., *Man and the Environment.* New York: New York Times Company, 1975.

McEvoy, James. "The American Concern for the Environment." In William Burch et al., eds., *Social Behavior, Natural Resources, and the Environment.* New York: Harper and Row, 1972.

Maga, Timothy P. *The World of Jimmy Carter: United States Foreign Policy, 1977–1981.* West Haven, Conn.: University of New Haven Press, 1994.

Mangrove, Gerald. *Marine Policy for America.* New York: Taylor and Francis, 1988.

Mayer, Carl J., and George A. Riley. *Public Domain, Private Dominion: A History of Public Mineral Policy in the United States.* San Francisco: Sierra Club Books, 1985.

Melosi, Martin. *Coping with Abundance: Energy and Environment in Industrial America.* Philadelphia: Temple University Press, 1985.

———. "Lyndon Johnson and Environmental Policy." In Robert A Divine, ed., *The Johnson Years: Vietnam, the Environment and Science.* Lawrence: University of Kansas Press, 1987.

Micklin, Philip. "The Environmental Hazards of Nuclear Wastes." *Science and Public Affairs* 30, no. 4 (April 1974): 36–44.

Miller, Douglas T. *On Our Own: America in the Sixties.* Lexington, Mass.: D. C. Heath and Company, 1996.

Mitchell, Robert Cameron, et al. "Twenty Years of Environmental Mobilization: Trends among National Environmental Organizations." In Riley Dunlap and Angela Mertig, eds., *American Environmentalism: The U.S. Environmental Movement, 1970–1990.* New York: Taylor and Francis, 1992.

Morris, Roger. *Richard Milhous Nixon: The Rise of an American Politician.* New York: Holt and Company, 1990.

Muhn, James, and Hansen R. Stuart. *Opportunity and Challenge: The Story of the BLM.* Washington, D.C.: U.S. Government Printing Office, 1988.

Nathan, Richard P. *The Plot that Failed: Nixon and the Administrative Presidency.* New York: John Wiley and Sons, 1975.

Nevin, David. *Muskie of Maine.* New York: Random House, 1972.

Paarlberg, Robert. "A Diplomatic Dispute: Clinton, Congress, and International Environmental Policy." *Environment* 38, no. 8 (1996): 16–20, 28–33.

Palmer, Tim. *Endangered Rivers and the Conservation Movement.* Berkeley: University of California Press, 1986.

Parmet, Herbert H. *Eisenhower and the American Crusades.* New York: Macmillan, 1972.
————. *Richard Nixon and His America.* Boston: Little, Brown and Company, 1990.
Petulla, Joseph M. *American Environmental History.* San Francisco: Boyd and Fraser, 1977.
————. *American Environmentalism: Values, Tactics and Priorities.* College Station: Texas A&M University Press, 1980.
Portney, Kent. *Controversial Issues in Environmental Policy.* Newbury Park, Calif.: Sage, 1992.
Price, Raymond. *With Nixon.* New York: Viking Press, 1977.
Primack, Joel and Frank Von Hippel. "Scientists, Politics and the SST: A Critical Review." *Science and Public Affairs* 28, no. 4 (April 1972): 24–30.
Pursell, Carrol, ed. *From Conservation to Ecology.* New York: Crowell, 1973.
Rathlesberger, James, ed. *Nixon and the Environment: The Politics of Devastation.* New York: Village Voice, 1972.
Rauber, Paul. "The Great Green Hope." *Sierra* 82, no.4 (1997): 40–43, 60–63.
Regenstein, Lewis. *America the Poisoned.* Washington, D.C.: Acropolis, 1982.
Richardson, Elmo. *Dams, Parks, and Politics: Resource Development and Preservation in the Truman-Eisenhower Era.* Lexington: University of Kentucky Press, 1973.
Riley, George. "The Mining Law of 1872." *Amicus Journal* 2, no. 4 (1981): 17–21.
Roberts, Malcolm. *The Wit and Wisdom of Wally Hickel.* Anchorage: Searchers Press, 1994.
Rosenbaum, Walter A. *The Politics of Environmental Concern.* New York: Praeger, 1974.
Roth, Dennis Murrow. *The Wilderness Movement and the National Forests.* College Station, Tex.: Intaglio Press, 1988.
Rothman, Hal. K. *The Greening of a Nation? Environmentalism in the United States since 1945.* Orlando, Fla.: Harcourt Brace, 1998.
Rowley, William D. *U.S. Forest Service Grazing and Rangelands.* College Station: Texas A&M University Press, 1985.
Sale, Kirkpatrick. *The Green Revolution: The American Environmental Movement, 1962–1992.* New York; Hill and Wang, 1993.
Sansom, Robert L. *The New American Dream Machine: Towards a Simpler Lifestyle in an Environmental Age.* Garden City, N.Y.: Anchor Press, 1976.
Scarce, Rik. *Eco-Warriors: Understanding the Alternative Environmental Movement.* Chicago, IL: Noble Press, 1990.
Scheffer, Victor B. *The Shaping of Environmentalism in America.* Seattle: University of Washington Press, 1991.
Shabecoff, Philip. *A Fierce Green Fire: The American Environmental Movement.* New York: Hill and Wang, 1993.
Shanley, Robert A. "Presidential Executive Orders and Environmental Policy." *Presidential Studies Quarterly* 13, no. 1 (Summer 1983): 405–16.
————. *Presidential Influence and Environmental Policy.* Westport, Conn.: Greenwood Press, 1992.

Smith, Thomas G. "John Kennedy, Stuart Udall, and the New Frontier Conserva-
    tion." *Pacific Historical Review* 64, no. 3 (August 1995): 329–41.
Solberg, Carl. *Hubert Humphrey.* New York: W. W. Norton, 1984.
Stacks, John F. *Stripping: The Surface Mining of America.* San Francisco: Sierra Club
    Books, 1972.
Stewart, William H., Jr. *The Tennessee-Tombigbee Waterway: A Case Study in the Pol-
    itics of Water Transportation.* University, Ala.: Bureau of Public Administration,
    University of Alabama, 1971.
Stine, Jeffrey K. "Environmental Politics in the American South: The Fight over the
    Tennessee-Tombigbee Waterway." *Environmental History Review* 15, no. 1
    (Spring 1991): 3–14.
———. *Mixing the Waters: Environment, Politics, and the Building of the Tennessee-
    Tombigbee Waterway.* Akron, Ohio; University of Akron Press, 1993.
———. "Regulating Wetlands in the 1970s: U.S. Army Corps of Engineers and the
    Environmental Organizations." *Journal of Forest History* 27 (April 1983): 60–75.
———. "Environmental Policy during the Carter Presidency." In Gary Fink and
    Hugh Davis Graham, eds., *The Carter Presidency: Policy Choices in the Post-New
    Deal Era.* Lawrence: University of Kansas Press, 1998.
Strum, Henry and Fred Strum. "American Solar Energy Policy." *Environmental Re-
    view* 7, no. 2 (Summer 1983): 135–53.
Switzer, Jacqueline. *Green Backlash: The History and Politics of Environmental Oppo-
    sition in the U.S.* New York: Lynne Reinner Publishers, 1997.
Terrell, John Upton. *War for the Colorado River.* Glendale, Ariz.: Arthur H. Clark,
    1965.
Udall, Stewart. *The Quiet Crisis.* New York: Holt, Rinehart and Winston, 1963.
Vietor, Richard. *Environmental Politics and the Coal Coalition.* College Station: Texas
    A&M University Press, 1980.
Vig, Norman, and Michael Kraft. *Environmental Policy in the 1980s.* Washington,
    D.C.: Congressional Quarterly, 1984.
Vileisis, Ann. *Discovering the Unknown Landscape: A History of America's Wetlands.*
    Washington, D.C.: Island Press, 1997.
Webb, LaVarr. "The Sagebrush Rebellion: Coming On Strong." *State Legislatures* 6
    (1980): 18–21.
White, Theodore. *The Making of the President, 1972.* New York: Atheneum, 1973.
Wicker, Tom. *One of Us.* New York: Random House, 1991.
———. "Waiting for an Environmental President." *Audubon* 96, no. 5 (1994): 49–54,
    102–3.
Wyatt, William K. *Westward in Eden: The Public Lands and the Conservation Move-
    ment.* Berkeley: University of California Press, 1982.

Index

301

DATE DUE

ILL. 6/10/06		
ILL. 10/10/16		

HIGHSMITH #45231